FROM GO TO WHOA

A Compendium of the Australian Turf

Peter Pierce

with Rhett Kirkwood

CROSSBOW
PUBLISHING PTY LTD

Published by

Crossbow Publishing Pty. Ltd.

Level 3, 150 Jolimont Road, East Melbourne, Vic. 3002

PHONE (03) 654 2900. FAX: (03) 654 5756

Crossbow Production Facility

2 Kembla Street, Cheltenham Vic. 3192

Phone: (03) 583 6511 Fax: (03) 583 7199

Distributed by HarperCollins

25 Ryde Road, Pymble, N.S.W., 2073

Phone: (02) 952 5000 Fax: 952 5555

National Library of Australia

Cataloguing-in-Publication-entry

From Go to Whoa

ISBN 0-646-19082-2

1. Thoroughbred Horseracing, Australian.

2. Social History 19th and 20th century, Australian.

I. Pierce, Peter (1950-)

Design, typesetting and film separations by

Fast Impressions Australia Pty. Ltd.

2 Kembla Street, Cheltenham, Vic. 3192

Proudly printed in Australia by

The McPhersons Printing Group, Victoria

Cover design by John Hillier

ABOUT THE AUTHORS

Peter PIERCE was educated at the Universities of Tasmania and Oxford and is currently Senior Lecturer in the National Centre for Australian Studies at Monash University. He co-authored the best-selling cookbook, *Donnini's Pasta* and *Vietnam Days. Australia and the Impact of Vietnam.* He edited *The Oxford Literary Guide to Australia*; anthologies of Australian war poetry and nineteenth-century verse, and currently is completing a book on Thomas Keneally. Besides writing regularly for the *Age, Bulletin, Canberra Times* and the *Sydney Morning Herald*, he is turf correspondent for the journal *Eureka Street*. He is married with a daughter, Catherine.

Rhett KIRKWOOD is a multiple award winner for racing journalism who spent most of his working life on newspapers before transferring to public relations. After joining the Adelaide *News* as a copy boy he became chief of the paper's Melbourne bureau and then worked with the *Sun* and the *Herald*. His passion for racing saw him write scripts for the videos 'This Fabulous Tuesday' (on the Melbourne Cup) and 'The Dominators' (on trainers Bart Cummings, Colin Hayes and Tommy Smith). He is married with two sons, Kristian and Harley.

ACKNOWLEDGEMENTS

Several desperates assisted in the making of this book by generously proffering information and advice. Foremost among them was Dr Robin Gerster, while Father Michael Kelly S.J., Gerry O'Brien and Lyn Verity also deserve a share of the credit and none of the blame. Numerous works were also consulted. *Turf Monthly* was indispensable, as was *Miller's Guide*. Other books used, and which can be recommended in their own right, were:
Bill Ahern, *The Melbourne Cup*; Margaret Benson, *Tommy Woodcock* D.L.Bemstein, *The First Tuesday in November*; Cashman et al, *The Oxford Companion to Australian Sport*; Bert Bryant and Neill Phillipson, *The Bert Bryant Story*; Maurice Cavanough and Meurig Davies, *Cup Day*; Maurice Cavanough, *The Caulfield Cup*; John Costello, *Galloping Greats*; Harold Freedman and Andrew Lemon, *The History of Australian Thoroughbred Racing*; Nat Gould, *On and Off the Turf in Australia*; Frank Hardy and Athol Mulley, *The Needy and the Greedy*; David Hickie, *Gentlemen of the Australian Turf*; Roy Higgins and Terry Vine, *The Professor*; Warwick Hobson, *The Golden Slipper Stakes*; *Racing's All-Time Greats*; H.Kreig and M.Appleton, *Great Australian Racehorses*; Michael McKernan (ed), *The Makers of Australian Sporting Traditions*; Mary Mountier, Douglas Barrie, Graeme Clark and Alister Taylor, *Notable Australian Thoroughbreds*; John Pacini, *A Century Galloped By. The First 100 Years of the Victoria Racing Club*; Martin Painter and Richard Waterhouse, *The Principal Club. A History of the Australian Jockey Club*; Brian Penton, *A Racing Heart*; Jack Pollard, *Australian Horse Racing*; Jim Shepherd, *Encyclopaedia of Australian Sport*; Jenny Tomlinson, *Born Winners, Born Losers. A History of Thoroughbred Breeding and Racing in Western Australia Since 1833.*

DEDICATION

FOR MY FATHER
Tom Pierce (1908-82)
'Second Again!'

INTRODUCTION

Thoroughbred horseracing offers drama without parallel. Rich in legend and superstition; replete with transitory triumphs and intense disappointments; it is an activity (and an industry) whose participants plumb depths of meanness and perfidy, but also reach heights of courage and grandeur. No other business offers such scope for idiosyncrasy, or for the cruel play of luck on the best-laid plans; no other forgets less and forgives more, so thrives on extreme reversals of fortune, better mirrors the society with which it is enmeshed.

From Go To Whoa depicts the long history as well as the contemporary scene of thoroughbred racing in Australia. Not an encyclopedia, it is a comprehensive compendium, an A to Z of the turf in Australia, which begins with the nineteenth century champion Abercorn and concludes with Zulu, a Melbourne Cup winner who ended his days pulling a milk cart. Here are stories of great and humble achievers; horses, jockeys, trainers, owners, urgers, punters, con-men; racecourses and clubs in all states; the finest events contested on the Australian turf as well as the incidents – glamorous and infamous – which have made the canvas of Australian racing so complex and brilliant.

Readers will find here the familiar and also the unsuspected: the eclipse of the sun on the day Surround won the 1976 Cox Plate; the streakers who led Tontonan down the Randwick straight in the 1974 Doncaster; Jim Pike, Roy Higgins, Darren Gauci, but also Jimmy Ah Poon who retired to China with his winnings on Poseidon and the Lady in Black who retired hurt after Bernborough's defeat in the 1946 Caulfield Cup. There are tales of ring-ins, of fortunes won and lost, of top rides and ordinary ones, of the long-term confidence which inspired the building of stud properties and the short-term kind which fuelled plunges. *From Go To Whoa* is designed to enthral and to aggravate. It is a book for punters and lovers of horseracing, for students of the turf and of the wider history of Australia. *From Go To Whoa* intends to settle thousands of arguments and to start thousands more.

Peter Pierce

A

ABERCORN

1884 ch horse Chester – Cinnamon

Bred and owned by James White, Abercorn was one of the best sons of Victoria Derby and Melbourne Cup winner Chester. From juvenile days he showed champion form, winning the A.J.C. and V.R.C. Sires'. At three he won the 1887 A.J.C. Derby and dead-heated with Niagara in the Victoria Derby behind The Australian Peer. Those two colts had run second and third behind Abercorn at Randwick. Both the A.J.C. and V.R.C. St Legers also fell to the horse, who quickly began to make his mark at weight-for-age as well. He won the three miles Champion Stakes at Flemington, besides the Essendon Stakes and the Melbourne Stakes of 1889. In Sydney his big wins included two Craven Plates and the 1889 Metropolitan which he won with 60.5kg. Trained by M. Fennelly, Abercorn was usually ridden by the leading jockey of his day, Tom Hales. Among his big race successes, Abercorn could boast three over Carbine, although he ran third to that horse in the 1889 Sydney Cup. At stud he sired the 1894 Caulfield Guineas winner Cobbity and Cocos who won the Victoria Derby of 1898. In that year Abercorn was sent to England to continue his stud duties.

ADAMS, GEORGE (1839-1904)

Born in England, George Adams came to Australia with his family in 1855; went gold-mining in Queensland; dealt in stock; drove Cobb & Co coaches; bought into a sheep station and set up as a butcher. Sydney's racing often lured him from the country, and when in town he stayed at The Mayor's Inn in Pitt Street. This was the headquarters of the Tattersall's Club, which had adopted the rules and standards of Tattersall's in London. Before long Adams had bought the hotel and began to run sweepstakes on race meetings for club members and friends. His first public sweep was held on the 1881 Sydney Cup. Opposition from church bodies to this form of gambling led to two interstate moves, first to Queensland and then to Tasmania, where the Tattersall's lottery was established from 1895. Long a patron of horse-racing, Adams was honoured posthumously when the mile race on the final day of the Flemington Spring Carnival was named (temporarily) the George Adams Handicap.

ADELAIDE CUP

The swift success of the Melbourne Cup led racing officials in Sydney and Adelaide to emulate it with two mile races of their own. The first Adelaide Cup was run at weight-for-age in 1864 when Falcon gave the two year old Roebuck 25kg, and a beating. First run at Thebarton, the Cup was staged at the Old Course (later Victoria Park) in 1869, before finally being established as an S.A.J.C. feature event at Morphettville. The amazingly versatile Malua, in 1884, was perhaps the first top-liner to win the Adelaide Cup, but he had plenty of successors. Not in the next year, however, when the ban on totalisator and off-course betting meant that South Australian racing was so near collapse that the 1885 Adelaide Cup was run at Flemington as a stop-gap measure. Lord Wilton beat Anchorite. The Cup was not staged in the next three years, but resumed with a win to The Lawyer over Harbinger in 1889. King Ingoda, Rain Lover, Hyperno, Just A Dash and Subzero won both the Adelaide and Melbourne Cups. Reckless was another distinguished winner, while Lord Reims – who took the Caulfield Cup in 1987, had won the first of an unprecedented three Adelaide Cups in succession in that year. The Bart Cummings-trained Mr Lomondy had completed the Adelaide-Caulfield Cups double in the previous year; Our Pompeii recorded successive wins in 1993-4. The Adelaide Cup remains one of the surer indices of staying ability on the Australian racing calendar.

AGUA CALIENTE

When big weights threatened the racing career of Phar Lap in Australia, his owner Dave Davis decided to take the horse overseas. Lured by the promise of $100,000 first prize, he set the horse for the Agua Caliente Handicap at a track of that name in Tijuana, Mexico. Tommy Woodcock took over the training of the horse, who was troubled before the race by a split heel, and

Billy Elliot had the mount. Carrying the 9 saddlecloth, and favourite at 6/5, Phar Lap raced wide and near the rear for most of the way, but won easily, by two lengths, in race record time for the 10 furlong event. Unfortunately for Davis, the winner's purse had been cut to just over $20,000. This win, on 20 March 1932, was Phar Lap's last. He died the next month at Menlo Park in California.

AJAX
1934 ch horse Heroic – Medmenham

Heroic's greatest son, and one of the finest horses of the inter-war era, Ajax was foaled at the Widden Stud on the night that Peter Pan won the 1934 Melbourne Cup. Unplaced only once in 46 starts, he won 36 of them. Famously, 18 of these victories were in succession, and all in Group races. Before this marvellous effort, spread over four preparations from the spring of 1937 until the autumn of 1939, Ajax had won the A.J.C. Sires' Produce and Champagne Stakes as a two year old. At three, he was second in both the A.J.C. and Victoria Derbies (to Avenger and Hua respectively). His great run then began, with the first of two victories in the Linlithgow Stakes. In his stretch of 18 wins, Ajax broke six race or course records, or equalled Australian records. He was not, as sometimes enviously alleged, a cotton-wool champion. In the autumn of 1938 he won the Futurity and then the Newmarket with 57kg, 3kg over weight-for-age. Sent to Sydney, he equalled the Australian record in the All Aged Stakes, a race which he won three times.

Ajax's sequence continued into the spring of 1938, when his wins included the Underwood Stakes, then run at Williamstown, another race which he would win three times; the Caulfield Stakes, the Cox Plate, Mackinnon and Linlithgow

Stakes and the C.B. Fisher Plate, the last completing three wins over the four days of the Flemington Spring Carnival. Back in the autumn of 1939, he won the second of three consecutive Futurity Stakes under 66.5kg, and a second C.M. Lloyd Stakes. Finally the run ended, and Ajax became the longest priced beaten favourite in Australian history when he went under at 40/1 on by half a length to Spear Chief in the Rawson Stakes. Regular jockey Harold Badger, who won 30 races on the horse, claimed that Ajax was off-colour that day. The evidence supports him, as Ajax won his next four races in a row. At a mile he won 13 of 14, while his weight for age record is one of the finest that the Australian turf has to show. Following his retirement, Ajax stood at stud both in Australia and, from 14, in the United States. His best son was Magnificent, winner of the Victoria and A.J.C. Derbies in 1945.

A.J.C. DERBY

The Randwick Derby Stakes was first run in 1861, when Kyogle won. The race was renamed the Australian Derby Stakes and first contested in September 1865 when A. Cheeke rode Clove to victory. The 1860s saw such top winners of the race as Yattendon, The Barb and Fireworks, while the filly Florence won in 1870 and the unbeaten Grand Flaneur a decade later. Navigator scored in 1882 (and like Fireworks and Grand Flaneur went on to the Derby double). Trident and Abercorn were other fine winners in the 1880s. Poseidon was the best winner early this century. In 1919 the only Derby dead-heat occurred between Richmond Main and Artilleryman. The 1920s was a vintage decade, when Heroic, Manfred, Trivalve and Phar Lap all won. The champion Peter Pan scored in 1932, the year from which

geldings (such as Phar Lap) were barred, as only horses eligible for the Stud Book could be entered for the Derby. That rule was rescinded in 1957, when another champion – Tulloch – was victorious. There had not been many quality winners to speak of in between. The 1973 Derby saw one of the greatest races in Australian turf history, when Imagele prevailed in the tightest of photo finishes from Leica Lover and Grand Cidium. Dulcify won in a controversial protest from Double Century in 1979 to complete the Victoria-A.J.C. Derby double. That year the race was run for the first time in the autumn, the notion being that more mature three year olds would be able to contest it. The decision has been vindicated by the quality of subsequent winners. The champion Kingston Town won in 1980, but that decade was more notable in the history of the race because no fewer than three fillies won: Rose of Kingston (1982), Tristarc (1985) and Research (1989). Other distinguished Derby winners of the 1980s were Bonecrusher and Myocard. The 1990s already boasts such fine A.J.C. Derby winners as Dr Grace, Durbridge, Naturalism (who beat Veandercross) and Mahogany, the first dual Derby winner since Dulcify. From 1995, the race will be known as the Australian Derby (the race of that name in Western Australia having been discontinued).

ALBION PARK

Brisbane's famous sand track, affectionately known as 'The Creek' (because of its proximity to Breakfast Creek), was officially opened in 1889 and used as a pony track. Meetings had evidently been held in the area for decades before this. A testing course for jockeys, it proved an invaluable learning ground for champions such as George Moore. John

Wren bought Albion Park in 1910 and later sold the track to the B.A.T.C. Some horses who were duds on Brisbane's grass tracks excelled at 'The Creek'. Red Seas was one such 'Creeker', winning 15 races there, while Auction twice won while carrying 76kg. Prone to flooding, and bedevilled by dwindling crowds, the track was sold to the Albion Park Trotting Club. The last race meeting was held there on 30 December 1981, when Mick Dittman rode a treble.

ALCIMEDES

1954 br horse Alycidon – Honey Hill

One of Australasia's great sires of stayers, Alcimedes was out of the top-line English horse Alycidon, winner of the King George VI Stakes by five lengths and of the Ascot Gold Cup. Much less successful on the track, Alcimedes won six races from seven to ten and a half furlongs and was placed 17 times from 34 starts before being sent to Seton Otway's Trelawney Stud in New Zealand. There he sired some of the finest middle-distance and staying horses of the 1960s and 1970s, prominent among them Galilee, Divide and Rule, Prince Grant and Silver Knight. This durable horse's last stakes winner was No Peer, who also ran second in the Caulfield Cup of 1981. On the questionable assumption that his sons would be too dourly in the staying mode to be in their turn successful sires, most of them were gelded.

ALISTER

1947 ch horse Whirlaway – New Flower

A slow starter, Alister was tenth at his first race start, and was placed only once – a third in the Gibson Carmichael – in six outings at two. Next season he won the Warriston Handicap at Caulfield, but even with little form behind him, started at only 7/1 in the A.J.C. Derby of 1950. He duly won, and headed south for the Caulfield Guineas in which he was second to Merry Scout. Thereafter the colt's improvement was dramatic. He won the Cox Plate from Delta (a weight-for-age star and the previous year's Victoria Derby winner) before taking the Derby at 7/4 on from Delta's full brother, Midway. Jack Purtell had the choice of Alister or Comic Court in the Melbourne Cup. Proving once more how jockeys are bad judges he chose the colt, who finished eighth at 3/1 favourite to Comic Court. In the autumn of 1951 Alister was placed in the V.R.C. and A.J.C. St Legers before his owner, A.G. Hunter, retired the horse to stud.

ALL AGED STAKES

An All Aged Stakes was part of the first V.R.C. Spring Carnival in 1864, raced over one mile. In 1914 the All Aged became the C.M. Lloyd Stakes and was run at weight-for-age, but that race has now vanished from the calendar. In Sydney the tradition of the All Aged Stakes has been long and honourably maintained. First run in 1866, when Falcon won, the All Aged Stakes at Randwick is now a Group One event over 1600m at the autumn carnival. Yattendon and Fireworks were other early winners, as was Tim Whiffler, who was second in 1869 and 1872 but won in the two intervening years. Briseis (in 1876) and Carbine (in 1889-90) were the greatest of nineteenth-century winners. Wakeful won in 1902, while Gladsome (1904-5) was a dual winner, succeeded by Malt King, Yaralla, Kilshery, Dalrello and Rough Habit (in 1992-3). Cetigne was placed four times in the race. The All Aged Stakes at Randwick has one of the finest roll-calls of any top event in Australia: from the 1920s, Limerick and Mollison; the 1930s, Amounis,

Winooka, Chatham and Peter Pan; Bernborough in 1946; Tulloch in 1958; from the 1960s Noholme, Sky High and Tobin Bronze; Abdul, Triton, All Shot, Tontonan and Belmura Lad in the next decade; Emancipation and Campaign King in the 1980s, while Shaftesbury Avenue saluted in 1991.

ALL LOVE

1939 br mare Double Remove – Beauvue

Trained by J.T. Cush, and usually ridden by Ted Bartle, All Love was a brilliant filly. At two she won six of her nine starts and ran second in two others. Her only unplaced run was against older horses in the Oakleigh Plate. In the spring of 1940 she won the Gimcrack Stakes in Sydney and the Maribyrnong Plate at Flemington. Next autumn she won the V.R.C. Sires' Produce at 13/8 on, from Primavera and Status Quo. Back in Sydney she was second to Yaralla in the A.J.C. Sires' before scoring in the Champagne Stakes of 1941 at 7/4 favourite. All Love trained on as a three year old to win the Hobartville Stakes in the spring of 1941.

ALL SHOT

1968 b gelding Idomeneo – Gambit

One of the finest sprinting and middle distance horses of the early 1970s, the under-rated All Shot has an imposing record in what are now classified as Group One races. Trained by Ian Saunders, All Shot enjoyed a brilliant spring in 1972. After running second to Latin Knight in the Spring Champion Stakes at Randwick, he won the Toorak Handicap with 58kg, was second to Gunsynd in the Cox Plate, and then during the Flemington carnival won the Linlithgow Stakes and the George Adams Handicap (with 59kg). Back in the autumn of 1973, he recorded the first of

successive wins in the William Reid Stakes. Later in the year he recorded three notable Sydney victories: in the All Aged Stakes (from Century and Longfella), the George Ryder Stakes (from Century and Triton) and the George Main Stakes. All Shot was also third in the Theo Marks Quality. In the spring he won a second Linlithgow Stakes, when once more he beat home Tauto and Century. In the autumn of 1974 his second William Reid came in record time, while he campaigned on in the spring to win the Craiglee and to confirm his capacity to compete at the highest level.

ALMAARAD

1982 ch horse Ela-Mana-Mou – Silk Blend

Winner of nine races in Europe before being brought to race in Australia, this high quality son of an English Derby winner performed with more distinction than have most imported gallopers. Trained by Colin Hayes, Almaarad had one brief and brilliant spring campaign in 1989, although it was sufficient to win him a Horse of the Year award. Beginning with an unlucky second in the Craiglee Stakes, he then won three Group One races in succession: the Underwood and Caulfield Stakes, and the W.S. Cox Plate in which he narrowly beat that season's Victoria Derby winner, Stylish Century and Empire Rose, winner of the previous year's Melbourne Cup. Almaarad broke down before he could start in the 1989 Melbourne Cup, and was retired to stud.

ALWAYS THERE

1965 ch horse Pipe of Peace – April Wonder

Owned by the controversial Filipino Felipe Ysmael and trained by Charlie Waymouth, Always There won the S.A.J.C. Sires' Produce in 1968 from Alrello. Sent east to campaign as a three year old he ran third in the A.J.C. Derby and then had a purple patch in which he won the Moonee Valley Stakes, the Victoria Derby with Geoff Lane up and the Sandown Guineas, in what was perhaps not a vintage year. Ysmael had no complaints, purportedly pocketing $300,000 from the Derby win. Always There stood with success at stud in Australia.

AMBERITE
1894 b horse Carbine – Duenna

One of the best sons of the champion Carbine, Amberite, who was leased to and trained by William Duggan, won the 1897 A.J.C. Derby. He then carried 61.5kg to victory in three year old company in the Duff Memorial Stakes. Sent to Melbourne, he failed in the Caulfield Stakes, but beat the favourite Parthenopaeus in the Caulfield Cup. A win in the Victoria Derby by four lengths from the unlucky odds-on favourite Aurum, meant that Amberite was the first horse to win the two Derbies and Caulfield Cup treble. He finished down the track in the Melbourne Cup, and never recovered his best three year old form, although he did win a V.R.C. Champion Stakes and A.J.C. St Leger in the autumn of 1898. He was also a good second in the Sydney Cup, carrying 56kg. In eight starts at four he won only once, in the three miles Randwick Plate.

AMIABLE
1934 blk mare Lord Quex – Agreeable

A top-line sprinting mare, Amiable progressed from handicap to weight-for-age company in the space of a season. She won the Standish Handicap in January 1938, a race in which she would be third to Manrico and Aurie's Star in the following year. Amiable was second in the Oakleigh Plate in the autumn of 1938 to Pamelus. In the summer of 1939 she won the William Reid Stakes and then added the Alister Clark Stakes, also at Moonee Valley, where she beat Judean and El Golea. In 1940 she beat the brilliant horses High Caste and Ajax in the C.M. Lloyd Stakes at Flemington; ran an Australian record for the mile and became the first horse to break 1.35 for that distance. Later Amiable was the dam of Aqua Regis, winner of the Stradbroke Handicap in 1951.

AMOUNIS
1922 br gelding Magpie – Loved One

This champion galloper raced with distinction until he was an eight year old, and at that age was the first leg of the ruinous 1930 Caulfield-Melbourne Cups double for bookmakers. Phar Lap won the second leg, but his was among the many great scalps that Amounis took, notably in the St George Stakes of that year, and in the All Aged Stakes at Randwick several months later. Trained by Frank McGrath, Amounis had classic form at three, winning the 1925 Rosehill Guineas. Next year he won the Epsom in record time and took the race again in 1928. Amounis' other big handicap wins included the 1928 Williamstown Cup, the Cantala Stakes in 1929 with 62.5kg, the 1930 Futurity Stakes where he carried 65.5kg to beat the top quality sprinter Greenline and the 1930 Caulfield Cup with 61kg. Amounis also won 18 races at weight-for-age. This tally included three Linlithgow Stakes, the Cox Plate of 1927 (in which he beat Limerick and Windbag), the 1929 Canterbury Stakes, the Caulfield Stakes and All Aged Stakes (when he beat Nightmarch) in 1930, Amounis' late vintage year. Few superior gallopers have raced in Australia, or been more versatile. Amounis won in the best company from 1200m to 2400m.

ANALIE

1970 b mare Sovereign Edition – Nalei

Equally credentialled in classic and handicap races, Analie enjoyed one outstanding year on the Australian turf. After a second in the South Australian Oaks of 1972, Analie went to Sydney where she was trained by T.J. Smith. In 1973 she won the A.J.C. Doncaster and Oaks in the autumn; went north to take both the Q.T.C. Derby and the Oaks; returned to Sydney in the spring to win the S.T.C. Cup and the Metropolitan Handicap, her fifth victory at Group One level.

ANGLES FAMILY

Two of the 11 children of Victor ('Lordy') Angles, a sometime cloakroom attendant at Randwick and bookie, made their mark on Australian turf history. Fred Angles (1903-60) was one of Sydney's largest punters from the 1930s through the 1950s. He began on the staff of Rufe Naylor, but soon set up as an independent punter. Successful plunges included those on Dark Felt in the 1943 Melbourne Cup and Carioca in the Villiers-Summer Cup double of 1952. Fred Angles was one of the first, and most prosperous, of careful analysts of form among professional punters.

His brother Cyril Angles (1906-62) worked as a clerk for Naylor, who secured him the position as race broadcaster with 2KY. These were the days when fig trees outside Warwick Farm, or a chair on a table on the back of a lorry provided vantage points for callers who were banned from the track. Angles won a court case which had been brought by Victoria Park (N.S.W.) to stop him from broadcasting its races. In 1935 he had switched to 2UW; in 1945 he went to 2GB as the highest paid broadcaster in Australian radio. He called many sports besides racing: athletics, boxing, cricket, wrestling, even ping pong and Walter Lindrum at billiards. He collapsed while broadcasting a Metropolitan; retired at the end of the 1950s and died in 1962.

ANNTELLE

1980 br mare Loosen Up – Soft Quest

On 3 July 1982, when Ideal Planet won the Rothman's 100,000 at Doomben and Airmond the Grand National Hurdle at Flemington, a first starter gave trainer Tommy Smith yet another racing record. In the Norman Ross Handicap at Canterbury, Anntelle, ridden by apprentice Jamie de Belin, scored by a short half head from the favourite Flighty Girl in a blanket finish. Anntelle, which came from 12th on the turn, had drifted in betting from 100/1 to 500/1. At those odds she was the longest priced winner in Australian turf history. By the first crop of Loosen Up to race in Australia, Anntelle faded into obscurity and her sire had to wait his turn for fame until his son Better Loosen Up began his career. Five years after Anntelle's win, Pablo's Pulse scored at Warwick Farm, also at 500/1.

ANONYME

1955 ch gelding Landau – La Patrice

Second in the 1960 Newmarket to Correct, Anonyme soon proved himself one of the finest sprinters of the early 1960s. In the spring of 1961, Anonyme won the Liston Stakes, was second to Lord in the Memsie and won the first of successive Invitation Stakes. His affinity for Caulfield was confirmed with a further win at the track, this time in the Toorak Handicap when Anonyme carried 61.5kg to victory. Later in the spring he won the Linlithgow Stakes from Aquanita and Webster. In the autumn of 1962 Aquanita beat him in the Futurity Stakes, where both horses were burdened with 66.5kg. In the spring,

Anonyme carried 59.5kg to victory over Samson in the Invitation Stakes: Alan Burton drew the ride this time, Billy Pyers had had the mount the previous year.

APPRENTICE, THE

A neglected novel of the Australian turf, alertly informed of stable and racing nuances, besides its commitment to moralising, Wilda Moxham's *The Apprentice* (1969) is another story which finds its climax with the Melbourne Cup. Juvenile criminal Rufe Dale is given his chance of rehabilitation as an apprentice jockey; he is then associated with the supposedly broken-down champion Pancho. The pair race into the burgeoning fictional history of the great event: read on.

AQUANITA
1956 br horse Wateringbury – Reinita

One of the finest horses ever bred in Western Australia, Aquanita won two races at two, and seven of eight starts at three, including the 1959 Railway Stakes. Sent to Melbourne as a four year old, Aquanita was trained by Roy Shaw. His first big win in Victoria was the George Adams Handicap. Wintering in Brisbane in 1960, he won the Healy Stakes and the Doomben 10,000 with 57kg. In the spring of 1961, Aquanita beat Dhaulagiri in the Underwood Stakes, before carrying 59.5kg to a second George Adams victory. Next autumn, he took the Futurity Stakes at Caulfield while carrying 66.5kg. A large, savagely tempered horse, Aquanita was a great weight carrier, and proved himself an outstanding galloper in an era of champions. At six he won eight weight-for-age races from 12 starts, including the Cox Plate of 1962, the Mackinnon Stakes, another Underwood Stakes and the St George Stakes. He also ran third in the Melbourne Cup with 59kg, thus underlining his ability over a wide range of distances. Other victories included a Turnbull and a Craiglee Stakes. Leg problems forced his retirement, and Aquanita returned to Western Australia where he had an indifferent career at stud.

ARCHER
1856 b horse William Tell – Maid of Oaks

Winner of the first two Melbourne Cups, Archer was trained by Etienne de Mestre. According to legend, his strapper Dave Power walked the horse 850km from Nowra on each occasion that he won the Cup. Archer almost certainly travelled by ship. In the inaugural Melbourne Cup, before a crowd of 4,000 which may have been depleted by the news of the deaths of Burke and Wills, Archer started at 6/1 second favourite and won by six lengths. The owner's prize was 710 pounds and a beaten gold watch, but the horse had been heavily backed as well. Together with de Mestre's Inheritor (whose chances the trainer preferred), Archer was one of two New South Wales horses in the race. Twilight delayed the start by bolting, while Dispatch and Medora were killed in falls.

Back at Flemington the next year, Archer carried 64.5kg to victory (second only to Carbine's winning weight in 1890) by eight lengths. Second once more was Mormon, the only time the Cup has been twice quinellaed by the same horses. A clerical mishap prevented Archer running in the Cup of 1863. His nomination arrived on the Separation Day holiday in Melbourne and Victoria Turf Club officials refused to accept it. De Mestre threatened never to race in Victoria again (although he did, and his horses won three more Melbourne Cups), and so many runners were scratched in sympathy, that only seven starters faced the judge – the smallest field in the history of the race.

Archer raced on until 10, when he went to stud after a race fall. In the 1984 film 'Archer' the horse suffered the celluloid mystification that was also the fate of Phar Lap. In a supposed dramatic improvement of events, strapper Dave Power replaced John Cutts as jockey in this film version, although in fact Cutts won both Cups on Archer.

ARCTIC EXPLORER

1954 b horse Arctic Prince – Flirting

Winner of five races in England, including the Edward VII Stakes at Ascot, Arctic Explorer was brought to Australia for stud duties in 1958. After six seasons here, he was sent to New Zealand for a further seven, before returning to finish his career in Australia. Best son of Arctic Explorer was Tobin Bronze, winner of a Victoria Derby, two Cox Plates, Caulfield Cup, Doncaster and numerous weight-for-age races. Arctic Explorer also sired the top stayers Arctic Symbol, who won the Sydney Cup in 1970; Igloo, who besides a Brisbane Cup won a Caulfield and Chipping Norton Stakes and was unlucky in other quality handicap events; Australian Cup winner Arctic Coast and Arctic Star, who won the V.R.C. Oaks in 1962 and the A.J.C. Oaks in the following year.

ARMANASCO, ANGUS (1912-)

The son of an Italian immigrant to Western Australia, Angus Armanasco was a leading rider in Perth in the interwar years, his best effort being 66 wins in the 1931-2 season. After retirement he trained in Perth until shifting his operation east in the early 1950s. He has trained at Caulfield for more than four decades. His first big Melbourne winner was Jovial Lad in the inaugural Invitation Stakes (now the Show Day Cup)

at Caulfield in 1951. Armanasco was leading Melbourne trainer on the first of six occasions in the 1963-4 season. His last premiership came in 1973-4. Especially renowned as a trainer of young horses, and of sires-to-be, Armanasco won the Blue Diamond Stakes three times: with Tolerance (in the first running of the race in 1971), Forina (1974) and Zeditave (1988). Twice he saddled beaten odds-on favourites in the Golden Slipper – Biscay in 1968 and Tolerance in 1971. While Star of Heaven and Star Affair were placed in the race in the mid-1960s, he had to wait till 1981 when Full on Aces gave him his first Slipper. His many top horses include Biscay, Bletchingly, The Judge, True Version (all of whom have gone on to further distinction as sires), Victoria Peak, Tetranate, Magic Ruler, Zeditave and – most versatile of all – Crewman. Among his remarkable training feats are to have twice trained all three placegetters in a metropolitan race, and within the space of a month: at Caulfield in November 1973, at Sandown in December. In the V.R.C. Sires' Produce Stakes of 1985, Armanasco not only trained the first two place-getters, True Version and Jackson Square, but he had also trained the sires and dams of both colts: Bletchingly-Fiction Star, Biscay-Red Rebecca. Armanasco still trains a small team.

ARTILLERYMAN

1916 br horse Comedy King – Cross Battery

Foaled during the Great War, and so topically, if grimly named, Artilleryman was by the imported sire and Melbourne Cup winner Comedy King. In 1919 he emulated his sire, when – as a three year old – he won the Melbourne Cup by six lengths, in record time, from his great rival Richmond Main. Artilleryman had won the Mona Nursery at his second two year old start; was third in the Maribyrnong Plate and second in the V.R.C. Sires'. At three he blossomed. After a win in the Memsie Stakes, he went to Sydney and ran third in the Rosehill Guineas, before dead-heating with Richmond Main in the A.J.C. Derby. The latter had the better of him in the Victoria Derby, but Artilleryman soon started a sequence of seven wins in succession, including the Caulfield Guineas and the Melbourne Cup, and culminating in the Segenhoe Stakes of 1920. In the C.B. Fisher Plate Artilleryman defeated the fine horse Cetigne, whom he beat again in the St George Stakes in the autumn. After his Segenhoe success, Artilleryman's form tapered off, with a second in the A.J.C. St Leger and unplaced runs in the Sydney Cup and All Aged Stakes. The explanation was unhappily forthcoming when he died of cancer only a year later.

ASCOT RACECOURSE

Set on a bend of the Swan River, Ascot is the site of all the classic events of the Western Australian turf calendar. The first race was run there in 1848, but the ground often proved too boggy for winter racing. Ascot, like Flemington, benefits from its riverside scenery and is subject to occasional inundation. In 1877 the course was leased to the Western Australian Turf Club for 199 years and is the headquarters of the club.

AT TALAQ
1980 b horse Roberto – My Nord

Among the best performed horses to be imported from the northern hemisphere to race in Australia, At Talaq tested trainer Colin Hayes' patience as he took time to acclimatise. By an English Derby winner, and an $800,000 yearling purchase, At Talaq had run fourth in the English classic.

His best European win was in the Group One Grand Prix de Paris over 3000m, where he showed his stout staying qualities. Hayes brought him along slowly, setting At Talaq for the Caulfield-Melbourne Cups double in 1986. In his lead up, the stallion ran second to Bonecrusher in the Underwood Stakes and to Mr Lomondy in the Caulfield Cup. Nearing his peak, he won the Mackinnon Stakes and then just lasted to win the Melbourne Cup. Brought back in the autumn, At Talaq won the Orr Stakes and was then a gallant and narrow second in the Australian Cup to Bonecrusher. Shortly afterwards he began a successful stud career.

AUSTRALASIAN CHAMPION STAKES
   see SPRING CHAMPION STAKES

AURARIA
1892 br mare Trenton – Aura

Bred at James Wilson's famous St Albans Stud, Auraria was bought by David James, a South Australian pastoralist and one of the owners of the Broken Hill silver mine. Auraria's 10 wins included the S.A.J.C. Derby in 1895 and the Flemington Stakes, but she is chiefly remembered for her deeds at the Flemington Spring Carnival of 1895. After a third to Wallace in the Victoria Derby, Auraria beat the favourite Hova by a neck in the Melbourne Cup. Starting at 33/1, she became only the second of her sex to win the race. The champion Briseis was the other. Next Auraria won the Oaks, before dead-heating with Wallace in a memorable contest in the C.B. Fisher Plate.

AURIE'S STAR
1931 b gelding Stardrift – Aurie Anton

Trained by J. Doyle, this champion sprinter was a prolific winner at the highest level and raced until he was 13. Bred in South Australia by his subsequent owner,

E.D. Murphy, Aurie's Star ran time of 1.07.8 down the 'straight six' (1200m) course at Flemington in the Whittier Handicap on 7 September 1940, a record that stood so long that it unwarrantably became the object of scepticism. But Aurie's Star had also been smart enough to win the Oakleigh Plates of 1937 and 1939 (the latter with 63kg), the Newmarket of 1937 and a Railway Highweight on Melbourne Cup day, carrying 71.5kg, when he was an eight year old. He was also second in the 1939 Newmarket, carrying 63kg, and won the 1940 Goodwood Handicap with 63.5kg, giving 10.5kg to the second horse, Dreamsome.

AURUM

1895 b horse Trenton – Aura

Trained by W. Wilson, this outstanding juvenile was beaten a head in the Oakleigh Plate as a two year old. In other contests at that age against older horses, he won the Electric Stakes at Caulfield by six lengths and the V.R.C. All Aged Stakes. Against his own age group, Aurum won the Ascot Vale Stakes, the V.R.C. Sires' (from The Hypnotist) and the A.J.C. Champagne Stakes. As a three year old he won the Caulfield Guineas (with The Hypnotist again runner-up), the V.R.C. Flying and Spring Stakes, the C.B. Fisher Plate and the V.R.C. St Leger. Aurum also ran second in the Victoria Derby to Amberite (whom he had beaten in the Champagne), and had thirds in the Melbourne and Australian Cups. Sent to England to continue his racing career, he did not acclimatise and was unsuccessful.

AUSTRALASIAN OAKS

One of the newest classic events on the Australian racing calendar, the Australasian Oaks – run over 2,000m at Group One level

– at Morphettville in May – was first contested in 1982. Originally it was run in February, to coincide with the Adelaide yearling sales, but was moved in 1993 to become a feature of the Adelaide Cup carnival. The South Australian Oaks is run two weeks later, over the classic distance of 2400m. In 1993 Our Tristalight, trained by Bart Cummings, won both Oaks. Rose of Kingston proved a top quality winner of the first Australasian Oaks, while Imposera in 1988, and Mannerism in 1991, both of whom went on to win Caulfield Cups, have set their seal on the race.

AUSTRALIAN CUP

One of the oldest, and in recent years one of the best races on the Australian calendar, the Australian Cup was first contested at Flemington over 18 furlongs in 1863, when Barwon won. A couple of years later Woodman became the first dual winner (in 1865-6). He was second the next year to Tim Whiffler, as an index of the early quality of the race. In 1872 three starts were necessary to decide the Australian Cup winner. Saladin dead-heated twice with Flying Dutchman, before winning the third run-off. The unlucky Flying Dutchman had also been second to Norma in the 1870 Cup. Subsequent dead-heats were let stand: between Prizefighter and Saxonite in 1912, Yootha and Cyron in 1969.

Formerly a handicap, the Australian Cup is now a weight-for-age Group One race over 2000m and – with the Newmarket – a feature event of the Flemington autumn carnival. It was not until the 1960s that it became the race noted for the calibre of its winners that it had been in the 19th century. Both Welkin Prince (1962-3) and Craftsman (1965-6) scored in the 1960s, while the good Cup winners Grand Print, Bore Head and Arctic Coast were also victorious in that decade. Beaten in the 1970 Newmarket, Crewman controversially atoned in the Australian Cup. Gay Icarus won the next year. From 1975-81 a superb array of horses saluted: Leilani, Lord Dudley, Ngawyni, Ming Dynasty, Dulcify, Ming Dynasty again and then Hyperno. Bonecrusher won in 1987, but could only finish third the next year behind the 140/1 bolter Dandy Andy and Vo Rogue. The latter had his turn in 1989-90, before finishing a distant second to Better Loosen Up in 1991, when that horse was at the peak of his form. Let's Elope, Veandercross and Durbridge won from 1992-4, to confirm the status of the Australian Cup.

AUSTRALIAN DERBY

In 1972 the W.A.T.C. decided to establish a national Derby as one of the features of its summer racing carnival. Horses would run by invitation, and those eligible included the four first home in the Victoria and South Australian Derbies, the A.J.C. Spring Champion Stakes, as well as the first six placegetters in the W.A. Derby. Bart Cummings won the inaugural Australian Derby and the first of his four with Dayana. In the following year his horse Leica Lover atoned for seconds in the A.J.C. Derby (to Imagele) and Victoria Derby (to Taj Rossi). Several other Victoria Derby winners went on to take the Australian Derby: Haymaker in 1974, Sovereign Red in 1980 and Bounty Hawk in 1983. Tommy Smith's filly Denise's Joy was the first of her sex to win the event, on protest in 1975 from another filly Ace Queen. Smith won again with Show Ego in 1977 beating the Victoria Derby winner Stormy Rex. The first horse owned and trained in Western Australia to win the Derby was Satanate in 1982. Recent years have seen a decline in the quality of the horses entered and in

particular fewer top horses from the eastern states have contested the race. The W.A.T.C. therefore discontinued it after 1993 and the A.J.C. took over the title for its 1995 Derby.

AUSTRALIAN GUINEAS

The Australian Guineas (a Group One event over 1600m) was added to its autumn programme by the V.R.C. in 1986, as a classic contest for three year olds, a stepping stone to the Australian Cup, and to the big races in the Sydney autumn carnival. The Angus Armanasco-trained True Version won the first running of the race, ridden by Darren Gauci. Three fine horses from the Hayes stable have won the race: Military Plume, King's High and Zabeel. The filly Triscay scored in 1991, before going on to win the A.J.C. Oaks. Equal third in Triscay's Guineas was Durbridge, who then won the A.J.C. Derby. Naturalism, second to Jolly Old Mac in 1992, also scored in the A.J.C. Derby, while in 1994 Mahogany became the first horse to win the Australian Guineas-A.J.C. Derby double.

AUSTRALIAN JOCKEY CLUB (A.J.C.)

In April 1828, members of the original Sydney Turf Club broke away to form the Australian Racing and Jockey Club during a meeting at Cummings Hotel in Sydney. The club's first meetings were held at Parramatta that spring. Its operations then moved to 'the Sandy course', that is the first Randwick from 1835-8. The poor quality of the course led to its abandonment, after which the club raced at Homebush, on land owned by the Wentworth family, from March 1841. At a meeting in January of the next year, the A.R.J.C. reconstituted itself as the Australian Jockey Club. Racing continued at Homebush until 1859, but the renovation of Randwick had begun in the previous year, and the A.J.C. was back there – in much improved circumstances – by 1860. From 1863 it paid an annual rent of one peppercorn for the right to conduct meetings at Randwick.

Throughout the remainder of the 19th century, the A.J.C. gradually established its control over most aspects of racing in metropolitan and country New South Wales. It had many battles in this century with the Associated Racing Clubs, and its authority was periodically but never successfully challenged by various State governments, usually of Labor persuasion. A second track, at Warwick Farm was acquired in 1922. The history of the A.J.C., titled without modesty *The Principal Club* (1992), has been written by Martin Painter and Richard Waterhouse.

AUSTRALIAN STUD BOOK

Stud books were published in Victoria and New South Wales late in the 1850s. The Australian Stud Book, administered by the Australian Jockey Club made its first appearance in 1878. It was published in Melbourne by the bloodstock agency of William Yuille until 1909, when copyright was sold to the A.J.C. and the V.R.C. That initial edition listed about 1200 broodmares, besides cataloguing the breeding records of Australian and New Zealand racehorses. In 1933 it was decided that only horses qualified for the Stud Book were eligible for classic races, a ban that was lifted by 1957.

AUTONOMY
1889 b horse Chester – Aveline

The J.B. Clark-trained Autonomy was one of the many fine sons of Chester, especially as a juvenile. He won seven of nine starts at two, including the V.R.C. and the A.J.C. Sires' Produce Stakes. He won the latter, in 1892, with 60kg on a heavy track and started at 7/4 on. His Flemington Sires' win also came on a heavy track, and at the prohibitive odds of 7/2 on. He also won the Champagne Stakes at Randwick.

B

BADGER, HAROLD (1908-82)

Born in Melbourne, Badger was apprenticed to Richard Bradfield and rode his first winner at Echuca in 1922; his last on Gay Saint at Flemington in 1948. On six occasions Badger was premier jockey in Melbourne, five times in a row from 1938-9 to 1942-3, and again in 1947-8. He was riding as strongly at the finish of his career as at the start. In 1948 he won the third of his three Cox Plates, on Carbon Copy. Earlier he had won with Chanak in 1947 and Ajax in 1938. Ajax was the best horse with whom Badger was associated. He won 30 races on him, but is best known for the defeat at 40/1 on in the Rawson Stakes in 1939. In that year Badger also astounded jockeys battling with their weight by advertising Energy chocolate. Other big wins included the Caulfield Cup with North Wind (1936) and Columnist (1947); three Newmarkets, a Moonee Valley Cup and Caulfield Guineas, two Epsoms and two Doncasters. In the year of his retirement, Badger had his 17th and last losing ride in the Melbourne Cup of 1948. He was on Howe, who broke down. Thereafter Badger lived off his property investments.

BAGHDAD NOTE
1965 gr gelding Kurdistan – Fair Note

From a handful of starts at two, Baghdad Note was placed at Riverton in his native New Zealand, and won a Canterbury maiden. At three he won a couple of moderate races at Wellington and Petone. At four, success was still halting, although Baghdad Note won the Great Autumn and was third in the Gloaming Stakes. Like so many stoutly-bred stayers, he came into his own at five, when his wins included the Navy Day Handicap at Flemington, a second in the Herbert Power at Caulfield to the tough Tasmanian Beer Street and a dead-heat for third in the 1970 Caulfield Cup with Royal Show behind Beer Street and Voleur. Baghdad Note's greatest triumph was only a couple of weeks away, for he carried 54kg to victory in the Melbourne Cup from Vansittart, with New Zealander Midge Didham in the saddle. At six Baghdad Note's racing was restricted, but he ran third to Gay Icarus in the Underwood Stakes. At seven he followed an unglamorous path to further victories, scoring at Seymour and at Sandown (with 63kg) before finishing second to Tavel in the Adelaide Cup of 1973, giving the winner 5.5kg. Taken to Queensland,

Baghdad Note won the O'Shea Stakes and was third in the Brisbane Cup to Irish Whip. Racing on as an eight year old, this grand campaigner was second in the Werribee Cup but beat The Bite in the Sandown Cup of 1973. That year's Melbourne Cup winner, Gala Supreme, wound up third. Nor were his travels over. Baghdad Note gave 12kg and a beating to Man-O'-Blue at Ascot in Western Australia at the end of the year, before running unplaced at yet another top quality 3200m essay in the Perth Cup of 1974. Baghdad Note, a much loved grey, ended his days as one of the clerks of the course's horses at Flemington and often participated in Melbourne Cup Day parades.

BAGOT, ROBERT (c1825-1881)

Born in County Kildare, Ireland, Bagot emigrated to Queensland as a teenager. After moving to Melbourne in 1848 to work as a civil engineer, he was invited to redesign the ground of the Melbourne Cricket Club in 1861. His first contact with Flemington came when he was engaged to survey the course with a view to improvements. Though no great student of the turf, Bagot's powers of organisation led to his appointment as secretary of the Victoria Racing Club in 1864. In this role, he caused massive renovation of the Flemington racecourse, draining its central swamp to create 'the Flat', which he opened free of charge to families on race days. The first stand built during his time as secretary seated about 3,000 people and was affectionately known as 'Bagot's Cowshed'. One of his shrewdest moves was to issue each member with two ladies tickets. Bagot's reckoning was that where ladies went, men would follow. A measure of Bagot's success in popularising race-going was the fact that the average Melbourne

Cup crowd of the 1860s was 7,000 people – that figure had reached 100,000 when he retired in 1880. This represented more than a third of the population of Melbourne. Bagot was an indefatigable worker and this hastened his death. When Flemington was flooded in 1881 he assisted workers to install emergency drainage; contracted pneumonia and died on 14 April that year. The Bagot Handicap, run each January at Flemington's summer meeting, is named in his honour.

BAGUETTE

1967 br horse Rego – Dark Jewel

Unbeaten in seven starts as a two year old, including one in open company at Canterbury, Baguette was the first horse to win the autumn two year old Triple Crown in Sydney. With a Maribyrnong Plate at Flemington and a Silver Slipper already behind him, he won the Golden Slipper of 1970 from Royal Show and Dual Choice while ridden by George Moore, the Champagne and A.J.C. Sires' Produce Stakes. At three and four he continued to compete with distinction at the highest level. He won the Newmarket, Doomben 10,000 and Hobartville Stakes at three, besides showing some staying ability (at least to 10 furlongs) by running second in the Champion Stakes and the Rosehill Guineas. At four, he added the George Main, Hill and Canterbury Stakes to his 15 wins. Retired to stud, Baguette sired the gay deceiver Bagalot and the fine horse Romantic Dream, who included the Q.T.C. Sires' Produce among his wins.

BALMERINO

1972 b horse Trictrac – Dulcie

Two fine horses of this name have raced in Australia. The lesser known of the Balmerinos won the Caulfield Guineas of 1928 and was third to Strephon and

Yodelist in the Victoria Derby. Nearly half a century later, the New Zealand-bred Balmerino established an international reputation. A winner of one of his four starts at two, Balmerino swept all before him at three, winning 14 of 18 starts and finishing second in three others. After winning the Guineas at Auckland, Wellington, Canterbury and Avondale, he won the Wellington Derby by four and a half lengths. Brought to Sydney, he took the Rawson and Tulloch Stakes before tracking north. A hat trick of successes followed in Brisbane, where Balmerino won the Grand Prix from Cheyne Walk, the P.J. O'Shea Stakes and then the Brisbane Cup with 54.5kg. After a short spell he was placed in the Feehan and Turnbull Stakes in the spring of 1976, but a disappointing fourth in the Caulfield Stakes saw the horse returned to New Zealand for a longer rest.

Resuming in March, Balmerino won the Air New Zealand Stakes in course record time, the Awapuni Cup and then beat Gold and Black (who would win that year's Melbourne Cup) over 2000m in the Autumn Stakes. Just over a month later, Balmerino was racing in the United States, where five runs yielded a single minor win at Hollywood Park. Transferred to John Dunlop in Britain, Balmerino was a five lengths winner at Goodwood before running a great second, beaten one and a half lengths, by the champion Alleged in the Prix de l'Arc de Triomphe. He was relegated to second in a 2400m weight for age race in Milan for waywardness in the last 200m, before being invited to run in the Washington International at Laurel Park, where he finished a creditable fourth. Balmerino's last win was over 2000m at Goodwood, following placings at Epsom, Ascot and Sandown. Returning to stud in New Zealand, Balmerino was a success. His best son was the Victoria Derby winner Bounty Hawk.

BANKER
1860 b horse Boiardo – Jeannette

Banker has a place in the history of the Melbourne Cup as the winner who carried the lightest weight and beat the smallest ever field. No other deeds of his earned fame. In the 1863 Cup, depleted because of the scratching of Archer and the consequent absence of any interstate runners, Banker carried 33.5kg. His full brother Barwon, a Derby and St Leger winner, had top weight of 59.5kg. The weight difference turned the trick for Banker. To everyone's surprise, he won again the following day, in the Metropolitan Handicap, but never afterwards troubled the judge.

BARTLE, TED (1900-72)

Five times premier jockey in Sydney, Ted Bartle was a natural light-weight and one of the best 'money' riders in Australia. Apprenticed to Tom Scully in 1915, he graduated quickly from bush to pony to metropolitan racetracks. His first big win was on Braille in the Summer Cup of 1920; Bartle won the event again in the following year and on three more occasions. He made his mark emphatically on Sydney racing, although he partnered High Caste to many big race wins in Melbourne. Bartle won three A.J.C. Derbies and four Rosehill Guineas, four Metropolitans and three Sydney Cups. He had the mount on Ajax when he won the Cropper Plate and also rode Peter Pan. His best day's performance was to ride six winners and a second at the old Moorefield track on 22 March 1930. Bartle retired in July 1947 to go fishing, and died after a long illness in February 1972.

BATTALION

1891 ch gelding Battailous – Nancy Till

A champion Queensland-bred stayer at the end of last century, the S.G. Hatton-owned Battalion carried 65kg to victory in the Brisbane Cup of 1897. He followed up with victory in the Moreton Handicap under the crushing burden of 71kg. In that campaign he also won the Charters Towers Town Plate which was worth as much as the Brisbane Cup, a fair indication of the strength of provincial racing in Queensland in those years. Taken to Melbourne in the spring, Battalion won the Melbourne Stakes, before carrying 59kg into 10th place in the Melbourne Cup. He came back hard with a second in the Fisher Plate and then a win, under 59kg, in the Williamstown Cup. Back the following autumn in Melbourne, Battalion was second to Ayrshire in the Australian Cup with Aurum third. In the spring he had Bobbie Lewis as a regular jockey. Battalion won the Loch Plate and a second Melbourne Stakes from The Grafter and Amberite. He was then mid-field, carrying 61.5kg, in the 1898 Melbourne Cup won by The Grafter. Seeking another success in the Williamstown Cup, Battalion had to be content with second to Auriferus, to whom he conceded 22kg. Late in 1898, Battalion accompanied his old rival The Grafter to England. In 1900 he was killed in a jumping race.

BATTLE HEIGHTS

1967 br gelding Battle Waggon – Wuthering Heights

The tough and high quality New Zealand stayer Battle Heights raced until 10 (when he broke down in the 1977 Mackinnon Stakes); had 115 starts and won a fifth of them, most in top company. He had 16 wins in New Zealand, seven on his various Australian campaigns. Unraced at two, he won a couple of minor events at three in his home country. His progress was steady if unspectacular until he was six, when Battle Heights won the Wellington Cup, beat Glengowan in the Trentham Stakes and won the International Invitation Stakes at Waikato from Peg's Pride. Taken on his first outing to Australia in the autumn of 1974, he ran a moderate fourth to Igloo and Dayana in the Autumn Stakes, while underdone. Two days later he failed to please punters when he won the Sydney Cup at 30/1 from Grand Scale. But Battle Heights soon became a crowd favourite. In the A.J.C. Queen Elizabeth Stakes, at the end of the Randwick carnival, he scored by four lengths from Igloo and Dayana. At seven he downed the star three year old Taras Bulba in the Cox Plate and was still around two years later, as a nine year old, to beat that horse narrowly in a grinding finish in the Craven Plate. In between he carried 56.5 to victory in the A.J.C. Metropolitan. Nor was Battle Heights done with yet: he ran second to How Now in the 1976 Caulfield Cup and was being prepared for the Melbourne Cup in the next season, when he broke down. He last saw a racetrack as a 24 year old, when paraded in New Zealand.

BEAU GEM

1944 ch horse Helios – French Gem

Out of the 1938 V.R.C. Oaks winner and prolific broodmare French Gem (also the mother of Royal Gem), Beau Gem won three races at two, including the Byron Moore Stakes at Flemington. At three he resumed on a winning note in his home state of South Australia, winning a 1600m welter before taking the Port Adelaide Guineas. Sent to Melbourne again, Beau Gem won over 1600m at Caulfield before scoring narrowly from Chanak in the 1947

Victoria Derby. Other wins followed at weight-for-age over 1600m in Adelaide and then in the South Australian St Leger which Beau Gem won by four and a half lengths. In 1948 he was back in the spring to win the Turnbull Stakes. Beau Gem's half brother Royal Gem won the Underwood Stakes that year, and the durable Beau Gem kept the race in the family by winning in 1949 and 1950.

BEAU VITE

1936 br horse Beau Pere – Dominant

Excellently credentialled in New Zealand, Beau Vite came to Australia in 1940, when – in the care of Frank McGrath – he won four weight-for-age races besides an A.J.C. Metropolitan. Having won the Cox Plate from Ajax and the Mackinnon Stakes in that year, he repeated the dose in 1941. In between Beau Vite had returned to New Zealand where he won the Auckland Cup. While Beau Vite ran third in the Melbourne Cup of 1941, he had had a more sensational involvement with the race in the previous year. Trainer McGrath learned of threats by criminals to nobble Beau Vite (who eventually started favourite at 7/4). They were taken seriously, but in the week before the cup, and on the night of a thunderstorm, shots were fired through a hole drilled in one of the stalls at McGrath's Glenhuntly stables. The wrong horse suffered – another brown entire, El Golea, who survived his wounds. Beau Vite went on to run fourth, after suffering interference, in a Cup won by the 100/1 shot Old Rowley. In a career of 60 starts, Beau Vite won 31 races and was placed on 14 other occasions. Twenty three of his wins were at weight-for-age.

BEAU ZAM

1985 b horse Zamazaan – Mia Belle

An expensive yearling purchase at $200,000, Beau Zam repaid that outlay tenfold. Trained and part-owned by Bart Cummings, Beau Zam began his career with a win in a mid-week event at Canterbury in 1987. He failed to qualify for the Golden Slipper, but showed staying mettle with a win in the 1600m Fernhill Handicap. In the spring he beat older horses in the weight-for-age Hill Stakes, then took the Spring Champion Stakes at 6/4 on in record time. Taken to Melbourne, he was most unluckily defeated by Lord Reims in the Caulfield Cup on a bog track. Beau Zam's form tapered off and he was spelled until the autumn of 1988.

In the purple period of his career, the horse came back to win five races in a row. He began with the Group One Rawson Stakes where he defeated Bonhomie and Myocard by five lengths. Next contesting the Group One Tancred Stakes for $1,000,000, Beau Zam met outstanding overseas horses in Le Glorieux, Highland Chieftain and Vaguely Pleasant. The latter two secured second and third places, but Beau Zam won by five and a half lengths at 6/4 on. The Derby at (4/1 on) and St Leger (16/1 on) were processions as the horse kept extending his winning margins. Although due for a spell, Beau Zam was kept up to run at Canberra in the Queen Elizabeth Stakes before the person of that name. In a thrilling race, Beau Zam just accounted for the grand New Zealand horse Bonecrusher. Thereafter he suffered a frustrating and worsening series of injuries. Despite them, Beau Zam won the Apollo Stakes of 1989 and another Rawson Stakes. Sent to stud in Australia, Beau Zam failed to attract the attention that his deeds warranted, and was sold to Japanese interests.

BEGG FAMILY

Neville Begg (1931-) was apprenticed as a jockey to Maurice McCarten at Randwick. Soon beaten by weight, he stayed to work for the trainer for 22 years. In 1967 he went out on his own with a small team at Randwick which word of his skills soon augmented. His first big success came with Divide and Rule in the A.J.C. Derby of 1969. Begg was renowned as a conditioner of fillies, particularly for classic races. His horses won two A.J.C. and two V.R.C. Oaks, four Queensland and two W.A.T.C. Oaks, besides four Wakeful Stakes. He also took the 1980 Golden Slipper with Dark Eclipse. November Rain was a triple Oaks winner for Begg, but he rated another mare – Emancipation – the multiple Sydney weight-for-age winner, as his best horse. In 1990 Begg was granted permission to train at Hong Kong, where he has worked since. His place at Randwick was taken by his son Graeme, who has enjoyed early success.

BEGONIA BELLE

1965 ch mare Court Sentence – Near Belle

A top flight sprinter and 'miler', Begonia Belle won 13 of 35 starts and was placed in 13 others. Trained by A. E. 'Meggs' Elkington, she won three of six starts as a juvenile before being narrowly beaten in the Merson Cooper Stakes by her stablemate, Quezette. After an unlucky second to Sweet Embrace in the Golden Slipper of 1967, Begonia Belle returned in the spring of that year in fine form. Second in the Edward Manifold Stakes, she then beat Manina and subsequent Oaks winner Chosen Lady in the Thousand Guineas. She topped off the campaign by turning the tables on Quezette in the Sandown Guineas. The high class stayer Lowland was third. In the autumn of 1968 Begonia Belle won the Lightning Stakes and was third to Manihi in the

Newmarket. Her form tapered off during a winter campaign in Brisbane, but the following autumn she was at her peak. Beaten a head in the Oakleigh Plate by the brilliant but erratic Iga Ninja, she won the Newmarket from Black Onyx and then the Alister Clark Stakes.

BELMONT RACECOURSE

For long in use as a proprietary racetrack, owned by the Cockram family, Belmont is situated on a bend of the Swan River, near the Bunbury bridge. The Western Australian Turf Club tried to buy the course unsuccessfully in 1920, but eventually secured it in 1944. Thus the pressure of racing and training on the facilities at Ascot were alleviated, and one of the most attractive of metropolitan courses in Australia was developed.

BELMURA LAD

1974 b gelding Belmura – Fairaleana

A versatile and under-rated galloper, Belmura Lad won three minor races up to 1,850m as a two year old. But he blossomed at three, winning the Canterbury Guineas, defeating Pelican Point in the A.J.C. Derby and being placed in top company in the Rawson, Chipping Norton, Australian Champion and Queen Elizabeth Stakes. Belmura Lad won a quality handicap at Doomben and then ran second in the Queensland Grand Prix and Derby, on both occasions behind Lefroy. Bart Cummings brought Belmura Lad back at four to win the Doncaster in course record time; the All Aged Stakes; the National Stakes at Canberra and – back in Brisbane – the O'Shea Stakes at Eagle Farm in course record time. Belmura Lad did not race at five and won only once at six, but it was at the highest level, when he beat Family of Man in the Mackinnon Stakes at

Flemington, Still not a spent force, Belmura Lad was good enough to win the Metropolitan in the spring of 1981 and to repeat the dose in that year's renewal of the Mackinnon, this time from no less an opponent than Kingston Town.

BEN BOLT

1881 b horse Newbold – Lady Baldwin

In some respects, Ben Bolt's trajectory to fame anticipated that of the 20th century champion Bernborough. His career began in north Queensland, where he won nine of 10 races as a three year old, a sequence which culminated in victory in the Vice-President's Cup at Bowen where he carried 76kg and gave nearly 30kg to the second horse. On Boxing Day 1885 he ran third in the A.J.C. Summer Cup and second in the Tattersall's Cup before winning the Carrington Stakes. With prize money of 1,000 pounds, this was the richest race contested in Sydney at the time. Owner W. Strickland then sent Ben Bolt to Melbourne, where he was put in the care of the wily, Irish-born illiterate Pat Kelly. The trainer leaked a false telegram to the effect that the horse had gone wrong and would miss his spring engagements. Ben Bolt's price for the Caulfield Cup went out to 50/1 at which point the stable plunged. On Cup day he started at 8/1 and won narrowly. After that coup, Ben Bolt's connections had to wait until 1888 when he won the St Kilda Cup and, remarkably, the Doncaster, in which he carried 59.5kg to victory.

BERNBOROUGH

1939 b horse Emborough – Bern Maid

Bernborough, whose trademark was an exhilarating finishing burst despite carrying huge weights, was lost to metropolitan racing for four years because of an ownership wrangle that involved the Queensland Turf Club. He still ranks as one of the greatest Australian thoroughbreds. Bred by Harry Winten, Bernborough was originally sold to Frank and John Bach for 150 guineas. In turn they sold him to A.E. Hadwen. The Q.T.C. would not accept nominations for horses owned by the Bachs, and because they suspected Hadwen to be in collusion with the Bachs, would not accept his nomination of the horse either. In consequence, Bernborough's first four years of racing were confined to Toowoomba, where racing was not under the control of the Q.T.C. At Toowoomba Bernborough won 11 from 19, but for puny stakes of not much more than 1,000 pounds. Because of the weights the horse was being forced to carry, Hadwen decided to sell him so that Bernborough could run in town.

Trainer Harry Plant was a keen prospective buyer, as was colourful Sydney restaurateur Azzalin Romano. In the event Romano won the bidding, but Plant was given the horse to train. The Q.T.C. ban was eventually lifted, but Plant never started Bernborough at a Q.T.C. meeting. Given 58.5kg in a Canterbury Flying, Bernborough finished powerfully but could only manage fourth. Plant blamed 'Digger' McGrowdie's ride, and so began Athol Mulley's association with the horse. After a hat trick in Sydney, Bernborough came to Melbourne and won the 1946 Futurity Stakes by five lengths with 64.5kg. He then beat 27 others to win the Newmarket with 63kg, a weight-carrying record for the sprint down the Flemington straight. Back in Sydney, the big horse won the Rawson, Chipping Norton and All Aged Stakes (for what would now be five Group One wins on end). Plant now set Bernborough for the B.A.T.C. winter double of the Ahern Memorial Handicap (soon to be the Doomben 10,000) and the Doomben Cup.

In the first leg he carried 65.5kg, came from last on the turn in a field of 27 and won by two lengths in record time. He was then penalised to 68.5kg but stormed home from the tail to score a double never achieved since, let alone with such imposts.

After a trio of Sydney weight-for-age successes in the Warwick, Chelmsford and Hill Stakes, Bernborough was readied for the Spring Carnival in Melbourne, notwithstanding that he had been allocated 68kg in the Caulfield and 67.5kg in the Melbourne Cup. Despite the weight he had to carry, Bernborough was 7/4 favourite in the Caulfield Cup. After a chequered passage, he came home hard, but too late, and was beaten into fifth place. His great string of 15 wins had ended. Ever afterwards Plant blamed Mulley for losing the race and he was replaced by Billy Briscoe for the Mackinnon Stakes. Odds on, Bernborough was travelling easily to the turn when he shied and fractured a sesamoid. His racing career had reached its sad conclusion, but at least the horse was saved for the stud. Bernborough was sent to stand at Spendthrift Farm in Kentucky, where his best sons were Berseem (champion American sprinter of his year) and Bernwood (who held the world 1600m record for a time). Bernborough died in 1960. The racing world, which he electrified in 1946, will not forget him.

BEST, FRED (1912-90)

Fred Best began his career in racing as a jockey in the Townsville area. After the Second World War he set up as a trainer at Eagle Farm with a single horse, but ended by winning the Brisbane trainers' premiership no less than 16 times. Among his best winners were Book Link, who won the Queensland Guineas and Derby in 1956, and then with George Moore up the

Doomben Cup two years later. Best also trained Prince Medes to win the Stradbroke in 1969 (a race in which he had been third the previous year) and Bengalla Lad, winner of the 1972 Doomben 10,000.

BEST WESTERN

1978 ch horse Bletchingly – Grease Paint

A winner of his only two starts at two, while under Neville Begg's care, Best Western showed notable potential for his three year old year. Transferred to the Bart Cummings stable, the colt surpassed the expectations of his optimistic owners by winning five of six starts. The only blot on his record was a fifth first up in the San Domenico Stakes. A fortnight later, Best Western took the Up and Coming Stakes at Randwick and then strolled home in the Peter Pan, first leg of the 1981 Sydney spring Triple Crown. In the second leg, Best Western won even more easily, by five lengths over the 1900m of the Gloaming Stakes. With two down and one to go, Best Western earned fame and a $100,000 bonus by taking the Spring Champion Stakes from Brewery Boy. Spelled, he returned on a winning note in the autumn of 1982, winning the Royal Sovereign Stakes before being retired to stud.

BETTER BOY

1951 b horse My Babu – Better So

While a sound performer at the track, winning nine races from 1200m to 2400m, the Irish-bred Better Boy never reached the heights there that he later managed as a sire. In England he won only once in each of his two and three year old seasons. Brought to Australia in 1954 by David Whiteside and sent to be trained by Barney Warke, Better Boy won at Kilmore; took the Seymour Cup and recorded his best win in the 1955 Hotham Handicap. This was not the horse's most popular win. He started at 40/1 after failing as favourite in the Werribee Cup the previous run. In the following year, Better Boy also had the distinction of being first past the post in the 1956 Caulfield Cup, but unfortunately had lost his rider. Better Boy won the Woodend Cup in 1957 and took the Gardenvale Handicap at Caulfield in 1958.

Retired to Whiteside's Range View Stud at Carrum Downs, Better Boy sired a series of top-line performers. Among the best of them were the Newmarket winner Cap D'Antibes, Chosen Lady (who won a V.R.C. Oaks for Tommy Woodcock), Woodcock's top stayer Reckless, Epsom winner La Neige, Craftsman (a Victoria Derby and dual Australian Cup winner), the brilliant sprinter Tolerance and the multiple Group One winner Century. Better Boy was champion sire on four occasions between 1965-6 and 1976-7. Of his 479 foals, 307 were winners, including 36 stakes winners. He was also an outstanding sire of dams. Progeny of daughters of Better Boy number Better Loosen Up, Rose of Kingston and Spirit of Kingston, Full on Aces and So Called. Better Boy was put down in 1975.

BETTER LOOSEN UP

1985 b gelding Loosen Up – Better Fantasy

Late maturing, Better Loosen Up proved himself to be a horse of the highest international quality. The early part of his story is bound up with the misfortunes of his first owner and trainer, Les Theodore. Better Loosen Up was the second champion who had been in Theodore's care. Earlier he had trained Campaign King, then sold him to Bart Cummings in order to pay off his property at Berrigan. Shortly after he bought Better Loosen Up for $10,000. Sixth at his first start at Bendigo, the horse was spelled and gelded. He came back in April

1988 to win at the same track. Theodore sold his Berrigan property at a loss so substantial that he was eventually forced also to part with his share in Better Loosen Up, again to Cummings. Now racing in Sydney, the horse won a mid-week race at Canterbury and was later placed behind subsequent Group One winners Comrade and Livistona Lane. In January 1989 he won three metropolitan races in a row; ran second to Riverina Charm in the Canterbury Guineas and then sixth in the Rosehill Guineas. It was later diagnosed that he was suffering from a hairline pelvic fracture, and so he was turned out.

David Hayes was the third trainer of Better Loosen Up. Back at the track for a minor event on Caulfield Cup day, the horse was narrowly beaten. He then ended a dismal Flemington Carnival run for Hayes by winning the Group One Honda Stakes on the final day. Sent to Perth, he scored further last stride Group One wins in the Winfield and Railway Stakes. Reappearing stronger than ever in the autumn, he beat Vo Rogue and Super Impose in the Blamey, before finishing second to the former in the Australian Cup. Sent to Sydney, Better Loosen Up beat an outstanding field in the Rawson Stakes. It included Sydeston, Dr Grace, Horlicks, King's High and his old rival Vo Rogue. Wet tracks led to Better Loosen Up's undoing in the Tancred and Queen Elizabeth Stakes, but his best season was yet to come.

In the spring of 1990, Better Loosen Up won seven races in a row, after a first-up fourth in the Liston Stakes. He took the Feehan and Turnbull Stakes, before equalling the Moonee Valley track record in a thrilling win over Sydeston in the Cox Plate. This was followed by a win in the Mackinnon Stakes which ensured an invitation to the Japan Cup. Better Loosen

Up became the first Australian horse to win the race, coming from a seemingly hopeless position on the turn to achieve a characteristically late, narrow, but remarkable win. Campaigning on into the autumn of 1991, he won the Blamey, before defeating Vo Rogue by what was – for him – the luxurious margin of five and a half lengths in the Australian Cup. His winnings now amounted to more than $4.5 million, and there they stayed after this grand horse broke down and was retired.

BETTING SHOPS

In an attempt better to regulate gambling, the government of Tasmania legalised off-course betting shops for bookmakers in 1932. They remained a feature of the local racing scene, particularly the Murray Street premises in Hobart, until the long-delayed and controversial introduction of the T.A.B. to the state in 1974. South Australia briefly legalised betting shops from 1933-42. In other states, off-course gambling in the form of illegal S.P. bookmaking had flourished instead, notoriously in New South Wales.

BIG PHILOU

1965 b gelding Le Filou – Pink Lady

One of the most controversial horses to race in Australia, the New Zealand-bred Big Philou was taken along gently by trainer Bart Cummings. He did not race at two, but won five of 11 at three. In the spring of 1969 he ran second to Shorengio in the Feehan Stakes, took the Patrobas Welter and then surprised by running last of six to Wings of the Morning in the Anglesey Handicap. Big Philou redeemed himself in the Caulfield Stakes, going under narrowly to the long shot Hamua. Accordingly, he started favourite in the Caulfield Cup. In a sensational race, Big Philou was beaten a

neck by Nausori. Jockey Roy Higgins confidently protested and Big Philou was awarded the race. The only previous time that this had occurred was in the 1893 Caulfield Cup, which was won on protest by Sanfoin over Tim Swiveller. Big Philou's topsy-turvy carnival continued. Second to Roman Consul in the Mackinnon Stakes, he was strongly supported to take the big Cups double (for which he had been backed to win $600,000). Shortly before the Melbourne Cup, Big Philou was found to be scouring badly and was scratched. He had been nobbled with the purgative Danthron. Charges were laid, but no prosecutions resulted.

Big Philou was back in the autumn, where he defeated Rain Lover by a half head in the famous two horse Queen Elizabeth Stakes. In the spring of 1970, Big Philou won the Underwood Stakes and was installed as favourite to win a consecutive Caulfield Cup. But he was injured in a track gallop and Cummings intended to scratch him. Big Philou's owner the Honourable Charles Gawith disagreed, withdrawing the horse angrily from Cummings' stables. Big Philou was scratched anyway. Not that his part in the Cups' story was done. In 1971 he ran a distant third to the top-line gallopers Gay Icarus and Igloo in the Caulfield Cup. In the Melbourne Cup he badly interfered with Gay Icarus and cost that horse any chance of a famous victory.

BILL STUTT STAKES
see MOONEE VALLEY STAKES

BIRCHLEY, EDWARD ('THE FIREMAN') (1931-)

One of the most flamboyant of gamblers in the 1960s and 1970s, Birchley was an ardent swimmer, a former professional boxer and had been a Queensland fireman for 17 years before he took properly to the punt. His bank-roll came from land speculation on the Gold Coast, and from early success in the risky business of preferring to plonk on short-priced favourites. While 'The Fireman' had some massive collects (and became too difficult for the Brisbane ring to accommodate), his luck ran out. In December 1974, after a bad losing spell, he complained that bookies and jockeys were colluding to pull the short-priced horses who he had supported. No evidence was forthcoming, and Birchley came less and less often to the track. The last reported sighting of him was at Warwick Farm in 1983.

BIRTHDAYS OF HORSES

In 1860, an Australian Jockey Club plan was adopted whereby 1 August would become the notional birthday of all Australian racehorses. At the same time, this became the first day of each new racing season.

BISCAY

1965 ch horse Star Kingdom – Magic Symbol

Scintillating sprinter and prepotent sire, Biscay along with his high-class brothers – Star of Heaven and Tattenham – was raced by his breeder Stanley Wootton and trained by Angus Armanasco. Like another Star Kingdom prodigy, Todman, Biscay opened his career by running an Australian record: in his case over four furlongs in the Debutant Stakes at Caulfield in 1967. He backed up with a spectacular victory in the Maribyrnong Plate and – in the autumn of 1968 – with a courageous win, under duress, in the Merson Cooper Stakes. Biscay then campaigned without success in Sydney. He returned to the track as a three year old in the spring of 1968 and was unbeaten in three runs. But it was as a sire that Biscay

left his mark on Australian racing, outranking every other son of Star Kingdom, except Todman's internationally renowned brother Noholme, in creating a dynasty of his own. In his first crop, Biscay produced the champion sire-to-be Bletchingly, and the remarkably successful Zephyr Bay. From that start, he established himself as a 'sire's sire'. In mid-career he sired the record-breaking producer of precocious horses, Marscay. He also sired the dams of such outstanding gallopers as Marauding, Our Poetic Prince and Schillaci. As a sire of racehorses, Biscay was both consistent – regularly appearing in the list of leading stallions – and versatile, producing such brilliant juveniles as Shaybisc and the Golden Slipper victors Marscay and Bounding Away; winners of three year old classics, among them Bounding Away and Lowan Star; open-age sprinters of the calibre of Bletchingly, Zephyr Bay, Ubetido and Scarlet Bisque. Suffering from an incurable foot disease, Biscay was put down in his 22nd year at the Bhima Stud, Scone, in 1987.

BLACKLOCK, WALTER (1862-1935)

Until increasing weight forced his retirement in 1890, Blacklock had been one of Queensland's leading jockeys. His wins included the Queensland Derby on Goldfinder in 1882, the Brisbane Cup on Mozart the next year and the Queensland Cup of 1895 when he rode My Love. Blacklock set up as a trainer at Drummond Lodge next to the Eagle Farm racecourse and was at the head of his profession for many years. With an outstanding record in classic races in his home state, Blacklock also trained the winners of six Stradbroke Handicaps and won the Brisbane Cup with his own horse, Yelverton, in 1894. Forays south netted some big victories, but they were well spaced. Togo took the Doncaster in 1908, while perhaps Blacklock's best horse, Gold Tie, won the Futurity in 1920, having won the Stradbroke in the two previous years. A notable horseman, Blacklock was less at home in the mechanised world, and his notion of stopping a car was to pull the steering wheel and cry 'Whoa!'

BLACK ONYX

1965 gr gelding Pipe of Peace – Organdie

A small and courageous sprinter, Black Onyx was trained throughout his Australian career by T.J Smith, and owned by the Bootle family of Narromine in western New South Wales. Unfancied at 33/1 in his first two year old start, at Rosehill in January 1968, Black Onyx beat Royal Parma by two and a half lengths. He defeated that horse again at his next start, and won a third in succession, thus ensuring a high place in the Golden Slipper market. The Melbourne colt Biscay started at 10/9 on favourite; Black Onyx and his stablemate Flying Fable were on the second line at 13/2. George Moore was obligated to ride Black Onyx for Tommy Smith, but the colt finished down the track behind Royal Parma. The grey made amends quickly, winning the A.J.C. Sires' at 14/1. In the autumn he returned to run second to Begonia Belle in the Newmarket. Taken north, he gave Moore a 46th birthday present with victory in the 1969 Doomben 10,000. Tried over an unsuitably long distance, Black Onyx still managed second in the 2200m Doomben Cup. Once more sent to Melbourne for the autumn, Black Onyx carried 57.5 to victory over Tauto in the Newmarket. After third placings later that year in the Doncaster and Stradbroke Handicaps, Black Onyx took a second successive Doomben 10,000 under 59kg. Other top class wins for the horse

included the Tramway and Hill Stakes in Sydney, the Lightning and Orr Stakes in Melbourne. He bled in the 1970 Hill Stakes and the problem recurred in a Melbourne track gallop. Given the benefit of the doubt, Black Onyx bled badly in the Futurity Stakes and was banned forever from racing in Australia. His career ended obscurely. Sent to America, Black Onyx – racing on drugs to prevent bleeding – won a couple of minor races, but deserves more honour in his own country.

BLAZING SADDLES

1974 br horse Todman – Lady Simone

A beautifully bred grandson of Star Kingdom, Blazing Saddles was a brilliant two year old who won the Debutant Stakes by 10 lengths. Trainer Tommy Smith sent the colt along an unusual path to the Blue Diamond Stakes, by running him in the Barton Handicap against older horses. Blazing Saddles ran down the track, but back against his own age, won the Blue Diamond at his next start by three lengths. Taken to Sydney for the Golden Slipper, he could only manage third to the outstanding juvenile Luskin Star. Blazing Saddles was retired to stud. He stood first at Woodlands Stud in New South Wales, but in 1984 was removed to Derisley Wood Stud in England. Best of his sons was Mr Brooks, winner of the Group One July Cup at Newmarket over six furlongs. Subsequently the horse returned to Australia, standing first in South Australia and then in Queensland.

BLETCHINGLY

1970 br horse Biscay – Coogee

Bred and owned by Stanley Wootton and trained by Angus Armanasco, Bletchingly was lightly raced, but won four of his five starts. The wins included a course record of 56.8 for 1000m at Flemington in the Moomba Handicap, and the Group One Galaxy at Randwick over 1100m. Those performances hardly prepared observers for Bletchingly's resilience and versatility when he went to stand at the Widden Stud. Of his 423 progeny, more than 75% were winners, and 45 of them stakes winners. He was leading sire for three seasons in a row from 1979-80. Among the outstanding gallopers he sired were Canny Lad and Canny Lass, Coronation Day, Emancipation, Lord Ballina, Spirit of Kingston and True Version. Foremost among his progeny was Kingston Town, one of the greatest of all Australian racehorses. Bletchingly, while proving to be a great sire of winners, and of broodmares, did not pass as much of his ability on to his sons. He died in July 1993.

BLUE DIAMOND STAKES

The premier two year old race in Victoria was established in 1971 in response to the success of the S.T.C.'s Golden Slipper Stakes. Run in the autumn at Caulfield, the race was first won by Tolerance, giving Roy Higgins the first of four winners in the race, the others being Lord Dudley (1975), Blazing Saddles (1977) and Star Shower (1979). He was also beaten a short half head on Century by John's Hope in the second running of the Diamond. A good race for fillies, it was won by 40/1 shot Out of Danger in 1976, who edged out the favourite and Colin Hayes' stablemate, Desirable. Bounding Away won by four lengths in 1986. Among colts, Manikato's win in 1978 was notable, while Rancher (who went on to become a top sire) beat War Chest and Grosvenor in 1982. John's Hope, Manikato, Bounding Away and Courtza progressed from the Blue Diamond to annex the Golden Slipper.

BLUE SPEC
1899 br horse True Blue – Specula

Bought in Sydney by erstwhile prospector and drover Paddy Connolly, Blue Spec was taken to Western Australia to race. In 1904 he won the Kalgoorlie and Perth Cups. Connolly was persuaded to try his luck with the horse in Melbourne, and Blue Spec was sent to be trained by Walter Hickenbotham. Thriving in the east, Blue Spec completed the unusual double of the Moonee Valley and Melbourne Cups of 1905, the latter in what was then record time. Connolly evidently had a large share of the attractive odds of 10/1 about his horse. Blue Spec became the first horse from Western Australia (by one reckoning) to win a Melbourne Cup until Black Knight in 1984. He raced on with success in the west, taking the Helena Vale Cup of 1907 under 63.5kg.

B.M.W. STAKES

Premier weight-for-age distance race in the Sydney autumn carnival, the B.M.W. (formerly the Tancred) Stakes is run over 2400m at Group One level. Its beginnings were modest. In 1963 Maidenhead beat Kwatcha and Ruato. Two solid handicapping stayers were among the winners in that decade: Striking Force in 1966, Prince Grant three years later. In 1972 Tails won and Apollo Eleven followed him the next year. By the end of the 1970s the race had gained more lustre. Hyperno won in 1978, while in 1979 Shivaree beat Dulcify. Kingston Town saluted in 1980 from Double Century and Gold and Black, Sydney and Melbourne Cup winners respectively. Trissaro won in 1983, was second to Hayai the following year, while in turn that horse was second to Alibhai in 1985. Now the race briefly became the preserve of brilliant staying three year olds.

Bonecrusher won in 1986, followed by Myocard and Beau Zam in the next two years. Our Poetic Prince in 1989, Sydeston and then Dr Grace maintained the standard of the B.M.W. as one of the toughest of all weight-for-age tests on the Australian racing calendar.

BOBADIL

1895 br horse Bill of Portland – She

A brilliant racehorse who became a top sire, Bobadil won the 1898 A.J.C. Champagne Stakes from Essex and Cocos. At three he won the All Aged Stakes at Randwick before being sent to Melbourne where he was victorious in the Ascot Vale Stakes, then defeated Cocos and Cordite in the Caulfield Guineas. Returning in the autumn of 1899, Bobadil – who had run second in the race the year before – scored in the Futurity Stakes. He then won the St Leger, Australian Cup and the three mile Champion Stakes. Retired to stud, he had a fine career, notably as a sire of dams: from the Bobadil mare Bob Cherry came the champion Eurythmic, from Polacca came Whittier.

BONECRUSHER

1982 ch gelding Pag-Asa – Imitation

This aptly named New Zealand galloper, by the unfashionable sire Pag-Asa, was one of the best and toughest competitors of the mid-1980s. Winner of 18 of his 43 starts, the Frank Ritchie-trained gelding was placed in 16 others. Bonecrusher was particularly brilliant at three and four. He won the New Zealand Derby in the spring of 1985 and the Air New Zealand Stakes before being sent to Sydney for the autumn carnival in the following year. Bonecrusher promptly won the Tancred Stakes and – coming from last on the turn – the A.J.C. Derby. Put away for the spring, he was back better than ever. He won the Underwood Stakes from At Talaq (whose string of second placings that spring would eventually end when he won the Melbourne Cup), scored by five lengths in the Caulfield Stakes and then fronted for one of the most famous of all runnings of the Cox Plate. Bonecrusher started at 10/9 on favourite and duelled with fellow New Zealand champion Our Waverley Star from well before the turn, finally prevailing by a neck. This was Bonecrusher's seventh Group One win from seven attempts. Arguably neither he nor Our Waverley Star was ever as good again, and neither enjoyed a happy trip overseas for the Japan Cup soon afterwards.

But Bonecrusher was back in the autumn. Again he met At Talaq, and again finished in front of him – by a short half head in a great race for the Australian Cup. Though no longer as sound as he had been, Bonecrusher was third in the 1987 Segenhoe Stakes to Myocard and Our Waverley Star. Then he ran a fine third in the 1988 Australian Cup (a race which had been tipped to be a match race between him and Vo Rogue, until Dandy Andy spoiled the fun). Next Ritchie set him for the Queen Elizabeth Stakes in Canberra, where he was just beaten by Australia's best horse of the time, Beau Zam, to whom Bonecrusher was spotting a couple of years. With earnings of over $2,000,000, Bonecrusher was retired.

BOOKMAKERS

Bookmakers began operating in Australia at the first officially recognised race meeting, which was held at Hyde Park in Sydney on 15 October 1810. Several men set themselves up in booths to accept bets from a crowd estimated at 11,000. In those times bookmakers did not issue tickets. They entered clients' bets in pocket books (hence the term bookmaker) and settled after the meeting. Eventually people started betting in cash, with the result that many set up as bookmakers, hoping for a quick killing. No regulations were in force, so unscrupulous operators frequently decamped with the money in the bag, with punters left lamenting. There were honest, big betting bookmakers, wagering fortunes from the 1870s. One was Robert Siever, who in the early 1880s became the first in his calling to use a bag for his dealings, the first to issue tickets for each bet and the first to call the odds while a clerk recorded the wagers. Siever, who went on to several more colourful careers in England, was said to have won 80,000 pounds in his first year.

Welching bookmakers still caused problems, with the result that the V.R.C. imposed a registration fee of 25 pounds a year in 1882 for those operating in the Paddock at Flemington. Next year Hill bookmakers were required to pay a 10 pound fee. Registered bagmen were identified by a silver lapel badge. The A.J.C. followed suit, with Randwick bookmakers registered three months later. Welchers were still common, though the violent end of one of them – Donald McLeod in 1906 – at the hands of the Flemington crowd, caused uproar. The profession is now very tightly controlled. All bookmakers and clerks are registered and the Bookmakers' Guarantee Fund ensures that all gambling debts can be met. But the game is harder than ever, and the number of bookmakers has steadily dwindled, through the competition of the totalisator and multiplication of gambling attractions. Sports betting and on-course telephones may give some bookmakers a lease of life into the next century, but their colour is in danger of being lost to the world of racing.

BOOTS, LES (c1915-1987)

Adelaide jumps jockey Les Boots happily admitted that he was perhaps the worst at his trade in the world. He had 39 starts over obstacles for 41 falls. On one occasion he fell, remounted the horse, only to be dislodged again. His next fall came almost immediately afterwards, when he came off the stretcher upon which he was being taken to the casualty room. Boots' record as a jumps rider was so consistently unfortunate that his wife packed his pyjamas with his riding gear on the reasonable expectation that he would regularly end up in hospital. Boots never rode a placegetter during his flat racing career, and seldom travelled more than half a mile before parting company with his jumps mounts. Apprenticed in 1929 to Harry Butler at Geelong, he retired in 1947 with two unfulfilled ambitions: to win a race, and to ride over fences in England (notwithstanding that he was worried about drowning at the water jump). A jumping career, which had begun with a bonebreaking fall off Umtalia at Cheltenham ended when he came off Paola at Victoria Park, sustaining injuries which sidelined him for two years. Racing lost a wonderful raconteur and true turf character when Les Boots died in 1987. His advice to aspiring jumps riders was succinct: 'Stop where you are. Get a job outside'.

BOUGOURE, GARNET (1923-)

Garnet Bougoure rode with moderate success in Australia, his best win being on Prince of Fairies in the 1951 Brisbane Cup. He and George Moore had married sisters, and it was Bougoure who set an example that Moore would follow by deciding to try his luck overseas. In 1952 he moved to Europe. Based mainly in Ireland, he rode for Vincent O'Brien and Paddy Prendergast.

His big race wins included the English Oaks on Ragusa, the St Leger and two Irish Derbies. He also had a stint in Malaya, winning the jockeys' premiership there in 1958. Bougoure rode with success in continental Europe and in India, emulating the adventurous Australian jockeys who had taken similar paths and risks since Frank Wootton at the turn of the century.

BOUNDING AWAY

1983 gr mare Biscay – Who Can Say

Trainer Tommy Smith's favourite filly, Bounding Away won six of seven starts as a two year old, beaten only by Diamond Shower in the A.J.C. Sires' Produce. In this campaign Bounding Away won the Blue Diamond Stakes by four lengths; with Mick Dittman up won the Golden Slipper at 5/4 and then the Champagne Stakes from Myocard and Diamond Shower. At three she enjoyed a lesser strike rate, failing to win in open company, although she took the Orlando Wines Classic in the autumn of 1987 against fillies and mares. Nevertheless she competed at the highest level, and besides second placings in the Ascot Vale and Veuve Clicquot Stakes, and a second in the Rosehill Guineas, she won the Flight Stakes in the spring of 1986 and had a final big race triumph when she took the 1987 A.J.C. Oaks, before being retired to stud.

BOUNTY HAWK

1980 b or br gelding Balmerino – Marie's Daughter

Injured as a yearling, Bounty Hawk's start in racing was delayed until his three year old year. While he won at Warwick Farm, he was last in the Spring Champion Stakes. Nevertheless trainer Bart Cummings was convinced of his staying promise and sent Bounty Hawk to Melbourne. There he was placed in the Norman Robinson Stakes at Caulfield and in the Geelong Derby Trial, before Harry White saw him home in the Victoria Derby. Now Bounty Hawk followed a familiar path for Cummings' stayers of that period and headed west. Second in the W.A. Derby (when he split Old Currency and Old Spice), Bounty Hawk won the Western Mail Classic and the Australian Derby. In the autumn of 1984 he was second in the Hobartville Stakes and second to Beechcraft in the Canterbury Guineas. At four Bounty Hawk progressed to weight-for-age company, winning the Underwood and Mackinnon Stakes in the spring of 1984, besides finishing second to Affinity in the Caulfield Cup and running unplaced as 4/1 favourite in the Melbourne Cup. Bounty Hawk was retired after five unplaced runs at five.

BRADFIELD, RICHARD (1862-1944)

Born near Bendigo, Bradfield was established as a private trainer at Elsternwick when only 20. His career lasted almost six decades. First of Bradfield's four Melbourne Cups came when Patron won in 1894. His later winners were The Victory (1902), Night Watch (1918) and Backwood (1924). Bradfield won the 1918 Caulfield Cup with King Offa and believed that the galloper would give him the Cups double. King Offa, starting at 7/2 in the Melbourne Cup, was defeated by his stablemate Night Watch at 12/1. Perhaps Bradfield's most remarkable training feat was the 1919 Caulfield Cup in which he trained the first three place-getters: Lucknow, Night Watch and Chrome. Known as a masterly trainer of apprentices as well, Bradfield superintended the early careers of such later champion jockeys as Harold Badger.

BRAVO

1883 b horse Grand Flaneur – The Orphan

Bred near Braidwood, Bravo was the first Melbourne Cup winner to be sired by a Melbourne Cup winner, in his case the brilliant, unbeaten Grand Flaneur. Bought by the stockbroker W.T. Jones, Bravo was trained at Dowling Forest, Ballarat, by Tommy Wilson. He showed staying class in the spring of 1888 by winning a 14 furlong race at Flemington and was a good thing beaten when third at 7/1 equal favourite in the Caulfield Cup. A year later he dead-heated for third in the Caulfield Stakes and was again unfortunate when third once more as a beaten favourite (this time at 3/1) in the Caulfield Cup. Unsound throughout his career, he was lame after that race, so that a Melbourne Cup start was in doubt. But Wilson's perseverance got him to the post. Rumours that the lameness had been staged to get a big price about the horse persisted. Bravo started at 8/1 and beat the champion Carbine, whose turn it would be next year, and the unlucky Melos.

BREASLEY, ARTHUR EDWARD ('SCOBIE') (1914-)

Born at Wagga Wagga, Breasley was apprenticed at the age of 12. He gained his nick-name from the famous trainer James Scobie, a friend of Breasley's father, who was also a trainer, if not on the same scale. After moving to Melbourne, Breasley rode his first winner in town in 1928; his first feature race on Cragford in the Metropolitan of 1930 at Randwick. He won a Williamstown Cup on the perennial Melbourne Cup place-getter, Shadow King, in 1933. During the Second World War, he won four Caulfield Cups in succession beginning with the brilliant mare Tranquil Star in 1942. He also won the Victoria Derby, V.R.C. Oaks, Epsom and Sydney Cup during the 1940s. A trip to England in 1950 persuaded Breasley to try his luck there, and he rode with a success unparalleled abroad by any other Australian jockey. He was back at Caulfield in 1952 to win a fifth Cup on Peshawar, but soon returned to ride in England. A bad fall at Alexandra Park threatened to paralyse Breasley, but he recovered so completely that he won a first British jockeys' premiership in 1957, while riding for the stable of Sir Gordon Richards. He won the title again from 1961-3, on the last occasion riding 176 winners to defeat his great rival, Lester Piggott, by one. In all Breasley rode 3,251 winners, more than 2,000 of them in England. Twice he won the English Derby: in 1964 on Santa Claus, two years later on Charlottown. Ballymoss gave him the 1958 Prix de l'Arc de Triomphe. He never won a Melbourne Cup: Gold Chick, in 1964, was his 17th and last losing ride in the race. After retiring in 1968, Breasley trained in England. His best winner was Steel Pulse, who took the Irish Derby of 1972. After short training stints in France and the United States, Breasley retired to the Bahamas, although he makes regular visits to Australia.

BRIBERY

1901 b gelding Malvolio – The Gift

Trained by D.J. Price, Bribery was one of the top jumpers of the early years of this century. He carried 75kg to victory in the Caulfield Grand National of 1907 (later the Australian Steeple) and in the same season won the Grand National Hurdle at Flemington with 81kg. Sustaining that form, Bribery won the Grand National Steeple two years later (with F. Burn up), and carried 81.5kg to beat Confederate (who was in receipt of 14kg from him) by 15 lengths on a heavy track. Only Sussex (with 82kg in 1881) and Redleap (with 83.5kg in

1892) have won the Steeple with more weight.

BRISBANE AMATEUR TURF CLUB

Formed by a group of businessmen led by newspaper owner G.M. Dash in January 1923, the Brisbane Amateur Turf Club raced first at Albion Park. Viewed with some suspicion by Queensland racing authorities, who believed that John Wren was behind its operations, the club fairly soon established respectable credentials. It took up an option to buy Albion Park, and then leased Doomben, a track owned by Wren across the road from the Q.T.C. course at Eagle Farm. Racing began at Doomben in May 1933 and the course is now the headquarters of the B.A.T.C. and site of its premier events the Doomben 10,000 and Doomben Cup. Albion Park was closed in 1981.

BRISBANE CUP

The first race to be known as the Brisbane Cup (in honour of the governor of New South Wales, Sir Thomas Brisbane) was run in 1826 at the Grose Farm racecourse near Sydney. Victor was the champion early colonial Arab stallion, Junius. The first Brisbane Cup proper was contested over 18 furlongs at Eagle Farm in 1866 and won by Forester. It is now a 3200m Group One event. Fitz-Grafton was the first dual winner in 1904 and 1905. In his second victory he carried 63.5kg and gave James McGill his seventh winner of the Brisbane Cup. Battalion, with 65kg in 1897, is the highest weighted winner of the race. Subsequent outstanding horses to annex the Brisbane Cup have included Redcraze (1956), Igloo (1974) and Balmerino (1976). Macdougal won the Brisbane-Melbourne Cup double in 1959, but the horse who received the greatest reception was Tulloch in 1961 when he defeated Sharply, who was in receipt of 10kg from him, in this, Tulloch's last race.

BRISCOE, BILLY (1911-)

After learning his trade on bush and unregistered tracks in Queensland, Billy Briscoe moved to town and was five times leading rider in Brisbane in the 1930s and 1940s. Following the Second World War he tried his luck in Sydney. He was rewarded with immediate success, and controversy. On the good colt Prince Standard, Briscoe won the 1946 Hobartville and Rosehill Guineas, and then the Victoria Derby. The Derby win took place on the same afternoon that he had ridden the odds on favourite Bernborough in the Mackinnon Stakes (replacing Athol Mulley, after the latter's defeat on the horse in the Caulfield Cup) only to have him shy at a crossing and break down. In this season Briscoe's good fortune overcame that ill luck. He won one of the divisions of the Cox Plate on Leonard (Flight took the other) besides the Thousand Guineas, Sydney Cup, Villiers, Chipping Norton and All Aged Stakes.

BRISEIS

1874 br filly Tim Whiffler – Musidora

A filly whose deeds now inspire incredulity, the James Wilson-trained Briseis won the Doncaster as a two year old, with the featherweight of 35kg. Despite a record of three minor placings from five starts, she ran 4/1 equal favourite. The filly then proceeded to win a Flying and the All Aged Stakes. Taken to Melbourne for the spring of 1876, Briseis raced on all four days of the Flemington carnival. In an unprecedented performance, Briseis took the Victoria Derby, the Melbourne Cup and the Oaks, before running second to Pride of the Hills in the Mares' Produce Stakes. In an era when young horses, let alone potential broodmares are more tenderly treated, these feats have never been emulated. Briseis was unplaced in four more runs in the autumn of 1877. Sent to the stud in 1879, she was put down after falling and fracturing her skull.

BRITT, EDGAR (1913-)

One of the first Australian jockeys to establish an overseas reputation, Britt was originally apprenticed to Mick Polson at Moorefield. A highlight of his early years as a jockey was a trip to the United States with Polson in 1933, where he won several races, including the Baltimore Handicap at Pimlico, on Winooka. A year later Britt accepted a retainer to ride in India, where in little over a decade he won seven jockeys' premierships. The Maharaja of Baroda, for whom Britt had ridden with success, invited Britt to ride for him in England in 1945. There he rode the winners of about 1,200 races, among them seven classics: two Oaks, two St Legers, two One Thousand Guineas and a Two Thousand Guineas. After retiring in 1959, Britt returned to Australia, where he abandoned thoughts of training to write a racing column for the *Daily Telegraph*.

BROKER'S TIP

1970 ch horse Summertime – Fatehpur Sikri

Winner of the Canterbury Guineas in 1968, Broker's Tip recorded three other wins at three. In the spring of 1969 he was second to Black Onyx in the Tramway Stakes, before Darby McCarthy saw him home over Alrello in the Epsom. In the autumn of 1970, Broker's Tip won the Rawson Stakes and then beat Alrello by a neck in the Doncaster. That unlucky galloper was also second behind Broker's Tip in the All Aged Stakes. In the spring Broker's Tip returned to the winning list in the Canterbury Stakes, and was runner-up

to Planet Kingdom in the Craven Plate and to Ricochet in the George Main Stakes.

BROWN, JOE (1919 -)

One of Australia's leading and longest serving racecallers, Brown was born in Dandenong, but went to Tasmania to further his career, broadcasting there for the A.B.C. He was transferred to Melbourne, where he called about 20,000 races in a 35 year career, including 33 Melbourne Cups. He retired in 1981 after calling the Moonee Valley Hurdle. Less flamboyant than such contemporaries as Bert Bryant, Brown was an accurate and respected caller and course broadcaster.

BROWN, JOHN (1850-1930)

The Newcastle coal magnate John Brown began to race horses under the name 'J. Baron' in the 1890s and enjoyed outstanding success as an owner. Prince Foote, son of the stallion Sir Foote who Brown had imported from England, won both the A.J.C. and V.R.C. St Legers and Derbies as well as the Melbourne Cup in the 1909-10 season, thus equalling the feat of Poseidon in 1906. In 1919 Brown's colt Richmond Main dead-heated with Artilleryman in the A.J.C. Derby, before winning the Victoria Derby. Brown seldom enjoyed cordial relations with those who worked for him, whether they were racehorse trainers or miners. His affections were rather directed towards animals, especially the 240 brooodmares and seven stallions who – at their peak – he maintained on his stud properties.

BRYANT, BERT (1927-1991)

Most loved of all Australian racecallers because he never failed to 'talk through his kick', to side with punters rather than racing authorities, Bert Bryant was born in Dubbo.

A victim for the punt from his tender years, Bryant talked his way into calling country races for the local station when manager Wally Grant gave him a break. Bryant's first assignment was at Geurie: 27 Melbourne Cup calls were at that stage well over the horizon. After numerous misadventures, Bryant answered an advertisement which led to his appointment as assistant racecaller to Tom Moon at Melbourne's radio station 3UZ. He began work in November 1948 and was employed there (besides stints with Melbourne television channels 9 and 0) until his retirement in 1977. It was Bryant who described horses parked rearwards as 'seeing more tails than Hoffman', others scouting wide as 'covering more ground than the early explorers'. His 'Turf Talk' programme was a never emulated highlight of race coverage (and much else) in Australian radio. His broadcast of the two horse race for the Queen Elizabeth Stakes between Big Philou and Rain Lover in March 1970 is arguably the classic call of them all. And yet he fudged the 1975 Melbourne Cup and gradually found that the strain told. A mild stroke in April 1977 was followed by a brief and unsuccessful comeback to the microphone. Bryant retired and collaborated in a genial memoir with Neil Phillipson, *The Bert Bryant Story* (1978). He died on 3 April 1991.

BUCKINGHAM, BEVERLEY (1965-)

Born in England, Buckingham is the daughter of the trainer Ted Buckingham. Apprenticed to her father in Tasmania, she first rode in the 1980-1 season. Only a year later, while still an apprentice, Buckingham became the first and so far the sole woman to win a senior jockeys' premiership in Australia, when she took the Tasmanian title with 63 winners from 337 rides. Dark Intruder gave Buckingham her biggest win

in the 1986 Hobart Cup. In 1989 she moved to the mainland where she rode in an atmosphere less tolerant to women riders, and with diminished success. She is currently riding again in Tasmania.

BULLOCK, FRANK (1885-1947)

Among the first Australian jockeys to try his luck in European racing, Frank Bullock initially went to England in 1900. He was back in Australia a few years later, and piloted Blue Spec to victory in the Perth Cup and the Melbourne Cup. Other wins in the Perth Cup came with May King in 1906 and on Eurythmic in a dead-heat in 1919. Eurthymic was probably the best Australian horse he rode. Germany had been his base from 1908-14, and he was leading rider there on several occasions. When the Great War was imminent he moved to England, but not before securing the top German horse Cyklon for Australian interests, for whom he stood with success at stud. Bullock won the first Prix de l'Arc de Triomphe ever contested, on Comrade in 1920, and was successful in the race again two years later, aboard Ksar. His best results in England came on the filly Saucy Sue, on whom he captured the 1,000 Guineas-Oaks double in 1925.

BUNDAMBA RACECOURSE

Opened at Ipswich in December 1886, the Bundamba Racecourse was for long a flourishing rival of the Brisbane metropolitan tracks. John Wren leased it before the Great War and attracted much patronage with the running of the rich Ipswich Cup in 1911. That event continues to be the main attraction on the Bundamba calendar, and good horses have won it. Sharply, Tulloch's conqueror in the 1961 Sydney Cup, won the Ipswich Cup later that year. Sometime deadheated with Conference in 1963 before going south to win the Caulfield Cup, while Bore Head figured in another dead-heat the following year, with Isaacson, but had to wait till 1965 to win the Caulfield Cup. Lloyd Boy (1978) and Donegal Mist (1992) have been other notable winners of the race.

BUNRATTY CASTLE

1964 gr horse Henry the Seventh – Winter Solstice

In seven starts in England, the brilliant but erratically tempered Bunratty Castle won three races and was second twice. Raced by the daughter of the Duke of Norfolk, he attracted the attention of Australian jockey Ron Hutchinson, who was then riding for the Duke. Hutchinson arranged for Bunratty Castle to be sold to Australian interests. A winner at Caulfield over 1200m in the spring of 1967, Bunratty Castle failed to impress thereafter, managing only to win a welter in Adelaide. Sold, he found a new trainer in Kevin Wynne at Bendigo. Now he began to show staying form. After victory in the Patrobas Welter at Caulfield, he was second to Shorengro in the 1968 Feehan Stakes at Moonee Valley (in the first of three wins in a row for that horse in the race). Then Bunratty Castle ensured a Caulfield Cup start with a fast-finishing and unlucky second to Tried and True in the Toorak Handicap after he had missed the start badly. Next week Mick Mallyon led all the way on the grey to win the Caulfield Cup untroubled by three lengths. Bunratty Castle was the second grey (after Grey Boots in 1950) to win in the race's long history; and only the second to lead all the way (after Yangtze in 1964). When his racing career was over, Bunratty Castle stood with success at the Balbethan Stud, Oaklands Junction.

BYRNE, TED (1934-72)

A daring and flamboyant jumps jockey, Ted Byrne rode more than 500 winners before his career was tragically cut short in a fatal car accident. He rode only one Grand National Hurdle winner, Rose in 1964, and never won a Grand National Steeple, although he finished second on Blacksmith behind no less than Pedro's Pride in 1957 and second to Redfield on Penang the following year. In 1962 Byrne was swamped with offers for the Steeple and chose Odd Boots who was fifth. Two of the rides which he turned down ran first and second. Tom McGinley, another top jumps rider, was sharing a hospital ward with Byrne in the week leading up to the 1965 Steeple after they had both fallen in a race. McGinley booked himself out and told him he would win the Steeple on Royal Rennie. He was as good as his word, and was back with a bottle of champagne to celebrate. Despite the fact that the Grand National Steeple eluded him, Byrne was leading Melbourne jumps rider on five occasions, with 15 wins in the 1963-4 and 14 in the 1970-1 seasons.

C

CABOCHON

1963 ch horse Edmundo – Dark Jewel

After Baguette, the best produce of the great broodmare Dark Jewel, Cabochon won 15 races and was placed 23 other times, usually in the best company, often after enjoying little luck. He was a restricted class galloper when beaten a short head by the champion Tobin Bronze in the 1967 Doncaster. When trainer Fil Allotta brought him back in the spring, Cabochon reeled off four victories in a row, including the Epsom, which he won by three lengths. He also won the Theo Marks Quality Handicap, a race in which he would be placed in 1968 and 1970. While being taken to Melbourne, Cabochon injured his back, and was perhaps never quite as good again. In 1968 he was again second in the Doncaster, beaten by the roughie Unpainted. However, in Brisbane he won three races in a row, culminating with a victory in the Stradbroke Handicap, when he carried 57.5kg. Besides his Doncaster defeats, Cabochon was also second in a Craven 'A' and All Aged Stakes, and in the Doomben 10,000 of 1970 which Black Onyx won. He was also runner up in that last campaign to Boy Dandy in the George Ryder Stakes, a race in which he had been third two years before.

CAMER, BILL (WILLIAM) (1931-)

One of the many crack Sydney jockeys who came originally from Queensland, Camer was a natural lightweight who rode at 48kg. In a career in which he rode more than 2,000 winners, he retired just short of his 60th birthday. His first winner was at Toowoomba on Antagonist in 1949, his first in Sydney on Perform at Canterbury in 1951. After a lean spell, Camer won his initial feature race, the Caulfield Guineas of 1953, on Barfleur. Next year Karendi gave him the Doncaster and Stradbroke double, while he took the V.R.C. Oaks on Lady Mogambo. In 1955 he won the Cox Plate on Kingster, but received a two months' suspension a week later for causing interference in the Victoria Derby on the same horse. Divide and Rule gave him more success in Queensland by winning the Stradbroke and Doomben Cup in 1970. Nearly three decades after his first win in a feature race, Camer was successful on Grey Receiver in the Galaxy of 1981.

CAMOOLA

1892 ch horse Chester – Copra

Out of the top broodmare Copra (who was in turn by Robinson Crusoe), and by the top sire Chester, Camoola was a brilliant young horse. He won the Oakleigh Plate of 1892 as a two year old. That spring he won the Ascot Vale Stakes, the A.J.C. and Victoria Derby double. In addition he won the Caulfield Stakes. Next year, in the autumn of 1893, Camoola won the A.J.C. St Leger, the Cumberland Stakes and Randwick Plate. He also ran third behind Realm in the Sydney Cup. The V.R.C. Champion Stakes was his other big win of that year. Camoola's dam Copra also produced Cobbity (a Caulfield Guineas winner), Coil (who won the Champagne Stakes, V.R.C. Sires', Oakleigh Plate and Australian Cup) and the Victoria Derby winner Cocos.

CAMPAIGN KING

1982 ch horse Saarond – Acid Queen

This brilliant sprinter-miler, originally trained by Les Theodore, blossomed when transferred to the stables of Bart Cummings, who had previously bought a part share in him. As a three year old Campaign King ran third in the Moonee Valley Stakes, and in the spring of 1986 gave the first indication of his class by winning the William Reid Stakes by a breath from King Phoenix. That campaign also saw victory in the Futurity. In the spring, Campaign King ran second to the top filly Special in the Moir Stakes, before winning the Linlithgow during the Flemington carnival. He continued to improve with age and found the Sydney way of going to his liking in 1987 when he won the Chelmsford and George Main Stakes, the All Aged Stakes and the first of successive George Ryder Stakes. In 1988 he was second in the Futurity and the All Aged, but this time found success further afield. Campaign King won the Stradbroke Handicap, before lumping 58kg to beat the good galloper Rancho Ruler (in receipt of 6.5kg from him) in the Doomben 10,000.

Campaign King was still competing in the best of weight-for-age company as a seven year old.

CAMPTON, NEIL (1936 -)

One of the most durable and serviceable of Sydney jockeys, Campton won at his last race ride on Pied Piper at Wyong in March 1992, after 30 years in the saddle. His first winner had come at Kembla Grange on The Scribe at his third race ride. A big race win followed soon afterwards, on Cele's Image in the Warwick Stakes. Rides refused by George Moore gave Campton two of his biggest successes: on El Gordo in the A.J.C. Derby of 1966 and Royal Parma in the 1968 Golden Slipper. Two years later, in December 1970 at Rosehill, Campton suffered the worst of the falls which punctuated his career and made racing history by successfully suing the S.T.C. for damages. On the brighter side, he scored numerous weight-for-age and handicap wins, among them the Sydney Cup of 1985 on Late Show, a Liverpool City Cup on the fine John Hawkes-trained mare Toltrice and three Hill Stakes, including the 1981 renewal on Canarthus, who was unwanted at 100/1. Campton rated the injury-prone Strausbrook as his best horse. He won a Pago Pago, Canterbury and George Ryder Stakes on Strausbrook before his career ended. Campton rode in Hong Kong in the early 1980s. He married a daughter of Les Coles, who had taken the Caulfield-Melbourne Cup double on Even Stevens in 1962, and appointed his father-in-law as stable manager when he turned to training after his retirement.

CANNY LAD

1987 br horse Bletchingly – Jesmond Lass

The Rick Hore-Lacy-trained Canny Lad showed his quality as a spring two year old in 1989 when he won the Maribyrnong Plate at Flemington after earlier wins there and at Caulfield. In the autumn he won a Sandown Blue Diamond Prelude but was beaten by Mahaasin in the Blue Diamond. Canny Lad atoned with a win in the V.R.C. Sires' Produce Stakes. Hore-Lacy sent him to Sydney where he found a heavy track to suit him in the Golden Slipper, and Canny Lad scored with authority from With Me to end his two year old season with six wins and a second from seven starts. Returning in the spring of 1990, Canny Lad was third in the Ascot Vale to Bureaucracy and Storaia, but then won the Bill Stutt Stakes at Moonee Valley. Perhaps his finest run came at the same track where he was a gallant third in the Cox Plate behind the seasoned champions Better Loosen Up and Sydeston. Canny Lad came back in 1991 to win the Autumn Stakes, but never recovered his two year old form.

CANNY LASS
1982 ch mare Bletchingly – Jesmond Lass

The beautifully-bred Canny Lass was given no easy assignments by trainer Rick Hore-Lacy. At two and three the filly raced in all six mainland stakes, and she continued to perform at the top level as a four year old, particularly in Melbourne. At three, Canny Lass won the Veuve Cliquot at Moonee Valley. In that season she was also placed in three Oaks, running third to Just Now at Randwick, third in the S.A.J.C. and second to Miss Clipper in the Australasian Oaks in South Australia. In May 1986 she had some revenge for those defeats by taking the Sedgwick Premium Classic at Morphettville. That spring two of her biggest Group One wins came at Caulfield where she won the Marlboro Cup with 54.5kg and followed up with victory in the Toorak Handicap, carrying 55kg. In the

autumn of 1987, Canny Lass showed her affinity for Moonee Valley with a win in the William Reid Stakes, before putting in another fine performance to run third to Placid Ark and Special in the Lightning Stakes.

CANTALA STAKES
see HONDA STAKES

CANTERBURY GUINEAS
This Group One race for three year olds over 1900m, is the most important event contested at Canterbury, besides being an important lead-up to other Sydney autumn classics. First run in 1935, when Hadrian won, the Canterbury Guineas has been won by numerous horses who have gone on further to distinguish themselves. They include Todman, Martello Towers, Persian Lyric, Royal Show, Imagele, Mr McGinty, Beechcraft, Spirit of Kingston, Riverina Charm and Veandercross in 1992. And as is often the case in three year old classics, the list of place-getters bears an equally impressive air.

CANTERBURY RACECOURSE
Situated on the Cooks River, south-west of the centre of Sydney, Canterbury Park was opened for proprietary racing in January 1884. Six decades later, when the New South Wales government legislated to make the Sydney Turf Club the body that took over all the old proprietary clubs, Canterbury was sold. Its last meeting under the old dispensation was held on 9 December 1944. Thereafter it has been the site of important innovations in Australian racing: barrier stalls were used for the first time there in 1946 and the photo finish camera in March of the same year. The first legal, off-course, totalisator betting took place on the occasion of the Canterbury

meeting of 9 December 1964. While George Moore refused to ride at the track for a time in this decade, claiming that it was unsafe, Canterbury is well established as the S.T.C.'s second track.

CAP D'ANTIBES

1971 ch mare Better Boy – Tereus

A top quality and versatile galloper, Cap D'Antibes was one of the many fine mares to go through Bart Cummings' hands. As a two year old she won three minor races, two in Adelaide and one at Moonee Valley and was third in the S.A.J.C. Sires' Produce Stakes. Cummings set Cap D'Antibes an ambitious programme in the spring of 1974. She won in three states: at Morphettville, Randwick and Flemington before running second in the V.R.C. Oaks to Leica Show and third in the Sandown Guineas behind Shiftmar. Cap D'Antibes blossomed in the autumn of 1975, winning in succession the Lightning Stakes and the Newmarket (in each of which Aurealis was second) and then taking the Kewney Stakes from Classic Conquest. Sent again to Sydney, Cap D'Antibes ran into Taras Bulba on a day when he consented to do his best and was second to him in the Spring Champion Stakes. Unplaced in the A.J.C. Oaks, Cap D'Antibes was let down till the spring. Again she performed with distinction. After a second to Dark Ruler in the Bobbie Lewis Handicap, Cap D'Antibes carried 55.5kg to beat no less than Tontonan in the Marlboro Cup. Once more she headed to Sydney, where she was burdened with 56kg but finished a gallant second to Authentic Heir (who had only 48.5kg) in the Epsom. After an unplaced run in the Caulfield Cup, Cap D'Antibes was spelled and later retired to stud.

CARANNA

1952 b horse Valognes – Connette

Caranna's spring campaign of 1955 marked him as a champion in the making, but it was a promise never fulfilled. The run of minor placings which he racked up in high class events is almost without parallel in our racing history. Caranna was second to Aboukir in the Canterbury Guineas, and then won the Rosehill Guineas and A.J.C. Derby in 1955. Taken to Melbourne, Caranna won the Caulfield Guineas. He was second to Kingster in the Cox Plate, before finishing third to Sailor's Guide and Arlunya in the Victoria Derby, when he started as an even money favourite. The following year was even more frustrating for Caranna. In the autumn he was third in the All Aged Stakes and second to Redcraze in the Brisbane Cup. Back in the spring he was second to Advocate in the Chelmsford Stakes and third to El Khobar and Syntax in the Warwick Stakes. Perhaps his luck would turn in Melbourne? It was not to be: Caranna was third to Ray Ribbon and Rising Fast in the Cox Plate. He backed up in the Melbourne Cup and wound up third after running erratically down the straight, thus earning jockey George Moore a two month holiday. The year of 1957 was less productive, but Caranna was back running against the best in 1958. In the autumn he was second to Tulloch in the Rawson Stakes; third in the Queen Elizabeth Stakes to Tulloch and Baron Boissier; second (with 56kg) to Straight Draw in the Sydney Cup. In another tilt at the Brisbane Cup, Caranna carried 56kg into third place behind Timor and Baystone. In the spring he ran second to Prince Darius in the Colin Stephen Quality (the previous year Baron Boissier had beaten him); third to Prince Darius and Bold Pilot in the Chelmsford; second, with 57.5kg, to Monte Carlo in the

Metropolitan. Caranna's is the exemplary story of a top quality horse who kept finding ones slightly better.

CARBINE
1885 b horse Muscat – Mersey

'Old Jack' was in most estimations the greatest Australian thoroughbred before Phar Lap. Unbeaten as a young horse in New Zealand, Carbine was unlucky to lose in the Victoria Derby. There followed a change of owners, and Walter Hickenbotham took over the horse's training. Now Carbine won seven races in succession as a three year old, including the Sydney Cup. In the Melbourne Cup of 1889 he ran unplaced for the only time in his career, because of suffering from a split heel.

Returning in 1890, Carbine won 15 races in a row. A second Sydney Cup was one of them, while he took the A.J.C. Cumberland Stakes and All-Aged Stakes in the same afternoon. In all, he four times contested two races in a day. With a record 66kg on his back in the Melbourne Cup, Carbine beat the largest field then assembled – 38 rivals – and ran record time. As a five year old, Carbine won 10 of 11 races before his heel problems forced retirement. He won 33 of 43 starts and was placed nine times.

A successful sire in Australia for four years, Carbine's best son was the Victoria Derby and Sydney Cup winner Wallace. Carbine was bought by the Duke of Portland to stand beside St Simon at the Welbeck Abbey stud in England. A cheering crowd farewelled 'Old Jack' at Melbourne in April 1895. Racing novelist and journalist Nat Gould, who travelled to England with the horse, captured the scene in his memoirs, *On and Off the Turf in Australia* (1895). At stud Carbine proved a notable success, much enhancing the reputation of the Australasian

thoroughbred. He sired the English Derby winner Spearmint, who in turn sired another winner Spion Kop, who sired Felsted, to give the progeny of Carbine classic success in three generations. Carbine's blood can also be found in many of the winners of cup races and classics in Australia throughout the 20th century.

CARBINE CLUB

First formed in Melbourne in 1961, this is a sportsmen's club limited to 40 members which takes its name and its colours from the great 19th century Australian thoroughbred Carbine. Sister clubs have subsequently been established in every Australian state and territory, as well as Hong Kong, New Zealand and Papua New Guinea. Highlights of the club's calendar are lunches before the Australian Football League Grand Final and the Victoria Derby.

CARBON COPY
1945 ch horse Helios – Havers

Carbon Copy was the great rival of Comic Court, whom he could usually beat in Sydney, but not the Melbourne way of going. A top-line three year old, Carbon Copy won the A.J.C. Derby from Vagabond and then took the Cox Plate, a race in which Comic Court ran fourth. Accordingly Carbon Copy was 7/4 favourite for the Victoria Derby, but could manage only third to Comic Court. In the Melbourne Cup he struggled home eighth behind the longshot Rimfire. In the autumn of 1949, Carbon Copy beat Comic Court in the St George and was second to that horse in the V.R.C. St Leger. The tables were turned in their duel in the A.J.C. St Leger. Carbon Copy had one big win left. He carried 53.5kg – a big weight for a three year old – to victory over Vagabond in the 1949 Sydney Cup, with Comic Court out of a place. His other wins included the 1949 Craven Plate; two Randwick Plates and the 1950 Chipping Norton Stakes. At stud Carbon Copy sired Grand Print who emulated his father by winning the Sydney Cup, in 1962.

CARIOCA

1947 b horse Felt Yet – Sing Again

Plagued by ill-health, Carioca had only six starts for three restricted wins up to the age of four. But his fifth year showed his mettle. At his third run in the spring of 1952, Carioca began a winning sequence of seven, in the course of which he broke three time records. The run of wins included the Villiers Stakes and Summer Cup by four lengths. Resuming after a spell he equalled the course record for 1400m at Warwick Farm before Tarien beat him a short half head in the Rawson Stakes. Carioca made amends with victory in the Chipping Norton Stakes, before defeating Advocate in the 1953 Sydney Cup. The new season began for Carioca with seconds in the Warwick and Chelmsford Stakes, before an unlucky third in the Epsom, won in record time by Silver Phantom. Carioca's versatility and courage were emphasised when he came out to beat Hydrogen in the Metropolitan a few days later. Turned out after an unplaced run in the Cox Plate, Carioca resumed to win the S.T.C. Club Stakes in world record time of 1.30 for the seven and a half furlongs. Then he ran records to win at Warwick Farm and Rosehill. A heavily backed favourite, he carried 60.5kg into third place in the 1954 Doncaster. The toll of racing began to tell, and in his seventh year Carioca won twice: at Eagle Farm, and again in the Chipping Norton. Retired to stud next season, he did not receive the patronage that his racing record warranted.

CARLITA

1911 b or br mare Charlemagne II – Couronne

Foaled in New Zealand, this top-line staying mare was sent to race in New South Wales. Her best wins in Sydney included the Rosehill Guineas of 1914 and the Craven Plate, although she also won an Easter Stakes, a Grantham and a Randwick Plate. In Melbourne she enjoyed even more success, annexing the Victoria Derby and V.R.C. Oaks, a rare double for a filly. She also won the three mile Champion Stakes, besides the C.B. Fisher, King's and Loch Plates. A fine handicap performer as well, Carlita won the Williamstown Cup, but was also seasoned enough to run third in the 1915 Melbourne Cup to Patrobas.

CARSLAKE, BERNARD ('BROWNIE') (c 1890-1946)

The Australian-born 'Brownie' Carslake had one of the most eventful careers of any of the top jockeys from this country who have sought their fortunes abroad. At the outbreak of the Great War he was interned by the Austrians, but escaped to Rumania, disguised as a stoker on a steam engine. Between the wars he won half a dozen English classic races, despite troubles with rising weight: they numbered two 1,000 Guineas, a 2,000 Guineas and an Oaks, besides three St Legers. In addition Carslake was runner up in the Derby on Zionist in 1925 and on Scottish Union in 1938. After his death, Carslake's ashes were scattered on one of the Newmarket training tracks.

CASTLEMAINE STAKES

A Group One event over 1600m for two year olds, run at Eagle Farm in the Brisbane winter carnival, the Castlemaine Stakes was inaugurated in spectacular fashion in 1976 when Romantic Dream beat none less than Family of Man and Surround. Luskin Star quickly confirmed the quality of the race when he won the next year. Flotilla, Zeditave and Prince Salieri won from 1987-9; the high quality filly Slight Chance scored one of her numerous Group One wins in the Castlemaine in 1992, while the colt Mahogany gave a taste of his ability when he scored the following year. A selected list of placegetters is also instructive, for so many went on to become top stayers: Karaman, Our Paddy Boy, Cossack Prince, Riverdale, Red Anchor, Dr Grace, Kinjite.

CASTLETOWN

1986 b gelding One Pound Sterling – Mona Curragh

One of the great stayers of modern times, Castletown clinched his third Wellington Cup in 1994 (at his 13th race start over 3200m) having previously won in 1991 and 1992. Doing so, he equalled the feat of Great Sensation, who won the race between 1961-3. Trained by Paddy Busuttin, Castletown was a classic winner at three, when he scored in the 1989 New Zealand Derby. He won the 1992 Auckland Cup, was placed in a New Zealand Cup, and on regular forays to Australia, ran second in the 1991 Sydney Cup and third the following year under the burden of 59.5kg. Nor was weight for age competition beyond him, as he proved in a slogging win in the wet in the 1992 Caulfield Stakes. He ran right up to that form with a third in the Melbourne Cup to Subzero and Veandercross. The third Wellington Cup win took Castletown's earning beyond $2.5 million. He failed to flatter in a Brisbane winter campaign in 1994; his best days clearly behind him.

CAULFIELD CUP

A Group One event run over 2400m in mid-October, the Caulfield Cup is one of the great events on the Australian racing calendar. Maurice Cavanough, in his book *The Caulfield Cup*, called it 'the most exacting handicap run south of the equator'. The Caulfield Cup was first contested in the autumn of 1879, when Newminster overcame difficulties in running to emerge as a worthy winner. In 1881 it was switched to the spring, so that there were two winners that year: Blue Ribbon in the autumn, Master Avenel in the spring. There were also dual winners in 1943, when pressure of numbers led the Cup to be divided. The winners were Skipton and Saint Warden, and the Caulfield Cup was run at Flemington – as it had been since 1940, Caulfield being used as an army barracks. The Cup was back home in 1944, when Counsel beat Lawrence. Controversy has long attended the Caulfield Cup. In Grace Darling's year, 1885, 16 of the 44 runners fell in a shocking incident which left jockey Donald Nicholson dead. Seven runners came down in 1906, and Robin Hood's rider, James Flanagan, died. Paris – in 1892 and 1894 – was the first galloper to win the race twice. He was succeeded by Hymettus, whose well-spaced wins came in 1898 and 1901, the champion Poseidon (1906-7), Uncle Sam (1912 and 1914), Whittier (1923 and 1925), another champion in Rising Fast in 1954-5 and most recently Ming Dynasty, in 1977 and 1980. That grand grey was at bolter's odds of 50/1 when he gave Bart Cummings yet another big cup victory. Galilee had been his first, in 1966, and then Big Philou won on protest from Nausori in 1969. The brilliant mare Leilani won for him in 1974, while Let's Elope – victor in 1991 went on to complete the Cups double, as had Galilee.

The Caulfield Cup has seen one dead-heat, between Aborigine and Blue Book in 1909, though the desperately close finish in which Imposera (at 50/1) beat Congressman in 1988 was almost another. Riding honours belong to Scobie Breasley, who won the Caulfield Cup five times, first on the fine mare Tranquil Star in 1942, last on Peshawar in 1952, and in between them three years in a row from 1943-5 on Skipton, Counsel and St Fairy. Eurythmic and Manfred were outstanding winners in the 1920s; Amounis and Rivette (which went on to the Melbourne Cup) in the 1930s. Redcraze set a weight-carrying record when he won with 63.5kg in 1956, while Tulloch's victory in Australasian record time the following year is one of the fabled performances on the Australian turf. Even Stevens and Galilee were matched in the 1960s by Tobin Bronze, who – after being beaten at odds on in 1966 – scored a triumphant win the next year. That was the decade when both Yangtze and Bunratty Castle led all the way. Mares won the race for four years in a row from 1973-6, courtesy of Swell Time, Leilani, Analight and How Now, but the year before Sobar had recorded a win almost to be spoken of in the same breath as Tulloch's. Steady handicappers and a succession of wet tracks took some of the lustre from the race in the 1980s, but in the 1990s three top-liners won in succession: Sydeston, Let's Elope and Mannerism (1990-2). The Caulfield Cup remains one of the sternest tests of a thoroughbred in this part of the world.

CAULFIELD GUINEAS

Since 1881, when Wheatear won the first Caulfield Guineas, this Group One 1600m event has been one of the great races on the Australian calendar. Winners in the 1890s alone included Strathmore, Autonomy, Patron, Wallace and Aurum. Early in the new century the good fillies Sweet Nell and Lady Wallace won. Patrobas

won during the Great War, Artilleryman just after it. The 1930s saw Young Idea, Ajax, Nuffield and High Caste in the winners' stall. Attley won in 1945, Royal Gem in 1946; the latter showed his liking for the track by winning the Caulfield Cup the same year, while Attley won the Futurity of 1947. Hydrogen scored in 1951, Tulloch in 1957. The 1960s was a vintage decade for the race, with winners including Lady Sybil, Coppelius, Time and Tide, Yangtze, Star Affair, Storm Queen, Rajah Sahib and Vain. That line-up was followed in the 1970s by Dual Choice, Sobar, Grand Cidium, Surround, Luskin Star and Manikato. Since then, the Caulfield Guineas honour roll bears an altogether more chequered appearance. Runaway Kid won on protest from Bold Diplomat in 1979; Marwong the same way and controversially – from Our Poetic Prince in 1987. While the period 1982-4 saw Grosvenor, Beechcraft and Red Anchor win the Guineas, several previously ill-performed gallopers have recently saluted. Binbinga won in 1981, Abaridy at 250/1 in 1986, Procul Harum, Centro, Chortle, Palace Reign between 1989 and 1992. Some of the lustre was restored to the event when Mahogany (who would go on to win two Derbies) scored in the Caulfield Guineas of 1993.

CAULFIELD RACECOURSE

'The Heath' is the principal course of the V.A.T.C. and is located in Melbourne's south-east. Races were held there in bush conditions from 1859 and the area was swampy and snake-infested. Nearly sold for development as a cemetery in 1861, Caulfield was taken over by the V.A.T.C. which held its first meeting there on 5 August 1876. The Caulfield Cup has been run there since 1879. The V.A.T.C.'s spring carnival precedes that at Flemington, as does its autumn carnival, when the Oakleigh Plate and Futurity are the principal events. Caulfield lost its members' stand in a suspicious fire on the morning of the 1922 Caulfield Cup. From 1940-44 the course was taken over as a World War Two barracks. More recently its spring carnival has suffered from the worst of Melbourne's weather at that time of the year. But in 1993 an ambitious plan of rebuilding was completed and Caulfield is now perhaps the most comfortable and attractive of all the Melbourne metropolitan courses. It is also an important centre for a number of Melbourne trainers.

CAULFIELD STAKES

Over-shadowed in prize-money by the Cox Plate, and by the pre-Melbourne Cup hype of the Mackinnon Stakes, the Caulfield Stakes yet has claims to be the greatest spring weight-for-age contest in Melbourne. It was first run in 1886 when Isonomy beat Malua and The Nun, and is now a Group One event held over about 2000m. The great mare Wakeful scored in 1901-2; Eurythmic went one better with three victories in succession between 1920-2 – in each case Tangalooma followed him home. Manfred, Heroic, Gothic, High Syce, Amounis, Chatham, Hall Mark, Young Idea, Ajax and High Caste were other high quality winners between the wars. Tranquil Star and Bernborough scored in the 1940s; while winners in the next decade included Rising Fast, Prince Courtauld, Redcraze and Lord. The latter won in 1958, 1959, and dead-heated for first with Dhaulagiri in 1960, in a remarkable race where third place also resulted in a dead-heat, between Nilarco and Webster. Sky High won in 1961-2, while Winfreux equalled Eurythmic's feat with victories from 1965-7. Arctic Symbol and

Gay Poss in 1970, Zambari and Guest Star in 1975 continued the tradition of dead-heats in the Caulfield Stakes. Gay Icarus, Gunsynd, Glengowan, Igloo, Family of Man added to the honour roll of the race in that decade. Proving that he could handle the Melbourne way of going, and the particular vagaries of Caulfield, Kingston Town was second to Hyperno in 1980 and won the next two years. Best recent winner was Shaftesbury Avenue, who in 1991, ridden by Darren Gauci, broke two minutes for the race journey and left the likes of Super Impose, Sydeston (winner in the previous year) and Rough Habit behind him.

CENTURY

1969 br horse Better Boy – Royal Suite

Trained by Bart Cummings and usually ridden by Roy Higgins, Century was a top-line sprinter of the 1970s. He won 11 of 29 starts and was placed on 12 other occasions. At two he won the V.R.C. Sires' and was beaten a breath by John's Hope in the 1972 Blue Diamond Stakes. Sprinting was his strength. Century aptly won the 100th running of the Newmarket in 1973 as a three year old with 55kg in race record time; beat 25 others with 59kg in the Craven 'A' Stakes in the spring of the same year. Other big wins included the Ascot Vale, Lightning, Moonee Valley and Freeway Stakes. His second placings are further testament to his ability. Besides the Blue Diamond they numbered the Doncaster, All Aged Stakes, Oakleigh Plate, Toorak Handicap and Caulfield Guineas. Century went on to a distinguished career at the stud. In 1979 he sired both a Golden Slipper winner (Century Miss) and a Sydney Cup winner (Double Century).

CETIGNE

1912 b horse Grafton – Pretty Nell

Perhaps the most under-rated of the top horses to race during the Great War, Cetigne was bred at the Rylstone Stud. After finishing second at his first start, he won a Nursery Handicap and a December Stakes, before returning in the autumn to underline his class with a victory in the A.J.C. Sires' Produce Stakes. Beaten by Wallace Isinglass in the Rosehill Guineas of 1915, Cetigne took the Hawkesbury Guineas. He then convincingly out-stayed Wallace Isinglass in the A.J.C. Derby, when ridden by A. Wood, who also won the Clibborn Stakes on the horse at the Randwick spring carnival, despite a 14lb penalty. After the Derby win, Cetigne's owner, George Barnett donated 100 pounds to a subscription list for the widow and eight children of Sergeant-Major Lamont, who had been killed in the Dardanelles. A most durable galloper, Cetigne's other feature wins included the Rawson Stakes in 1916, the Villiers in 1917 and two Melbourne Stakes in 1917 and 1919. Cetigne's versatile command of different distances was emphasised by a win in the 1918 Newmarket, while he was placed in successive All Aged Stakes from 1917-9.

CHAMPAGNE STAKES

Two races of this name were run in Sydney in 1860. The next year a five furlong race for two year olds carried the Champagne name, while in 1862 the distance was increased to a mile. The Champagne Stakes in its recognisable form dates from 1866, when it became a complementary event in the autumn Sydney Cup programme and was won by the good horse Fishhook. Now established as a Group One fixture in the Randwick Easter carnival, and third leg of the two year old Triple Crown, the Champagne honour roll boasts many outstanding winners. Fireworks and Florence joined Fishhook as early winners; Robinson Crusoe, Navigator and Chester were also winners in the 19th century. Thereafter Woorak, Furious, Heroic, Manfred and Mollison, Hall Mark, Young Idea and Ajax all scored before the Second World War – and all proved capable of running over a distance. Since then Sky High and Storm Queen, Vain and Baguette, Luskin Star and Red Anchor have been among the top-class juveniles to win the Champagne Stakes.

CHAMPION STAKES

For more than half a century, the Australasian Champion Stakes of three miles was the longest flat race of importance on the national racing calendar. It was first run in Victoria in 1859, at Randwick the next year, at Ipswich in Queensland in 1861. This established the pattern of rotating the race around the Australian colonies. Eventually it was run as a regular fixture of the V.R.C. autumn carnival. Carbine's daughter La Carabine won the race in 1901 and 1902, the great mare Wakeful in 1903 and Trafalgar was another dual winner in 1911-12. The race was abandoned after Carlita won the 58th running at Flemington in March 1915.

CHATHAM

1928 b horse Windbag – Mysotis

Bred by Percy Miller at the Kia Ora Stud, by the first-rate galloper Windbag, Chatham was trained by F. Williams. He proved to be one of the greatest ever Australian 'milers', winning a dozen of 21 races at that distance. They included two Epsoms, in 1932 and 1933 (with 61.5kg) and the 1934 Doncaster, where jockey Jim Pike overcame difficulties to win despite the horse's burden of 65.5kg. Chatham equalled Marvel's weight-carrying record, set in 1892, with this victory. Trying for a third successive Epsom in the spring of 1934, he was beaten carrying 67.5kg. His lead-up form had been solid enough, with one of his two Warwick Stakes wins and a Hill Stakes victory as well. Subsequently he beat Peter Pan in one of his three successes in the Craven Plate and Hall Mark in the Cox Plate of 1934. He had won the latter race as a four year old in 1932, besides finishing second to Phar Lap the year before. Other top class victories for Chatham numbered a Rawson Stakes, two Linlithgows, an All-Aged and a Caulfield Stakes. By any reckoning, his ability to combine weight-carrying feats in top-class handicaps with the talent to compete at weight-for-age at the highest level stamp Chatham as among the best horses of the inter-war period. At stud his performance was moderate, but his son Craigie won the 1945 Sydney Cup.

CHELTENHAM RACECOURSE

Eager to establish itself in South Australian racing, the Port Adelaide Racing Club leased land at Woodville for a new track. Called Cheltenham after an English course, the first meeting was held there on Boxing Day 1895. Its main events are conducted in the summer: the Port Adelaide Cup (which earlier this century rivalled the Adelaide Cup in prize-money) and the Christmas Handicap. The Port Adelaide Guineas was inaugurated in 1917, while the Lightning Stakes is an important winter sprint at Cheltenham. The P.A.R.C. bought the freehold of the course after the Great War and continued its improvement of amenities there.

CHESTER
1874 br horse Yattendon – Lady Chester

Trained by Etienne de Mestre and owned by the Honourable James White, Chester won three of four races in a week as a two year old, including the A.J.C. Sires' Produce and Champagne Stakes. In the A.J.C. Derby he was beaten a short head by Woodlands after an ill-judged ride, then had revenge on that colt in the Mares' Produce Stakes. Taken to Melbourne, he was victorious in the 1877 Derby. The Melbourne Cup of that year was notable for a sensational plunge on Savanaka, whose well-disguised abilities secured tasty odds early in pre-post betting. Chester started at 5/1 equal favourite with Savanaka and beat that horse narrowly. Although not known as a betting man, White had plunged also, and collected 10,000 pounds on the Cup. Savanaka went on to win a Sydney Cup. Chester won 16 of his 29 starts and was retired to stand at White's Kirkham Stud. He was leading Australian sire on four occasions. The best of his progeny were Abercorn, the dual Derby winner Camoola, Stromboli and Titan.

CHICQUITA
1946 blk mare Blank – Sir Faithful

A brilliant and durable staying mare, Chicquita's three year old season was the highlight, but by no means the conclusion of her career. Unplaced in one run at two, she won eight in a row in 1949, including a rare clean sweep of the four main fillies' races in Melbourne: the Manifold Stakes, Thousand Guineas, Wakeful Stakes and the Oaks, in which she started at 7/4 on. In the autumn of the following year she returned strongly to racing, winning the C.M. Lloyd Stakes, besides running second to Comic Court, a horse who would prove her nemesis, in the St George Stakes and

Alister Clark Stakes. Trained by Tony Lopes, Chicquita was set for the Caulfield Cup of 1950. She won the Feehan and Craiglee Stakes in her lead-up and ran a gallant second, at 15/1, to Grey Boots in the Cup. She then found herself second again to Comic Court in both the Mackinnon Stakes and the Melbourne Cup. In 1951 Chicquita continued to compete in the highest class and won the Alister Clark and Liston Stakes, besides seconds in the Memsie and – to Comic Court once again – in the Orr Stakes. He would later be one of the first horses to serve Chicquita when she went to stud. Lopes (who died in July 1994) named his training premises, near the six furlong pole at Flemington, Chicquita Lodge.

CHIPPING NORTON STAKES

Now a Group One event contested at the autumn carnival at Randwick over 1600m, the Chipping Norton Stakes is named after the training property of A.J.C. committeeman William Long, across the Georges River from the Warwick Farm racetrack. First contested in 1925, when Wallace Mortlake beat Windbag, the race boasts a top line-up of winners. Windbag atoned in 1926. No less than Amounis, Limerick, Strephon and Phar Lap followed him into the winner's stall in the Chipping Norton. Lough Neagh won three times during the 1930s, a decade in which Rogilla also saluted. Tranquil Star beat High Caste and Beau Vite in 1941. Katanga scored twice during the Second World War, while the Chipping Norton was one of the 15 races that fell to Bernborough during his great campaigns in 1946. Carbon Copy won in 1949-50, Comic Court the next year. Carioca became another dual winner in 1955, after scoring two years before. Tulloch also spaced his wins: in 1958 and 1960. Sky High, Prince Grant and Rain Lover were

top winners of the race in the 1960s; Gay Icarus, Apollo Eleven (in 1973 and 1975), Igloo and Taras Bulba in the next decade. More recent winners include Emancipation and Our Waverley Star, Dr Grace in 1990 and the champion Super Impose in the next two years.

CHIRNSIDE FAMILY

Few families have had as long an association with Australian racing as the Chirnsides. Andrew and Thomas Chirnside emigrated from Scotland in 1839 and established themselves as Victorian pastoralists. Both Andrew and his son A.S. Chirnside were involved in the creation of the Victorian Amateur Turf Club. At its first meeting, held in March 1876 at Dowling Forest, Ballarat, Andrew Chirnside's Sailor, ridden by his son, won the Victoria Gold Cup. The same result occurred in a race of the same name at the first V.A.T.C. Caulfield meeting in August that year. Andrew Chirnside owned the 1874 Melbourne Cup winner Haricot, but perhaps obtained more satisfaction when his horse Newminster won the inaugural Caulfield Cup in 1879. The Chirnside Stakes, at the Caulfield spring carnival, remembers the contribution of the family to Victorian racing and to the V.A.T.C. in particular. In July 1991, Mrs Sally Chirnside created Australian racing history by becoming the first woman to be elected to the committee of a Principal racing club. She won her seat on the committee of the Victoria Racing Club in a tight election which went to preferences, having been defeated the previous year by leading racehorse owner Lloyd Williams.

CITIUS
1962 b mare Star Kingdom – Rich and Rare

This brilliant sprinter from the 11th crop

of Star Kingdom won nine races. In the autumn of 1965 she won the V.R.C. Sires' Produce Stakes. Taken to Sydney, she was a creditable third in both the Golden Slipper and Champagne Stakes. Tried (again) over a mile in the spring, she found the distance just beyond her, but was a gallant third in both the Edward Manifold Stakes and the Thousand Guineas. Citius' turn in the big time came the next year. She won the Lightning Stakes from Bowl King and Star Affair; beat Star Affair in the Oakleigh Plate and then was third to Bowl King and Peace Council in the 1966 Newmarket. Although that rare treble just eluded Citius, she went to Sydney where she carried 54.5kg to victory in the Doncaster, before running third to Pterylaw and Maritana in the Doomben 10,000. Citius was perhaps the best daughter of Star Kingdom to race.

CLARK, ALISTER (1864-1949)

Lawyer and landowner, Alister Clark was master of the Oaklands Hunt and first chairman of the Moonee Valley Racing Club at its foundation in 1917. Before then he had raced some steeplechasers, but his main interests were in racing administration and, more particularly, in the development of new varieties of roses. Appropriately, the Group Two event which is named after him and run at Moonee Valley in the autumn, is popularly known as 'The Run for the Roses'.

CLARKE FAMILY

Former jockey cum trainer Arthur Clarke, based at Epsom in Victoria, is the father of three sons who became jockeys – Peter, Gary and Michael Clarke. Arthur, who rode in Indonesia and briefly in the United Kingdom, won such races as the Bagot Handicap, and Albury and Wagga Cups; rode against his sons before taking up training in 1976. Peter Clarke, who was

apprenticed to Bon Hoysted and rode more than 400 winners in his career, is now taking up a trainer's licence. Brother Gary, whose biggest win was the 1988 Victoria Derby on King's High, is now number one rider in Adelaide for the David Hayes stable. But Michael has enjoyed most success. Apprenticed to his father in 1978, he rode his first metropolitan winner two years later. Colin Hayes took over his indentures in 1982. After Darren Gauci went freelance in 1985, Clarke became stable jockey for Hayes, and in the 1986-7 season secured the first of four consecutive Melbourne jockeys' premierships. His tally of 85 winners in 1986-7 broke Roy Higgins' record, although Clarke had had nearly twice as many mounts. Michael Clarke's biggest wins were on At Talaq in the 1986 Melbourne Cup and Better Loosen Up in the 1990 Cox Plate and Japan Cup. After a productive association he split with the Hayes' stable in 1993 to ride freelance. In 1994 he took up an offer to ride in Hong Kong.

CLASSIC MISSION
1968 b gelding Persian Garden II – Angelet

Owned in Singapore by Bob Goh and Les Wong, Classic Mission was trained in New Zealand by Sid Brown. Riskily named, the horse had high expectations to realise. At three he crossed the Tasman and ran second to Baguette in the Hill Stakes, before scoring a narrow and controversial victory in the A.J.C. Derby. It had been suggested that Classic Mission was in fact a four year old. Stipendiary stewards were sent to New Zealand where they established that Classic Mission was indeed a 1968 foal, and so eligible for the Derby, even though his teeth were, remarkably, those of a four year old horse. In Melbourne, Classic Mission ran unplaced in the Cox Plate, but still started at 6/4 in the 1971 Victoria Derby. Tempted once more out of retirement, George Moore had the ride, and he saw Classic Mission home from Column and Altai Khan. Now Moore retired for good: Classic Mission had given him an 11th Derby winner, 10 of them in Australia, the other being Royal Palace at Epsom in 1967. Classic Mission won the C.B. Fisher Plate on the last day of the spring carnival and in 1972 was retired to stud in South Australia.

CLAUDETTE
1937 br or blk mare David – Crowfoot

One of the most versatile mares to race in Australia, Claudette, owned by D. McRae, campaigned against the best on offer over the jumps and on the flat in the Second World War period. She won the Grand National Hurdle in 1943, carrying 64.5kg to beat Gay Invader and giving jockey F. Douglas his fourth success in the race. Later that year she ran a gallant third to Spearfelt in the Melbourne Cup. A week later, Claudette won the Williamstown Cup from the fine stayer Skipton. Campaigning on in the following year, she started 8/1 equal favourite in a very open Caulfield Cup, but could finish no better than ninth. She still had enough dash to win a division of that year's Herbert Power Handicap at the Caulfield spring carnival. Sirius, who won the other division of that race in 1944, went on to win the Melbourne Cup. Claudette, who was fourth in the Cup, protested unsuccessfully against the third placegetter, Cellini. She made another try for the Williamstown Cup a week later, finishing second to Peter, who was in receipt of 6kg from this game mare.

CLEAN SWEEP
1897 blk horse Zalinski – Benzine

The tough stayer Clean Sweep was trained by James Scobie. In the spring of 1900 Clean Sweep won the Coongy Handicap and the Moonee Valley Cup. Next start was the Melbourne Cup in which, starting at 20/1, he beat his equally unfancied but much better performed stablemate, Maltster. This was the first of four Cup wins for Scobie. The colt took out the V.R.C. Spring Stakes at the end of the carnival. Next year he won the St George Stakes and the V.R.C. Loch Plate. Clean Sweep was the first of only four horses to complete the Moonee Valley-Melbourne Cup double.

CLIBBORN, THOMAS (1837-1910)

Born in County Westmeath, Ireland, Clibborn came to Australia in 1860. His success as secretary of the Ballarat Turf Club led to an invitation to become secretary of the Australian Jockey Club. Despite Ballarat's efforts to lure him back, Clibborn remained with the A.J.C. until his retirement in 1910, effecting in that time a wholesale reorganisation of its administration, superintending a notable increase in prize money and the establishment of the A.J.C. headquarters at Bligh Street in Sydney. Clibborn's work is remembered in the Clibborn Handicap, run at Randwick during its spring carnival.

COLLINS, WILLIAM HENRY (1928-)

Long known as 'The Accurate One' because of his ability to pick the winner in the tightest of finishes (and as his station's counter to the flamboyance of Collins' friendly rival Bert Bryant), Collins prepared for his future career while a child in Gippsland. Inspired by established callers Jim Carroll and Eric Welch, he would practise by racing marbles against each other down an inclined table. He learned the colours of the 150 marbles in his 'stable' in an invaluable piece of self-teaching. Collins' career in radio began with 3TR Sale. He moved to 3DB in 1953 and took over from Welch as its premier caller the following April. In 1954 he called his first Melbourne Cup. Rising Fast won. Collins' last Cup call was of Kensei's victory in 1987; his last race call on Easter Saturday of the next year. In a long career, he also called races in the United States, England, New Zealand and South Africa. The call that Collins will always ruefully remember was when he declared what everyone else thought – that the black champion Kingston Town 'can't win' the 1982 Cox Plate. He did, a third victory in succession. Two of Collins' calls, both towards the end of his career, stand out for the drama that he injected: when Bonecrusher beat Our Waverley Star in the gruelling 1986 Cox Plate, and when Bonecrusher pipped At Talaq in the 1987 Australian Cup.

COLUMNIST
1942 ch horse Genetout – Pen Name

Best of the horses owned by Frank Packer, Columnist was by the imported French sire Genetout and was trained in the most lucrative period of his career by Maurice McCarten. In all he won 17 races. Campaigning in 1946, he was second to Bernborough in the Caulfield Stakes, before running second to Royal Gem next start in the Caulfield Cup, the race in which Bernborough was controversially unplaced. At five, Columnist won 10 races. After victory in the Hill Stakes at Randwick, he was third in the Epsom. In Melbourne he went one better than the previous year by winning both the Caulfield Stakes and the Caulfield Cup. In the Cup a clever ride by Harold Badger saw Columnist home at 9/2 favourite. At the Flemington Carnival the horse won the Linlithgow Stakes and Fisher Plate, adding the Williamstown Cup with 60.5kg to round off his spring. In the autumn of 1948, Columnist won the Rawson and Autumn Stakes and the S.T.C. Cup, before running second in the Sydney Cup to Dark Marne. As a seven year old Columnist could still mix it with the best, winning the Chelmsford Stakes.

COMEDY KING
1907 blk or br horse Persimmon – Tragedy Queen

Bred in England, and by the Derby winner Persimmon, Comedy King was imported to Australia as a foal with his dam Tragedy Queen by bookmaker/studmaster Sol Green. He proved a top-line race horse, winning the A.J.C. Spring and Autumn Stakes, the V.R.C. All-Aged Stakes, and at Caulfield the Futurity, Eclipse and St George Stakes. He won the latter event in 1911, beating his old rival Trafalgar, to whom he finished second the following year. But in the most important event in which they clashed, Comedy King was victorious, beating Trafalgar by a half head in the Melbourne Cup of 1910. Thus Comedy King became the first imported horse to win Australia's greatest race. The win was the second in a row for jockey W.H. McLachlan, who had won the previous year on Prince Foote and would win again on Westcourt in 1917. At stud, Comedy King sired the champion Artilleryman, a second Melbourne Cup winner, King Ingoda (1922), the dual Derby winner Biplane and the unluckiest runner in the long history of the Melbourne Cup, Shadow King.

COMIC COURT
1945 br horse Powerscourt – Witty Maid

One of the most versatile and brilliant horses to race in Australia, Comic Court was bred at the Bowe Neire Stud in South

Australia. He was trained by Jim Cummings, who had owned both his parents. At his first start in Adelaide, Comic Court won the Fulham Park Plate, and was then purchased by the three Lee brothers. In another seven starts at two, he won four and finished second in the rest. He won both the Victoria Derby and the V.R.C. St Leger and managed fourths in the Cox Plate and Melbourne Cup of 1948. Racing the Sydney way, in the A.J.C. St Leger, Derby and Sydney Cup, he found Carbon Copy his master. Blossoming at four, Comic Court won eight races in Melbourne, including the first of successive Memsie and Mackinnon Stakes and the St George, in which he brought to an end the winning streak of nine races of Chicquita. At five he won the Turnbull and took the Caulfield Stakes on protest from Playboy. Chicquita was again behind him in the Mackinnon.

When Comic Court was unplaced in the Caulfield Cup, jockey Jack Purtell got off him to ride the Derby and Cox Plate winner Alister in the Melbourne Cup. The ride went to Pat Glennon, who took Comic Court to the front seven furlongs out and had three lengths to spare over Chicquita at the finish, in course record time. This supposed non-stayer ran the last six furlongs in the time that Commentator had taken earlier in the day to win the Railway Highweight. With Irish jockey Michael Kinnane, Glennon is the only man to ride the winners of the English Derby, Prix de l'Arc de Triomphe and the Melbourne Cup. Comic Court was no spent force. Remarkably at his first run back after the Cup victory, he won the William Reid Stakes at six furlongs and broke the Moonee Valley track record! He had four more wins at weight-for-age: in the Orr, St George and Ercildoune Stakes before he beat Grey Boots in the Chipping Norton. Comic Court

earned retirement and duties at stud following a third in the 1951 Sydney Cup, where he gave 16kg to the winner. Comic Court won 28 of his 53 starts. Chicquita was one of the mares which he served at stud.

CONNELL, CORNELIUS MYLES (1881-1958)

Born at Araluen, Connell learned to round up cattle in the same high country where 'Banjo' Paterson's 'The Man From Snowy River' had his apprenticeship. He is also touted as one of several Australian riders who adopted the crouched style of riding before the example of the American jockey Tod Sloan became well known. After riding at Sydney's pony tracks during the first decade of this century, Connell was licensed to ride at official tracks in 1907. His success was immediate, including a dead heat in the Caulfield Cup on Blue Book in 1909, as well as major races in other states: the Brisbane Cup and Doncaster among them. Salitros gave him the A.J.C. and Victoria Derby double in the spring of 1920. Weight problems forced his retirement in 1921, but an aversion to gambling had left him well set-up from the income of Sydney properties. After retiring as a jockey he moved to South Australia, where he was licensed as an owner-trainer. Connell rode more than 1,000 winners in his career.

CONNOLLY, ERIC (1880-1944)

One of Australia's most famous punters, Connolly came from a racing family. His brother Harry was a trainer who won the Grand National Hurdle with Aquarius (1900) and Jackstaff (1924). Eric Connolly's first big winning plunge was on The General, a horse that he trained, in the Grand National Steeple of 1904. Another of his big training successes was with Celerity in the 1910 Oakleigh Plate. In

1913, Connolly backed his horse Anna Carlovna for a fortune in the Caulfield Cup. Bookmaker Sol Green, who was to be the biggest loser, cunningly convinced Fred Merton, the owner of Aurifer, to start that horse in the Caulfield Cup. Aurifer duly beat Anna Carlovna by three quarters of a length. Connolly got even to an extent when the mare won the Mackinnon at her next start. Among his innovations in the punting game was to advertise a tipping service. And as a trainer, winners kept coming. With Rostrum he won the Newmarket and Epsom in 1922; took the Newmarket again with Sunburst in the following year. Murillo won the Metropolitan for Connolly in 1929. One of his biggest winning plunges came late in his career, when he backed Nightmarch to win the 1929 Epsom and Melbourne Cup. This unusual double was successful. Nightmarch beat Phar Lap by six lengths in the Cup. The following year Connolly was reputed to have won 200,000 pounds on the Amounis-Phar Lap Cups double. Towards the end of that decade his luck changed and he died in 1944 with little to show for the vast wealth that had passed through his hands. Nevertheless, Connolly is remembered for his resonant maxim on the gambler's life: 'Money lost, nothing lost; courage lost, everything lost'.

CONNOLLY, PATRICK (1866-1946)

Born at Ophir in New South Wales, Connolly grew up in the bush; worked as a stockman; followed the gold rush to Western Australia in 1894 and made his fortune there from carrying and from hotels. When his horse Blue Spec took the 1905 Melbourne Cup, Connolly reputedly won 30,000 pounds. Other big race wins included the 1908 Sydney Cup with Dyed Garments and the Doncaster of 1913 with

Jolly Beggar. Back in the West, Connolly's horses won seven Perth Cups and three W.A. Derbies. Before the Great War he bought the Helena Vale race course, which led to frequent battles with the W.A.T.C. over racing dates. In his later years Connolly became suspicious and paranoid, and spent much of his time holed up in a shack behind his Kalamunda Hotel.

COOK, BILLY (1910-85)

Son of a Hornsby butcher, Billy Cook learned about horses while delivering meat by cart. Apprenticed to J.S. Donohue, he rode his first winner at Canterbury and had his initial big race win on Crucis in the 1929 Sydney Cup. He had to wait until 1953 to win that race again, when he partnered one of his favourite horses – Carioca – to one of the 16 victories that they shared. Cook won his only Caulfield Cup, on Amounis in 1930, and then in 1932 headed off for the first of three profitable trips to India. On the second of them he won the Bombay Jockeys' Premiership and upon returning home married Rae Fisher, who had starred in the film adaptation of C.J. Dennis's *The Sentimental Bloke*. Tough as he was, Cook was rejected by the Australian army because of flat feet. The war years proved to be one of the most productive times of his career. He won the first of two A.J.C. Derbies on Pandect in 1940, the first of two Victoria Derbies on Great Britain in 1945, besides the 1941 and 1945 Melbourne Cups on Skipton and Rainbird respectively. His two V.R.C. Oaks came on Primavera in 1941 and Sweet Chime in 1946, while he had to wait until 1950 to win the first of two A.J.C. Oaks, on Elusive. Cook went to England to ride in 1950; hated the cold but was second to Gordon Richards on the jockeys' premiership when his wife's illness summoned him home to Australia. Cook set a Sydney riding record which still stands in the 1939-40 season of 124 wins and three dead-heats (although some were on tracks no longer used for metropolitan racing). This was the first of four premierships. Famous for his ability to land the last winner of the day, particularly at Randwick, Cook retired in 1958. He had the satisfaction of seeing his son, Peter, emulate his feat of riding two Melbourne Cup winners. The only previous father-son combination to be successful were the Dawes: as 'H. Chifney', Henry Dawes won the 1863 Cup on Banker. His son Harry scored in 1894 on Patron. 'Last race Billy' Cook died in January 1985.

COOK, PETER (1950-)

Son of the champion jockey Billy Cook, Peter Cook was apprenticed to his uncle Reg, a former top jockey cum trainer. A brilliant judge of pace, Cook wore a fashionable beard and long hair during the 1970s. This was a highly productive decade for him. He won the 1971 Sydney Cup on Gallic Temple: it had also been the race that gave his father his first big win. Cook was to win the Cup again in 1983 on Veloso, in 1988 on Banderol. Once more following the pattern of his father's career, Cook won two Melbourne Cups – on Just a Dash in 1981, Black Knight three years later. The Cooks were only the second father-son combination to land the Cup. The 1970s and 1980s saw Peter Cook ride with success all over Australia: in 1973 he took the Perth Cup on Dayana, the Australian Derby on Leica Lover; he won Doomben Cups in successive years (1979-80); two Cox Plates on Surround in 1976 and Kingston Town in 1982; while in Sydney he won two Metropolitans (like his father), three Rosehill Guineas to Billy's

four, two A.J.C. Oaks (as his father had), consecutive Australasian Champion Stakes in 1974-5 on Asgard and Taras Bulba. Peter Cook won two A.J.C. Sires' Produce Stakes to his father's five, but Binbinga gave him the lone family success in the race when he scored at bolter's odds in the 1981 Caulfield Guineas. Cook's career suffered a severe reversal when he was stricken by a heart attack, and in recent years the memories of his marvellous riding skills have not been enough to secure him regular mounts on city tracks.

CORRIGAN, TOM (1854-1894)

A champion jumps rider and trainer of the 19th century, Corrigan was born in Ireland and came to Victoria with his parents in 1864. After he rode his mare Juliet to win a hack steeplechase at a publicans' picnic race meeting, his father allowed Corrigan to become an apprentice jockey at Warrnambool. He first rode in Melbourne at the age of 13, finishing second on B.A., and had a Cup ride five years later on Emblem, but he was essentially a jumps rider, based first at Ballarat and then at Caulfield. Between 1866 and 1894, Corrigan had the astonishing strike rate of 239 wins and 230 placings from 788 rides. He won both the V.R.C. and the V.A.T.C. Grand National Steeplechases three times, and the V.R.C. Grand National Hurdle. Chasing a fourth V.A.T.C. Grand National Steeplechase in August 1894, Corrigan suffered a fatal fall from his mount Waiter, a last minute ride after the scratching of his original mount Daimio. His boots and racing jacket were placed on the coffin. One hundred jockeys and trainers led a funeral procession which was three km long. Small, unfailingly honest and game, besides being immensely popular with punters, Corrigan was celebrated in a poem by A.B. 'Banjo'

Paterson :

But Corrigan would ride them out, by danger undismayed,

He never flinched at fence or wall, he never was afraid.

COUNSEL

1937 br gelding Law Maker – Open Mind

The stylishly named Counsel took a few seasons to reward his owners' patience. He was in fact a poorly performed horse until he surprisingly won a division of the 1943 Toorak Handicap from Dark Felt. He followed that success with a strong second to Dark Felt in the Melbourne Cup. Counsel's late-blooming versatility was emphasised when at his next start – in the autumn – he won the 1944 Futurity Stakes at 50/1. Switched to the stables of Ray Webster in the spring of 1944, Counsel won a Quality Handicap at Moonee Valley from the mare Claudette. After four years of army occupation, racing resumed at Caulfield in August 1944. Starting at 8/1 equal favourite in the Caulfield Cup (with Lawrence and Claudette), and ridden by Scobie Breasley, Counsel won well before a crowd of more than 87,000. His 5,000 pound purse was augmented by a 150 pound war bond. Nor was Counsel done with: subsequently he defeated Lawrence in the Melbourne Stakes. In 1945, as an eight year old, Counsel was good enough to win both the V.R.C. Handicap and the Williamstown Victory Cup.

COURTNEY, BRIAN (1923-77)

Brian Courtney's maternal grandfather, Dan Larkins, was an owner-trainer at Avoca, while his father, Ned Courtney, held a jockey's or trainer's licence for more than 60 years. The natural first step was for Brian to become an apprentice jockey, an enterprise which weight soon curtailed.

Forced to quit the saddle, without having ridden one winner, he became involved with horses to assist his father. After Courtney gained his own trainer's licence in 1951, he was helped along early by the horse Maori Peak, who won 25 races for him. President of the Victorian Trainers' Association for seven years, Courtney also won the trainers' premiership three times in a row, from 1960-1 to 1962-3. Dhaulagiri, who won the 1961 Cox Plate was a star of his team, as was the runner-up in that race, 1961 Victoria Derby winner New Statesman. He also had the Derby winner of the following year Coppelius, the 1964 St Leger winner Better Lad, and the good sprinters My Peak and Small Time. A tenacious worker for fellow trainers, Courtney is remembered by a race at Flemington named in his honour.

COURTNEY, JIM (1946-)

One of the most durable of racing partnerships was that established in Adelaide between the Colin Hayes stable and jockey Jim Courtney. The latter served his apprenticeship in Melbourne, and shared the apprentice jockeys' premiership with Harry White in 1964. Lack of opportunities, together with weight problems, led him to ride for several years in Mauritius. When he returned, he was offered the job as stable jockey for Hayes in Adelaide. In subsequent years he rode an estimated 1300 winners for Hayes (or roughly a quarter of the stable's Australia-wide successes). He won almost every major race in South Australia, the Derby excepted, and had the sit on such champions as Dulcify and So Called before they went east in search of richer pickings. Courtney's first big win for Hayes was on Romantic Son in the 1971 Goodwood Handicap. He also had his share of successes in Melbourne, winning the Lightning

Stakes on Sportscast in 1980 and the Blue Diamond for Hayes on Midnight Fever in 1987 from Rancho Ruler. A bad fall in January 1990, in which he broke his back, ended Courtney's long career.

COURTZA

1986 b mare Pompeii Court – Hunza

Few fillies have progressed more quickly to top class than Courtza. At her first start she was second to Signorelli at Caulfield, and then second to the brilliant but unsound filly Confederate Lady in a Sandown Blue Diamond Prelude. Next start the Bob Hoysted-trained Courtza won the Caulfield Blue Diamond Prelude, and at only her fourth start won the Group One Blue Diamond from Sculptured Arch. Hoysted sent her to Sydney where from one start she won the Golden Slipper Stakes from Paris Opera and Show County. Courtza's great promise was not fully realised as a three year old, for although she beat Prince Salieri in the Ascot Vale Stakes; won the Laurent Perrier at Moonee Valley and was third in the Moonee Valley Stakes to Zabeel and Dr Grace, her form tapered off and she was retired. Courtza and Bounding Away are the only fillies to have won the Blue Diamond-Golden Slipper double.

COX FAMILY

When Murray Cox retired as Secretary of the V.R.C. in 1986, after 16 years in the position, he brought to an end a century-long association of his family with racing administration in Victoria. Murray Cox's great grandfather, William Samuel Cox (1831-95) owned Imperial who won the Sydney Cup of 1873, and part funded his purchase of land at Kensington Park in Melbourne where he staged race meetings from October 1874 until 1882. In 1880 Cox bought land at Moonee Ponds, opening the

Moonee Valley racecourse in 1883. The prospects of private racing on inner city tracks continued to appeal to him, and he started one at Maribyrnong in 1891. When Cox died in 1895, his son A.H. Cox took over as secretary of the private Moonee Valley Club. In turn he was succeeded by his brother-in-law, Arthur Hiskens. In 1929, during his term of office, the Moonee Valley racecourse was purchased from the Cox family. Another of Sam Cox's sons, W.S. Cox junior, was a successful jockey and trainer. He rode the great jumper Redleap; trained Realm to win the Sydney Cup in 1893. Sam Cox's grandson, W.S. (Bill) Cox, succeeded Hiskens as secretary of the M.V.R.C. in 1935 and his eldest son Murray assumed that position in 1966. In 1970 Murray Cox left to become secretary of the V.R.C. W.S. Cox is honoured by the naming of the richest weight-for-age race in Australia, the W.S. Cox Plate. It is run on the Saturday before the Flemington Spring Carnival, a date in the racing calendar that Cox cannily secured for the lasting benefit of the course which he established.

COX PLATE

Named for the founder of the Moonee Valley racecourse, W.S. Cox, this Group One weight-for-age race over 2,040m owes its present celebrity to Cox's shrewdness. He secured a date between the Caulfield and Flemington Spring Carnivals for Moonee Valley, thus attracting the best three year old horses and Melbourne Cup contenders. In 1922 the first Cox Plate was run over nine and a half furlongs. The fine galloper Violoncello beat Easingwold and Furious, to set a pattern of quality scarcely equalled by any race in the Australian turf calendar. Easingwold won the next year, to be followed by The Night Patrol in 1924, Manfred, Heroic, Amounis, Highland and

Nightmarch. Phar Lap won in 1930-1, Chatham in 1932 and 1934, his victories split by Rogilla in 1933. Young Idea was another dual winner in 1936-7, while Ajax won in 1938 and then ran second to Beau Vite, who won the Cox Plate in 1939 and 1940. During this inter-war period, the race was worth much less than the Moonee Valley Cup.

The champion mare Tranquil Star won in 1942 and 1944, Flight in 1946. Second in 1951, Hydrogen won the Cox Plate in the next two years. Rising Fast, Kingster, Redcraze and Noholme saluted later in the 1950s, while Tulloch saw the 1960s in when he beat Dhaulagiri, who won the following year. Star Affair beat Winfreux in 1965 and Winfreux was runner-up again the next year to Tobin Bronze, who won successive Cox Plates in 1966-7. Rajah Sahib and Daryl's Joy rounded out that decade's winners. Gunsynd, Taj Rossi and Battle Heights won from 1972-4, before Fury's Order won on a bog track in 1975, the meeting being called off soon afterwards. The champion filly Surround won in 1976, Family of Man and So Called in the next two years, before Dulcify went home by seven lengths to record an unprecedented winning margin in 1979. Nor was there a precedent for what followed, when one of the greatest of all Australian thoroughbreds, Kingston Town, won three Cox Plates in a row from 1980-2. The international champion Strawberry Road followed him into the winners' circle in 1983. Three years later the Cox Plate saw one of the most famous of all Australian races when Bonecrusher and Our Waverley Star duelled for furlongs before the former got home by a neck. Next year Rubiton won from Our Poetic Prince in a race when Vo Rogue set a suicidal pace and hung on for fourth. Our Poetic Prince scored in 1988, from the unlucky mare Horlicks. Almaarad

beat the Derby winner Stylish Century in 1989, Better Loosen Up scored from Sydeston in 1990 and then went on to win the Japan Cup. While Super Impose went under to Surfers Paradise in 1991, he scored the following year in a roughly run race. Starting at 20/1, he was nonetheless one of the most popular winners of the greatest of all Australian weight-for-age races.

CRAFTSMAN

1960 br horse Better Boy – Blue Gypsy

One of the best sons of Better Boy, Craftsman beat Sir Dane and Future in the 1963 Victoria Derby, the first of 18 victories, a number of them at the highest level. He won the Liston Stakes in 1964 and – in Sydney – two A.J.C. Autumn Stakes, but his best was to come. In 1965 he won the Turnbull Stakes and then ran third to Bore Head, beaten a length in the 1965 Caulfield Cup. Carrying 60kg, and backed from 12/1 to 7/1, Craftsman was most unlucky not to win, having almost fallen at the five furlong mark. Multiple big race wins included the Queen Elizabeth Stakes in 1965 and 1966 and the Australian Cup in the same years. He also won a C.B. Fisher Plate and was still good enough at seven to run second to Winfreux in the 1967 Caulfield Stakes and third to Tobin Bronze in the Cox Plate.

CRAIG, WALTER (1825-1870)

The popular publican of the hotel in Ballarat which still bears his name, Walter Craig, born in England, is best remembered for his contribution to one of the earliest legends of the Melbourne Cup. Owner of the aged gelding Nimblefoot, who he had set for the Cup, Craig dreamed that his horse won the race, but that its jockey was wearing a black armband. Persuaded that Nimblefoot would indeed win, but that he would not live to see it, Craig was laid 1,000 pounds to eight drinks by the bookmaker Slack about his horse's chances. In August 1870 Craig died. Two months later, Nimblefoot, with only 40kg, scrambled home to beat Lapdog by a half head. Jockey J. Day wore a violet jacket and black armbands on the winner, as Craig had dreamt. Slack honoured the bet with Walter Craig's widow. Craig's Hotel has a notable place in Australian racing history for at least two other reasons: as the site behind which poet and steeplechase jockey Adam Lindsay Gordon ran livery stables in the late 1860s, until ruined by fire; and as the location of the bibulous establishment of the Victoria Amateur Turf Club, in October 1875.

CRAVEN 'A' STAKES
see GADSDEN STAKES

CREWMAN
1965 b horse Todman – Royal Lark

Perhaps the most versatile horse who Angus Armansco trained, and certainly one of the finest, Crewman competed against the best throughout his career. As a two year old he was second to Flying Fable in the V.R.C. Sires' Produce. At three he seemed destined to remain a bridesmaid, as he finished third to Always There in the Moonee Valley Stakes, second to Rajah Sahib in the Caulfield Guineas and third to Always There in the Victoria Derby. But in the following spring, in 1969, Crewman broke through for a win in the Toorak Handicap. In the autumn of 1970 he won the William Reid Stakes, then carried 63kg to victory over Black Onyx in the Futurity. This performance saw him start favourite in the Newmarket, but Black Onyx won and Crewman finished down the line. The Flemington crowd was unamused two days later when the horse backed up and won the Australian Cup from Cyron. Crewman

campaigned on without major success in the spring of 1970. After retirement he enjoyed moderate success at stud in Queensland.

CRISP
1963 b or br gelding Rose Argent – Wheat Germ

Perhaps the greatest of Australian jumpers, despite never winning a Grand National, Crisp was bred and owned by VRC and founding TAB chairman, Chester Manifold. His career began modestly, with five runs at two and three for one win in the bush. At four he took to hurdling. Beaten a head at Kyneton at his first try, he then won three in a row, including the Redditch and Pines Hurdles at Flemington. At five he won hurdles at Flemington and Caulfield, fitted in an Encourage win on the flat at Moonee Valley and then switched brilliantly to steeplechasing. Crisp finished his season with wins in the Redleap and Hiskens steeplechases. Four wins followed in the next season, including a second Hiskens Steeple when, with 76kg and with Tommy McGinley up, Crisp gave an exhilarating exhibition of jumping to win by 12 lengths in course record time.

It was decided late in 1970 to send Crisp abroad for his future racing. In the Colonial Cup in South Carolina he ran down the track. England would suit him much better. Crisp stepped out first in a minor race at Wincanton in March 1971 and won convincingly. Less than a week later he took the prestigious Champion Chase at Cheltenham. Other wins followed in top flight company before it was decided to try him over the four and a half miles of the Grand National Steeplechase at Aintree. In arguably the greatest performance ever in this famous race, Crisp showed unsuspected stamina besides his usual brilliance and courage, leading almost all the way until run down just before the post by Red Rum. He gave that horse (ultimately a triple winner of the event) 10kg and a course record was posted. At their next meeting Crisp thrashed Red Rum, by way of minor compensation, and he continued to be a star of the National Hunt racing in England before injury forced his retirement.

CROPPER, CHARLES WILLIAM (1859-1932)

Dissatisfied with a long and stodgy career in the New South Wales Public Service, despite having twice been tennis champion of the State, Cropper moved west in 1894. From 1900-1910 he was secretary of the Kalgoorlie Racing Club in what were literally golden years. His abilities were noticed in his home town and he was invited to succeed Thomas Clibborn as secretary of the Australian Jockey Club. In that role Cropper superintended the purchase of a second racecourse for the club, at Warwick Farm, as well as the refurbishment of facilities at Randwick. He was still secretary on his death in 1932. A race was named in his honour at the Randwick Easter carnival.

CUMMINGS, JAMES BARTHOLOMEW (BART) (1927-)

The South Australian-born Bart Cummings earned the sobriquet 'Cups King' before he reached his present tally of nine victories in the Melbourne Cup. But he could also be known as 'Oaks King', 'Derby King', 'Weight-for-Age' or 'Sprint King'. Son of the top Adelaide trainer Jim Cummings, Bart learned to ride at nine; flirted briefly with the idea of being a jockey till weight beat him; and fortunately for Australian racing ignored the advice of a specialist treating his asthma who advised him to stay away from horses and chaff. At 17 Cummings became a strapper for his father, tending Comic Court in his 1950 Melbourne Cup victory. Three years later Cummings was a trainer in his own right, after the S.A.J.C. committee told him that if he continued to look after his father's horses in the latter's extended absence, he needed a ticket of his own.

Cummings's first classic winner came with Stormy Passage in 1958 in the South Australian Derby. He has won this race 10 times, besides five Victoria, three A.J.C. and four Australian Derbies. In addition, he has won 17 Oaks, seven in Victoria, six in Sydney, many of them ridden by his sometime stable jockey, Roy Higgins. And Cummings collects cups as others do ties. Light Fingers gave him his first Melbourne Cup (and Cup quinella) in 1965 and Let's Elope his ninth in 1991. Cummings has also won six Caulfield, four Adelaide and three Sydney Cups, as well as nine Australian Cups. Taj Rossi gave him his sole Cox Plate success in 1973. At sprint distances his horses have also performed with distinction, collecting eight Newmarkets, four Gadsden Stakes and four Golden Slippers.

In 1968-9 Cummings was the first trainer to win two state premierships (in South Australia and Victoria) in the one season; in 1974 he was the first to train winners of $1,000,000 in stakes. Cummings shifted his main operation to Sydney in 1985. When he won the trainers' premiership there in 1989-90, he became the first person to do so in three states. For good measure, Cummings-trained horses have won the title of Australia's Champion Racehorse on seven occasions. Stung by the collapse of his ambitious yearling syndicate deal in the early 1990s, Cummings finally reached agreement with creditors in 1993. His son Anthony now trains in his own right, his best horse having been Gold Trump, winner of the Newmarket in 1990.

D

DALRAY

1949 b horse Sire Balloch – Broiveine

Bought for only 460 guineas because of what appeared to be a suspect joint, Dalray blossomed into a top-line stayer. Unplaced in three outings at two, he won a Hack Handicap at Westport (NZ) in his second start at three, and a similar event at his next start. After this unpromising beginning, he won the New Zealand Derby easily two starts later. His brilliant campaign now saw him take the Great Northern Derby, the Gloaming and Trentham Stakes and the New Zealand St Leger. Brought to Australia in 1952, Dalray ran third in the Chipping Norton Stakes at Warwick Farm before winning the Randwick Autumn Stakes. Unluckily beaten in the Sydney Cup, he returned to New Zealand. He was back in Sydney in the spring, winning the Colin Stephen Stakes and the A.J.C. Metropolitan. Dalray's less than popular owner, Cyril Neville, persistently denied that the horse would start in the Melbourne Cup. However after he won the Mackinnon Stakes, Dalray took his place in the Cup field, with Bill Williamson riding after Keith Nuttall had been 'jocked off'. Evidently Neville had backed his horse heavily for the Cup before the Mackinnon was run. With 61kg, Dalray won by half a length from the 200/1 shot Welkin Sun. Only Phar Lap with 62.5kg among four year old winners of the race, carried more weight to victory. Returning to Melbourne the next autumn, Dalray broke down in the Carbine Stakes and was retired to stud in Queensland, where his best son was the dual Metropolitan winner, Tails.

DALRELLO

1970 br horse Aloe – Delegraphy

A versatile and under-rated Queensland galloper, Dalrello mixed sprinting and staying with aplomb. After winning the Queensland Guineas in 1973 and the Queensland Newmarket, he was second to Count Rapier in the Queensland Derby. A second to Asgard in the 1974 Grand Prix Stakes followed. Think Big, who would win that year's Melbourne Cup, was third. In the autumn of 1975, Dalrello warmed up with two wins in Doomben Flying Handicaps before downing Purple Patch in the George Ryder Stakes. He followed with his biggest win – in the Doncaster – from Sizzler and Martindale. Freshened up, Dalrello was second behind Spedito in the Doomben 10,000 and then fourth to Golden Khan in the Doomben Cup. In 1975 Dalrello also annexed the Craven Plate from the luckless Leica Lover. Next year his big wins included the Apollo and All Aged Stakes (the latter from Wave King and Leica Lover). In the autumn of 1977 Dalrello was still competing honourably in the highest class, winning a second All Aged Stakes and running third in the Doncaster.

DAREBIN

1878 b horse The Peer – Lurline

Bred by Samuel Gardiner, Darebin was owned by William Guesdon, sometime treasurer of the Tasmanian Racing Club. When Darebin won the Victoria Derby of 1881, it was the second fastest time (2.41.5) recorded in any Derby run in the world. In consequence, Darebin started equal favourite with Waxy at 3/1 for the Melbourne Cup, but was unplaced in a rough race which saw a stray dog bring down the A.J.C. Derby winner, Wheatear, and another fall in which jockey Dodd was killed. Zulu won at 50/1, carrying a mere 41.5kg. But Darebin had plenty of racing left in him. He won the Melbourne Stakes in the spring of 1882 and then ran fourth to The Assyrian in the Melbourne Cup under 61kg. Interstate wins included the Adelaide Birthday Cup and the S.A.J.C. St Leger, while Darebin lumped 61kg to victory in the 1883 Sydney Cup. An early success at stud, he got The Australian Peer (an A.J.C. Derby and Sydney Cup winner) before being sold in 1886 to stand in California.

DARK JEWEL

1953 ch mare Star Kingdom – Red Lace

One of the greatest broodmares in Australian history, Dark Jewel produced 11 colts and fillies, of whom 10 raced. Between them they won 69 races. All were trained by Fil Allotta, who had trained Dark Jewel in her moderate racing career (three wins at

two and three). After her retirement, Allotta bought Dark Jewel, but later sold her to Peter and Daisy Tait. Her first foal was Ginger Bread, a chestnut colt who won three races in Sydney, before being injured and subsequently sold to Malaysia. Powella, who won one race from 15 starts, was next, but the bay filly Heirloom, by Rego, gave a better indication of the strength of the Dark Jewel line. Heirloom won five races at two, including the Maribyrnong Plate, and four races as an older filly, including a dead-heat in the Thousand Guineas with Anna Rose. She was also placed in the A.J.C. Sires', Craven 'A', Epsom and Stradbroke Handicaps. Dark Jewel's fourth foal, a filly, was destroyed at three months. Her fifth was the good colt Betelgeuse, whose 13 wins included the Shorts Handicap. Cabochon was next from Dark Jewel. By Edmundo, Cabochon won 15 times and was placed on 23 other occasions. A winner of the Stradbroke in 1968, Cabochon was beaten a half head by Tobin Bronze in the 1967 Doncaster. Birthright followed, and became Dark Jewel's second Maribyrnong Plate winner, among eight victories. Lucie Manette struggled for two wins, but ninth was the champion Baguette. Unbeaten at two, including a third Maribyrnong Plate for Dark Jewel's offspring, Baguette also won the two year old Triple Crown in Sydney; the Newmarket and Doomben 10,000 at three, and other weight-for-age races at four. Facet and Briolette were moderate performers, but the lustre of Dark Jewel's performances in the breeding barn are undimmed, and unequalled.

DARYL'S JOY

1966 br horse Stunning – Rutha

Owned by the Singapore hotelier Robert Goh, and trained by Sid Brown, Daryl's Joy won seven times as a two year old in New

Zealand. Accordingly, he came to Australia with a top reputation. At his first three year old start here he was third to the champion Vain in the Ascot Vale Stakes of 1969 with fellow New Zealander, the fine filly Wood Court Inn, splitting them. But with American jockey John Sellers up, Daryl's Joy caused an upset by defeating Vain in the Moonee Valley Stakes. Their duel continued in the Caulfield Guineas, which Vain won convincingly, but then the paths of the two top colts diverged. Vain went on to triumph over sprint and middle distance courses; Daryl's Joy first beat the New Zealand star Ben Lomond by two and a half lengths in the Cox Plate, and then won the Victoria Derby by three lengths, with W. Skelton in the saddle. This was the last that Australasia saw of the brilliant galloper, whose future racing took place in the United States. There he won six races from 11 starts, the best of them the Oak Free International at Santa Anita, before being retired to stud.

DAWKINS, RODNEY (1943-)

In a long career in the saddle, Dawkins rode 1700 winners in several countries. Apprenticed to Ken Hilton, Lord was the best horse he rode as a young jockey. His first big success was a pick-up ride on Prince Grant in the 1965 A.J.C. Derby. Unwanted at 50/1, Prince Grant scored by eight lengths. Shortly afterwards Dawkins left Australia for an eight year riding stint (1967-75) in Singapore and Malaysia. On one return visit to Australia, he rode Kenmark to victory for Bart Cummings in the 1974 Caulfield Guineas.

DAYANA

1969 br gelding Oncidium – Dicidiana

Only horse in Australia to win four Derbies, Dayana was owned by the former Test cricketer H.C. 'Slinger' Nitschke. After winning the South Australian Derby, Dayana – trained by Bart Cummings – began his campaign in the spring with a victory in the Geelong Derby Trial. Then he beat the odds-on favourite Sobar in a controversial running of the Victoria Derby. Dayana now headed west, where he won the West Australian Derby. On Boxing Day 1972 he took the inaugural Australian Derby, and went on to win the Perth Cup in the new year. He was the first three year old to win the cup for 20 years. Dayana's great staying abilities found little further expression, because he was injured and retired.

DAYBREAK LOVER

1980 b horse Namnan – Rising Sun

Aptly named, the brilliant Queensland sprinter Daybreak Lover served a season at stud with a strong book of mares in between wins in the Group One Stradbroke Handicaps of 1984 and 1986. The other six dual winners of the race Babel, Gold Tie, Highland, Petrol Lager, Lucky Ring and Rough Habit have all done so in successive years. After winning the Stradbroke (then the Elders) in 1984, Daybreak Lover was set for the race again the following year. After winning the 1000m White Lightning Stakes, he was a disappointing 11th to Canterbury Belle in the big race. Now sent to stud, Daybreak Lover did so well that it was decided to give him one last campaign. Sceptics were silenced when he won the White Lightning again first up; was second – beaten a short half head after stargazing in the Ansett Cup – and then won his second Stradbroke by a length from Goldorme. After an ordinary run in the Prime Minister's Cup, Daybreak Lover bowed out in style with a second to Between Ourselves (who had 8kg from him) in the Doomben 10,000.

DE LA SALLE

1944 br mare Speardale – Fossil

Few horses have made a more spectacular transition from the bush to the city than De La Salle. Her career began at three with a win at Manilla (New South Wales) in October 1947. Taken around the northern New South Wales circuit, De La Salle had wins at Quirindi, Tamworth, Newcastle, Barraba and Glen Innes. Her owners decided to try their luck in town and the mare was sent to Lou Burke to be trained in Sydney. She won twice at Rosehill and at Randwick. In the spring of 1948, De La Salle took the Tramway, then in succession the Epsom, the George Main and Caulfield Stakes, before running third to Red Fury and Howe in the Caulfield Cup. Although she won again at Randwick in the autumn, De La Salle's form fell away and from 14 more races she recorded a solitary win, in 1950.

DELTA

1946 br horse Midstream – Gazza

One of Australia's finest stayers in the immediate post-war period, Delta was bred at the Kia Ora Stud near Scone, and was owned by the Sydney jeweller Adolph Basser and trained by Maurice McCarten. At two he was successful in a couple of minor races, but he starred at three. In Sydney he won the Canterbury Guineas, but was second in the Rosehill Guineas, and beaten by Playboy in the Derby. The Melbourne way of going proved more congenial. Delta beat Comic Court in the Cox Plate before winning the Victoria Derby. That form was good enough to send Delta out as 6/1 favourite for the 1949 Melbourne Cup, in which he ran a creditable fifth. In the autumn of 1950 he won the V.R.C. St Leger and King's Plate. His spring campaign began with weight for age wins in Sydney in the Chelmsford and

Colin Stephen Stakes and the Randwick Plate, but an unplaced run in the Cox Plate and a second to Playboy in the C.B. Fisher Plate in Melbourne convinced McCarten to give the horse a spell that lasted almost a year.

This was a shrewd move, as Delta's five year old season was his best. He won 11 of 14 starts, opening with successive wins in the Chelmsford and Colin Stephen, victory in the Metropolitan with 59.5kg and – in Melbourne – a win in the Mackinnon Stakes. He was at good odds in the Melbourne Cup, but with Neville Sellwood up, Delta won strongly at 10/1. Sellwood's "sling" was a Rolls Royce from Basser. Campaigning on in the following year, Delta won another half dozen weight for age races, including a St George and Chipping Norton Stakes. He was retired in 1952, after winning his third Chelmsford Stakes, to conclude a notable career in which he won 22 of his 41 starts.

DELVILLE WOOD

1942 br horse Bois Roussel – Everlasting

By the 1938 English Derby winner Bois Roussel (who was in turn descended from Carbine), Delville Wood was imported by Percy Miller to stand at the Kia Ora Stud from 1947. In England he had solid staying form. The top-line horse Hydrogen came from his first crop. In 1953, when he had only three crops racing, Delville Wood became Australian champion sire for the first of no fewer than five consecutive occasions. He sired 21 stakes winners, of whom the best besides Hydrogen – were Birchwood (winner of the Oakleigh Plate and Newmarket) and the 1956 Melbourne Cup winner Evening Peal.

DE MESTRE, ETIENNE (1832-1916)

First of Australia's great racehorse trainers, de Mestre was the seventh of 10 children of an American merchant who had settled in Australia. After training his first winner, Sweetheart, at Bathurst at the age of 15, de Mestre established a stud and a racetrack on the Shoalhaven River during the 1850s. With Archer in 1861 and 1862, de Mestre won the first two Melbourne Cups. The following year he was chagrined when Archer was scratched because the telegram signalling his acceptance for the race arrived late. Tempted out of a threat never to race his horses again in Melbourne, de Mestre won the Cup of 1867 with Tim Whiffler; lost the chance of a fourth in 1876 when the ship City of Melbourne, which was carrying his string of horses south, was damaged in a gale. Nine horses died, including the early Cup favourite Robin Hood.

De Mestre's luck soon turned. He trained the winners of the 1877 and 1878 Cups with James White's Chester and with Calamia. This fifth Cup win was a record which stood for almost a century, until surpassed by Bart Cummings. Then de Mestre's luck turned again. Drought in Queensland caused him severe losses. In the time-honoured fashion of the turf, he attempted to punt his way out of trouble. While his fine horse Navigator won the Victoria Derby of 1882, Gudarz, with whom he had coupled it in a heavy wager, could only manage third in the Cup. Much reduced, de Mestre, spent his last three decades quietly on a farm at Moss Vale, his finances buoyed by a benefit meeting organised at Randwick by his friends.

DEMPSEY, FRANK (1899-1977)

Apprenticed to his father Tom, Frank Dempsey was one of the best apprentice jockeys that Australia has seen, and thereafter rode with distinction until 1939, when he had his last mount on Contact at Moonee Valley. When only 16 Dempsey won the 1915 Caulfield Cup on the imported horse Lavendo for Lou Robertson. Two years later he scored on Bronzetti, while the Caulfield Cup of 1920 was one of numerous big races in which he partnered the Western Australian champion Eurythmic to victory. Thus at 21, Dempsey became the first jockey to win the Cup three times. He had begun to collect jockeys' premierships in Melbourne as an apprentice as well, winning the first of four in a row in 1915-6, a fifth in 1923-4. He won four V.R.C. Oaks – on Frances Tressady, Miss Disraeli, Ninbela and Gallantic – and two Victoria Derbies – on Frances Tressady and, in 1925, on the wayward but brilliant Manfred. During the 1920s Dempsey successfully emulated many Australian jockeys before and since by riding in England and Europe. His other big Australian wins included two Futurity Stakes, an Australian Cup, a V.R.C. Sires' Produce Stakes. Several years after his retirement as a jockey, Dempsey succeeded Rupert Greene as starter at Caulfield and sent away the 1945 Caulfield Cup which St Fairy won.

DENHAM FAMILY

Another of the Sydney training dynasties, the Denham family has been associated with racing for much of this century. Joe Denham trained at Campsie from 1933-9, when his son Mick took over. Jack Denham (1924-) was apprenticed as a jockey at 14, but by season 1948-9 he had turned to training. His first winner, Eloquent, saluted at Newcastle's Broadmeadow track. Mick Denham was disqualified for life in 1948 after his horse

Frontal Attack became the first ever to return a positive swab in A.J.C. dope testing. The suspension was lifted in 1951, but Mick never trained again, becoming foreman to his brother Jack. In 1968 the latter was made private trainer to Stan Fox at Nebo Lodge, Rosehill. Later Denham had his own establishment there, and has trained more than 3,000 winners, besides finishing second on seven occasions on the Sydney trainers' premiership. With Fair Summer he won the Canterbury and Rosehill Guineas; Ricochet won an Epsom, while Purple Patch was one of his best performers. In April 1978 Denham was suspended for six months over the running of Bold Akkadian, and his notoriously sour and taciturn demeanour with the racing press may date from that time. But he bounced back, with such class performers as Flotilla and Triscay. Denham also trained the 1982 Golden Slipper winner Marscay. His son Alan Denham gained his training licence in the 1986-7 season and took stables next to his father's. The sprinting brother of Rubiton, Euclase, has been the best of his horses.

DENISE'S JOY

1972 b mare Seventh Hussar – Fun For All

Trained by Tommy Smith, Denise's Joy was a high quality horse who competed at the top level throughout her career and won 13 races. As a two year old, she ran second to Toy Show in the 1975 Golden Slipper Stakes. Denise's Joy would be placed in no fewer than nine Group One races, apart from those which she won. After winning the 1975 Moonee Valley Stakes, Denise's Joy took the V.R.C. Oaks at 14/1 from Ace Queen. In that spring, Denise's Joy was also placed in the Thousand Guineas (again behind Toy Show) and the Sandown Guineas. On Boxing Day that year, Denise's Joy beat Ace Queen again, but this time on protest, in the W.A.T.C. Australian Derby. The fine horse Ngawyni was third. In the following autumn, Denise's Joy ran third in the Champion Stakes and the A.J.C. Oaks, before heading to Brisbane, where she won the Q.T.C. Oaks and ran second to Cheyne Walk in the Derby. During the spring of 1976, Denise's Joy ran third in the Underwood and won the Turnbull Stakes. She was still up to competition in the best company as a five year old, when she won the 1977 renewal of the Underwood Stakes from Vice Regal and How Now.

DERBY, ENGLISH

Neither the richest race in the world, nor the oldest thoroughbred classic, and run on a course that offers little more than rudimentary amenities to patrons, the English Derby, contested in early June each year at Epsom Downs, is the greatest of horse races. It was first run on 1 May 1780, and named after the racing patron Edward Stanley, 12th Earl of Derby. (Anthony St Leger had originated the oldest English classic named after him four years earlier). From 1780-3 the Derby was contested over a mile; the distance was increased to (about) one and a half miles from 1784. Geldings were eligible until 1904. Following the Second World War Australian jockeys enjoyed remarkable success in the Derby. 'Togo' Johnstone won on My Love in 1948, with Galcador two years later, and on Lavandin in 1956. Neville Sellwood saw Larkspur home in 1962, while 'Scobie' Breasley, who had already been premier English jockey on four occasions, enjoyed his first Derby success with Santa Claus in 1964; won again in 1966 on Charlottown. In his all-conquering English season of 1967, George Moore rode Royal Palace to victory. At least one era of the history of the

Derby at Epsom is indelibly marked by the presence of Australian jockeys.

DESERT GOLD
1912 b mare All Black – Aurarius

The 36 successes which the top mare Desert Gold notched from her 59 starts include a stretch of 19 in a row. This is an Australasian record that she shares with Gloaming. Desert Gold began her sequence of wins on 1 May 1915 in her last two year old run. At three she won at all 13 starts, and not in easy events. Desert Gold's victories included the New Zealand Derby and Oaks, the Ellerslie Royal Stakes and the Great Northern Derby. She won the Great Northern Oaks by an official margin of 'over 150 yards' and the Great Northern St Leger by 50 yards. Resuming as a four year old, Desert Gold won the Hawkes Bay Guineas, the Trentham Champion Plate and two other races. Eventually she was defeated at Wellington on 19 April 1917. After winning four of her first five starts as a five year old, Desert Gold was sent on her first campaign outside New Zealand. She won the 1918 St George Stakes at Caulfield; was narrowly beaten in the Futurity and then won the Governor's Plate at Flemington. In Sydney she had two starts at Randwick for victories in the Autumn and All Aged Stakes. Back in New Zealand she won the Awapuni Cup. Tried in the 1918 Melbourne Cup, Desert Gold was eighth behind Night Watch when asked to carry 60kg. Thereafter her form faded and she was retired at the end of 1919.

DHAULAGIRI
1956 b horse High Peak – Solar Circle

Elegantly named for one of the highest mountains in the Himalayas, Dhaulagiri raced during one of the golden eras of the Australian turf. For instance he pushed Tulloch right out in the 1960 Cox Plate, and the champion had to run an Australian record to beat him. Victory in the race came next year by way of consolation, when Dhaulagiri beat two Victoria Derby winners, New Statesman and Sky High. His 17 victories also numbered two Blamey and two St George Stakes, the V.R.C. Queen Elizabeth Stakes besides the Tattersall's Cup in Queensland. In addition, Dhaulagiri – always competing at the highest level – ran second 18 times; was twice placed in the Caulfield Cup; ran third and fourth in the Melbourne Cup. Another top-line effort was his dead-heat for first with Lord in the 1960 Caulfield Stakes (a race that Lord had won the two previous years); Webster and Nilarco dead-heated for third. In 1963 Dhaulagiri was sold to breeding interests in France, continuing a practice of sending Australian horses overseas to stand at stud in the northern hemisphere which had begun in the previous century. Because of his low fertility rate, Dhaulagiri was put down in 1968 and – according to a Francophobic legend – sold as horse-meat for the table. After Dhaulagiri's death, his son Dhauvedi won the Prix Royal Oak (the French St Leger).

DIAMOND SHOWER
1980 b mare Zephyr Zip – Jewel Flight

In a brief, but brilliant career, Diamond Shower raced against the best of her age and in open company. Her contemporary, Bounding Away, was sometimes a stumbling block, but Diamond Shower recorded her first big race win in the 1986 A.J.C. Sires' Produce Stakes, when she relegated Bounding Away to second. She then ran third to that filly in the Champagne. In Melbourne for the Spring Carnival, Diamond Shower's form peaked when she won the Wakeful Stakes and followed up with victory in the V.R.C. Oaks from Shackle. She campaigned on in the autumn of 1987, recording honourable placings in the Rosehill Guineas, the Flight Stakes (second to Bounding Away) and the Chipping Norton (second to Our Waverley Star), before being retired for duties as a broodmare.

DIDHAM, ERNEST ('MIDGE') (1944-)

Son of the New Zealand trainer Arthur Didham, Midge Didham enjoyed his first big success in Australian racing on the grey Baghdad Note in the 1970 Melbourne Cup. The following year he ran second on Igloo in both Cups. Soon afterwards he was enticed to ride in Australia by Tony Lopes, and was thus among the first of the many top-line New Zealand jockeys to make that decision. Didham settled in Australia in 1973. He enjoyed big wins in both staying and sprinting races. In 1978 he won the Moonee Valley Cup on Clear Day after Roy Higgins dropped his hands near the post on Hyperno. Tai Salute gave him a second victory in the race two years later. He had a pick up ride on another grey horse, Ming Dynasty, in the 1980 Caulfield Cup and saw him home at 50/1 from Hyperno and Kingston Town. Silver Bounty gave him two Caulfield Cups in a row the next year. Didham also won a Marlboro Cup on the Bart Cummings-trained Cap D'Antibes; William Reid Stakes with Leica Show and Lord Dudley; a Mackinnon Stakes on Belmura Lad. He retired in 1985 to take up training, and his son John followed his father's career as a jockey.

DITTMAN, LEONARD ('MICK') (1952-)

Born in Rockhampton, and one of six children, Leonard Dittman (known Australia-wide as 'Mick' or 'The Enforcer') was five times leading rider in Brisbane

before establishing a permanent base in Sydney. He won his first Brisbane premiership while a 17 year old apprentice and was not out of his time when he scored his first big race win, in the 1972 Doomben Cup on Knee High. A winner of more than 1700 races, Dittman has also been three times leading jockey in Sydney. An earlier attempt to settle in Melbourne as stable rider with Angus Armanasco was unsuccessful, but Dittman has continued to ride with profit all over Australia. He ranks third behind George Moore and Roy Higgins in terms of feature race wins. They include the 1982 Melbourne Cup on Gurner's Lane, the 1990 Caulfield Cup on Sydeston, Cox Plates on Strawberry Road and Red Anchor, A.J.C. Derbies with Strawberry Road, Research and Naturalism. He won Golden Slippers with Full on Aces and Bounding Away, the latter for Tommy Smith, with whom he has often had a profitable association. Bounding Away gave him a Blue Diamond Stakes as well, a race he had previously won on Aare. Perhaps the most admired of modern Australian jockeys, Dittman rode a winner at Hollywood Park in an invitation race in 1994, further whetting his appetite for the long-deferred welcome to ride in the lucrative Hong Kong racing scene.

DIVIDE AND RULE

1966 b gelding Alcimedes – Beehive

Bought by Felipe Ysmael at the 1968 New Zealand yearling sales, Divide and Rule was sold along with Ysmael's other horses following his disqualification. Divide and Rule was bought by Dick Roden (who trained him) and his wife. In a brief, but brilliant career on the Australian turf, Divide and Rule won the A.J.C. Derby in the spring of 1969. Roden brought him back the next year with Brisbane plums in mind and the horse did not disappoint him. In one of the worst months in the memory of Australian bookmakers, they were caned by Divide and Rule's victories in the Stradbroke and the Doomben Cup. The latter might have been thought a more suitable distance, but Divide and Rule had shown his sprinting qualities with a win at Rosehill in June over five and a half furlongs. In the Stradbroke he was backed from 10/1 to 5/1; in the Cup from 5/2 to even money, when he carried 57kg to victory. Black Onyx's victory in the Doomben 10,000 (and his coupling with Divide and Rule) compounded bookmakers' woes.

DOIRAN

1913 b gelding Sojourner – Hibernia

Good enough to run third in successive Grand National Steeples in 1920 and 1921, Doiran's place in the history of Australian jumps racing lies with his performances at Oakbank. Trained by J. McKinnon, he holds the record of four victories in the Great Eastern Steeplechase. The first of these came in 1918, then again in 1919, 1922 and 1923, when he carried 79.5kg. Later that year, Doiran added the Warrnambool Grand Annual Steeplechase to an imposing record.

DOMINO

1891 gr gelding Landsborough – Belgravia

A grand late 19th century jumper, Domino was trained by G. Russell. He carried 82kg to victory in the Great Eastern Steeplechase of 1899 and later that year ran second in the Grand National Steeplechase at Flemington with 80.5kg, conceding no less than 23.5kg to the winner, Mysore. Towards the end of this season, Domino lumped 85kg to victory in the Caulfield Grand National Steeple (later the Australian Steeple).

DONCASTER HANDICAP

One of the two great 1600m (one mile) handicap races run at Randwick, the Doncaster was first staged in 1866. It is the autumn counterpart of the Epsom, staged in the spring. Each takes its name from a famous English racecourse. Dundee won the first Doncaster, as he had the first Epsom. The weight-carrying record for the race – an astounding 65.5kg – is shared by Marvel (victor in 1892) and Chatham (1934). The latter also won two Epsoms. Indeed a number of horses have enjoyed multiple success in both events. In an unprecedented feat, Super Impose won the Doncaster in 1990-1 and the Epsom in the same years. In 1992 he ran a gallant sixth in the Doncaster under 62.5kg. The champion grey Gunsynd won the Doncaster with 60.5kg in 1972, and was first and second in Epsoms. Twice two year olds have won the Doncaster, easily the more distinguished being the great filly Briseis in 1876. Wakeful was another top class female to win the race, in 1901. Dual winners include Hall Mark, Mildura, Blue Legend, Slogan II, Tudor Hill and Fine and Dandy. Prize-money for the Doncaster was lifted dramatically to $1,000,000 in 1990, to the pleasure of the connections of Super Impose. Controversy has attended the race from its early days: Tippler won in 1869. Although he had finished second, Falcon (first) and Circassian (third) were disqualified because their jockeys came to blows. Tommy Smith has trained seven winners of the Doncaster, but the disqualification of Tarien in 1953, after she returned a positive swab, cost him another. Jockeys Jack Toohey and Jack Thompson have each won four Doncasters.

DOOMBEN CUP

Now a Group One weight for age race run over about 2000m at the Brisbane winter carnival, the Doomben Cup was originally a handicap, and one of the first features to be run at Doomben after the track opened in May 1933. Pentheus scored by four lengths in the first running, only to be disqualified, along with his owner-trainer C.P. Brown, on the grounds that he had not run on his merits the previous start. Seriodi beat the Queensland crowd favourite Lough Neagh in 1935 with a big pull in the weights. Bernborough carried the record and improbable weight of 68.5kg to victory in 1946. Winfreux enjoyed regular trips to Brisbane and won the Cup in 1966. Top winners in the next decade numbered Divide and Rule (1970), Tails (1971), Cheyne Walk (1976). After the race's conversion to weight-for-age, the New Zealand star Rough Habit won in three consecutive years, from 1991-3, while Durbridge concluded a great autumn with victory in the 1994 Doomben Cup.

DOOMBEN RACECOURSE

Situated across the road from Brisbane's other racetrack, Eagle Farm, and near the airport, Doomben was bought by a private company before the Great War with the intention that it should become a race course. During the war it was secured by John Wren, who was then the dominant figure in proprietary racing in Queensland. The Brisbane Amateur Turf Club leased the Doomben track from Wren and the first meeting there was held on 20 May 1933. The main event was the Doomben Newmarket (later Doomben 10,000). A week later the Doomben Cup was run for the first time. They are still the main events on the Doomben racing calendar. The B.A.T.C. bought the track in 1953 after Wren's death. It was the deeds of Bernborough in particular, when he won the Doomben 10,000-Cup double in 1946 under huge weights, that ensured the popularity of the track.

DOOMBEN 10,000

Since 1933 one of the key events of the Brisbane winter carnival, the Doomben 10,000 is run at Group One level over 1350m. After various changes of name it has reverted to the best known of them, which indicated a purse of 10,000 pounds for the race. Wallun won the race called the Doomben Newmarket down a straight six furlong course in 1933, backed in from 33/1 to 12/1 and surviving a protest. The top Queensland galloper Lough Neagh won the following year. In 1942 the race was lengthened to seven furlongs, but this came back 93 yards in 1946 when the race was known as the Ahern Memorial Handicap and the winner, Bernborough, carried 65.5kg to a resounding victory. In 1947 the race adopted its now familiar style: Doomben 10,000. Aquanita and Winfreux were top winners during the 1960s, while Black Onyx won in successive years, 1969-70, carrying 59kg to beat Cabochon on the second occasion. Baguette won the next year, while Charlton Boy – second in 1972-3 – was rewarded with a win in 1974. Maybe Mahal set a weight-carrying record for a mare in the race when she won with 56.5kg from Romantic Dream in 1977. The champion Manikato humped 58kg to win two years later. Campaign King, in 1988, was the best winner in recent years, although Prince Trialia scored in 1990-1, albeit with light weights.

DOUBLE CENTURY

1975 br horse Century – Hello Love

Trained by Ron McDonell, a former foreman for Bart Cummings, Double Century was one of the best performed sons of the top sire Century. But unlike his father, he excelled over long distances. Placed twice at two, he had a brilliant, but unlucky three year old term which resulted in seven wins and six placings from 21 starts. The wins included the 1979 Sydney Cup by seven lengths, the Queensland Derby and Grand Prix Stakes (in record time) at Eagle Farm. The biggest disappointment was when Double Century was first past the post in the A.J.C. Derby, only to be relegated to second after a protest by Dulcify. Double Century was also placed third in the Brisbane Cup. At four, he had an exasperating campaign, racing 12 times for five seconds and a third, all against top company. His seconds came in the Underwood Stakes, behind Ming Dynasty in the Australian Cup, Kingston Town in the Tancred, Iko in the Queen Elizabeth Stakes and then Kingston Town in the Sydney Cup. Sent to stud, Double Century's best son has been the multiple Group One winner Stylish Century.

DR GRACE
1986 br horse Sir Tristram – English Wonder

This handsome entire proved himself one of the high quality horses of his era. As a two year old he had wins at Kembla Grange and Eagle Farm. Still in Brisbane, the Geoff Chapman-trained youngster ran third in the Castlemaine Stakes. In the spring of 1989 he was second in the Moonee Valley Stakes and third to Stylish Century in the Victoria Derby. But his credentials to race in top company were being established. In the autumn of 1990 Dr Grace won the Chipping Norton Stakes before scoring in the A.J.C. Derby. Later that campaign, sent to Queensland again, he was placed in the P.J. O'Shea Stakes and the Queensland Guineas. In the autumn of 1991 Dr Grace won the first of successive Manion Cups, besides running third in the Chipping

Norton and Ranvet Stakes. Then he proved too strong for Shuzora and Castletown in garnering another Group One victory, in the BMW Stakes. In Melbourne in the spring of 1991 Dr Grace won the Liston and Underwood Stakes, and ran second to Rasheek in the Dalgety. Chapman gave the horse no easy assignments. Dr Grace was back in 1992 for another Manion Cup victory, a second to Let's Elope in the St George Stakes and then, in the spring, a victory in the Chelmsford Stakes as a fine career neared its conclusion.

DRONGO
1920 b horse Lanius – Lys d'Or

Named for a species of bird, Drongo's deeds on the racetrack, where he was unable to win in 37 starts, etched his name into the Australian vernacular. Ever afterwards, 'drongo' has signified someone useless and slow. Yet the horse was second in the Victoria Derby of 1923 to Frances Tressady, besides being placed in two St Legers. Drongo also ran in two Melbourne Cups, and the Argus was moved to remark before the 1924 Cup that 'Drongo is sure to be a very hard horse to beat', however, he finished near last. After 17 starts for 11 placings at four, Drongo was retired to stud as the most famous non-winner in our racing history. His owner, Mrs Woods, may have aimed too high with the horse, but enriched the Australian language by doing so. In 1977 the V.R.C. named a race the Drongo Handicap.

DUAL CHOICE
1968 ch mare Showdown – Unit

From her early two year old days, the Ken White-trained Dual Choice showed outstanding sprinting ability. Her six wins from eight starts at two included the V.R.C. Sires' Produce, in which she beat Royal

Show, while she finished third in Baguette's Golden Slipper. Her three year old campaign began with wins in the Freeway Stakes (which she would annex again the following year) and the Edward Manifold Stakes, which she won by four lengths. She then defeated Eastern Court in the 1969 Caulfield Guineas. At the Flemington spring carnival she beat Tauto by a half head in 1.9 in the Craven 'A' Stakes. The following autumn Dual Choice won the Lightning Stakes, the William Reid and the first of two Oakleigh Plates. Baguette had the wood on her again in the Newmarket of 1971. The following year, after a second Oakleigh Plate victory, Dual Choice ran perhaps her greatest race when although carrying 60.5kg (a record weight for a mare in the event) – she was narrowly beaten by Crown, who was in receipt of almost 7kg from her in the Newmarket. Dual Choice was retired with the career record of 16 wins and seven placings from her 28 starts.

DULCIFY

1975 b gelding Decies – Sweet Candy

Foaled in New Zealand, the parrot-mouthed colt Dulcify was bought by C.S. Hayes for a modest sum, gelded and put out until he turned three. His progress in 14 starts during that year was remarkable. First-up he won an Adelaide Graduation at the odds of 300/1! Beaten in the S.A.J.C. Derby, he was sent to Melbourne where – with Brent Thomson up – he easily beat Karaman and Turf Ruler in the 1978 Victoria Derby. Sixth in the Sandown Cup after a luckless run, some of the shine went off the horse when he failed twice in a Perth campaign. Floated back across the Nullarbor, because of an aversion to air travel, the horse nearly died of dehydration when the float broke down and was kept alive by being swum in the Great Australian Bight.

Eleventh at his first start in Caulfield in the autumn, Dulcify's stocks sank further. He went out at 80/1 in the Australian Cup in which Manikato was 7/4 on favourite. Ridden by John Miller, Dulcify won decisively. Sent to Sydney he found Manikato again an odds on rival, in the Rosehill Guineas, and again Dulcify beat him. Defeated by Shivaree in the Tancred Stakes, Dulcify then ran second to Double Century in the A.J.C. Derby before winning a controversial protest. Returning in the spring of 1978, Dulcify proved his weight-for-age class with a win in the Craiglee Stakes. Third in the Underwood, he then took the Turnbull from Karaman. In the Cox Plate, Thomson let the horse go at the 1,000m mark and he streeted his rivals by a record margin of seven lengths for one of the most astonishing wins in the history of the race. In the Mackinnon he beat Shivaree, who had been second in the Cox Plate, but only by a neck after a battle up the Flemington straight. Dulcify was 3/1 in the Melbourne Cup, against a field which Thomson unwisely described as 'a jumpers' flat'. In the event Dulcify was galloped on by Hyperno the eventual winner, broke his pelvis and was destroyed. This was the only occasion that he was not victorious at Flemington, where he had five Group race successes. Trainer Colin Hayes thus lost the horse whom he has always rated as his finest, with many of his greatest deeds perhaps before him.

DUNCAN, BILL (1900-1983)

A natural lightweight, and a feisty competitor who was frequently suspended, Bill Duncan won the Melbourne jockeys' premiership on 11 occasions, a record that he shares with Roy Higgins. The first premiership came in the 1919-20 season. Before then he had enjoyed one of his biggest wins, while still an apprentice, on Night Watch in the Melbourne Cup of 1918. A Moonee Valley Cup on Wirraway followed in 1921; the Sydney Cup on Lilypond in 1925; successive Caulfield Cups on Maple and High Syce in 1928-9, while Duncan was up when the great horse Peter Pan won the first of his two Melbourne Cups in 1932. In that season he won the 11th and last of his jockeys' premierships, in the space of 14 years. Highland, on whom he won the 1928 Cox Plate and Cantala Stakes, and the 1929 Toorak Handicap, was another of the top gallopers he rode. Perhaps the greatest was Manfred, for whom Duncan had not fond feelings. This brilliant, foul-tempered horse was badly left at the barrier in the 1925 A.J.C. Derby, but when he consented to race, gathered in the field and recorded an astonishing win. In 1933 Duncan unexpectedly retired. Jack Holt, for whom he rode regularly, was perplexed, but Duncan was not altogether lost to racing. He turned for a while to training, and in later life was licensee of the Inkerman Hotel, not far from the Caulfield track.

DURBRIDGE

1988 ch horse Durham Ranger – Arcona

Originally trained by B.D. Murphy at Morphettville, Durbridge won two minor two year old races in South Australia. Taken across the border for the spring of 1990, he won the Hardy Brothers at Flemington before beating Pre Record in record time in the Sandown Guineas. Placed behind the top filly Triscay in the Australian Guineas and the Tattersalls Classic in the autumn of 1991, Durbridge beat her in the Alister Clark Stakes. Sent to Sydney, Durbridge thrived, winning the Tulloch Stakes and the A.J.C. Derby. He was back in Melbourne for the spring and won the Craiglee Stakes,

before a bleeding attack looked likely to end his career. Out for a year, Durbridge was transferred to the care of Lee Freedman. He had a couple of weight-for-age placings in the spring of 1992, then won the Orr Stakes the next autumn. A year later his greatest campaign again occurred in the autumn, as Durbridge reeled off victories in the Chester Manifold, Blamey and St George Stakes before beating his stablemate Mahogany in the Australian Cup of 1994. In Sydney he earned his keep. An inexplicable failure in the Tancred Stakes was followed by another decisive Group One victory, in the Queen Elizabeth Stakes at Randwick. Taken to Brisbane, he rounded off a sensational term with victories in the Hollindale Cup and the Doomben Cup.

DUVAL, FRANK (1909-81)

Colourfully, if inappropriately named the 'Hong Kong Tiger', Duval was one of Australia's biggest punters in the 1960s. Born in Narrandera, the son of a chemist, Duval abandoned prospecting for accountancy; served in the Middle East, New Guinea and with the occupation forces in Japan during and after the Second World War. Electing to remain in Japan after 1949, he set up an import-export business. Australia became a holiday resort, and a place to bet. Duval also raced horses. The first smart one was Our Fun, who won first up at 66/1 and was good enough to beat Ripa in the Edward Manifold Stakes. The filly also ran third in the Oaks and she later threw the Rosehill Cup winner Such Fun and the Stradbroke winner Go Fun. Duval's duels with the bookmaker Bill Waterhouse were a feature of the Sydney ring in the 1960s. Winning $150,000 from Waterhouse on Oaks Day in 1966, Duval ended up behind when his filly What Fun was easily beaten by Farmer's Daughter in the Oaks.

On the first day of next year's Wagga Cup meeting, Duval lost $193,000, but won it back when What Fun took the Wagga Cup at 3/1. Duval moved to Hobart in 1974; was knighted for his services to industry in 1977; was bankrupt in 1980 – not because of the punt but from the failure of several of his companies – and died in 1981.

DYE, R.S. (1967-)

Raymond Shane Dye had racing in his blood. His grandfather, Vic, won such races as the Avondale Cup in New Zealand, and his father, Vic junior, was also a jockey. Young Shane helped out around the Dave O'Sullivan stables at Mata Mata from the age of 10 and was apprenticed to O'Sullivan four years later. In his initial year as an apprentice, Dye rode 78 winners, the first of them coming at Rotorua in 1982. He moved to Australia in 1985 and was third to Mick Dittman on the jockeys' list. But another feature of his career was evident: Dye's eagerness cost him seven suspensions in his first 12 months in New South Wales. Dye was leading Sydney jockey for the 1990-1 season. Highlights of his career include four successive victories in the Golden Slipper from 1989-92 on Courtza, Canny Lad, Tierce and Burst. Dye also won the 1989 Melbourne Cup, on Tawriffic. Many believe that he should have added the 1992 Caulfield Cup to his big race wins, but Dye remains unrepentant about taking Veandercross so wide that Mannerism was able to come through nearer the rails and win narrowly. A dual winner of the V.R.C. Oaks with Slight Chance and Arborea, Dye has also won Doncasters on Lygon Arms and Magic Flute, three A.J.C. Sires' Produce and three Champagne Stakes; Queensland Derbies on Dorset Downs and Air Seattle; a Queensland Oaks in 1993 on Slight Chance.

E

EAGLE FARM RACECOURSE

An inner city track, just to the north of the centre of Brisbane, Eagle Farm is situated near the airport, and across the road from the Doomben course. Its first race meeting was held in August 1865, in a swampy and heavily timbered setting, by the Queensland Turf Club. The first Brisbane Cup was run here in May 1866. In the 19th century the Tattersall's Club held meetings at Eagle Farm besides the Q.T.C., and the course hosted trotting events as well. Eagle Farm is now the site of some of the main races on the Australian racing calendar, particularly in the late autumn and early winter, when it hosts the Brisbane Cup, Sires' Produce Stakes, Q.T.C. Derby and Oaks and the Stradbroke Handicap.

EASINGWOLD

1918 ch horse Eaton Lad – Bahloo

Trained by Jack Marks of Kalgoorlie, Easingwold was an outstanding three year old in Western Australia, winning the Derby in 1921 and the St Leger in the next year in a time which stood for 48 years. Taken east, Easingwold – trained there by Jack Holt – was placed second in the first W.S. Cox Plate of 1922; came back to win the Kalgoorlie Cup under 60kg that year;

and then returned to Moonee Valley to win the 1923 Cox Plate. At Caulfield in that year he won the St George Stakes, the Herbert Power Handicap and was second in the Caulfield Cup. He added another Herbert Power to his impressive tally in the following year, to prove himself a top class galloper, even if somewhat overshadowed by his contemporary from the West, Eurythmic.

ECLIPSE OF THE SUN

On 23 October 1976, Moonee Valley's main day of the year, the Cox Plate meeting, was interrupted for an hour by an eclipse of the sun. A crowd of nearly 40,000 enjoyed the opportunity to reflect on form at the bar under the illumination of the course lights. When the sun returned to view, the programme was boisterously resumed. The Cox Plate that day went to the champion Surround, first filly to win the event.

EDSER, GEORGE SAMUEL ('HOLLYWOOD GEORGE') (1919-)

Born in Maitland, Edser was frequenting racetracks before he entered his teens and stayed on them until warned off in 1961. He sold racebooks at the Broadmeadow course in Newcastle and earned his famous nickname 'Hollywood George' there after an extravagant winning run (allegedly Edser turned three pounds into 6,000) led a bookmaker to tell the good-looking lad to go to Hollywood and leave him alone. Edser moved to Sydney, where he was the biggest punter of the 1950s. A setback occurred when he was shot outside his Elizabeth Bay flat in March 1958. Then in June 1961 the A.J.C. warned Edser off all courses, without explanation. Betting in secret, Edser went on what he was pleased to call 'the biggest, craziest betting spree in Australian racing history'. In 1966 he was found guilty of receiving stolen liquor, but received a surprisingly lenient suspended sentence. By 1974 he had been admitted back to greyhound tracks in Sydney, and the A.J.C. lifted its life ban in 1979. Seeking immortality through his words as well as his wallet, Edser once declared that there were 'more heartbreaks in racing than hoofbeats'.

ELEPHANT JUICE

The drug etorphine was so nick-named because it is potent enough to tranquillise an elephant. It also has the capacity to act as a powerful stimulant when administered to racehorses. In 1987, stewards of the W.A.T.C. disqualified Perth trainer George Way for 20 years for doping two of his horses – Brash Son and Hollydoll Girl – with elephant juice. To the club's embarrassment, the latter was owned by its chairman, John Roberts. After an inquiry, Roberts was cleared of any involvement in the doping.

EL GOLEA

1934 br horse Eastern Monarch – Versatile

But for Ajax, El Golea – a top performer in the 1930s – would have a much higher ranking. He was second to Ajax on five occasions – including successive Memsie and Underwood Stakes – and was third to him four times, twice in the Futurity and once in the Newmarket. But despite this frustrating record, El Golea won in top company. At two he won a single race at Williamstown; at three he was five times a winner, besides Futurity and Newmarket placings. At four, El Golea dead-heated with Ena in the Toorak Handicap, before finishing well back in the Caulfield Cup. Resuming in the autumn of 1939, he was placed in the Futurity before beating Aurie's Star in the Newmarket, at last to gain a well-deserved outright victory in a big race. Further placings behind Ajax in the Lloyd Stakes and Amiable in the Alister Clark followed. In the spring, El Golea was placed in the Memsie and the Underwood. The autumn of 1940 saw him fourth behind Mildura in the Newmarket; third to that horse in the Doncaster. Wins in Melbourne followed, in the Rosny and Moondah Plates, before further minor placings to Ajax in the spring. In the lead-up to the 1940 Melbourne Cup, two men broke into the stables of Fred Foulsham at Glenhuntly and fired shots at a horse who they believed was Beau Vite, the ruling favourite for the Melbourne Cup. But they picked the wrong stall and shot El Golea. This gallant, unlucky horse recovered. In 1941 he won the Mentone Cup, was second in the Mackinnon to Beau Vite and recorded further minor placings in the Williamstown Cup and Eclipse Stakes. Brought back once more in 1942, El Golea was third in the 1942 Caulfield Cup. His form tapered off and he earned retirement, but not oblivion. El Golea's name went into rhyming slang for racegoers as a beer.

ELLIOT, BILL (1908-41)

Best known for his victory on Phar Lap in the Agua Caliente Handicap in 1932, Bill Elliot had already ridden the champion to six Australian victories, in New South Wales, South Australia and Victoria. In the Agua Caliente, Elliot's instructions from Tommy Woodcock were to keep the horse wide and out of trouble. A famous victory in course record time resulted. Back in Australia, Elliot proved himself a top-line jockey and won the premiership in Melbourne in 1936-7 and 1937-8. In 1939 he broke his leg in a race fall and was out for six months. He resumed race-riding on New Year's Day 1940 but broke his leg again in trackwork soon afterwards. In 1941, debilitated by these accidents, Elliot contracted pneumonia and died in hospital.

ELLIOTT, JACK (1922-)

A racing writer for 56 years, Jack Elliott is the only member of his fraternity to have been honoured with the Medal of the Order of Australia, which he received in 1988 for services to the racing industry and racing journalism. Elliott's career began on the *Truth* in 1938. By 1946 he was chief racing writer for the *Argus*, held the same position on the *Sporting Globe* and then on the *Herald*, which he joined in 1958. Elliott worked for that paper for 30 years, until his semi-retirement in 1988. President of the Australian Racing Writers' Association for 14 years, Elliott has reported on 53 Melbourne Cups. He has collected a string of awards for his racing journalism, and now writes for a Melbourne Sunday paper, as well as for overseas newspapers and magazines. His pen is still used to effect when racing officialdom becomes too pompous.

ELWICK RACECOURSE

After the Tasmanian Racing Club was established in Hobart in 1874, its members decided to secure land for a racecourse. They leased a property at Elwick, north of the city, from Samuel Travers, whose homestead remained a feature of the track for many years. It was decided to race anti-clockwise (the Melbourne way) in the hope of attracting Victorian horses. A new grandstand was built in 1908, and the course was often praised for the beauty of its setting, by the Derwent River and beneath Mt Wellington. In the 1950s racing shared the course with Hobart's first drive-in theatre, while in the spring of 1986 Pope John Paul II was almost blown away as he addressed the faithful at Elwick. The Hobart Cup meeting is run there in the summer.

EMANCIPATION

1979 gr mare Bletchingly – Ammo Girl

In a remarkable career, Emancipation won 19 of her 28 starts, and recorded one second placing: in essence, it was win or nothing for her. Ten of those wins came at weight-for-age. They included the Canterbury, Chelmsford and Hill Stakes in 1983; the first of successive George Ryder Stakes in that year (she beat Manikato in 1983, Sir Dapper in 1984) and the Doncaster. Trained by Neville Begg, and out of a Gunsynd mare, she came up just as well in 1984, when feature wins included the Chipping Norton, another victory over Sir Dapper in the All Aged Stakes and a win in the Orlando Classic with 60kg. Melbourne fans never saw the best of one of the most talented mares of the modern era.

EMPIRE ROSE

1982 ch mare Sir Tristram – Summer Fleur

The giant dimensions of the mare Empire Rose finally gave her the Melbourne Cup victory her connections had long sought, if only by a half head. Bart

Cummings had charge of her campaign in 1986, when she was second in the Dalgety to Sea Legend and then a creditable fifth to At Talaq in the Melbourne Cup. Returning to Australia the next year, Empire Rose was a close second to Kensei in the Melbourne Cup. Now back in the care of Laurie Laxon, she won the 1987 New Zealand Cup. Faster times in the Auckland and Wellington Cups saw her run down the line, but Laxon persevered with another Flemington mission. Empire Rose's lead-up to the 1988 Cup was unpromising. She finished last at Te Rapa and then third at Hawera in the Ferndale Dairies Cup before being sent to Melbourne. There she at once sent her odds tumbling by upsetting Vo Rogue and Sky Chase in the Mackinnon Stakes. It was enough to earn her equal favouritism at 5/1 with Natski and with T. Allan up the mare triumphed narrowly. At 17 hands she was easily the biggest starter in the race, and she set a weight carrying record for a mare with her 53.5kg. As a seven year old, Empire Rose was back for a fourth tilt in the Cup; started at 9/2 favourite, but found the weight beyond her and finished 15th. She was retired soon afterwards.

EPSOM HANDICAP

A Group One event run over 1600m at the Randwick spring carnival, the Epsom was named after the course in England where the Derby is run, because it was an addition to the A.J.C. Derby programme from 1865. Later the Derby was shifted to the spring. Dundee won the first Epsom, as he won the first Doncaster, contested in the autumn of the following year. Atlanta and Kingfisher dead-heated in 1873, there would not be another until 1925 when the judge could not split Metellus and Boaster. Masquerade was the first dual winner, in 1882-3, while Melodrama won in 1907-8,

the champion Amounis in 1926 and 1928, Chatham in 1932-3, Toi Port in 1963-4. When Super Impose won his second successive Epsom in 1991 he completed a unique double, for he also won the Doncaster in 1990-1. The brilliant Marvel set a weight carrying record in the race when he humped 64.5kg to victory in 1891. Woorak (1915), Wolaroi (1919), Nightmarch (1929), High Caste (1940) and Shannon (1945) were outstanding winners of the race. After the Second World War such winners as Noholme in 1959, Sky High (1961) and Gunsynd (1971) added lustre to the Epsom. It has been a race for roughies too, with long-shots Citadel and La Neige scoring in the 1970s. In recent years the deeds of Super Impose are best remembered.

EPSOM RACECOURSE

Situated in the southern Melbourne suburb of Mordialloc, 'down the line' from the city, Epsom was a private racetrack which was opened in October 1889 by J.S. Jenkins. The Mordialloc Cup was the feature event of the first meeting. J.L. Reilly took control of the course in 1906, but between the wars he sold it to the newly formed Epsom Turf Club, although he continued to act as secretary. The club was sufficiently prosperous for a new grandstand to be built and opened in 1936, but unhappily it burned down after a meeting in December 1938. Epsom was never used again as a racetrack. After the Second World War, the surviving Melbourne racing clubs bought Epsom and Mentone for use as training tracks, and Epsom still fulfils that role today.

ESKIMO PRINCE
1961 blk horse Todman – Chicquita

The beautifully bred Eskimo Prince was owned by dashing punter Perc Galea, who celebrated the colt's victory in the 1964 Golden Slipper Stakes by throwing banknotes into the crowd. Eskimo Prince won his first start by four lengths and then scored in the inaugural Silver Slipper Stakes. Resuming in the autumn he was beaten first up, but still started favourite in the Golden Slipper, which he won by four lengths from Farnworth and Star of Heaven. The colt rounded off the season with victory in the A.J.C. Sires' Produce. In the spring of 1964, Eskimo Prince won the Canterbury Stakes, but was defeated in both the Canterbury Guineas and the Hill Stakes. Undeterred, Galea supported his horse heavily in the Rosehill Guineas, which Eskimo Prince duly won by five lengths. Galea tipped his winnings back into bookies' bags when Eskimo Prince was unplaced in the Derby. After Galea lost plenty when his horse was again beaten, this time in the Stradbroke Handicap, trainer Cecil Rolls asked that Eskimo Prince be transferred to another trainer to take the pressure off him. New mentor Fil Allotta won the Hill Stakes at Eskimo Prince's second run for him, but after two unplaced efforts, Galea sold the horse to American interests, who subsequently discovered throat and lung problems which made Eskimo Prince's performances the more remarkable. At stud, Eskimo Prince was unable to emulate his track success.

EURYTHMIC

1916 ch horse Eudorus – Bob Cherry

One of the greatest of Australian gallopers, and without peer among horses bred in Western Australia, Eurythmic began his career indifferently. However later in his two year old term he won the Karrakatta Plate and the Sires' Produce. At three, he won six races in a row, among them the W.A. Derby, the Perth Cup (in which he

dead-heated with Rivose) and the St Leger. No other horse has won the four two and three year old classics in Western Australia, let alone the Perth Cup as well. Eurythmic was trained in Perth by J.J. Kelly, but his owner, Sir Ernest Lee-Steere decided to send the colt to Melbourne under Jack Holt, 'the wizard of Mordialloc'.

At his first Victorian start, Eurythmic was unfancied at 20/1 in the Memsie Stakes but won by three lengths. This was one of his favourite races, for he won it in 1920, 1921 and 1922. At four, Eurythmic won 12 of 13 starts, missing only in the Melbourne Cup where he ran fourth to Poitrel. His wins numbered the 1920 Caulfield Cup, the 1921 Sydney Cup with 61kg, the C.B. Fisher Plate in the same year. At weight for age, Eurythmic won 21 of his 30 starts and was placed on eight other occasions. His Memsie sequence was repeated at his preferred track in the Caulfield Stakes which he also won from 1920-2. Each time Tangalooma ran second. Again at Caulfield, Eurythmic won the Futurity Stakes of 1922 with the maximum weight of 66.5kg. At Flemington the Mackinnon Stakes fell to him in successive years, 1920-1. Retired to stud in the West, and evidently debilitated by his deeds under big weights, Eurythmic died in 1925 in his first season as a sire. He had won 31 of 47 starts and been placed in 10 of the others.

EUSEBIUS

1915 ch horse Eudorus – Lager

A winner of one race at two, Eusebius proved himself a high quality performer in the following year. He began his spring campaign in 1918 with a win in the Memsie Stakes; scored comfortably from Clever Jim in the Caulfield Guineas and then lasted to beat Outlook by a head in the 1918 Victoria Derby. On either side of that classic win he had been third in King Offa's Caulfield Cup, near the rear in the 1918 Melbourne Cup which Night Watch won. In the autumn he added the V.R.C. St Leger to his big race wins and beat Chrome in the Eclipse Stakes in the spring. Thereafter Eusebius lost form and his only other success was a 1400m handicap at Flemington; he was winless at five and six.

EVENING PEAL
1952 br mare Delville Wood – Mission Chimes

Bred at the Kia Ora Stud, Evening Peal was owned by Mr and Mrs R. White of Collarenebri. Trained by E.D. Lawson, she was very slow to mature, not winning until her ninth start in a maiden in the winter of 1955. At three, Evening Peal won one of four races but showed enough for Lawson to reserve her for longer fillies' events in Melbourne. His judgment was acute: Evening Peal won the Wakeful Stakes by three lengths, and then the Oaks by two. Taken to Queensland, she won the Q.T.C. Oaks by five lengths at 5/2 on. The Oaks treble was completed when Evening Peal won the 1956 Adrian Knox Stakes, beating Arbolado (second to her at Flemington) who went out at 6/4.

In the spring of 1956 Evening Peal surprisingly won first up at Canterbury over six furlongs at 33/1. The run may have flattened her. She was beaten in the Newcastle Cup; ran fifth in the Epsom; went under to Redcraze in the Metropolitan. Taken to Melbourne, the mare was third in the Caulfield Stakes to Redcraze and Rising Fast; beaten four lengths by Redcraze in the Caulfield Cup before running fourth in the Mackinnon Stakes which Red William won in a boil-over. The form was still sound enough to make her Melbourne Cup odds of 15/1 look generous. Receiving 14kg from Redcraze, Evening Peal, ridden by her regular jockey George Podmore, beat him narrowly in a roughly run race. Rising Fast was fifth under 64.5kg. George Moore was suspended for two months for his ride on Caranna. The mare's owners had taken the Evening Peal-Redcraze Cups double at 160/1, but unfortunately had the horses in the wrong order. Evening Peal won only once more, in the Canterbury Cup, and never passed on to her offspring the qualities which she had shown on the racecourse.

EVEN STEVENS
1957 ch horse Fair's Fair – Amaroo

A flashy chestnut with a flaxen mane, Even Stevens was trained by Archie McGregor, who had been the colt's first owner. Even Stevens won first up at Te Awamutu, but after a protest was relegated to third. He won at his next start at Ellerslie and then again in hack company before being unplaced in the Great Northern Derby. Next start he had his revenge on the Derby winner, Stipulate, when with a pull in the weights, he took the Queen's Plate. At four Even Stevens was lightly raced, but showed staying promise with a victory in the Avondale Cup in September 1961. Resuming in August 1962 he won the Jellicoe Handicap before again contesting the Avondale Cup, in which he ran third on a heavy track. The Caulfield-Melbourne Cups double was his mission, and although there were doubts whether transport could be arranged, Australian bookies kept Even Stevens' price tight. Eventually he came by Qantas charter flight. Someone close to the stable had taken him for 50,000 pounds to win both cups.

Without much fuss Even Stevens obliged. Third in the Iolo Welter on a heavy track, he set a course record for a mile on the middle day of the Caulfield carnival.

The track was again rain affected for the Caulfield Cup, but Even Stevens strolled in by four lengths at 6/1. McGregor gave him his next start in the Werribee Cup, and this odd choice was rewarded with another win. Despite a 4.5kg penalty for the Melbourne Cup, Even Stevens (with Les Coles up again) repeated his four lengths Caulfield Cup success. For good measure, he won the weight for age C.B. Fisher Plate on the last day of the Flemington spring carnival of 1962. McGregor kept the horse up for New Zealand summer racing, but eventually a sesamoid problem saw Even Stevens retired to stud, where his success was moderate.

F

FAMILY OF MAN
1973 b horse Lots of Man – Colleen

Not always the favourite horse of punters, the George Hanlon-trained Family of Man performed with distinction for six seasons, before going to stud. He won seven Group One and four Group Two races. A winner of five of 10 two year old starts, Family of Man was third in the Victoria Derby of 1976, second in the Western Australian Derby and then won the Australian Derby. Next year he dead-heated with Surround in the Alister Clark Stakes (a race he won outright in 1979); took the Caulfield Stakes and the Cox Plate (he ran second the following year). Nor was sprinting beyond him – a William Reid Stakes victory came up in 1978. He also recorded handicap wins in top class: winning the George Adams in 1978. In that spring, he also won the Craiglee and Mackinnon Stakes. His peripatetic career saw Family of Man win the National Stakes at Canberra in 1978, set a Flemington course record for 1400m in the House of Windsor Stakes in 1977 (the monarch in attendance) and win his 78th and last start in the Pinjarra Sunspeed Stakes back in Western Australia in 1980. This was the 21st win for Family of Man and it came after he had already commenced his duties at the stud of recent owner Robert Holmes à Court.

FERRY, MICHAEL (1872-1943)

One of the most versatile of Australian turf personalities, Ferry failed as a grazier near Hanging Rock in Victoria; went to Perth where he worked as a racecourse detective from 1901 and filled in as a wool-classer. In 1905 he went overseas to look for bloodstock on behalf of the owner of Perth's Belmont Park racecourse, A.E. Cochran. His next incarnation was as a Wagga Wagga horse-dealer, in which capacity he took a team of buck-jumpers to England. When well into middle-age, in 1925, he persuaded the Sydney radio station 2FC to allow him to broadcast track gallops and then races, beginning at the Randwick Easter carnival. In those days broadcast positions often had to be improvised outside the course, and Ferry's location for Canterbury races was a fowlyard. He switched to broadcasting for the A.B.C. in 1932, and was employed there until shortly before his death.

FINE AND DANDY
1956 ch gelding Star Kingdom – Shading

A brilliant juvenile, the Harry Plant-trained Fine and Dandy won seven from eight starts at two in three different states. They included the Maribyrnong Plate, the Golden Slipper of 1959, in which he started at 11/8 on, the A.J.C. and Q.T.C. Sires' Produce Stakes. As a three year old he won a Flying Handicap at Randwick and was second in the Stradbroke Handicap (a race in which he ran third two years later). Later in his career Fine and Dandy developed into a champion miler. He won the Doncaster in 1961 and was second to Sky High in that year's Epsom, carrying 59kg. In 1962 he was placed in top class weight-for-age events, while in the autumn of 1963 Fine and Dandy came back to win a second Doncaster, with 55kg.

FINE COTTON RING-IN

When jockey Gus Philpot was legged on to the poorly performed Fine Cotton in the Second Commerce Novice Handicap over 1500m at Eagle Farm in August 1984, he was at a loss to know why his mount had been heavily backed. Had he been aware that those well-informed of its chances stood to win $2,000,000, he might have been more disconcerted. In the event, Philpot got 'Fine Cotton' home in a photo from Harbour Gold. Stewards were immediately suspicious. They sought the horse's papers from trainer Hayden Haitana but he promptly walked off course and next showed up on the television programme '60 Minutes'. Haitana alleged that there had been a ring-in forced on him by the same criminal interests that were responsible for the murder of the Sydney trainer George Brown. 'Fine Cotton' was disqualified, and the winner of the race was identified as Bold Personality, who with four metropolitan successes behind him, was well out of novice company. Long inquiries by stewards and by the police led to gaol sentences for Robert

North, John Gillespie and Haitana. In addition bookmakers Peter McCoy and the famous father and son pair of Bill and Robbie Waterhouse had their licences revoked. Several others were warned off, including the Catholic priest Father Edward O'Dwyer, but criminal charges against them were dropped. There has been no more sensational ring-in attempt in Australian turf history, nor one more disastrous for its alleged perpetrators. Attempting a comeback in June 1994, Haitana was escorted from the Mildura racecourse.

FIREWORKS
1864 b horse Kelpie – Gaslight

Owned by John Tait, Fireworks is in the record books as a triple Derby winner, although in peculiar circumstances. In 1867 he won the A.J.C. Derby and then took the Victoria Derby. However the V.R.C. changed the date of the Derby to 1 January, so that it was run twice in the 1867-8 season. Fireworks duly turned up again on New Year's Day 1868 and won in quicker time than on the previous occasion. To cap off that feat, he won the Midsummer Handicap on the same afternoon. Returning from a spell, Fireworks went to Launceston where he won the Champion Cup and St Leger. He added a V.R.C. St Leger in the autumn of 1868, but missed out on another treble when second in the A.J.C. St Leger to Glencoe. Later in that campaign, Fireworks won three good races in Sydney, best of them the 1868 All Aged Stakes. He became the first Victoria Derby winner to sire a winner of the same race when his son Robin Hood won in 1875.

FIRST UP WINNERS

Some gallopers have been remarkably successful when racing fresh. Manikato won at his first start and subsequently he had a remarkable nine further first-up successes. Kingston Town was last at his first start, for which he was punished by being gelded. He won his next five first-up starts. Other champions of different eras, Ajax and Gunsynd each won seven of eight initial runs in their numerous campaigns. The Sydney mare Joanne had a perfect record of seven from seven first time in. The capacity to perform consistently well first-up is one of the more reliable indicators for punters.

FISCOM

1916 b or br gelding Comedy King – Lady Fisher

Owned in South Australia by C.L. Moorhouse, Fiscom was probably the best jumper to be sired by a Melbourne Cup winner (in his case, Comedy King). He won the Grand National Hurdle as a four year old in 1921, ridden by A. Doy who had recently returned from a successful stint riding over the jumps in India. Fiscom was back again the following year, with a 14kg weight rise, but was still good enough to beat Roisel. A jumps race was named in his honour. There was not another dual winner of the Grand National Hurdle until Robert, 51 years later.

FISHHOOK

1863 b horse Fisherman – Marchioness

Intent on improving the quality of thoroughbred racing in colonial Australia, Hurtle Fisher imported the English sire Fisherman and the 1855 English Oaks winner Marchioness and set up a breeding establishment at Maribyrnong. In his first race, Fishhook ran last in the Ascot Vale Stakes of 1865, which was then run on Melbourne Cup day. But he soon found form, winning the Essendon Stakes on New Year's Day 1866 and the Flemington Stakes soon afterwards. When Hurtle Fisher

decided to sell his horses, his brother Charles (C.B.) Fisher paid a record 3,600 guineas for Fishhook. The horse's daunting assignment was to travel north to tackle The Barb. At Homebush Fishhook defeated his great rival and then won the Champagne Stakes. He was beaten by The Barb at Randwick and was then third to him in the A.J.C. Derby.

Prone to bolting, and needing a strong rider, Fishhook ran off the track in the Champion Stakes at Flemington on New Year's Day 1867. His owner then sent him to Launceston, where he won the Champion Cup over three miles at Mowbray at the tasty odds of 10/1 and the St Leger, beating John Tait's horses Volunteer and Warwick. He returned to Melbourne to win the V.R.C. St Leger. Back in Sydney, he renewed acquaintance with The Barb (Tait's most famous horse) and beat him in the A.J.C. St Leger, before winning the Sydney Cup by four lengths from Rose of Australia and Tim Whiffler, who would be third at the next two runnings of the race as well. Fishhook next beat Yattendon by 10 lengths in the Queen's Plate. After an unsuccessful dispersal sale in 1867, Fisher decided to raffle his horses the following year. This bold notion yielded 20,000 pounds. Fishhook was won by the bookmaker Austin Saqui and sent to stud at Woodstock, north of Melbourne. His racing career had ended after he pulled up lame in the 1868 Sydney Cup.

F.J.A.

1900 b horse Wallace – La Tosca

This small, tough horse was owned by Sir Rupert Clarke and trained by James Scobie. His unusual name reflected a fashion of the time for around the turn of the century horses called AZ, PDO and ABCDEF were in training. As a two year old F.J.A. won the

Gwyn Nursery and the Oakleigh Purse among five wins from 13 starts. As a three year old he won the S.A.J.C. Derby and then the Toorak Handicap. In the Derby he led all the way to beat his more fancied stablemate Sweet Nell, before being unplaced in the Melbourne Cup. Back in the autumn of 1904, F.J.A. was second in the V.R.C. St Leger, but then won the All Aged Stakes at Flemington and the S.A.J.C. St Leger. His form then fell away, and he was unplaced in eight starts at four.

FLEMINGTON RACECOURSE

Biggest of Australia's courses and home to the country's most famous race, the Melbourne Cup, Flemington has hosted racing since 1840. The origins of its name are contested; there are popular and patrician explanations. The name may come from a Van Diemen's Land butcher, Robert (or Tom) Fleming whose establishment of a business here led to the area being called Fleming Town; alternatively it may have been named after the Flemington Estate in Scotland, managed by the father-in-law of the Victorian pastoralist Tom Watson. The ambiguity is fitting, because Flemington is genuinely a democratic course, at carnival time, while also catering for the social pretensions of Australian quality.

The Melbourne Race Club shifted its rough track from the stretch between the present sites of the North Melbourne and Spencer Street railways stations to Flemington, by the Saltwater Creek (now the more dignified Maribyrnong River) in 1840. The course was leased in 1848 to the Victoria Turf Club, which held the first Melbourne Cup there in 1861. After the amalgamation of the V.T.C. and the Victoria Jockey Club, the Victoria Racing Club took over the management of Flemington in March 1864. The transition from rudimentary facilities to excellent on-course amenities was principally the work of Robert Bagot, first secretary of the V.R.C. and Henry Byron Moore, who took over from Bagot in 1881. From 1866 a spur railway line linked the course with the centre of Melbourne, a few kilometres to the south-east. Most spacious of Australian tracks and possessed of such distinctive features as the 'straight six' (a 1200m chute which joins the straight), Flemington is accordingly not always the most welcoming or intimate of race-going venues. But it has been the site of some of the most dramatic moments in the history of the Australian turf and no course matches the crowds drawn there for the spring carnival. A total of 118,877 people saw Spearfelt win the Cup in 1926; crowds of 90,000 are usual on Cup Day; of 45-50,000 on Derby and Oaks days.

FLIGHT
1940 b mare Royal Step – Lambent

Bred at the Mirradong Stud, New South Wales, Flight was bought by Brian Crowley, later Chairman of the A.J.C., and sent to the stables of Frank Nowland. Evidence of her ability came early, when she won at her first start, in December 1942, at 33/1. This was the first of 24 victories from 65 starts. With Ted McMenamin up, Flight's best win of her two year old season was in the Champagne Stakes. Jack Thompson had the mount in the filly's three year old campaign which saw her win the Hobartville Stakes, run third in the Rosehill Guineas, take the Craven Plate and then finish a most creditable second to Moorland in the A.J.C. Derby. Back in the autumn she won the Adrian Knox Stakes before running a gallant and narrow second with 57kg to Goose Boy in the Doncaster. In the spring Flight won the Warwick and Colin Stephen Stakes, but failed to win in the autumn. She did run third in the Sydney Cup after her saddle had slipped.

At five Flight started slowly, before brilliantly winning the Craven Plate from Shannon and Russia. She then went to Melbourne and beat two-time winner of the race, Tranquil Star by a head in the Cox Plate. Flight would win again the next year, in 1946, when the race was divided. Her autumn campaign began with victories in the St George, Essendon and C.M. Lloyd Stakes before she was beaten a long head by Bernborough in the Chipping Norton Stakes. Her last hurrah on the race track came in the spring of 1946 when she won the Mackinnon Stakes (in which Bernborough broke down) besides the Cox Plate. The Group One Flight Stakes for three year old fillies run at Randwick in the spring is named in her honour. None of the five foals who Flight produced was any good on the track, but one of them ensured her continuing fame. The prosaically named Flight's Daughter was the dam of the Derby winners Sky High and Skyline.

FLORENCE
1867 b mare Bolardo – Rose of Denmark

One of the many champion horses trained by John Tait, Florence won the Victoria Derby in 1870, beating her stablemate Pyrrhus, who had also run second to her two months before in the A.J.C. Derby. Not content with that, Florence added the Q.T.C. Derby to her tally, to become one of Australia's few triple Derby winners, and the only filly to bring off that feat. In addition she won the V.R.C. Oaks in her triumphant three year old campaign. At four her form never reached the same heights, although she was placed in four of seven starts.

FLYING HALO
1947 br horse St Magnus – Saint Trilby

A largely forgotten hero of the early 1950s, Flying Halo won 24 races and was placed on another 27 occasions. After four minor wins, he showed signs of better things to come by winning the Yan Yean Stakes on Melbourne Cup Day 1951. Second in the Standish Handicap on New Year's Day 1952, Flying Halo shifted gear sharply to win the William Reid Stakes later that month. It was to be the first of three victories in the race, a performance topped only by Manikato. In 1953 he went one better by winning the Standish with 59kg from New Britain and then beat Laurie Hussar in his second William Reid. A second to Ellerslie in the C.F. Orr Stakes followed. In the spring of 1953, Flying Halo showed his capabilities over more ground. He won the Underwood and Caulfield Stakes, beating Olympic Girl and Advocate respectively. In 1954 Flying Halo's wins included the Orr Stakes in the autumn and then another Underwood victory, this time over Rising Fast, in the spring. Back once more in the autumn of 1955, Flying Halo showed how well he had maintained his form in top class company with a win in the William Reid (his third) and a victory over Rising Fast in the St George.

FORESIGHT
1964 ch horse Wilkes – Ptolemy

After disappointing in good company as a two year old, the Arthur Ward-trained, Frank Packer-owned colt Foresight landed a big plunge at Hawkesbury. Graduation to city class now proved easy. Foresight won the Carrington Stakes at Randwick. In the spring of 1967 he beat Legal Boy in the Linlithgow Stakes; won the Newcastle Newmarket in 1968; had his biggest year in 1969 when he was beaten by Bye Bye in the

Doncaster, but won the Rawson and the All Aged Stakes, to prove himself one of the top horses of his day up to 1600m. In all Foresight won 17 races.

FOULSHAM FAMILY

The Brighton-based trainer Isaac (Ike) Foulsham (c1860-1943) was involved in the racing game for 70 years. Originally a jockey, he trained with notable success for such owners as John Tait. In 1884 he had charge of the Tasmanian champion Malua, when that horse won the Melbourne Cup. An amazing three decades later, Foulsham led in another Cup winner, Kingsburgh. In between he had won many big races, for instance the 1891 Caulfield Cup with G'naroo. Foulsham's notorious superstition was that none of his horses should be photographed before a race. His son Bill Foulsham (1890-1979) was a jockey during and after the Great War, and he won such races as the 1915 Adelaide Cup on Naxbery, the V.R.C. Oaks of 1920 on Mufti and the 1921 Caulfield Cup on Violoncello. As a trainer, Foulsham was a renowned mentor of young jockeys.

FOXBRIDGE

1930 blk horse Foxlaw – Bridgemount

Imported from England to Seton Otway's Trelawney Stud at Cambridge in New Zealand in 1935, Foxbridge became one of that country's most influential sires. He was leading sire for 11 seasons in a row from 1940-50 and was leading broodmare sire nine times on end. Foxbridge is responsible for the Trelawney Stud's special place in the history of the Melbourne Cup. Seven Cup winners can be traced to Trelawney sires. Foxbridge mares produced Hiraji, Foxzami, Macdougal, Hi Jinx and Silver Knight, while the grand dam of the 1964 winner Polo Prince was also a Foxbridge mare.

Trelawney's other resident stallion was Alcimedes, sire of Galilee, brilliant winner of the 1966 cups double. Of all the horses bred at the Trelawney Stud, Tulloch stands out as the greatest. But breeding remains a chancy business. In his 90s Otway conceded that 'It's all a fluke... in the lap of the gods'.

FRANCES TRESSADY

1920 b mare Tressady – Thorima

No filly since Frances Tressady in 1923 has won the Victoria Derby (although much more recently the A.J.C. Derby has fallen to the fillies Rose of Kingston, Tristarc and Research). With Frank Dempsey up, Frances Tressady beat Drongo in the Derby; finished fourth in the Melbourne Cup behind Bitali before taking the Oaks a few days later at 4/1 on. She was also placed in both the V.R.C. and A.J.C. St Leger during her three year old season. That form was never regained, and Frances Tressady finished near last in the 1924 Melbourne Cup.

FREEDMAN FAMILY

The powerful Lee Freedman stable is in fact a training partnership of four brothers. Besides Lee, who is in charge of the Flemington operation, Richard runs the stable at Caulfield, Anthony that in Sydney, while Michael works with Lee. Since training its first Group One winner in 1986, the stable has become one of the strongest in Australia. Towards the end of the 1993-4 season the Freedmans had produced more than 900 winners, and around 100 at Group level. They included the Melbourne Cup winners Tawriffic and Subzero, Golden Slipper winners in successive years Bint Marscay and Danzero, Mannerism's Caulfield Cup, the Victoria-A.J.C. Derby double of Mahogany, besides the Cox Plate and dual Doncaster and Epsom victories of Super Impose. Freedman also trained the champion sprinter Schillaci, and the top weight-for-age and classic performers Naturalism and Durbridge.

The Freedman brothers' great grandfather was the champion jockey Bill McLachlan, who rode three Melbourne Cup winners (Prince Foote, Comedy King and Westcourt); their grandfather Alan Freedman was a successful racehorse owner and their father Tony an owner and trainer, who ran a breeding farm from 1972 until his death in 1984. Lee Freedman (1957-) managed the breeding operation from 1975 until 1983 when he took up training, first at Warwick Farm and then at Flemington from the following year. The stable quickly expanded and now includes a pre-training and agistment property at Avenel, four stables and a full time staff of about 50 people. In 1992-3 Freedman became the first trainer to win the Caulfield and Melbourne Cups, Cox Plate and Golden Slipper in the one season. He has also trained two of Australia's three highest money winners: Super Impose (1) with $5,659,358 and Naturalism (3) with $3,285,606. Lee Freedman is also consultant in a joint Australian-Chinese project to build a commercial racetrack in Fujian province. In the 1993-4 season he became the first person to train 10 Group One winners in three consecutive racing years.

FULLARTON, ALEX (1910-64)

Twice leading Victorian apprentice, Fullarton's best win as a flat race jockey was in the inaugural King's Cup at Flemington in 1927 on Spear Maiden, trained by his master Bill Leyshon. Increasing weight led Fullarton to switch to jumps riding, where he enjoyed immediate and spectacular success. At his second ride over the jumps he won the 1929 Grand National Steeplechase on Sandhurst. Other big race

wins as a jockey included the Grand National Hurdle of 1932 on Polygonum, a second Steeple on Woodlace in 1934 and two Australian Hurdles. The first of these was with Dark Suit in 1937. The second came in 1944, four years after Fullarton had handed in his jockey's licence to train. He won – as an amateur – on Benghazi. During his riding career Fullarton won 700 races, 200 over the jumps. He was on Redditch when the horse fell and died in the 1935 Grand National Steeple.

As a trainer, Fullarton preferred to school his own jumpers. His big race wins included four Great Eastern Steeplechases at Oakbank (a race he had also won as a jockey). Two of these fell to The Feline, who also won an Australian Hurdle, a Grand National Hurdle and a Grand Annual Steeple. Fullarton trained another Australian Hurdle winner, Elastin (1949), and part-owned the Grand National Hurdle winner of 1943, Victory March. He is the only person who rode, trained and owned Grand National winners.

FURIOUS

1918 ch mare The Welkin – Danaide

Raced by Ernest Clarke and trained by F. Marsden, Furious won the A.J.C. Sires' and Champagne Stakes in the autumn of 1921. Later in the year she began a triumphant three year old campaign which yielded five wins and seven placings from 16 starts. Those victories included the Rosehill Guineas, the rare double of the Victoria Derby and V.R.C. Oaks (in each of which Furious ran favourite), and the V.R.C. St Leger. She was also third the next year to Violoncello in the first Cox Plate. A three year old fillies' race is named in her honour at Randwick.

FUTURITY STAKES

Now a Group One race run at weight-for-age at Caulfield in the autumn over 1400m, the Futurity was originally a weight-for-age race with penalties, so that many of its illustrious winners carried plenty of lead in the saddlebags. First run in 1898, the Futurity was won by W.R. Wilson's Resolute, who took the Oakleigh Plate in the next week. With prize money of 3,000 pounds, the Futurity in that year was worth almost as much as the Melbourne Cup. Gladsome won twice, in 1905-6, Eurythmic carried 67kg to victory in 1922, while the honour roll from 1928-31 read Gothic, Mollison, Amounis and Phar Lap. Ajax won three on the trot from 1938-40, while Bernborough scored an astonishing win in 1946, coming from the rear to win by five lengths under 64.5kg. The little known Attley scored with two kilograms more the next year. Lord's win in 1959 set off a run of champions: Todman, Sky High, Aquanita, Wenona Girl, Future, Sir Dane and Star Affair saluting in the next seven years. After Gunsynd's win in 1972, Idolou took the Futurity in successive years. Manikato has the most remarkable record in the race, with victories from 1979-81, a second to Galleon in 1982, before a fourth win the following year. Other top winners of the 1980s include Campaign King, Rubiton, Vo Rogue and Zeditave (1986-9). Mannerism won in 1992, while the high class sprinter Schillaci was victorious in 1993.

G

GADSDEN STAKES

One of the first races to be sponsored in Australia, the W.D. & H.O. Wills Hallmark Stakes was added to the spring programme of the V.R.C. in 1960. Next year it became the Craven 'A' Stakes. The vicissitudes of sponsorship saw it known as the Pure Pak from 1980-4, since when it has been the Gadsden, a Group One event run down the 'Straight Six' at Flemington. Karina won in 1960. In that decade he was followed by the likes of Samson, Ripa, Star of Heaven, Marmion and Vain, who in 1969 carried 54kg and beat Dollar's Double and Our Faith by an astonishing 12 lengths! Dual Choice won the next year, Century in 1973. River Rough was a dual winner in 1984-5. The top filly Special scored in 1988, while Planet Ruler scored in successive years, 1989-90, in this – after the Newmarket – the toughest of sprinting tests in Victorian racing.

GALEA, PERCIVAL JOHN (1910-77)

One of the biggest punters in the history of the Australian turf, Perce Galea was born in Broken Hill, and he came to Sydney with his family when four. He worked as a paperboy, had a milk run and then became a wharfie. His first big win was on Peter Pan in the 1934 Melbourne Cup, after which he turned avidly to punting. His fortune was not made on the track however, but as boss of several of Sydney's biggest illegal casinos. After he won a 12,000 pound lottery in 1957, Galea started to increase the volume of his wagers, so that 25,000 pound bets were not uncommon. The lucky Galea also won $200,000 in a Sydney Opera House lottery in October 1975. A keen surfer all his life, Galea allegedly saved the bookmaker 'Sharkey' Dwyer from the surf at Clovelly in 1961, only to be told that he could still settle up the following day. Stories of legendary wins and losses accompanied Galea everywhere: of how he needed to borrow a bag to carry his winnings off a track in Brisbane; of how he showered the crowd with 10 pound notes after his favourite horse, Eskimo Prince won the Golden Slipper in 1964. 'The Prince of Punters' suffered his first heart attack soon after he bought Eskimo Prince, but gambled on against doctors' orders. Galea finally expired in August 1977, leaving a legend, many sound gambling maxims, and an estate worth more than $400,000.

GALILEE
1963 b gelding Alcimedes – Galston

One of the great stayers of Australian turf history, Galilee was bred at the Trelawney Stud in New Zealand; sold at the yearling sales and sent to South Australia to be trained by Bart Cummings. The gelding was taken along quietly, racing only once as a two year old for a second in a Gawler maiden on the last day of the season. At three he proved himself to be at least a better than average handicapper, winning seven of his 11 starts in South Australia, including the Birthday Cup. But at four his greatness became apparent. Taken across the border, he won the Patrobas Welter at Caulfield before Cummings sent him to Sydney. Galilee was unplaced in the Hill Stakes and then second – by five lengths – to Chantal in the Epsom. Back in Melbourne, he came from second last before the turn to win the Toorak convincingly. Promoted to favouritism for the Caulfield Cup, he lost that place when his odd, pigeon-toed walk started a rumour that he was unfit.

So it was that Galilee went to the post at 14/1 for the 1966 Caulfield Cup (Tobin Bronze was odds-on favourite) and scored a decisive win. Regular jockey John Miller took the horse into third place in the Mackinnon Stakes behind Tobin Bronze and Prince Grant. Well primed, Galilee scored a magnificent win in the Melbourne Cup from Light Fingers and ended the carnival with a win in the Fisher Plate. In the autumn of 1967 he finished second twice to Tobin Bronze at weight-for-age, before reeling off four wins in succession: the Queen's Plate and Queen Elizabeth Stakes in Melbourne, the A.J.C. Autumn Stakes and then the Sydney Cup. The latter was one of the finest staying performances ever seen in Australia. Not only did Galilee

become the first horse to win the Caulfield-Melbourne-Sydney Cups treble in a season, he carried 60.5kg to a six lengths victory over Prince Grant. This triumph was followed by a severe reverse: Galilee developed a foreleg splint and was sidelined for 17 months. Returning at six, he won the Memsie and Turnbull Stakes, ran three thirds at weight-for-age and finally a gallant eighth to Rain Lover in the 1968 Melbourne Cup, under the burden of 64kg. At seven, Galilee was transferred to the stables of Len Smith and came back in the spring of 1969, but after two weight-for-age runs he broke down again and went for a well-earned retirement.

GAUCI, DARREN (1966-)

Perhaps the most brilliant young rider of the post-war era, Gauci followed his elder brother Mick into the racing game. Apprenticed to Frank King, he became the first apprentice jockey in 62 years to win the senior riders' premiership in Melbourne. He won the title three seasons in a row, from 1983-4 till 1985-6, and was also the first jockey to win four riding titles in one season: apprentice and senior jockeys' premierships in the city and in the country. These feats were more remarkable because Gauci did not ride his first winner until 18 December 1982. Less than a year later he was the first apprentice to ride a treble on Derby Day. In that carnival he won Group One races on River Rough (Pure Pak) and Taj Eclipse (V.R.C. Oaks). In the course of 1983 he set another riding record by winning at 18 consecutive metropolitan meetings. While still an apprentice Gauci became leading rider for the Colin Hayes stable, for which he won his first Newmarket – on Red Tempo in 1985. Another came in 1991 on Shaftesbury Avenue with whom he also teamed to win the Caulfield Stakes in the spring of that year. Gauci was the first apprentice to ride 500 winners; the first to win more than $1 million. In 1985 he split with the Hayes stable to ride freelance. Big race wins came in all south-eastern states: the Doomben Cup on Abstraction in 1989 and Q.T.C. Sires' on The Guida in 1990; the Goodwood Handicap on Daring Jon and South Australian Derby on Shark's Fin in 1987; the A.J.C. Oaks on Just Now in 1986 and 1990 Epsom on Super Impose. He has also won two Australian Guineas – on True Version and Jolly Old Mac. Gauci took up a three year retainer to ride in Hong Kong in 1992, but has made successful hit and run returns to Australia.

GAY ICARUS

1967 b gelding Icarus – Gay M'selle

Trained and part-owned by Cyril Beechey, Gay Icarus was a brilliant and unlucky stayer. Four starts as a two year old yielded a single placing. At three he progressed rapidly from an Intermediate win at Werribee to second placing in the 1970 Moonee Valley Stakes behind Eastern Court. After winning the Burwood Handicap, Gay Icarus ran a sound second to Silver Sharpe in the Victoria Derby. In the autumn the scope of his ability was revealed, as he won in succession the Blamey and St George Stakes and the Australian Cup, before running second to Fileur in the Queen Elizabeth Stakes. Taken to Sydney, Gay Icarus triumphed in the Chipping Norton Stakes, the inaugural Champion Stakes (beating Baguette and Gunsynd) and the Queen Elizabeth Stakes. He had earned his big impost of 57.5kg in both the Caulfield and Melbourne Cups.

Set for those races in the spring of 1971, Gay Icarus ran into the money at his first two starts before winning the Underwood and Caulfield Stakes. The Caulfield Cup field which he confronted was of high quality, with Igloo, Beau Sovereign, Gunsynd, Baghdad Note, Big Philou, Arctic Symbol and Oncidon among Gay Icarus's rivals. Carrying the highest weight for a four year old apart from Manfred and Poseidon, Gay Icarus won brilliantly from Igloo. In consequence he started at 7/4 favourite in the Melbourne Cup, but his winning chance was ruined by a bump from the egregious Big Philou. Gay Icarus now suffered an injury which blighted his future racing career. After a partnership disagreement, the horse left Beechey's stables and Tony Lopes took over his training. While Gay Icarus won the Craiglee Stakes at six, his halcyon days were behind him.

GEORGE ADAMS HANDICAP
see HONDA STAKES

GLENNON, PAT (1927-)

Weight problems hampered the brilliant international career of jockey Pat Glennon. Born in Melbourne, he was apprenticed to his father, Tom, and rode his first winner on Alares at Bacchus Marsh in 1941. In 1945 Glennon re-established himself in Adelaide, but raided east frequently. Late engagements were responsible for both his Melbourne Cup wins, on Comic Court in 1950, Macdougal in 1959. Next year he moved to Ireland and won the jockeys' premiership in his first season. By 1964 he was based in France, where he rode for Etienne Pollett. His greatest victories came at the end of his career. Glennon rode Sea Bird II, one of the best horses of this century, when he won the English Derby in 1965 and the Prix de l'Arc de Triomphe later in the year. Thereupon he retired. Until Irish jockey Michael Kinnane scored on Vintage Crop in the Melbourne Cup of 1993, Glennon was the only jockey to have ridden the Melbourne Cup, English Derby and Arc treble. He returned to Adelaide where he went into racing administration.

GLOAMING

1915 b gelding The Welkin – Light

When racing authorities turned down Celestial as the name for The Welkin-Light colt, he was called Gloaming instead and had a spectacular career in Australia and New Zealand. Gloaming was bred at Melton in Victoria, before being sold to New Zealand. He won 57 of his 67 starts, was second in nine others, missing out on prize money on one occasion only, following a barrier mishap. He equalled Desert Gold's Australasian record of 19 wins in succession. Gloaming's sequence ran from October 1919 until December 1921.

Shin-sore, Gloaming did not race at two, but once on the track he showed his ability through the remarkable feat of winning a weight-for-age race – the Chelmsford Stakes – at his first start. He followed with the A.J.C. Derby of 1918, the year in which geldings were again made eligible for the race. One of Gloaming's 15 crossings of the Tasman Sea saw him victorious in the New Zealand Derby as well. Back in Sydney in 1919 he won the first of three Craven Plates. At seven he had four great duels with Beauford, each horse winning two races, Gloaming's another Craven Plate and the Hill Stakes. No other horse beat him twice. Still a high quality performer at nine, Gloaming's last contest was a match race in May 1925, where he beat The Hawk in the Ormond Gold Cup at Hastings. He was then allowed a well-merited retirement. The Gloaming Stakes, a 1900m Group Two event for three year olds run at Canterbury is named in his honour.

GODBY, CECIL (1879-1963)

A gifted trainer, Cecil Godby was renowned for careful placement of his horses and for the big betting plunges of his stable. His principal clients were Jack Corteen and George Tye who raced about 20 horses in partnership. The only horse excluded from the partnership was the glamour two year old Heroic, owned solely by Corteen, but trained by Godby. In the spring of 1924 the stable was in top form. Heroic had won the A.J.C. Derby and he came south with the eight year old gelding Purser, also a recent Sydney winner. Starting at a short quote in the Coongy Handicap, Purser ran 11th. Godby had him entered for the Caulfield Cup, together with the better fancied The Monk, but to the consternation of punters, he scratched The Monk on Cup morning; replaced Hughie Cairns (who had had the Coongy mount) with George Young and saw stable followers back Purser from 50/1 to 14/1. Purser obliged by winning the Cup. Godby gave a convoluted explanation of the scratching of The Monk (which involved the horse's possible sale to a sportsman in India) but stewards opened an inquiry into the Coongy Handicap. In consequence, Tye, Corteen, Godby, Cairns – and Purser – were disqualified for 12 months. Heroic, owned by Corteen, had to be scratched from the Victoria Derby and Melbourne Cup. Heroic was sold to Charles Kellow, in whose colours he won a string of weight-for-age races before becoming a champion sire. Godby hit back. He won two more Caulfield Cups – with Gaine Carrington (1933) and the 66/1 shot Northwind in 1936. He also 'lost' a Melbourne Cup winner when Colonus was sold out of his stable in 1942. To show that all was forgiven, the V.A.T.C. named a welter in Godby's honour.

GOGONG

1977 gr gelding Rangong – Lumley Queen

The tough little gelding Gogong, trained by Leo Robinson who had won the 1976 Melbourne Cup with Van Der Hum, arrived from New Zealand in 1984. After a first up third on the flat, he bolted in with the Grand National Steeple by eight lengths. Two weeks later he led the field home by an astonishing 20 lengths in the Hiskens Steeple. Back the following year, Gogong was kept up to the mark by Robinson with three flat runs in eight days, culminating in a win over 2,600m at Moonee Valley. Two weeks later Gogong became one of only a handful of dual Grand National Steeple winners (and the first since McEwan, 1968 and 1966) when he carried 68kg to defeat Region by a length. Set for a second Hiskens, Gogong carried 70.5kg into second place, 10 lengths behind the fine Tasmanian jumper Monsist, who had 62kg. Few chasers in recent years have shown the strength and stamina that Gogong amply exhibited.

GOLDEN SLIPPER STAKES

The world's richest two year old race (worth $2,000,000 in 1994), the Golden Slipper Stakes was the brainchild of thoroughbred breeder and S.T.C. committeeman George Ryder, who argued that his club needed a prestige event to compete with those on the A.J.C. calendar. Some of his colleagues thought that he was acting self-interestedly, in the hope of breeding a winner himself, but Ryder prevailed and the first Slipper was run in 1957. It could have had no more brilliant winner, for Todman bolted in at 6/1 on. Star Kingdom, his sire, would have four more winners of the race in a row: Skyline, Fine and Dandy, Sky High and Magic Night. More than half the winners of the Golden Slipper have had Star Kingdom's blood in them.

Some of the victors have been topline racehorses in future years, notably Manikato, Vain and Storm Queen, while other brilliant winners include Todman, Sky High, Baguette, Tontonan, Toy Show, Luskin Star, Sir Dapper, Bounding Away and Courtza. But a "bad" horse has never won the race, which is Sydney's answer to the Melbourne Cup, on the criteria of attracting public attention.

Underpinning the race has become the stud value of winners and for that reason many of them retire early. Apart from being successful general sires some have in turn sired Slipper winners. Todman got Eskimo Prince and Sweet Embrace; Baguette, Dark Eclipse; Vain got Sir Dapper and Inspired; while Marscay was the sire of 1993 winner Bint Marscay.

The list of placegetters also recalls some of Australia's best known gallopers with the likes of Wenona Girl, Impulsive, Proud Miss, Ripa, Star of Heaven, Star Affair, Citius, Begonia Belle, Dual Choice, Denise's Joy, Desirable, Rose of Kingston, Grosvenor and True Version.

Trainer Tommy Smith says the Slipper is his favourite race, and little wonder, considering he has won it six times with Fairy Walk, John's Hope, Hartshill, Toy Show, Bounding Away and Star Watch. Bart Cummings is a four time winner. The most successful owners have been the Ingham brothers, who have been involved with five Golden Slipper winners. Jockeys Ron Qinton and Shane Dye share the riding honours with four wins apiece, with Dye's coming in successive years between 1989-92.

GOODWOOD HANDICAP

South Australia's only Group One sprint, the Goodwood Handicap has been run at Morphettville since 1881. Then it was an Adelaide Cup lead-up over a mile; in 1889 it came back to six furlongs (now 1,200m). D.O.D. with only 36.5kg on its back won the first Goodwood. The horse had formerly raced as Alarm, which aptly reflected punters' reaction to the result as one person walked away with the entire tote pool. Mostyn was the first dual winner of the race, in 1894-5, before going on to win the Toorak Handicap of 1895. The only other two-time winner was Musket Belle in 1911-12. Former stud master at St Albans, near Geelong, John Crozier had winners in successive years: The Despised (1891) and Fulham (1892). In 1904 Latchkey and Phaedra could not be split, but Latchkey (by Padlock) won the run-off. Aurie's Star set a weight-carrying record when he carried 63.5kg to victory in the race in 1940. The fine and under-rated galloper Royal Gem won in 1946 and went on to take the Caulfield Cup. Top sire-to-be Matrice was victorious in 1956. Since then such horses as Crown Lad, Romantic Son, Tango Miss, Kenmark, Mighty Avenger, Boardwalk Angel and Jolly Old Mac have won the Goodwood both before and after big race success in the eastern states.

GORDON, ADAM LINDSAY (1833-70)

Born in the Azores, Adam Lindsay Gordon's youthful misbehaviour led his parents to send him as a remittance man to Australia in 1853. Working as a mounted policeman, Gordon became a renowned amateur steeplechase rider on the South Australian circuit. His most famous exploit was jumping his mount onto a ledge 60m above the Blue Lake at Mount Gambier. A member of the South Australian parliament for a time, Gordon moved to Victoria where he ran a livery stable behind Craig's Hotel in Ballarat. Like all his business ventures this failed, and Gordon shifted with his family to Melbourne. On 10 October 1868

he set a record which has never been equalled, by riding three steeplechase winners on a single day at Flemington. They were Babbler, Viking and Cadger. In June 1870, the day after the publication of his volume of verse, *Bush Ballads and Galloping Rhymes*, Gordon shot himself on Brighton Beach. His fame was established by such racing poems as 'How We Beat the Favourite'. Gordon is the only Australian author to be honoured with a place in Poet's Corner in Westminster Abbey in London.

GOTHIC

1924 blk horse Tracery – Sundrilla

Bred in England, and imported by Sol Green, Gothic was slow to acclimatise to Australia, running last in his only start as a three year old. His two wins at four included the Newmarket, while he was placed in the Toorak Handicap and the Cantala Stakes. Next season Gothic was placed in the Epsom and the Cox Plate, however he posted wins in the Futurity and the C.M. Lloyd Stakes and again won the Newmarket. In that race he overcame difficulties to score with 61.5kg. Jockey Jim Pike's investment of 1,000 pounds on his mount ensured a desperately committed ride.

Tried over more distance at six years by his trainer Lou Robertson, Gothic won the Memsie and Caulfield Stakes, and was third in the Caulfield Cup when ridden too patiently by Pike. A few weeks later he triumphed at Flemington, becoming the first horse to win the treble of the V.R.C. Melbourne Stakes, the Linlithgow Stakes and the C.B. Fisher Plate. Victorious in 14 of 30 starts, Gothic died of intestinal illness a couple of years after his retirement.

GOULD, NAT (1857-1919)

Born in Manchester, Gould was a newspaper reporter who decided in 1884 to try his luck in Australia. He worked for the *Brisbane Telegraph*; edited the *Bathurst Times* and contributed regularly to the Sydney sporting paper, the *Referee*. Gould's lucrative notion was to combine racing with mystery: he published more than 100 novels to this formula. First was *The Double Event* (1891), which had originally been serialised as 'With the Tide' in the *Referee* and which was turned into a stage play in 1893, with the highlight a running of the Melbourne Cup. Although Gould returned to England in 1895, many of his novels had Australian racing settings. *The Roar of the Ring* (1900) was based in Bathurst; *A Racing Sinner* (1902) was one of a number set at Flemington while *The Dark Horse* (1899) had Randwick as its backdrop and *The Miner's Cup* (1896), Coolgardie. Perhaps Gould's most important work was his memoirs of Australian racing, and especially of Carbine, *On and Off the Turf in Australia* (1895; reprinted by Libra Books in 1973).

GRACE DARLING
1879 ch mare The Diver – Zoe

Named for the heroine of a British shipwreck, Grace Darling was a moderately performed mare before the spring of 1885. In the 1885 Caulfield Cup she was sent out at the long and unusual odds of 28/1. The field of 41 was the second largest ever in a race in Australia and nearly half of it came to grief in the worst multiple fall in the country's racing history. Before the turn 16 horses fell. The Scottish-born jockey David Nicholson (who had won the previous five Epsom Handicaps) was killed in his fall from Lord Exeter. Frank McGrath, later to be a leading trainer, fell with Prince Imperial. Uarah was killed instantly and numbers of other horses involved in the disaster never raced again. Kept wide, Grace Darling won handily. Good judges were not impressed

with the form and the mare was 20/1 for the Melbourne Cup. Twice checked, she was most unluckily beaten a head by Sheet Anchor. It should perhaps have been Grace Darling, rather than Poseidon who is in the record book as the first dual Cups winner.

GRAFNAX
1903 b gelding Grafted – Xanthippe

This Frank McGrath trained jumper was one of the finest steeplechasers in the early years of this century. He won a Maiden Steeplechase at Flemington in 1909, but quickly moved through the grades. He won two chases at Randwick before being set for the 1910 Flemington Grand National. With F. Burn up, Grafnax carried 75.5 kg to a comfortable victory, and started at 4/1 favourite. McGrath backed him up over the 6,400m journey of the Australian Steeple at Caulfield a month later, and Grafnax humped 82 kg to beat 14 others at 5/2 favourite. Set an even tougher task in 1911, he was third in the Grand National Steeplechase with 85kg, giving 20kg to the winner, Confide.

GRAND FLANEUR
1877 b horse Yattendon – First Lady

Perhaps the finest of the horses never to be beaten on the racetrack in Australia, Grand Flaneur was bred by the Hon. E.K. Cox at Fernhill Stud near Sydney, and trained by W. Forrester. He won the Normanby Stakes at Flemington on New Year's Day in 1880 at his only start at two; went lame and was spelled. Taken north, he was well-backed for the A.J.C. Derby after news of the engagement of Tom Hales. Grand Flaneur won the Derby and the Mares' Produce Stakes. Campaigning on in the spring of 1880 he beat Progress in the Victoria Derby beginning a sequence of five races in which the hapless Progress could make none, finishing second to Grand Flaneur on each occasion. Next Grand Flaneur won the Melbourne Cup, giving Hales his first success in the race. Because he was giving a stone in weight to Progress, that colt started at 3/1 favourite, but Grand Flaneur beat him comfortably by a length. The horse's owner, W.A. Long, reputedly won 20,000 pounds on the Derby-Cup double. Grand Flaneur's winning run continued, and he took the Mares' Produce and Champion Stakes, the V.R.C. St Leger and the Town Plate before breaking down. Progress now gave a true measure of the ability of Grand Flaneur, when he won the A.J.C. St Leger by 20 lengths and the 1881 Sydney Cup. Grand Flaneur further enhanced his standing at stud, where he became the first Melbourne Cup winner to sire a Cup winner, when his son Bravo won in 1889. He then became the first to sire two Cup winners when Patron was victorious in 1894. Another son, Merman, won three of the great staying races in England: the Ascot Gold Cup, Cesarewitch and Goodwood Cup.

GRAND NATIONAL HURDLE(S)

When, in 1881, the V.R.C. decided to move its main jumps meeting from mid-summer to the winter, the Grand National Hurdle was added to the programme. On 23 July a six race card was run, which included a Maiden Hurdle and Steeplechase, a Selling Hurdle, one flat race over a mile, together with the Grand National Hurdle and Grand National Steeplechase. Sir Peter won the first Grand National Hurdle while champions saluted at the end of the decade: Malua in 1888 and Redleap the following year. Don Quixote set the weight-carrying record of 76kg for the race as long ago as 1884. Fiscom won the race in 1921-2 but it was half a century before another dual

winner: Robert in 1973-4. Thereafter the feat has been repeated, if not in successive years, by Airmond (1980 and 1982) and Sir Agrifo (1987 and 1989). Mosstrooper won in 1930 and Green Cape just before the Second World War. The mare Claudette and The Feline were good winners of the Grand National in the 1940s. In 1969 Brother Bart ended Lots of Time's nine race winning streak by relegating him to second, while in 1972 – the last pre-metric Grand National – Our Leo ran a world record for a three mile hurdle. Other states have had their Grand Nationals with races of that name being run at Deloraine in Tasmania, at Randwick, and at Victoria Park in South Australia.

GRAND NATIONAL STEEPLECHASE(S)

Named for the illustrious English Grand National at Aintree, the Australian version of the Grand National Steeplechase was first run at Flemington in mid-summer 1866. For the first few years its cast was familiar: Reindeer had two wins and a second placing; Ballarat two seconds; Firetail a first and second and Babbler two thirds; Viking a first and a second. The last two named were ridden on another occasion by Adam Lindsay Gordon when he made history by taking three steeplechase events on a single day at Flemington in 1868. The Grand National was not contested between 1871-4, nor from 1876-80. In 1881 the V.R.C. switched the Grand National Steeplechase to mid-winter, and complemented it with a Grand National Hurdle. In that year Sussex won with the impost of 82kg, a weight exceeded only by the 83.5kg which the champion Redleap carried in 1892. The race has had many subsequent distinguished winners: Bribery and Grafnax before the Great War; the dual winner Mountain God in 1921 and 1922; Mosstrooper, Redditch and Green Cape in the 1930s; the mare

Pedro's Pride in 1957. Sir Cameron, Somoy and Gogong all were good enough to take this gruelling 5000m race twice. The Grand National Steeplechase has had controversial moments: bookmaker 'Big Mick' McLeod was bashed to death for welching in 1906; W.H. Sweeting did perhaps the first radio broadcast of an Australian race as an experiment for A.W.A. in 1923; Miss Dorothy Shiel trained Precocious to win in 1932 and was promptly refused entry to the presentation and was the immediate cause of a V.R.C. by-law that forebade women trainers. Training horses, said V.R.C. Chairman, L.K.S. Mackinnon, was 'not their proper sphere'. Miss Shiel has, however, had distinguished successors in the jumping game. Around Australia there have been other events named Grand National Steeplechase, but none with the demands on horses or the honour roll of winners as that at Flemington.

GREAT BOOKIE ROBBERY

Melbourne bookmakers were in a benevolent mood at the Victoria Club in the city after a winning three days during the Easter racing in 1976. Ten were gathered in the settling room on the second floor, waiting for the return of monies held after the races by a security firm. Around lunchtime security employees arrived with the takings. Out of hiding came six men, some armed with machine guns. They overpowered the guards and the bookmakers, before escaping with an estimated $1.4 million in cash. Then the biggest robbery in Australian criminal history, the operation had been expertly planned and the perpetrators have not been caught. 'The Great Bookie Robbery' was subsequently the subject of a television mini-series.

GREEN SOL(OMON) (1868-1948)

A London-born publican's son, Green came to Australia at 15 and began bookmaking in 1887. After initial reverses he started a highly successful, nationwide mail-order doubles book. By the beginning of this century, he had opened the Melbourne Tattersall's Club. Later he established a stud at Warrnambool. Of the top horses that Green owned, Comedy King won the Melbourne Cup of 1910, while Gothic won successive Newmarkets in 1927 and 1928. Green had imported both horses from England. Strephon took the Victoria Derby and St Leger for him. Retired from bookmaking in 1913, when the scale of his operations became larger than he cared any longer to manage, Green thereafter devoted himself to property development in Melbourne and to philanthropy. A flamboyant character, Green favoured Havana cigars and often arrived at the track in a gold-plated Rolls Royce.

GREEN CAPE

1931 b gelding Ethiopian – Capeless

Trained by Bill Burke, Green Cape was among a number of high class jumpers in Victoria just before the start of the Second World War. In 1938, with only 61.5kg he won the Grand National Steeple by 30 lengths. Showing his versatility, Green Cape switched back to hurdling in the next season, winning the Grand National Hurdle and then the Australian Hurdle. Other good quality wins for Green Cape included the Hopetoun and Doutta Galla Hurdles and the Rothwell Hurdle at Moonee Valley.

GREENLINE

1925 blk horse Greenstead – Ayrline

This brilliant weight carrying sprinter, trained by J. Barden, was by the 1920 Epsom winner, Greenstead. His place in racing history comes principally from the 1930 Newmarket when – with Jim Pike up – he carried a record 64.5kg to victory. Two years later, he was third in that event with 66kg! Although he won 13 of 82 starts, many with huge weights, Greenline often ran into horses who were better weighted, or champions in their own right. In 1929 he was third to Mollison and Gothic in the Futurity, second the following year to Amounis. He was most luckless in the William Reid, running second in three consecutive years (1930-2), and dead-heating for third in the next. In 1931 he carried 67kg into second place in the Oakleigh Plate. Greenline raced often in Sydney, winning the Challenge Stakes at Randwick in 1928. There too he was a professional place-getter, albeit at the highest level, running third twice in the All Aged Stakes: to Limerick and Gothic in 1928, to Amounis and Nightmarch two years later.

GREY BOOTS

1945 gr gelding Nizami – St Cloud

Known in his early days as no more than a moderate sprinter, this spotted descendant of the English champion, The Tetrarch, finally showed some form when he won the 1950 Doncaster at 25/1. Stepping out next at weight-for-age, he ran second to San Domenico in the George Main Stakes. Then trekking south, he won the Toorak Handicap. Punters still entertained doubts concerning the stamina of Grey Boots, and in the 1950 Caulfield Cup he started at 7/1 in a wide betting race. With Neville Sellwood up, Grey Boots beat Chicquita by three quarters of a length. This win gave the author Frank Hardy the first leg of a big Cups double, but as he related in *The Hard Way* (1961), the second leg was Alister, who was no match at Flemington for Comic

Court. Hardy had been arrested on a charge of criminal libel in respect of his novel *Power Without Glory*, but a sympathetic detective allowed him to keep the doubles ticket. Grey Boots lost nothing with age, winning the C.M. Lloyd Stakes, the 1951 Rawson and Caulfield Stakes, besides the Orr Stakes of 1952.

GROSVENOR

1979 b horse Sir Tristram – My Tricia

One of the best sons of Sir Tristram, Grosvenor distinguished himself on the racetrack and at stud. As a two year old he had sufficient brilliance to run a fast-finishing third in the 1982 Blue Diamond Stakes to Rancher and War Chest and to fill the same place behind Marscay and Vaindarra in the Golden Slipper. Grosvenor won the V.R.C. Sires' Produce and was second to the rank outsider Mighty Manitou in the A.J.C. Sires'. At three, Grosvenor won the Gloaming Stakes and was second to Veloso in the Spring Champion Stakes in Sydney. He then began a brilliant campaign back in Melbourne, winning the Caulfield Guineas and the Victoria Derby, before pushing Kingston Town in that champion's third successive Cox Plate. Grosvenor wound up second. At stud in New Zealand Grosvenor promptly sired a Victoria Derby winner, Omnicorp (1987) and he has had four Oaks winners: Domino in New Zealand, Richfield Lady (V.R.C. Oaks), Trappings (W.A.T.C. Oaks) and Our Heavenly Body (S.A.J.C. Oaks).

GUNSYND

1967 gr gelding Sunset Hue – Woodie Wonder

One of the bravest, most popular and soundest horses to race in Australia, Gunsynd cost only $1,300 as a yearling. Owned by a group of friends from the Queensland border town of Goondiwindi,

Gunsynd was affectionately known as 'the Goondiwindi Grey', and so immortalised in a pop song of the 1970s. Under the care of Queensland trainer Bill Wehlow, Gunsynd won his first three starts in Brisbane, before scoring over 1400m at Warwick Farm at his first run in Sydney. He was only sixth to Baguette in the Golden Slipper of 1970, but a week later won the Fernhill Handicap, always a good pointer of success to come.

Back as a three year old, Gunsynd won twice in Queensland before finishing fourth in the Canterbury Guineas. He then beat Roman Consul in the Chelmsford Stakes and was third in both the Rosehill Guineas (to Royal Show) and the A.J.C. Derby (to Silver Sharpe). He was third to the same horse in the Queensland Derby, before winning three of his remaining runs in that preparation. Wehlow saddled Gunsynd for the last time at his first four year old start in September 1971, when he won a Doomben Flying. The horse's new trainer was T.J. Smith. In his care, Gunsynd was out of the money only once in 32 starts (when fifth in the 1972 Sydney Cup on a heavy track) and won 17 of them. In 1971 Gunsynd took both the Epsom and Toorak Handicaps, ran fourth in the Caulfield Cup and Cox Plate, before completing a remarkable 1600m Group One treble with victory over Tauto in the George Adams Handicap by five lengths. The unrelenting Smith then successfully set Gunsynd for the Sandown Cup.

Back in the autumn of 1972, Gunsynd's five straight wins included the Doncaster, in which he carried 60.5kg to victory over the good horse Triton. At five, he started 18 times for five wins, best of them the Cox Plate, in which he passed Tulloch's stakes-winning record in Australia. Arguably his greatest run came shortly afterwards, in the 1972 Melbourne Cup. Although not bred to stay 3200m, Gunsynd carried 60.5kg to a fighting third behind Piping Lane (who had 12.5kg from him). Gunsynd's swansong in Melbourne came in March 1973, when he won the Queen Elizabeth Stakes. His last race in Sydney was in the race of the same name, when he finished second to Apollo Eleven, to conclude the racetrack career of one of the gamest, most resolute thoroughbreds to grace the Australian turf since the Second World War.

GURNER'S LANE
1978 ch gelding Sir Tristram – Taiona

One of the few horses to win the Caulfield-Melbourne Cups double, the Geoff Murphy-trained Gurner's Lane was one of the toughest stayers of the 1980s. As a two year old, he won one minor race at Eagle Farm. Then he won both the V.R.C. and the A.J.C. St Legers at three, besides running third in the A.J.C. Derby and second in the Tulloch and Chelmsford Stakes. But it was his Melbourne spring in 1982 which set the seal on the reputation of Gurner's Lane. Supposedly averse to wet tracks, he won the Caulfield Cup by five lengths from Gala Mascot in heavy going, with Brent Thomson in the saddle. In the Mackinnon Stakes, Gurner's Lane was second to Mighty Kingdom. A few days later he triumphed in one of the most famous of all Melbourne Cups. After Kingston Town was let go by Malcolm Johnson before the turn, Mick Dittman forced a passage clear on Gurner's Lane (an action for which he received a long suspension) just in time to catch the champion and win by a neck. But he had carried the good horse's weight of 56kg and was a worthy winner of the great race, if never likely to be well loved because of the horse that ran second to him.

H

HALES, THOMAS (1847-1901)

The most celebrated of 19th century Australian jockeys, Hales ran away from home at 12. At Stockdale station, where he was in hiding, he met Adam Lindsay Gordon, the horseman and poet, who would later – as a mounted policeman – arrest Hales at Penola for throwing stones at a bullock. Hales won a 50 pound match race at 13 but little is known of his early career as a jockey until he ran second on The Ace to The Quack in the Melbourne Cup of 1872. Soon he was noticed and patronised by leading owners, particularly James White, for whom he won three Sydney Cups, six A.J.C. and seven Victoria Derbies, six A.J.C. and 10 V.R.C. St Legers. Hales also won two Adelaide Cups, seven Australian Cups and seven V.R.C. Champion Stakes. Two of the great horses with whom he was associated were Briseis on whom he won the Victoria Derby and V.R.C. Oaks in 1876 and the unbeaten Grand Flaneur, who he rode to victory in the A.J.C. and Victoria Derbies and the Melbourne Cup of 1880. From 1872-94 Hales rode 496 winners from 1678 mounts which earned owners the unprecedented prizemoney of a third of a million pounds. It was White who paid Hales what must have seemed to him the highest compliment, when he put the jockey on a par with the great Fred Archer of England.

HALL FAMILY

Jockey Greg Hall (1957-) belongs to a famous racing family. His father Ron won the 1953 Grand National Steeple on Japaddy. One of Greg Hall's four brothers, R.J. Hall, was also a jumps jockey, who won the Grand National Hurdles of 1973 and 1978 on Robert and Donbredean respectively. Each of Hall's five sisters married jockeys. Initially indentured to his father, Hall completed his apprenticeship with Jim Morgan and Tony Lopes. He rode regularly for Angus Armanasco early in his career. His first Group One winner, Innisfree in the 1978 Stradbroke, was trained by his father. Subsequently Hall teamed with Getting Closer to win the Railway Stakes in Perth in 1983 and the Doomben 10,000 the next year. He won the 1985 Brisbane Cup on Foxseal and the 1987 Sydney Cup on Major Drive. Two Blue Diamonds – on Zeditave (1988) and Lady Jakeo (1993) have come his way, besides V.R.C. Sires' Produce wins with True Version (1985) and Not Related (1991). He won Futurities aboard Zeditave and Ark Regal in 1989-90 and the A.J.C. Derby of 1991 on Durbridge. More recently Hall won the S.A. Derby and Adelaide Cup on Subzero and the Melbourne Cup on that horse in the spring of 1992; the Cox Plate on Super Impose; the V.R.C. and A.J.C. Derbies on Mahogany and the 1994 Golden Slipper on Danzero, all of the latter for the Freedman stable.

HALL MARK

1930 ch horse Heroic – Herowinkie

Trained by Jack Holt, Hall Mark was one of the best sons of Heroic. At two he won the A.J.C. Sires' and Champagne Stakes. In 1933 he took the A.J.C. and Victoria Derby double, besides running second in the Caulfield Guineas. Starting at 4/1 he beat 17 other runners in the 1933 Melbourne Cup. Despite never recapturing the form of his three year old campaign, Hall Mark won the Doncaster in 1934 with 61kg and took the Memsie Stakes in the following year.

HAMLET

1868 b horse Maribyrnong – Rose of Denmark

One of the top horses of his era, Hamlet won the A.J.C. Sires' Produce and Champagne Stakes as a two year old, beating The Prophet and Acorn in the first, Beatrice and The Prophet in the second. In the A.J.C. Derby, Hamlet had to be content with third behind Javelin and The Prophet. In the autumn of 1872, Hamlet won the V.R.C. St Leger, and then beat Javelin and The Prophet in the A.J.C. St Leger, to become the second horse after Fishhook to win what was a coveted staying double. He went on to beat no less than Tim Whiffler and Javelin in the All Aged Stakes, before running second to The Prophet in the Sydney Cup. Hamlet was back in the spring, when his best effort was second in the Melbourne Stakes to Contessa.

HANLON, GEORGE (1924 -)

One of 12 children, the laconic and witty Hanlon was born at Willunga Beach in South Australia and started his long training career in that state. In 1949 he established stables at Epsom, where he trained until 1985. One important innovation which he advised there was a wood-chip training track. Hanlon is renowned as a master conditioner of stayers. He has had Melbourne Cup runners in every year bar five since 1963 and won the race three times, with Piping Lane, Arwon and Black Knight. The Australian, Brisbane, Moonee Valley, Sandown, Sydney and four Adelaide Cups have also fallen to his horses. Among the best of them have been the dual Newmarket winner Correct; the moody Taras Bulba, who won the Rosehill Guineas and A.J.C. Derby of 1974; the star weight-for-age performer Family of Man and Lawman, who won a Doncaster, St George and two Feehan Stakes. In 1985 Hanlon moved his training operation (which has usually contained no more than 30 horses at a time) to Leopold outside Geelong. Often spoken of as 'the trainer's trainer', Hanlon is renowned for placing horses to perfection and shows great patience in bringing them back after reverses. Most recently his patience was rewarded when Our Pompeii won the 1994 Adelaide Cup after going winless since the same race in 1993.

HARDY, FRANK (1917-94)

With an aptness that he would have relished and turned into a yarn, the Australian author and tale-teller Frank Hardy died on 28 January 1994 with a form-guide in his hand. Not only a keen gambler, Hardy wrote his second novel, *The Four-Legged Lottery* (1958) about victims of the punt (and the S.P. bookie). His first and most famous book, *Power Without Glory* (1950) numbered among the nefarious exploits of its villain John West (a fictionalised version of John Wren) the rigging of Melbourne races and the buying of Carringbush (Collingwood) premierships. After the publication of this novel, Hardy was arrested on a charge of criminal libel. Taken to the cells, he was disconcerted to find a live Cups double ticket in his pocket. Hardy had taken the winner, Grey Boots in the Caulfield Cup, coupled with the eventual Flemington favourite Alister. Mercifully one Detective O'Connor let Hardy keep the ticket, but this was 1950 – the year in which Comic Court surprised most punters by proving that he could run two miles – as he won the Melbourne Cup by three lengths in record time at 25/1. Hardy would have a different kind of win later: acquittal. For a time Hardy ghost-wrote a Sydney newspaper column for the jockey Athol Mulley, who also combined with Hardy to outdo each other in a collection of racing yarns called *The Needy and the Greedy* (1975).

HAWKESBURY RACING CLUB

Racing had been informally conducted in the region of the Hawkesbury River before the first official race meeting in New South Wales, at Hyde Park in 1810. By 1829 Sir John Jamieson was patron of a Hawkesbury Racing Club and soon after, a meeting was held at Windsor. The club then raced at Killarney, where a three day meeting was held in August 1831. The present-day Clarendon course was built from 1866-71 and the H.R.C. 's first meeting there was in August 1871. Accorded metropolitan status, the club was given race dates by the A.J.C. prior to the spring and autumn carnivals in Sydney. However the rise of suburban, proprietary racing damaged the club from

late in the 19th century. Closed during World War Two, the course did not re-open until 1951. Now thriving, the club's main race is the Hawkesbury Gold Cup, run in December as a lead-up to the Randwick Christmas carnival.

HAYAI

1979 br horse Skyhawk II – Poppa's Girl

When the under-rated stayer Hayai retired, he was the highest stakes-winning entire to that time in Australian turf history with winnings of more than $800,000. In the spring of 1983 he won the first of back-to-back Metropolitans, on this occasion over 2400m at Warwick Farm. Then in Melbourne he beat Cossack Prince in the Caulfield Cup. The following year Hayai won the Group One Tancred Stakes, a race in which he would finish second in 1985. In the spring of 1984 he won the Chelmsford Stakes and a second Metropolitan (back at Randwick, back to 2600m) in which he carried 57.5kg. Other big race wins for Hayai included two Craven Plates. After his retirement in 1986 he went to the Stockwell Stud outside Digger's Rest, Victoria.

HAYES FAMILY

When a newly married Colin Hayes (1924-) decided in 1950 that he wanted to become a trainer, he told his wife that he needed five years in which to prove himself. When he retired 39 years later, he had a record scarcely equalled anywhere in the world. Interested in horses since school days, Hayes was an amateur jockey until weight beat him. A moderate galloper called Surefoot gave him a start in the training game. Hayes set up an establishment at Semaphore, before making the radical move in 1970 of establishing the Lindsay Park Stud in South Australia's Barossa Valley.

Some owners left the Hayes' stable, not believing that horses could be trained so far out of town and win. Hayes had the last laugh. In all he won 28 South Australian and 13 Victorian trainers' premierships. His 5,000th winner was Concordance in the 1989 N.E. Manion Cup. When he retired he had trained more than 5,300 winners. His world records include 10 winners in a day on metropolitan tracks (23 January 1982), five Group winners in a day (7 February 1987), six Group and black type winners in a day (12 September 1987). In 1989-90 he set a Commonwealth record by training 278 winners (57 black type) in a season.

Hayes' tally of big races included Melbourne, Caulfield and Sydney Cups, the Cox Plate, A.J.C., Victoria, South Australian and Australian Derbies, Golden Slipper and Blue Diamond Stakes. Three horses stand out of all those in Hayes' care. The arrival of the French stallion Without Fear to Lindsay Park confirmed its status as a breeding centre. The horse set a world record of 30 individual winners in 1975-6. In all, winners of 2,300 races have been bred at Lindsay Park. Dulcify was Hayes' best racehorse, a dual Derby winner, besides his victories in the Australian Cup, Mackinnon Stakes and the Cox Plate by seven lengths. Dulcify was injured and put down in the 1979 Melbourne Cup. Hayes also trained Better Loosen Up, a champion who won a Cox Plate, besides a Japan Cup. Those successes came for his son David, who took over the stable operations when Colin Hayes (who had survived heart by-pass surgery in the 1970s) retired in 1990. Such was the rapidity of David Hayes' success that he became the first trainer in the Commonwealth to train more than 300 winners in a season. In the autumn of 1994 he trained his 1,000th winner.

HICKENBOTHAM, WALTER (1848-1933)

The champion trainer was born in Sydney. Unhappily apprenticed as a bootmaker, he went to work for John Tait. Hickenbotham's first trip to Melbourne as a jockey came in 1870 when he accompanied Tait's Derby hope Pyrrhus, who ran second to Florence. Setting up as a private trainer for such owners as the Hon. D.S. Wallace, Hickenbotham became a public trainer at Flemington from 1886. His greatest horse was Carbine. Apparently Hickenbotham spent the evening of Carbine's Melbourne Cup triumph of 1890 in bandaging the horse's split heel rather than in celebration. Hickenbotham won other Melbourne Cups with Mentor (1888), Newhaven (1896), who was also a Victoria Derby winner and Blue Spec (1905). Other fine horses in his care were Fireworks (who won the Victoria Derby twice), Swiveller and Trafalgar.

HIGGINS, ROY (1938-)

One of Australia's greatest jockeys, Higgins was born near the Murray River town of Koondrook, when his mother went into labour while riding on her husband's cart. He became an apprentice jockey in the Riverina, having a first, and hapless ride at Deniliquin in October 1953. He soon recorded his first victory for his master Jim Watters. By the early 1960s Higgins was established in Melbourne, where in the 1964-5 season he won the first of 11 jockeys' premierships, equalling Billy Duncan's record. Throughout that period he battled weight problems, so that his final career tally of more than 2,300 wins (many of them in feature races across the country) is remarkable. Higgins won the first of two Melbourne Cups on one of his favourite horses, Light Fingers, in 1965, another with Red Handed two years later. His affinity with fillies and mares was notable: Leilani gave him numerous big race wins, including the last of no less than six A.J.C. Oaks in 1974. He also won five V.R.C. Oaks. Other classic victories came in plenty, among them four Victoria Derbies, three of these for Bart Cummings with whom he formed one of the most lethal partnerships in Australian turf history.

Sprinting and distance races came alike to this preternaturally skilled jockey. Higgins won the first Blue Diamond Stakes on Tolerance in 1972, and took the race on three more occasions that decade. He won two Newmarkets, five George Adams Handicaps, three Oakleigh Plates, five William Reid and three Lightning Stakes. No Melbourne-based jockey has ridden with more success or acclaim in the hard school of Sydney. Besides his Oaks victories, Higgins won the 1974 Metropolitan on Passetreul for Tommy Smith and that year's Doncaster on Tontonan for Cummings. Gunsynd, another favourite horse, had given him a Doncaster in 1972. He won two Sydney Cups, on Grand Print in 1962, near the start of his career, and the mare Lowland in 1969. Twice he took the Golden Slipper, with Storm Queen in 1966 and Tontonan in 1973, while he rode Beau Babylon to an upset victory over Vain in the A.J.C. Sires' of 1969. Two Cox Plates came his way, besides two Brisbane and an Adelaide Cup (one of each on Fulmen in 1967) and the Hobart Cup in 1972 on Piping Lane, whose rump he saw in the Melbourne Cup of that year. Higgins won a single Caulfield Cup, on protest, with Big Philou in 1969.

Higgins had his last ride, on In the Slot, in October 1983, before retiring early the following year. He declared that his next ambition was 'to be the little fat man that I'm meant to be'. His diet of caraway seeds and water, cigars and black coffee, had taken sufficient toll. An autobiography, *The Professor* by Terry Vine, appeared in 1984. Its title came from Higgins's affectionate nickname, drawn originally from the elocutionist in 'My Fair Lady'; confirmed by his mastery in the saddle. Higgins had ridden for a time in France in the late 60s, but it was in his home country that his renown was established. These days he works as a racecourse analyst of horses' conditions for the media, in which capacity he causes bookmakers pain in different ways than he inflicted in the saddle.

HIGH CASTE
1936 b horse Bulandshar – The Begum

A tough and brilliant horse, 'The Strawberry Bull' was one of the biggest thoroughbreds to race in Australia. After three two year old wins in New Zealand, he was bought to race in Australia by Harry Tancred. His quality was quickly evident with wins in the autumn of 1939 in the V.R.C. Sires' Produce and the A.J.C. Champagne Stakes. In classic contests in the spring, High Caste duelled with Reading. He beat that horse in the Rosehill Guineas and ran second to him in the A.J.C. Derby; repeated that pattern in the Caulfield Guineas and Victoria Derby. But High Caste would prove the more durable galloper. His feature wins included three Fisher and three Linlithgow Stakes. He won the Caulfield Stakes as a three year old in 1939 and again the following year. He took a Craven Plate and the St George Stakes of 1940 and 1942. Weight-for-age wins in Sydney included the Hill, Hobartville and Warwick Stakes. High Caste humped 59.5kg to victory in the Epsom of 1940 and was unluckily beaten the next year (under 63kg) after an interrupted preparation. This was the saddest defeat for his jockey Ted Bartle, who was on the horse in all his 32

Australian wins. In 1940 High Caste had run Ajax to a half neck in the Futurity, but he won the next year with 66kg. From 71 starts, High Caste won 32 and deadheated three times, besides being placed on 26 other occasions. After his retirement he stood at the Segenhoe Stud. Only the coincidence of his triumphs with the early years of the Second World War have prevented High Caste from being ranked with the greats of the Australian turf.

HIGH SYCE

1924 ch horse Highfield – Concise

The star Queensland-bred performer of the 1920s, High Syce underlined his class when a change of ownership led him to be sent south to the care of Jack Holt in Melbourne. Trained in Queensland by his part-owner W.J. Noud, High Syce won 20 of his 28 starts in that state, including its main classic races : the Q. T. C. Sires' and Derby of 1927, besides the Guineas and the St Leger. In Victoria his principal victories came in such races as the V.R.C. October and Melbourne Stakes, and the 1929 Caulfield Stakes. A week after that win, Bill Duncan secured the Caulfield Cup on High Syce who started 2/1 favourite and beat the fine horse Amounis, who would have his turn the next year. For Duncan and Holt it was a second successive Caulfield Cup, after victory with Maple in 1928. High Syce was retired in 1930.

HISKENS STEEPLECHASE

The premier jumping race at Moonee Valley is named after A.V. Hiskens, the first secretary of the Moonee Valley Racing Club. Run over 3600m, it is the last major event on the winter jumping calendar in Melbourne. Etymology won the first Hiskens in 1936. The champion mare Pedro's Pride carried a record weight of 80kg to victory in

1958. Another champion, Crisp, put on two of his greatest displays when he won the race in consecutive years, 1969 and 1970. Strasbourg was another top-line winner, in 1977, while in 1982 a star-studded field saw Airmond beat Light Horse and Somoy. Dual G.N. Steeple winner Gogong won in 1984 and was back to the following year to split the Ray Trinder-trained Tasmanian pair of Monsist and Tengah Hari. The latter had his turn the next year. Another Nugget, who won in 1992, confirmed the Hiskens form when he won the Grand National Steeple next season.

HOBART CUP

Now a Group Three event run at Elwick in the summer, the Hobart Cup was first contested in 1875 over two miles. The distance was shortened to one and a half miles in 1886. Early winners of quality were The Assyrian and Malua, both of whom won the Melbourne Cup. No other horse completed the double until 1972, when Piping Lane won the Hobart Cup, ridden by Roy Higgins, and went on to triumph in the Melbourne Cup at 40/1. Dual winners have included Mac O Roni (1939 and 1942), Seriki (1955 and 1956), Macdalla (1964 and 1965) and Brallos (1976 and 1977). Scobie Breasley won the Hobart Cup on Wingfire in 1947, foreshadowing the increasing dominance of mainland jockeys in the race.

HOLMES À COURT, ROBERT (1937-90)

Born in Natal in South Africa, Robert Holmes à Court studied agriculture in New Zealand before taking a law degree at the University of Western Australia. Businessman and lawyer, he established the Bell Group of companies and diversified his interests into thoroughbred horse racing. Holmes à Court ran the Heytesbury Stud outside Perth, where he stood the top class galloper Family of Man. He is also remembered for splashing out an Australian record price of $825,000 at a 1981 yearling sale on the Luskin Star-Visit colt who – racing as Paint the Stars – proved to be a dud. Holmes à Court had some recompense when his horse Black Knight won the Melbourne Cup of 1984.

HOLT, MICHAEL (JACK) (1879-1951)

Born at Berwick and licensed as a jockey in 1898, Jack Holt became a trainer in 1902. For several years winners were few, but from the 1918-19 season he established himself as Victoria's leading trainer, topping the premiership 13 times in the next 16 seasons, and earning the sobriquet 'The Wizard of Mordialloc'. Among many champions through his yard were Eurythmic (sent from Western Australia on the strength of Holt's reputation), Heroic, Hall Mark and 1938 Victoria Derby winner Nuffield; Caulfield Cup winners Maple and High Syce; Cox Plate winners Easingwold, Highland and Chanak. Holt was a bachelor, philanthropist and poker player who invested shrewdly in real estate and the stock market. He was a famed conditioner of horses, who attracted the best jockeys, Frank Dempsey and Billy Duncan among them, to ride for his stable. He retired following a heart attack in 1948 and on his death three years later left 200,000 pounds to St Vincent's Hospital to assist in the creation of its School of Medical Research.

HONDA STAKES

This Group One race over 1600m during the Flemington spring carnival was first run in 1919. From that year until 1960 it was known as the Cantala Stakes; thereafter it was the George Adams Handicap and then the Ampol Stakes. Chal won in 1919, and

soon afterwards such top quality gallopers as Violoncello (1922), The Night Patrol (1924), Highland (1928) and Amounis (1929) won the race. In the 1960s Aquanita and Heroic Stone were dual winners of what by then was known as the George Adams Handicap. Vain carried a record weight for a three year old of 55.5kg when he beat Our Faith in the last start of his outstanding career. Gunsynd, All Shot and Taj Rossi saluted between 1971-3, while Maybe Mahal (1976) and Family of Man (1978) were the best winners later in that decade. Since then, the Caulfield Cup winner Silver Bounty (1980), Riverdale (1984), Better Loosen Up (1989) and Shaftesbury Avenue – winner in 1990 and unlucky runner-up with 60.5kg the following year – have confirmed the reputation of the race known as the Honda Stakes until 1993, when it was renamed the Nissan Stakes.

HORLICKS

1983 gr mare Three Legs – Malt

The grand grey mare Horlicks retired with stake winnings of more than $3,000,000. Unraced at two, she won her maiden at Pukekohe in 1986, and three other events at three. Next season she won a string of minor events before finishing second to Bonecrusher in the Air New Zealand Stakes; winning the Awapuni Cup and beating Bonecrusher at Ellerslie. At five and six she would win Group One races at this, one of her favourite tracks. Australia saw too little of the mare. In 1988 she was a most unlucky second to Our Poetic Prince in a vintage Cox Plate. Bonecrusher was third. In 1989 Horlicks made a hit and run visit to Flemington and beat King's High in the Mackinnon Stakes. That set her up for the Japan Cup. Horlicks became the first Australasian winner of the race when she scored in the astonishing time of 2.22.2 for the 2400m. In the autumn of 1990 she sandwiched a third to Sydeston on a heavy track at Rosehill in the B.M.W. between Group One wins in New Zealand. She was retired in the spring of that year.

HORSE OF THE YEAR AWARDS

Two bodies now present annual awards to Australia's horse of the year – the V.R.C. and the Australian Racing Media Association. The V.R.C. Award to 'Australia's Champion Racehorse' is based on the votes of the secretaries of the principal racing clubs in each state and of the V.R.C. Racing Manager. All racing journalists can vote for the 'National Horse of the Year'. The V.R.C. prize was given first to Rain Lover, for his deeds in the 1968-9 season. Subsequent winners were Gay Icarus, Gunsynd, and then four in a row for Bart Cummings-trained horses: Dayana, Taj Rossi, Leilani and Lord Dudley. The Media Association Award began for the 1976-7 season. Surround won it, and the V.R.C. award. In subsequent years there have, remarkably, been only two disparities: Strawberry Road was 'Australia's Champion Racehorse' for 1982-3, Gurner's Lane 'National Horse of the Year'. In 1986-7 Bonecrusher won the former award, Placid Ark the second. The roll-call of winning horses includes such champions as Manikato, Kingston Town, Better Loosen Up and Let's Elope. From 1994, the two awards have been consolidated into one.

HOULAHAN, JIM (1913-)

Victoria's foremost trainer of jumpers, Jim Houlahan has had plenty of first hand experience with them while farming at Axe Creek, near Bendigo. He regularly rode horses during hunting forays on his property, clearing fences and any other obstacles on the way. His first involvement in racing was

with trotters, as a hobby owner-trainer, and the best of his square-gaiters was Maestro's Melody. A change from farming to the building trade led Houlahan to become involved with thoroughbreds as an owner. His first galloper, Bellaron, was a racecourse failure and Houlahan sold him to a hunt club enthusiast. When the new owner claimed that the horse was unsound, Houlahan bought him back, put him into work, and won eight races with him. That was a quarter of a century ago. Since then, assisted by his son Mark, Houlahan has won all the top jumping races in Victoria: three Grand Annuals at Warrnambool, two Great Eastern Steeples at Oakbank, Grand National Hurdles with Sharp As, Fun Verdict and Tennessee Blue, Grand National Steeples with Strasbourg and So and So (who Mark trained). Houlahan also added a second Australian Hurdle to that which he had garnered with Massuk in 1980 when Tennessee Blue won the 1994 renewal of the race.

HOWARD, GEOFF ('SAMMY') (1939-94)

Sammy Howard was a top-class jockey of the 1960s and 1970s, who battled weight problems that his own delight in the high life exacerbated. While still an apprentice he won the first of successive Doncasters on Tudor Hill (1959-60). Times became leaner thereafter, until he was coerced to lose weight so as to ride what became his favourite horse, Tails. In their association, Howard was first home on eight occasions from 23 starts, highlights being the 1971 Doomben Cup and a victory in the 1972 Queen Elizabeth Stakes at Randwick over Gunsynd. Howard retired as a jockey in 1980 and set up as a trainer at Gosford in a small way. Keen judge of a horse, and of a beer, he died at his home town of Deniliquin after a long period of illness.

HOWARD, KEN (1910-76)

With Melbourne's Bert Bryant, Sydney-based Ken Howard was the most colourful of Australian race-callers. His signature 'London to a brick on' for a certainty in running has gone into racing folklore. Howard worked for nearly 40 years as a caller, for stations 2UE, 2GB and 2KY. From outside the course (because of a ban on callers' presence inside) he correctly picked Blue Legend in the four horse finish to the 1946 Epsom. An Epsom 22 years later would give him one of his unhappiest race days. In 1968 Howard backed his judgment in tight finishes in the two feature races: the A.J.C. Derby and Epsom, and got both wrong (Royal Account did not beat Wilton Park, nor Joking, Speed of Sound). Howard enjoyed visits to England and gave Derby calls whose flair was an astonishment to local listeners. He retired in 1973 and died at Coffs Harbour three years later.

HOW NOW

1972 b mare In The Purple – Fair Diana

One of the finest mares to be trained by Colin Hayes, How Now's best performance as a spring three year old in 1975 was a defeat of Toy Show in the Wakeful Stakes. In the following autumn, she won the Kewney Stakes, was third in the Australian Cup to Lord Dudley, before being sent to Sydney where she won the A.J.C. Oaks. How Now's spring that year was a triumph. After wins at weight for age in the Craiglee, Underwood and Caulfield Stakes, the mare was installed at 3/1 favourite for the Caulfield Cup despite drawing barrier 16 in a field of 18. Jockey John Stocker took her across the field and she won decisively. At the end of this campaign, she was third in the Mackinnon Stakes to Gold and Black and Better Draw. In 1977 How Now never recaptured her best form. In the autumn she

was second to Ashbah in the St George Stakes and to Ngawyni in the Carlyon Cup. Back in Sydney she was third in the B.M.W., while her best run in the autumn was third in the Underwood Stakes at Caulfield, her favourite track. How Now was then retired to stud.

HOYSTED FAMILY

The story of one of Australia's most famous racing families began when Frederick William Hoysted and his wife (who was the cousin of Australia's first Prime Minister, Edmund Barton), arrived from Ireland in 1859. They settled in Benalla, where Frederick became the first in a distinguished line of trainers. One of his sons, Harry, who was based in Wangaratta, enjoyed success with his horses throughout north-eastern Victoria. In turn, two of his sons, Henry ('Tib') and Fred ('Father') Hoysted became trainers, inheriting their father's stables after his death in 1906.

Fred Hoysted (1883-1967) was apprenticed as a jockey at the age of 12 and rode his first winner, Wicket, at Bright in 1895. Travelling to Melbourne with his father's small team of horses, he won his first city race at Maribyrnong on Bosnia in May 1896. Soon afterwards he was suspended for failing to ride Wicket out. He told stewards that he would sooner flog them than a tired horse, and received a month's holiday. Fred's career as a jockey ended after a fall at Beechworth in 1911 and with his brother Tib, he took up training.

The pair had a disagreement at the Albury races in November 1926, when Fred's horse Rakwool beat the odds-on favourite, trained by his brother. Fred moved to Melbourne and took over stables at Mentone where he trained for 39 years. With up to 50 horses in work, this was the largest training establishment in Australia in the 1950s. Fred was leading Melbourne trainer in the 1932-3 season. In all he won 17 trainers' premierships (of which two were shared) including seven in succession from 1945-6 until 1951-2. Rakwool was one of the first of his many fine gallopers, winning the Grand National Steeple in 1931 with 73kg. Hoysted's best jumper was Redditch after whom he named his stables. Redditch won the Grand National Steeple in 1933 with 77.5kg as well as the Australian Steeples of 1933 and 1934 with 82kg! The public outcry after Redditch's death in a race fall at Flemington led to the replacement of post and rail by brush fences.

Renowned especially as a trainer of two year olds (he won 20 juvenile races in 1953-4), Hoysted had the pick of Melbourne's finest jockeys, among them Harold Badger, Scobie Breasley, Frank Dempsey and Bill Williamson. His horses won numerous feature races: the V.R.C. Oaks (True Course, Provoke), Newmarket (Gay Queen), Doomben 10,000 (Ungar), Adelaide Cup (Donaster), Oakleigh Plate (High Title). In 1955 he took over the training of Rising Fast who won his second successive Caulfield Cup and was unluckily beaten in his bid for a second Melbourne Cup in a row.

Three of Fred Hoysted's brothers were country trainers, another was a jockey. His nephew Des Hoysted (1924-) was for many years a leading race-caller in Sydney. A cousin John ('Long Bob') Hoysted was a bookmaker, while his brother Percy ('Duck') Hoysted trained Carioca, winner of the 1953 Sydney Cup. Two of Fred's sons became Melbourne trainers. When Norman ('Bon') Hoysted (1919-78) died, his brother Bob (1925-) took charge of the champion Manikato. Among Bob's other fine horses were the classic winning mare Rose of Kingston and the sprinter River Rough. The

eldest of Fred's sons, Walter, achieved turf notoriety in February 1966 when he bailed up the starter with a shotgun before the running of the Fulham Hurdle at Flemington. He was protesting against the whipping of horses in races, and after discharging the gun, and extracting a soon rescinded promise that no whips would be allowed in the hurdle race, he surrendered to police. The action earned him a month in gaol and sparked a long-running but unresolved controversy over the use of whips. Fred Hoysted died the following year. Latest trainer in the dynasty is Hal Hoysted, who is based like his forebears – at Wangaratta.

HUA
1934 b horse Heroic – Gladioli

One of the best sons of Heroic, Hua won the V.R.C. Sires' Produce Stakes of 1937 (with Ajax eighth) and was placed on four other occasions. At three he was third in both the Rosehill Guineas and the Caulfield Guineas, before beating Ajax by a head in the Victoria Derby. This gave Ernest Clarke his fourth Derby winner and the eighth for the 77-year-old James Scobie. Hua ran unplaced in the Melbourne Cup, but returned strongly in the autumn, with wins in the William Reid, Orr and St George Stakes. He ran second to Ajax in the Futurity and then won the V.R.C. St Leger. Soon afterwards Hua was sent to stand at the St Aubins Stud at Scone.

HUTCHINSON FAMILY

Ron Hutchinson (1927-) scored his first major winner while still an apprentice when he rode Spectre to victory in the 1945 Australian Cup. He was to win that race on three subsequent occasions. In a highly successful riding career in Melbourne, which also saw him premier jockey in 1958-9,

Hutchinson won three Moonee Valley Cups, the 1959 Newmarket on Gold Stakes, 1951 Futurity on Iron Duke, V.R.C. Oaks in 1956 on Innesfell, the Doomben Cup of 1956 on Fair Chance and, in 1959, the Brisbane Cup and Metropolitan on Macdougal. The following year Hutchinson decided to try his luck in Europe and was swiftly rewarded when he won the 2,000 Guineas on Martial. In 1961 he accepted a retainer to ride for the Duke of Norfolk, whose stable jockey he remained for the next 16 years. Hutchinson rode more than 1,000 winners in Europe, including a St Leger on Intermezzo, 1,000 Guineas on Full Dress, three Irish 1,000 Guineas and the Irish 2,000 Guineas on Kynthos, besides the Ascot Gold Cup with Ragstone. In 1964 he was second on the English jockeys' premiership to Lester Piggott. Hutchinson had decided to retire and return to Australia, but was persuaded to stop over in Malaysia and Singapore, where he won the 1978 jockeys' premiership.

Hutchinson had developed a keen interest in thoroughbred breeding while in England and had set up a bloodstock agency there. After coming back to Australia he worked in conjunction with Colin Hayes at Lindsay Park, of which he became a director and part-owner. Hutchinson was gratified to see his son Peter become a jockey. Apprenticed to the Hayes stable, Peter Hutchinson was premier jockey in Adelaide in 1989-90 and 1990-1 before moving to Melbourne. He recorded Group One wins for Hayes on Planet Ruler in the Gadsden and Canonise in the 1991 Blue Diamond Stakes, besides winning the A.J.C. Oaks in 1992 on the Russ Cleland-trained My Brilliant Star. Peter Hutchinson's best win nearly eluded him. In disfavour with the stable after dropping his hands and losing the Coongy Handicap on Maraakiz, he

retained the Caulfield Cup mount on Fraar, and saw that temperamental galloper home at 30/1 by a narrow margin in a race which his father never won.

HYDE PARK

While match races may have taken place privately before, Governor Lachlan Macquarie sanctioned the first official race meeting in Australia at Hyde Park in Sydney over three days, commencing on 15 October 1810. Keen to further horse-breeding, as well as what he may have thought of as a genteel sport, Macquarie also needed to placate the desire for entertainment of the officers of the 73rd Regiment. While Macquarie tried to ensure a seemly occasion by interdicting 'Gaming, Drunkenness, Swearing, Quarrelling, Fighting or Boxing', this effort to determine the future decorum of Australian racing foundered at once. The short-lived Hyde Park course was 2,000m in length. A ladies' stand was part of its appointments, while the winning post was placed between Park and Market Streets.

HYDROGEN
1948 br horse Delville Wood – Sweet Sound

Out of the top-line broodmare Sweet Sound (eight of whose foals were winners) Hydrogen was owned by E.R. Williams and trained by Ted Hush. In a career which was ended by a third bleeding attack, Hydrogen won 26 of 60 starts – half of these at weight-for-age – and was placed in 17 others. Third at his first start, two successive victories saw him promoted to 10/9 favourite in the A.J.C. Sires', in which he could manage only a moderate third. Spelled, he came back to win the Hobartville Stakes first up with Darby Munro aboard; easily won the Rosehill Guineas but was a disappointing fifth at 9/4 on in the 1951 A.J.C. Derby.

Hush persuaded the owner to persevere with Hydrogen's preparation, and the colt confirmed his judgment, but did nothing for the temper of punters, by winning the Craven Plate at his next start. Sent south, he convincingly won the Caulfield Guineas and Victoria Derby, in which he beat Bronton, his conqueror in the Cox Plate. This was Munro's fifth and last Victoria Derby win. In the Melbourne Cup, Hydrogen ran a creditable fifth. It would be as close as he came in the race.

In the autumn of 1952 he won the A.J.C. and V.R.C. St Legers; had a top handicap win in the Rosehill Cup before a second to Delta in the Chipping Norton. Back in the spring he raced in the best company. Second to Delta in the Chelmsford and to Dalray in the Colin Stephen Stakes, Hydrogen won the Hill Stakes and the Craven Plate, before travelling to Melbourne to win the first of two Cox Plates. Only Kingston Town has a better record in the race. After a poor run in Dalray's Melbourne Cup, Hydrogen relished the return to weight-for-age and won the Fisher Plate. In the autumn of 1953 his versatility was underlined with wins in the Alister Clark Stakes and then, in Brisbane, the P.J. O'Shea Stakes before a victory in the Brisbane Cup with the soft weight of 55kg. In the spring of that year he beat the odds-on shot Tarien in the Hill Stakes, ran second to Carioca in the Metropolitan before heading south once more. His main wins were a second Cox Plate and a Mackinnon Stakes, after which he ran a creditable sixth to Wodalla in the Melbourne Cup, before again winning the Fisher Plate. Bleeding attacks now threatened Hydrogen's career. After he bled twice in Sydney, he was given permission to race in Melbourne; ran third to Rising Fast in the Caulfield Stakes, but then was retired after two ordinary runs. At that stage he was Australia's highest stakes-winner, with almost $119,000 to his credit, and a turf record which belies what now seems a puny sum.

HYLAND, PAT (1941-)

One of the longest and most amiable associations between a jockey and a trainer is that which Pat Hyland established with Jim Moloney. Hyland was apprenticed to Moloney at Warrnambool in the late 1950s and was still riding for him until his retirement from the saddle in 1990. The pair's first metropolitan success was with Saranover at Caulfield in 1959. But it was a horse trained by Andy White who gave Hyland a crucial boost. He won 18 races on Craftsman, including the 1963 Victoria Derby, two Queen Elizabeth Stakes, two Australian Cups and a Liston Stakes. In 1964 Hyland won the Newmarket-Australian Cup double on Rashlore and Grand Print. A second Victoria Derby came his way with Silver Sharpe in 1970, while he won his first Oaks in 1982 on Rom's Stiletto. Before then Hyland had ridden the champion Vain in all his victories, including the Golden Slipper of 1969, and the unprecedented spring treble of the Craven 'A', Linlithgow and George Adams later in the year. In 1984 the crowd saluted Hyland's victory on Affinity in the Caulfield Cup. The win was more significant in that a heavy fall in Adelaide five months before led Hyland to consider retirement. In 1985 his career as a jockey was capped with victory on What A Nuisance in the Melbourne Cup. Two of Hyland's sons followed him to become jockeys, while as a trainer he has enjoyed considerable success.

HYMETTUS

1894 ch horse Eiridspord – Busy Bee

Hymettus came to prominence in the spring of 1898 at his favourite track,

Caulfield, when he won in succession the Heatherlie and Coongy Handicaps. He was among the fancied runners when 33 horses faced the starter in that year's Caulfield Cup. He duly won, although as in 1885, there was a shocking fall and Robin Hood's rider, the 13 year old James Flanagan, was killed. Hymettus was swift enough to run second in the Oakleigh Plate the next autumn, before leg problems put him off the scene for a year. His owner was keen to send Hymettus to stud, but trainer Phil Heywood entered him for both Cups in 1901. It was a smart decision. Relishing an outing at Caulfield, Hymettus won the Clark Handicap and the Memsie Stakes, and was beaten a head in the Eclipse Stakes. In the Caulfield Cup he came up against the champion mare Wakeful; raced her neck and neck down the straight; edged past when she faltered momentarily and won the race by a half head. The dual Caulfield Cup winner Hymettus now went to stud, where his best offspring was the Caulfield Stakes winner of 1913, Mornington Princess.

HYPERNO

1973 b or br gelding Rangong – Mikarla

Unplaced in a Werribee maiden in one start as a two year old, Hyperno steadily moved through his classes at three, winning a Bendigo maiden and four races in town, besides showing staying ability with a third in the 1977 St Leger. In his four year old campaign, Hyperno scored in the Newcastle Gold Cup, was third in the Melbourne Cup to Gold and Black and second behind Tom's Mate in the Sandown Cup. In the autumn of 1978 he won his first weight-for-age race, the Orr Stakes at Sandown and added the Carlyon Cup before heading to Sydney where he won the Tancred Stakes from Lazy Pat. A famous second placing followed – to Clear Day in the Moonee Valley Cup – when unaccountably Roy Higgins stopped riding the horse before the post. Hyperno capped off this season with victory over Muros in the Adelaide Cup. At five Hyperno was prevented by injury from racing more than twice, but finished second to So Called in the Liston Stakes and third behind Salamander in the Toorak Handicap. His great year was 1979. In a breathtakingly tight finish in the Melbourne Cup, Harry White saw him home from Salamander, ridden by Roy Higgins, who had no reason to love Hyperno. Other victories in this season came in the Queen Elizabeth and Blamey Stakes. Nor was Hyperno done with. At seven he ran third in the Underwood Stakes in the spring of 1980, then beat no less than Kingston Town in the Caulfield Stakes. He was beaten by the veteran Ming Dynasty in the Caulfield Cup, but won the Queen Elizabeth Stakes at the end of the spring carnival. Hyperno was nippy enough to run third to Manikato in the 1981 William Reid Stakes; dead-heated with My Brown Jug in the St George Stakes, won the Blamey and then the Australian Cup from Turf Ruler. In Sydney he won the Rawson Stakes, adding yet another of what is now a Group One race to the imposing record of a tough and highly talented galloper.

I

IGLOO
1967 ch gelding Arctic Explorer – Silver Rod

The career of top-line and unlucky stayer Igloo began modestly. At two he won three races in New Zealand; at three he won five, including the Metropolitan Handicap at Wellington, but seemed just short of top class. Brought to Australia in 1971 by owner-trainer Arthur Didham, he quickly showed his true mettle by winning the Turnbull Stakes and the Coongy Handicap. Roy Higgins had the mount in the Caulfield Cup, but Igloo had to be content with second behind the champion Gay Icarus. Big Philou was five lengths further adrift. Igloo proceeded to run second in the Cox Plate (to Tauto) and in the Melbourne Cup (to Silver Knight) in one of the most frustrating sequences in Australian turf history. Some consolation came when he won the Christmas Handicap at Rosehill. Set for the Perth Cup, Igloo broke down so badly that it was feared he would have to be destroyed, but the horse recovered gradually. He did not race at five, but at six – and now in the care of Tommy Smith – he returned to racing with a victory in the Castlereagh Handicap at Rosehill. His best effort in Melbourne that spring of 1973 was third in the Fisher Plate. In 1974 Igloo was to enjoy his best year. He ran a course record to win the Chipping Norton Stakes at Randwick; beat Dayana in the Autumn Stakes and was then third to Battle Heights in the Queen Elizabeth. Smith set him a yet more ambitious programme. Sent to South Australia, he carried 60kg into third place in the Adelaide Cup. Something like his due came Igloo's way when he gallantly won the Brisbane Cup with 57kg, thus capping a great comeback story.

ILUMQUH
1955 br gelding Sabaean – Sunbride

Owned by Alister Williams and trained by Eric Ropiha, Ilumquh was brought along with characteristic New Zealand patience. At two he ran twice for a win at Manawatu; had two starts at three for a third at Hawke's Bay, before being put out for a year. When he resumed in the 1959-60 season, Ilumquh won three hack races in a row, before victory in the Summer Handicap at Wellington in January 1960 indicated his staying scope. Ropiha set the horse for the Cups double in Melbourne, but although he won the Desborough Welter at Caulfield, his form was patchy, and he suffered an injury in the week before the 1960 Caulfield Cup. Ropiha nursed his horse to the post and Ilumquh won convincingly and ran time only a second outside Tulloch's record. Unluckily third in the Melbourne Cup behind Hi Jinx and Howsie, Ilumquh rounded off his spring by beating Macdougal in the Williamstown Cup. Thereafter he was plagued by serious leg trouble. It was a training triumph which brought him back three years later, when Ilumquh, carrying 55kg, was a gallant second to Gatum Gatum in the 1963 Melbourne Cup.

IMAGELE
1970 ch horse Sostenuto – Cele's Image

Trained by T.J. Smith, Imagele raced only at two and three, winning 11 of 20 starts and being placed in five others. Brilliant two year old form, which included a win in the V.R.C. Sires' Produce Stakes, saw Imagele start favourite for the Golden Slipper Stakes of 1973, but he fell in the race, leaving Tontonan a decisive victor. At three Imagele won the Canterbury and Rosehill Guineas and the Phar Lap Stakes. The Hobartville Stakes also fell to him in that season but his greatest win was in the 1973 A.J.C. Derby, one of the most thrilling ever contested. Imagele won by the narrowest of margins from Leica Lover and Grand Cidium. All raced with distinction later in the season, but were to a degree upstaged by the emergence of Taj Rossi. Imagele finished second to that horse in the Sandown Guineas, while Grand Cidium had the edge over him in the Caulfield Guineas. In the summer, Leica Lover finally had his turn when he beat Imagele in the Australian Derby in Perth. Imagele then went to stud.

IMPERIAL PRINCE
1971 b horse Sir Ivor – Bleu Azur

By the 1968 English Derby winner Sir Ivor, Imperial Prince raced without luck in the highest class in England. He won his first start, but none of the remaining seven. He did, however, run second in the 1974 Derby to the 50/1 shot Snow Knight, second to the same horse in the Irish Derby, second once more to the champion French mare Dahlia in the Benson & Hedges Gold Cup. In 1976 Imperial Prince was imported to stand at the Newhaven Park Stud in New South Wales, and was promptly best first season sire. His classic progeny include Research, winner of the 1988 V.R.C. Oaks and 1989 A.J.C. Derby and Oaks double, besides the Wakeful, Flight and Furious Stakes; Arborea, winner of the Melbourne fillies' triple crown of Thousand Guineas, Wakeful Stakes and Oaks in 1993; Victoria Derby winner of 1991, Star of the Realm. Imperial Prince's son Victory Prince won the 1984 A.J.C. Sires' Produce Stakes, which was one of the races of the Sydney two year old Triple Crown won by his son, Tierce, in 1991.

IMPOSING
1975 ch horse Todman – Hialeah

Despite his impeccable breeding, Imposing was slow to fulfil his promise. When trainer Tommy Smith sent him to Brisbane for the winter of 1979, Imposing had managed a win in a Rosehill Welter, and he won in similar company in his first start in Queensland. Nevertheless he showed enough to be well backed in the Stradbroke, which he duly won. The effort took something from Imposing, who could only run fourth to Manikato in the Doomben 10,000. Returning to Sydney for the spring of 1979, Imposing rapidly rose through his classes. He won the Tramway and Hill Stakes at weight-for-age before carrying 54.5kg decisively to win the Epsom. He rounded off the season with another Group One victory, in the George Main Stakes. Thereafter Imposing was retired and sent to the Ra Ora Stud in New Zealand, where he stood with success.

INDIAN SUMMER

1958 ch mare Edmundo – Condenser

A good quality two year old, Indian Summer won the Merson Cooper Stakes in 1961 and finished second to Emblem in the V.R.C. Sires'. The A.N. McCoy-trained filly blossomed in the spring of that year. She won all the main races for her sex and age: the Manifold Stakes, Thousand Guineas, Wakeful Stakes and the V.R.C. Oaks, when Jack Thompson saw her home by four lengths at 5/4 on. Before the end of the spring Indian Summer added the Sandown Guineas (then restricted to fillies) to an imposing record. Returning in the autumn of 1962, she gave Roy Higgins the first of a string of victories in the race by winning the A.J.C. Oaks by a remarkable 12 lengths on a heavy track. Indian Summer also proved herself up to weight-for-age class in a brief, but brilliant career.

INGHAM FAMILY

The 'Chicken Kings', Jack and Bob Ingham, have been involved in the racing game as recreation and business for four decades. Their first big winner was Sweet Embrace, who scored in the 1967 Golden Slipper at 33/1. Since then they have had an interest in four subsequent Slipper winners. A classic came the brothers' way when Gold Brick won the A.J.C. Derby in 1972. A diversification of the Inghams' business interests into breeding led to the purchase of the Woodlands Stud in the Hunter Valley in 1986. Quest For Fame (an English Derby winner) and the brilliant Australian stayer Dr Grace are the main sires at Woodlands. The Inghams' racehorses are trained from Crown Lodge at Warwick Farm, where John Hawkes was recently installed. The combination's first Group One winner came in the 1994 Sydney Cup, won by Cross Swords.

INVITATION STAKES

A feature of the Show Day meeting at the Caulfield spring carnival for a quarter of a century, the Invitation Stakes was first run in 1951. Jockeys from around Australasia competed, drawing their mounts by ballot. The first Invitation Stakes was won by E. Treffone from Western Australia on Jovial Lad. Horses also set their seal on the race. St Joel won three times: in 1953, with G. Hughes from New Zealand up, in 1956, when ridden by Jack Purtell from Victoria, and in 1959 with Sydney's Ray Selkrig in the saddle. Anonyme (in 1961-2) and Tauto (1970-1) were dual winners, while Roy Higgins won the race in three consecutive years from 1964-6 with Ripa, Nicopolis and Maritana. In 1975 the race was renamed the Marlboro Cup and Cap D'Antibes beat Tontonan and Kiwi Can in the first running. Private Talk was a two-time winner in 1976 and 1979, while Manikato, Canny Lass, Rancho Ruler and Mannerism were the best winners of a race that endured another name change, to the Show Day Cup, in 1989.

J

JOCKEYS, RIDING OVERSEAS

From the last decade of the 19th century, some of the best Australian jockeys have ridden with skill and success in a dozen overseas countries. Frank Bullock was among the first of them, as a leading jockey in England at the turn of the century and in Germany before the Great War. He won the first Prix de l'Arc de Triomphe to be contested, in 1920, besides English fillies' classics with Saucy Sue in 1925. Frank Wootton was the first Australian-born jockey to win an English jockeys' premiership, in 1909; after the Great War he made an unusual but highly profitable switch to jumps riding. It was almost half a century before another Australian, 'Scobie' Breasley topped the English jockeys' list. He did so again in the three consecutive years 1961-3, before the advent of Lester Piggott. In between, Wootton and Bullock, and Breasley, 'Brownie' Carslake and 'Togo' Johnstone had won many of the top races to be contested in Europe. Johnstone found his incident-packed way to England via India, a happy hunting ground for such Australian jumps jockeys as A. Doy at the start of the century. The 1960s was a golden era for Australian jockeys in Europe, with Garnet Bougoure, Ron Hutchinson, Neville Sellwood and Bill Williamson joining Breasley to seek the spoils of northern hemisphere racing, and winning their share of classics. Although Ron Quinton, among several others, rode with success in Europe (particularly in Ireland) in the 1980s, Australian jockeys found that their home pickings were easier and more lucrative. Asia has beckoned some more recently. Edgar Britt was a flat race jockey who rode with success in a number of Asian countries; so did 'Digger' McGrowdie, who was killed on his way to a race meeting in Malaya. In the 1980s and 1990s the rich racing scene of Hong Kong has attracted such Australian-born trainers as George Moore and Neville Begg; besides top jockeys, among them Gary Moore, Greg Hall, Brent Thomson and Darren Gauci.

JOHNSON, JAMES EDWARD (1929-)

Jimmy Johnson was born in Adelaide. His father, Alf, was a jockey who was killed in a fall at Oakbank when the boy was four. Undeterred, Johnson went on to a long and distinguished career, if sometimes marked by controversy over his strong whip riding. When he retired in 1976, he had ridden almost 2,200 winners. Three of them came in the Melbourne Cup, on Gatum Gatum in

1963 and then in consecutive years on Rain Lover in 1968-9. He won successive Caulfield Guineas on Storm Queen and Dark Purple in 1966-7 and in the 1966-7 racing season interrupted Roy Higgins's long run as leading jockey in Melbourne. Besides Rain Lover, Tobin Bronze was the best horse he rode. Apart from many weight-for-age wins, he scored on the horse in the 1967 Caulfield Cup and in the 1966 and 1967 Cox Plates.

JOHNSTON, MALCOLM (1956-)

Born at Forbes, Johnston was apprenticed to Theo Green, a fine mentor of young jockeys. His first win was at Newcastle in September 1973, his first in the city four days later. In that same eventful month Johnston incurred the first of a record 56 suspensions on Primal, his first ride for the T.J. Smith stable. He won the Sydney apprentices' premiership three times, in 1975-6 with a record number of wins – one hundred and seven and a half. That was enough to win him the first of three senior premierships as well. Johnston's success as an apprentice led the A.J.C. to change the rules of racing so that apprentices who ride 60 city winners now lose all their claim.

Johnston replaced Kevin Langby as Smith's stable jockey in January 1978 and rode for him until 1983. In a career which saw him win three Epsoms and a Doncaster, besides other top races, he partnered two champions for Smith. On Mighty Kingdom he won the 1979 Caulfield Stakes and Caulfield Cup, but achieved most renown for his partnership with Kingston Town. Johnston won 25 of 30 starts on the horse (Jim Pike had 27 wins on Phar Lap). They included a Sydney Cup, the A.J.C. and Q.T.C. Derbies, the Spring Champion Stakes and Rosehill Guineas, the Caulfield

Stakes and the Cox Plate of 1980. Johnston is unfortunately also remembered for going too early in the Melbourne Cup of 1982, in which Kingston Town was narrowly beaten, while carrying 60kg, by Gurner's Lane. It was not long afterwards that he split with Smith. Johnston rode in Singapore from 1983-5, surviving a bashing by vengeful punters. Back in Sydney he won the jockeys' premiership again in 1986-7. His opportunities gradually dwindled; suspensions remained a bane of his career; and he was forced to pay out $250,000 for injuries to another jockey in a fall at Wyong for which he was deemed to be responsible. After riding 1,960 winners, Johnston retired following a narrow second on Zaremba at Randwick.

JOHNSTONE, RAE ('TOGO') (1905-64)

Born in Newcastle, the swarthy 'Togo' Johnstone rode with success in Australia for a number of years until one clash too many with racing officialdom (on one occasion he received a two year suspension) led him to try his luck overseas. Like several Australian jockeys before and after him, he rode first in India, but in 1932 he ventured to England. Stewards there barred him on account of his record in Australia, so the skilled and colourful Johnstone crossed the Channel to begin a remarkable European riding career. Between 1934-56 he won no fewer than 36 European classics. Columbo gave him the 2,000 Guineas in 1934; Lavandin the last of three English Derbies in 1956. In all, he won more than 2,000 races in nine countries. Snapshots of two years' riding tell how brilliant was the impression that Johnstone made. In the month of June 1948, he won the English Derby and the Grand Prix du Paris on My Love, the Prix du Jockey Club (French Derby) on Bey, the Irish Derby on Nathoo and three feature races at the Ascot meeting. In 1950 he scored in no fewer than eight classics: winning the English Derby on Galcador in a near clean sweep of English classics which also included the 1,000 and 2,000 Guineas and the St Leger; the French Derby and the Irish 1,000 Guineas and Oaks. An inveterate gambler in his younger days, Johnstone quelled that passion after his marriage to the blonde Follies Bergeres dancer Marie Soubre. He lived in France after his retirement as a jockey and died of a heart attack while watching one of his horses work at Le Tremblay.

JONES, LINDA (1947-)

Born in Auckland, Linda Wilkinson's stepfather was a farrier and her love of horses was early established. In 1970 she won the second running of the Powder Puff Derby. The next year she married the North Island trainer Alan Jones. Her bid to be apprenticed to Jones was initially rejected (because of her age, marital status, and the threat to male jobs), but Jones persisted. Licensed for the 1978-9 season, she had her first win on Big Bickies at Te Rapa and was soon second on the New Zealand jockeys' list. At the summer carnival at Trentham early in 1979, she was second in the Wellington Cup on her husband's horse Northfleet, but won two races on the programme. On the second day of the carnival, Jones won the Wellington Derby on Holy Toledo and recorded a double that day as well. On the third day, she suffered a fall in the Oaks. Jones became the first woman to ride as a professional jockey in Australia when she was third at Rosehill in the Manion Cup on Northfleet. Later in the season she won the Labor Day Cup at Doomben on Pay the Purple and a race at Morphettville on the well-travelled Northfleet. Jones was awarded an M.B.E.

before she came out of her time. Her spectacular riding career was brief. Injured in a track fall, she retired not so many months after it had all begun.

JORDAN, ALBERT (1913-)

Born in Kalgoorlie, 'Abo' Jordan became one of Western Australia's leading trainers. As a teenager he whetted his appetite for all forms of racing and gambling when he owned a good whippet called Aurie's Star. By 1935, he was training at Kalgoorlie, where he was often to be found strolling around the town with a talking cocky on his shoulder. After a spell with the Second A.I.F. in Syria during World War Two, Jordan took up bookmaking at the trots. Failing at that endeavour, he returned to training with immediate success. He won races in every mainland state. In Western Australia he won four Perth Cups besides every other feature race. Six times he was leading trainer, and was honoured in 1977 by the W.A.T.C. when the Albert Jordan Handicap became part of its calendar.

JORROCKS

1833 b horse Whisker – Matilda

The part-Arab Jorrocks was by an imported English horse who had run wild for a time. In his turn, Jorrocks was used as a stock horse and did not compete in a race until he was five. Thereafter, he was heroically busy, establishing himself as perhaps the first thoroughbred of undeniable quality to race in Australia. Of approximately 113 starts he won 65 including walkovers and was placed on 26 other occasions. John Higgerson was his usual trainer and rider. Jorrocks won the Parramatta Town Plate five times; had one of his best seasons as a 14 year old when he won all 10 starts. Retired at 17, he was brought out of the paddock two years later and was unplaced in his final run, at Homebush, in October 1852. Jorrocks died in 1860.

JULIUS, SIR GEORGE (1873-1946)

Born at Norwich in England, George Julius came to Australia with his family in 1884, when his father was made archdeacon of Ballarat. He attended university in New Zealand, before becoming an assistant engineer with the Western Australian railways from 1896-1907. Thereafter he took a job with an engineering firm in Sydney, and in 1908 invented the automatic totalisator machine, based on another which he had designed to count election votes. His totalisator was first used at the Ellerslie track in Auckland in 1913. Constant refinements saw a world-wide demand for Julius' invention, which was to be found in England, France and India, besides Australasia, by the early 1930s. Julius's contribution to Australian life was much wider: in 1926 he accepted an invitation to become chairman of the C.S.I.R.O., which position he held until 1945.

JUNIUS

c1820 b horse Young Hector out of a Shark (Arabian) mare

One of the most famous of the racehorses of the earliest era of the Australian turf, Junius was owned by a publican, Andrew Nash. At the inaugural meeting of the Sydney Turf Club in April 1825, he won on both days. At the club's spring meeting in September of that year, he did so again, taking the Town Purse and the Town Plate, ridden by James Spinks. After Junius won Governor Brisbane's Cup in 1826 and 1827, his owner challenged all comers to a match race and put up 1,000 pounds. There were no takers. Junius continued to perform with distinction until his death in a stable fire in 1831.

K

KAORU STAR
1965 ch horse Star Kingdom – Kaoru

From the 14th crop of the champion sire Star Kingdom who also sired Rajah and Biscay in that year, Kaoru Star proved himself to be a quality racehorse. But his best deeds were reserved (as in his father's case) for the stud. Star Kingdom sired five Golden Slipper winners, but Kaoru Star managed two: the champion Luskin Star (1977) and Full On Aces four years later. Both have gone on to stud careers in turn. Kaoru Star also got the multiple Group One sprinter-miler Planet Kingdom, among many top quality racehorses.

KELLY, J.J

The leading trainer in Western Australia in the early part of this century, Kelly grew up at Maitland, where he became a jockey. In 1900 he leased horses from Dick Wootton and trained them in Sydney. After the Boer War, he went to South Africa to train for Wootton. Kelly came back to Melbourne where he trained for a time before deciding to re-establish himself in the West. His first exploit was remarkable. In 1908 he set Warmur to win the Great Western Steeplechase (the leading jumps event on the goldfields) and decided to ride it himself, despite having never ridden over the jumps before. Warmur won, and Kelly capitalised on that success. Training in Perth, he won five W.A. Derbies, eight Karrakatta Plates, two Railway Stakes and seven Perth Cups. He also had Eurythmic in his charge before that great horse was sent to Victoria.

KERR, 'ANDY' (DAVID) (1867-1955)

Born in Edinburgh, Kerr came to Australia as Lord Carrington's footman. His career as a bookmaker began at Sydney's pony racing tracks, but by early in the century he was fielding on metropolitan courses. Willing to lay huge sums on any sporting event, and rejoicing in the epithet 'Longest Odds Bettor on Earth', Kerr did much to create a colourful, showman's image for the Australian bookmaker. Always eager to accommodate long-shot punters, whom he regarded as mugs, Kerr heralded their appearance at his stand with the cry 'More fruit for the sideboard!'. Known as the Coogee Bunyip, apparently for his willingness to surf Sydney's beaches in all seasons, Kerr was badly hit by the Amounis-Phar Lap Cup double of 1930. He quit the game, nearly broke, in 1939.

KING INGODA

1918 br horse Comedy King – Ingoda

Bred by Sol Green, by the Melbourne Cup winner he had imported from England, King Ingoda did his early racing in Adelaide, without much distinction, before being sent to Melbourne to be trained by James Scobie. He soon showed staying mettle. After a second in the Easter Cup at Williamstown, Scobie sent the colt back to Adelaide, where he won the St Leger. Returning in the spring, King Ingoda won the Hotham Handicap, but still had only 45kg in the Melbourne Cup. In the event he won by a head to the heavily-backed, but ill-named The Cypher. At his next start King Ingoda won the Williamstown Cup, while the following year he carried 60.5kg to victory in the Adelaide Cup, an event in which he had run fourth in 1922.

KINGSTER

1952 br horse Star Kingdom – Canvas Back

Best of the first crop of the champion imported sire Star Kingdom, the awkwardly named Kingster showed early promise by his win in the Breeders' Plate at Randwick. Trained by Jack Green, Kingster went on to top class victories in every season that he raced. In the autumn of 1955 Kingster beat Knave in the A.J.C. Sires' Produce, then – giving away 6kg – ran second to that horse in the Champagne. In Melbourne he won the Merson Cooper Stakes. That spring he won the Hobartville Stakes, was second to Caranna in the Rosehill Guineas and to Somerset Fair in the Hill Stakes before defeating two fine horses, Caranna and Sailor's Guide, in the Cox Plate. Kingster backed up in the autumn of 1956 to emphasise his versatility as well as brilliance by winning the Newmarket. Taken back to Sydney he won the George Main Stakes. In the autumn of 1957 in Sydney, Kingster was

second to Redcraze in the Rawson Stakes, third behind Tulloch and Prince Jambo in the Warwick Stakes, but he won the All Aged Stakes. Kept up for a Brisbane campaign, Kingster capped off his career by carrying 59kg to victory in record time to win the 1957 Stradbroke by four lengths from Mandingos. Retired to stud, he died after only two seasons. Kingster's brilliant career would be better regarded if Star Kingdom had not gone on to sire such horses as Todman, Noholme and Sky High.

KINGSTON RULE

1985 ch horse Secretariat – Rose of Kingston

The imperially-bred Kingston Rule was one of the most unusual of recent Melbourne Cup winners. He won in 1990 as a five year old, after a career total of only a dozen starts. No horse that Bart Cummings brought to the great race was less seasoned, but owner David Hains – who had put his top-line A.J.C. Derby-winning mare Rose of Kingston to the outstanding North American racehorse and sire Secretariat – trusted to breeding. Kingston Rule's form leading in to the Melbourne Cup was also unusual. He became only the fourth horse and the first since Wodalla in 1953, to win the Moonee Valley-Melbourne Cup double. Splitting those victories was a tune-up in the Dalgety on the Saturday before the Melbourne Cup, where Kingston Rule was second to Mount Olympus. In the Melbourne Cup he ran course record time of 3.16.3 to defeat the fine New Zealand pair The Phantom and Mr Brooker. After his Cup victory, Kingston Rule was retired to stud.

KINGSTON TOWN

1976 blk gelding Bletchingly – Ada Hunter

One of the four greatest of Australian gallopers, fit to keep company with Carbine, Phar Lap and Tulloch, Kingston Town began unpromisingly. Bred by David Hain's career he failed to reach his reserve at the yearling sales. Deciding to race the colt himself, Hains sent Kingston Town to Tommy Smith. At his race debut at Canterbury in March 1979, Kingston Town was an inglorious last, half a furlong from the winner. And he pulled up shin-sore. Despite his breeding, Kingston Town was gelded. He resumed at the end of June, in the Round Table Handicap at Rosehill, where his natural ability soon belied his starting price of 33/1 and he scored by three lengths. In another race named for an overseas champion, the Sir Ivor Handicap, Kingston Town beat Bemboka Yacht by a head. Kept in training, he scrambled home by a half neck at odds on in a minor race at Warwick Farm. Although Smith set the horse for the spring Triple Crown in Sydney, it was with no high opinion of his ability. Kingston Town swiftly and decisively proved him wrong.

He won the Peter Pan, Gloaming and Spring Champion Stakes by emphatic margins, in each case beating better fancied stablemates – Spear, Shogun and Mighty Kingdom respectively. Smith sent him to Melbourne, where despite intense difficulties with the Caulfield track, the horse ran third in the Guineas, fourth in the Cup. He was then the unluckiest of seconds to Big Print in the Victoria Derby. Brought back in 1980, he raced 14 times in the calendar year for 12 wins and two placings. In the autumn he began with a 1200m victory in the Expressway Stakes; finished with a win over 3200m in the Sydney Cup, carrying 52.5kg. In between he won the Heritage Stakes, the Rosehill Guineas by four lengths, the Tancred Stakes by four and a half lengths, the A.J.C. Derby by more than three. Smith kept the horse up and in Brisbane he capped off an amazing three year old season by winning the Grand Prix Stakes and the

Queensland Derby. Leg problems, which gradually worsened, restricted Kingston Town's racing at four. Nevertheless he won the Warwick and Chelmsford Stakes and the S.T.C. Cup (now the Kingston Town Stakes). In the Caulfield Stakes he was beaten a neck by Hyperno and then carried 60kg into a creditable third place in the Caulfield Cup behind Ming Dynasty and Hyperno. Finally his turn in Melbourne came, and Kingston Town won the Cox Plate by five lengths. But he was lame after the race, and was turned out for 10 months. When he returned at five, it was to reel off wins in the Premiere, Warwick and Chelmsford Stakes, the S.T.C. Cup and George Main Stakes, the Caulfield Stakes (finally overcoming the nemesis of that track in a defeat of Sovereign Red and Hyperno) before he added a second Cox Plate to his record. By now an overtaxed champion, Kingston Town was second in the Mackinnon Stakes and near last in the 1981 Melbourne Cup. But he was back once more at six, winning a third Warwick Stakes to chalk up an astonishing 21st consecutive win in Sydney. Then he was an unlucky fourth in the Chelmsford, second in the Hill Stakes, before setting things right with a win in the George Main which equalled Limerick's record of 22 metropolitan victories in Sydney.

Kingston Town went to Melbourne again. He won a second Caulfield Stakes and then an unprecedented third Cox Plate, after being given away long before the turn. What followed was a gallant second, with 59kg, to Gurner's Lane in the Melbourne Cup. But for his two close defeats in the Derby and the Cup, Kingston Town would be challenging Phar Lap as the greatest of Australian racehorses. He had one win left in the 1982 Western Mail Classic in Perth. Thereafter he went amiss again. Despite attempts to bring him back into training – first in California, then in Sydney – the champion was finally retired in 1986. He was put down after a paddock injury in March 1991. His racing record stands at 30 wins and seven placings from 41 starts.

KIWI

1975 ch gelding Blarney Kiss – Malrayvis

From farm hack to Melbourne Cup winner: that is the New Zealand fairy tale rise of Ewen ('Snowy') Lupton's $1,000 yearling purchase, Kiwi. Bought to race, Kiwi did his preparatory work on Lupton's property, rounding up sheep and cattle. When it came to more serious workouts, Lupton rode Kiwi in his gallops at the nearby Waverley racecourse. Unraced at two, Kiwi won three moderate races at three. It was not until his Wellington Cup victory in 1983 that Kiwi's staying scope was evident. The race also gave Lupton a notion of Kiwi's racing style, for Jim Cassidy had the horse last into the straight. Famously he adopted the same tactics in the 1983 Melbourne Cup. Kiwi was a conspicuous last for most of the race, but once hooked out he finished as fast as any horse has in the long history of the race. Thus Lupton became the first hobby trainer to win a Melbourne Cup; Kiwi the first horse to win the Wellington-Melbourne Cup double in the same year. Brought back in 1984, Kiwi was withdrawn in controversial circumstances in the week leading up to the race when V.R.C. stewards ruled him unfit because of a leg injury sustained in New Zealand. Lupton did not agree, but showed no ill-feeling and brought the horse back in 1985, when Kiwi was 11th, and then third in the Sandown Cup with 57kg to Puckle Harbour before going home. Kiwi's fourth Melbourne Cup campaign saw him finish a fighting fourth to At Talaq, after which he was spelled for good to graze with the sheep and cows on the Lupton property.

L

LADY SYBIL
1957 br mare Count Rendered – Cassiopeia

Bred at the Sasanof Stud in New Zealand, Lady Sybil was trained at Ballarat by Arthur Smerdon. She enjoyed an outstanding three year old spring campaign in Melbourne in 1960, when the frequently wet tracks worked to her advantage. After beating Misty View by six lengths in the Berwick Handicap, Lady Sybil (with a young Roy Higgins up) accounted for Samson in the Moonee Valley Stakes. Geoff Lane was back on board the filly when she won the Edward Manifold Stakes by 10 lengths at 6/4 on. It was then Roy Higgins' turn once more when Lady Sybil started at 9/4 favourite and defeated the champion Sky High by three lengths in the Caulfield Guineas. A few days later Lady Sybil's winning run ended when she finished third to the fine mare Wenona Girl in the Thousand Guineas. She missed the Wakeful Stakes, but then led all the way to take the V.R.C. Oaks, relegating Wenona Girl to third. Lady Sybil capped off her remarkable season by winning the Sandown Guineas (again on a heavy track).

LADY WALLACE
1902 br mare Wallace – Lady Mostyn

An outstanding filly, Lady Wallace was the best daughter of the champion sire Wallace. In the 1905-6 season, her three year old campaign netted nine wins from 13 starts. They included three victories at weight-for-age. In classic events for her age group, Lady Wallace ran third in the A.J.C. Derby before winning the Caulfield Guineas. This made her odds-on favourite for the Victoria Derby, which she duly won. Less than a week later she added the V.R.C. Oaks to her spoils, starting at 5/1 on. Other victories included the V.R.C. and A.J.C. St Legers among a winning sequence of eight. As an older horse Lady Wallace was still formidable, winning the 1907 All Aged Stakes, a race in which she ran second in her triumphant three year old days.

LAKE, DES (1943-)

When weight forced Des Lake's retirement from the saddle in 1974, he had built an imposing record as a jockey in Australia and overseas. Originally apprenticed in Melbourne, he moved to Sydney, where his big race wins included a Metropolitan with Piper's Son, Doncaster on Time and Tide and three Epsoms, on Toi Port, Cabochon and Ricochet. He also partnered Cabochon to victory in the Stradbroke Handicap of 1968. In the following year the biggest sensation in Lake's career occurred when he was first past the post on Nausori in the Caulfield Cup, only to lose on protest. However, success came his way in Melbourne: an Oakleigh Plate with Time and Tide, the Newmarket and Toorak Handicaps on Ripa in 1965. Lake also rode with success in Ireland (for Paddy Prendergast) and in England (for Sam Armstrong), notching around 1,200 winners in all before he gave the game away.

LANE, GEOFFREY (1939-)

The 'Golden Boy', Geoff Lane, was apprenticed to Tommy Woodcock at Mentone in 1953. He was five times champion apprentice. In 1959-60 he won the senior Melbourne jockey's premiership, starting the season as an apprentice, but completing his indentures before the season finished. Among the many fine horses he rode were Dhaulagiri (on whom he won the 1961 Cox Plate), New Statesman (1961 Victoria Derby), Coppelius (Caulfield Guineas-Derby double in 1962), Webster and Lord, on whom he won the Futurity Stakes in 1959 and a string of weight for age races. Lane also won the A.J.C. Oaks on Chicola in 1959 and three V.R.C. Oaks, with Lady Sybil in 1960 and – for Woodcock – in 1957 with Amarco and 1967 with Chosen Lady. The latter came during a Melbourne comeback. Weight had forced Lane out of the game in the early 60s, but when he resumed riding towards the end of the decade his skills were undimmed. Another Victoria Derby, on Always There in 1968, came in this period. Eventually he was forced to go to Hong Kong where higher weight scales allowed him to continue riding. He had many successes there throughout the 1970s, before accepting a position in 1979 as deputy starter with the Hong Kong Jockey Club. He is now a trainer in Hong Kong.

LANGBY, KEVIN (1946-)

Born at Orange, Kevin Langby rode trackwork as a hobby for his father, Roy. In 1961 he was apprenticed to Rosehill trainer Fred Hood, but had to wait a year before his first winning ride – at Newcastle. His first big race success came while he was still an apprentice, on the Hood-trained Striking Force in the 1964 Doomben Cup. Once out of his time, Langby rode for the Arthur Ward stable, freelanced, and in 1972 succeeded George Moore as leading rider for the T.J. Smith stable. Langby won the Sydney jockeys' premiership in four consecutive years from 1971-2 to 1974-5. His many big races wins, for Smith and others, include the 1978 Doncaster on Maybe Mahal, Epsoms on Gunsynd and Speed of Sound, two A.J.C. Derbies – on Great Lover and Imagele, with whom he also combined to win the Rosehill Guineas. Langby won three Golden Slippers, the 1967 Doomben 10,000 on Bourbon Beau, the 1985 Cox Plate on Rising Prince. He also won no fewer than five Metropolitans – on Striking Force, Oncidon, Analie, Bon Teint and Ming Dynasty.

LANTERN

1861 br colt Muscovado – Nightlight

Owned and bred by the V.R.C. committeeman Hurtle Fisher, Lantern was trained by S. Mahon. He was a horse whose full abilities were never realised. Starting at 15/1, and carrying a mere 39.5kg, he won the 1864 Melbourne Cup in the rain from Poet. That year the race was run on a Thursday. Next day, Lantern showed his class by winning the Derby by six lengths. Thus he became the only horse to win the Melbourne Cup before the Victoria Derby. To show that none of this was a fluke, he won the Publicans' Purse on the Saturday after being left badly at the start. Fisher kept the horse in work. Lantern beat one other rival in the Ballarat Derby, but a month after his Melbourne Cup win he broke down with internal problems in the Ballarat Cup and died soon afterwards.

LAST GAMBLE, THE

One of the few Australian racing thrillers of recent years is *The Last Gamble* (1974) by 'John Goodwood' (B.A. Wicks). This is an entertaining tale of a desperate's efforts to clear his commitments, and avoid punishment by criminals or the law, in the course of a seven-race programme at Randwick.

LAUNCESTON CUP

A Group Three event, run at Mowbray in late summer, the Launceston Cup (in its various forms) has a venerable history which dates back to the victory of the imported English stallion Panic in 1865. Initially run over three miles, it steadily dropped back to the present distance of 2,600m. Regularly raided by mainland horses, like the Hobart Cup, the Launceston Cup has been won by some fine Tasmanian-bred horses: Seignorina in 1923 and 1925, Brallos (1976-7) among them. The great days of the race belong to its early history, when the relative affluence of Tasmanian racing attracted top mainland horses. Thus Fishhook won in 1867 and Fireworks the following year. The 1868 Melbourne Cup winner Tim Whiffler twice ran second in the Launceston Cup, in 1868 and 1871. Subsequent Melbourne Cup winner The Assyrian was second in 1883, but had the satisfaction of siring such future winners of the Hobart-Launceston Cups double as Chaldean and Macquarie. The most remarkable horse ever to contest the Launceston Cup was Panic's son Strop, who won on no fewer than four occasions between 1866-76 and was in the placings on several others. Swiveller, Watchful, Ordella and Vamos were other multiple winners of the event.

LAWMAN
1976 ch gelding Boucher – Quote

Owned by Robert Holmes à Court and trained by George Hanlon, Lawman held his own in a strong era. At two he was twice unplaced. Next season he progressed very rapidly, winning at Caulfield and Moonee Valley before running second in the Moonee Valley Stakes and third in Dulcify's 1979 Cox Plate. At four he won at Caulfield and Flemington, before scoring his biggest win in the 1981 Doncaster. In the spring, Lawman was third in the Memsie Stakes, won the first of consecutive Feehan Stakes and was an unlucky second to Kingston Town in the Cox Plate. Next year his best win was over Sovereign Red in the St George Stakes, besides another Feehan, and Lawman was also second in the Australian Cup to Kip, carrying 58kg, and third again in the Memsie.

LAWRENCE

1940 br horse Law Maker – Gay Element

A high class galloper, Lawrence won the Caulfield Guineas of 1943 from Precept and St Fairy. Third in the Derby to Precept and Valentino, he was withdrawn at the barrier in the Cox Plate. In the autumn of 1944 he won the St Leger, and in the spring rejoiced in his return to Caulfield, his favourite track, where he won the Memsie Stakes and then beat Counsel and Tranquil Star in the Caulfield Stakes. Burdened with 57.5kg in the Caulfield Cup, Lawrence started 8/1 equal favourite with Counsel and the versatile mare Claudette in one of the widest betting races ever seen in Australia. He was an unlucky second to Counsel in the Cup. Lawrence was back once more in the spring of 1945 when he recorded a second consecutive Caulfield Stakes victory. Thereafter he stood with success at the stud.

LEE-STEERE FAMILY

Associated with racing in Western Australia since the 1850s, members of the Lee-Steere family have been leading figures in the breeding and administration of the sport. Pastoralist and philanthropist Sir Ernest Lee-Steere senior (1866-1957) was Chairman of the W.A.T.C. from 1920-41. He won Caulfield Cups with Eurythmic in 1920 and Maple in 1928. Other wins included a Sydney Cup and – with Second Wind– two Williamstown and a King's Cup. Second Wind also ran second to Phar Lap in the Melbourne Cup of 1930. His son, also Sir Ernest Lee-Steere, served as Chairman of the W.A.T.C. for 21 years as his father had (from 1963-84). Less successful with his horses, he was a great promoter of racing in Western Australia. In his period as Chairman, facilities on metropolitan courses were improved. The winter course was relaid at Belmont; the Australian Derby was introduced and the Perth summer carnival became an essential part of the planning of trainers from the eastern states. The Lee-Steere Stakes and the Lee-Steere Classic are races named in honour of the family's contribution to racing in Western Australia.

LEICA LOVER
1970 b gelding Latin Lover – Miss Valeica

Trained by Bart Cummings, Leica Lover was – with Igloo – the unlucky racehorse of the 1970s. He won one race, at Victoria Park, at two, but at three won the Adelaide Guineas and two other races in Adelaide before Cummings sent him to Sydney. There he figured in the thrilling finish of one of the greatest A.J.C. Derbies, being narrowly beaten by Imagele. Taken to Melbourne, he was second again in a Derby, this time to Taj Rossi. Cummings kept this tough horse going and Leica Lover went west. Second in the Strickland Stakes, he beat Imagele in the

Caris Diamond Quality and was then second to Asgard in the West Australian Derby. Leica Lover had a long overdue big win when he beat Imagele in the Australian Derby. In 1974 Leica Lover's best win was the Hill Stakes. The following year produced an agonising run of minor placings: second in the Canterbury Stakes, second in the Warwick Stakes (giving llkg to Silver Shadow), third in the Metropolitan (with the winner, Bon Teint, in receipt of 10kg) and second in Analight's 1975 Caulfield Cup. Leica Lover had some recompense by winning the Chelmsford Stakes. In 1976 frustration continued, with placings in the All Aged, Chipping Norton and Queen Elizabeth Stakes in Sydney, before he again showed his versatility – and ill luck – by carrying 57kg to second place in Authentic Heir's Doncaster.

LEICA SHOW
1971 b mare Showdown – Miss Valeica

This highly-talented mare, trained by Bart Cummings, was second in the Edward Manifold Stakes and the Thousand Guineas in the spring of 1974, but she won the Wakeful Stakes and then beat Cap D'Antibes in the V.R.C. Oaks. In the autumn Leica Show was switched back to shorter distances. She beat All Shot in the William Reid Stakes, was second to Zambari in the Blamey and then won the Canterbury Stakes in Sydney. In the spring she was second to Skyjack in the Hill Stakes. Her autumn form was strong again in 1976, when she was second in the Lightning Stakes to Desirable, second to Toy Show, carrying 56kg, in the Newmarket and had some compensation by winning the Alister Clark Stakes at Moonee Valley.

LE FILOU

1946 b horse Valletor – Fileuse

The French-bred Le Filou was a champion sire of stayers, especially in the 1960s. The best of his progeny was the great mare Light Fingers, who won the 1965 Melbourne Cup. The 1967 winner, Red Handed, was another well-named horse by Le Filou (French for thief). Both were trained by Bart Cummings, long a fan of the Le Filou stock. Light Fingers's brother, The Dip, won the Metropolitan and Chipping Norton Stakes; Fulmen the Adelaide and Brisbane Cups and the South Australian St Leger; Weidersehn the Metropolitan; Wilton Park the 1968 A.J.C. Derby; Gay Poss the A.J.C. Oaks of 1970; the nicely-styled Peculator the S.A.J.C. Derby in 1966; and Skint Dip the 1971 Moonee Valley Cup.

LE GRAND

1881 b horse Epigram – Legend

Queensland-bred, this top-line stayer won high class races in the three eastern states. He took the Q.T.C. Sires' Produce Stakes before travelling south to win the A.J.C. Derby of 1883 and the St Leger. Other big wins in Sydney included Craven, A.J.C. and Randwick Plates, besides the Cumberland Stakes. In Melbourne he won the V.R.C. Champion and Royal Park Stakes.

LEILANI

1970 br mare Oncidium – Lei

This brilliant, but pint-sized staying mare was bought in New Zealand by Liberal politician Andrew Peacock and Ian Rice. Leilani did not race at two, and was slow to develop at three. Second at Morphettville at her first start, she won a maiden at Gawler, but a third at the same track persuaded trainer Bart Cummings that she was too immature

to contest the top fillies' races. Leilani was put away, therefore, until the autumn of 1974. She won first up at Caulfield, before running three good placings, including a third in the Kewney Stakes and a second in the Queen of the Turf at Rosehill. Success then came quickly. Leilani won the Princess Handicap and the A.J.C. Oaks on heavy Randwick tracks, thus for a time earning her a limiting reputation as a wet-tracker. In the Oaks, Leilani injured a hock and was spelled till the springtime.

At her third preparation, Roy Higgins saw the mare home in the Turnbull Stakes. But he could not make the weight for the mare's next engagements. Accordingly, Mick Mallyon rode Leilani to a three lengths victory in the Toorak Handicap over the boom country horse Arama, and then to an easy victory at 9/4 favourite in the Caulfield Cup. When both Mallyon and Higgins were suspended, Peter Cook had the sit when Leilani won the Mackinnon Stakes and was beaten by her stablemate Think Big in the Melbourne Cup. In the Queen's Cup at the end of the carnival, Higgins was back to combine with Leilani for a two and a half length victory. The autumn of 1975 was an even more successful campaign: Leilani ran track records in the Orr and St George Stakes, won the Queen's Plate and then carried a weight record of 58.5kg for a mare in the Australian Cup. Thereafter she ran two seconds in Sydney before again being injured. Racing was taking a toll. Leilani managed only one more victory – in the St George Stakes in the autumn of 1976 from Authentic Heir. In the last race start of a superb career that yielded 14 wins and 13 placings from 29 starts, Leilani broke down in the Tancred Stakes at Rosehill and was retired.

LET'S ELOPE

1987 ch mare Nassipour – Sharon Jane

From being a moderate performer in New Zealand, Let's Elope – once under the care of Bart Cummings across the Tasman – proved herself to be one of the greatest mares to race in Australia. In the spring of 1991 she failed first up when well supported. Next time, her backers gained their reward. Let's Elope won the Turnbull Stakes at Flemington, followed with a last stride win from Ivory Way in the Caulfield Cup and then proved that weight-for-age competition at the highest level was not beyond her with a decisive win in the Mackinnon Stakes from Super Impose and Prince Salieri. That remarkable lead-up was enough to send Let's Elope out as 3/1 favourite for the Melbourne Cup, which she duly won, with Steven King up, surviving a protest from Shiva's Revenge (her stable-mate: this was yet another Cummings' Melbourne Cup quinella). Let's Elope showed champion qualities by returning even better in the autumn, when she won the St George Stakes and the 1992 Australian Cup in record time. Underdone, she ran boldly in the Cox Plate but a multiple protest saw her relegated from second to fifth placing. Because of a wet track, Let's Elope was a late scratching from the Melbourne Cup in the spring of 1992, and in the Japan Cup she bled and ran down the line.

Let's Elope would never win again in Australia. Shortly after the Japan Cup failure she was sent to America, where laws concerning anti-bleeding drugs are more lenient. She won first up, before enduring a succession of ill-fated runs in top company. Let's Elope beat the champion American mare Flawlessly at Group One level, only to end up third after a protest. Never averse to using her size to shoulder through, she cost herself a race which would have sealed her greatness. Thereafter she bled again, and was finally retired early in 1994. Only Rivette before her, among mares, had won the big Cups double; few horses of the modern era deserve to be mentioned in the company of Let's Elope.

LETTS, JOHN (1943-)

Born in Adelaide, Letts was apprenticed as a jockey in 1956 and would be premier rider in the state on eight occasions. He also rode with notable success around Australia, as well as in South Africa and Singapore. In Adelaide his big wins included five Goodwood Handicaps, five S.A.J.C. Sires' Produce Stakes and six Auraria Stakes. He also won three Adelaide Cups, with Rain Lover (for trainer Graeme Heagney with whom he enjoyed a long association), Grand Scale and Amarant; two Australasian Oaks, and the 1968 S.A.J.C. Derby on Dale Lace. At his first ride in Melbourne, he won the 1972 Melbourne Cup on the Tasmanian outsider, Piping Lane. Eight years later he repeated the dose on the Robert Sangster-owned and Colin Hayes-trained Beldale Ball. These were among the 97 cups victories in a career which saw Letts kick home about 1500 winners. For instance he won an Australian Cup on Ming Dynasty in 1980; the Hobart-Launceston Cups double in 1976 and 1977 on the fine local stayer Brallos and Hamilton and Warrnambool Cups on Favoured Bay. With Galena Boy he won the Victoria Derby in 1975, while Cheyne Walk gave Letts his only Australasian Champion Stakes. He won the Epsom on Raffindale in 1977. Before retirement he was trebly occupied: as jockey, trainer and as driver of pacers, in which latter capacity he had some success. Letts now trains at Morphettville, and has recently been a guest television commentator during the Flemington spring carnival.

LEWIS, ROBERT (BOBBIE) (1878-1947)

Ninth child of a Welsh miner, Lewis was born at Clunes, where he won his first race, in 1892. One of the most celebrated of Australian jockeys, Lewis began to ride in town soon afterwards. He had sufficiently impressed the trainer J.E. Brewer that the latter took him to England in 1898 with The Grafter. Lewis did not settle happily in England and soon came back to Australia where he forged his long and lucrative association with the trainer James Scobie. The Victory, while an ordinary horse, gave Lewis his first big race win in the Melbourne Cup of 1902. Three others followed from a total of 33 rides. The last was Trivalve in 1927 (a horse who had given him a record eighth Victoria Derby), while in between he scored on the fine gallopers Patrobas (1915) and Artilleryman (1919). Only once suspended, Lewis was highly respected as a judge of pace and for his gentle touch with horses. The incident in which he sued the V.A.T.C. handicapper, R. Kelly, for slander in 1900 (when the latter had too publicly and unwisely impugned Lewis's abilities) was a rare indecorous episode. Aptly, the matter was settled out of court. Besides his record tally in the Victoria Derby, Lewis won four A.J.C. Derbies, numerous St Legers in both New South Wales and Victoria as well as seven V.R.C. Oaks. He retired at 60, after 48 years as a jockey, and farmed at Glenroy until his death.

LIGHT FINGERS

1961 ch mare Le Filou – Cuddlesome

After three minor wins as a two year old, trainer Bart Cummings set this marvellous staying filly an ambitious spring campaign. She won the Edward Manifold Stakes, was second to the Sydney filly Reveille in the Thousand Guineas, won the Wakeful Stakes and then the Oaks. She capped off that cam-paign by winning the Sandown Guineas (then restricted to fillies). Back in the autumn, she campaigned in Sydney where she won the Princess Handicap before easily taking the A.J.C. Oaks at 9/4 on. Light Fingers could sprint brilliantly fresh. She won first up at four over five furlongs at Victoria Park, and on another occasion ran third in the Lightning Stakes to Marmion and Star of Heaven over the same distance in course record time. After winning the Craiglee Stakes, Light Fingers was well on course for the 1965 Melbourne Cup, but she was injured in the Caulfield Stakes in which she ran third, and thus scratched from the Caulfield Cup. A third in the Mackinnon Stakes saw her kept safe at 15/1 in the Melbourne Cup. There she scored a coura-geous win, in a race marred by the fall of Matloch and Borehead, beating her stable-mate Ziema by a short half head. Light Fingers carried a record 52.5kg for a mare to victory, and endeared herself to jockey Roy Higgins as his favourite horse. Next autumn, Light Fingers beat Tobin Bronze in the St George but was then injured and put out to spell. Back in the spring, she ran four weight-for-age placings, including a third in Tobin Bronze's 1966 Cox Plate. With 57kg she ran one of her greatest races in the Melbourne Cup, beaten only by the champion stayer Galilee. She carried the same weight to vic-tory in the Sandown Cup at her next start. Injuries restricted Light Fingers's future cam-paigns, and she was retired and sent back to New Zealand, where she was a failure at stud. Light Fingers lived on to the grand age of 28 before being put down in 1989.

LIGHTNING STAKES

In 1955 the V.R.C. introduced two new weight-for-age races to its autumn pro-gramme: the Blamey Stakes (then run over one and a half miles) and the Lightning

Stakes, now a Group One 1,000m sprint. Winners of the Lightning have been a roll call of champions, and it has been won by horses who could also get more ground. For instance the Victoria Derby winner Sky High twice won the Lightning (in 1961-2) and was third the following year when Wenona Girl won the race for the first of successive occasions. Maybe Mahal (1977-8), River Rough (1984-5) and Schillaci (1992-3, and a narrow second in 1994) are other distinguished dual winners of the event. Todman saluted in 1960 and in that decade there was a run of top class winners: Marmion, Citius, Storm Queen, Begonia Belle, Mister Hush. The grey Black Onyx won in 1970, while in the next year Dual Choice beat Tauto and Baguette. Brilliant sprinters Century and Desirable also won in the 1970s. In 1987 the champion Placid Ark beat Special, but in 1988 the mare had her turn, running a course record of 55.5 that still stands. She was back again in 1989, finishing second to Zeditave. Proving once more that the Lightning is within the scope of middle distance champions, Shaftesbury Avenue won the race in 1991.

LILLYE, BERT (1919-)

One of Australia's foremost racing journalists, Lillye was involved in the game for his working life of half a century, save five years of military service in the Second World War. Even then he was liable to be found on a racetrack, whether on leave, or AWOL. Indeed he once took leave from his unit and travelled 1,000 miles to see Modulation win the 1944 Epsom. On another occasion he discovered a champion at the Cluden racecourse near Townsville – jockey Neville Sellwood. Beginning as a copy boy at 15 on *Smith's Weekly,* Lillye progressed to work on the *Sydney Morning Herald* and then

switched to the *Daily Mirror.* After five years he returned to the *Herald,* where he remained until his retirement in 1984. A prolific award winner for his journalism, Lillye is also a great racing raconteur, as evidenced in his collection of anecdotes, *Backstage of Racing.*

LIMERICK

1923 br gelding Limond – Medley

Bred in New Zealand, Limerick won three starts there as a two year old. He became a regular visitor to Australia from 1926, being especially successful in Sydney and at weight-for-age. He won the A.J.C. St Leger and was second in the Derby. Other wins included three Warwick Stakes (Phar Lap running third to him in 1929), three Chelmsford and two Rawson Stakes, two Hill Stakes, a Chipping Norton and an All Aged Stakes. He was a star soon, if unfortunately, to be eclipsed by Phar Lap. However he shares with Kingston Town the remarkable record of 22 metropolitan wins in Sydney.

LISTON, JOHN JAMES (1872-1944)

Sometime barber, publican and entrepreneur, Liston served seven terms as Mayor of Williamstown between 1901 and 1913. After the Great War, he was Mayor of Melbourne on five occasions. He was Chairman of the Williamstown Racing club from 1931 until the course was closed on 10 February 1940, because of the Second World War. It never re-opened. From 1929 until his death, Liston was President of the Victorian Football Association. His memory is honoured by two sports. The V.F.A. best and fairest award is the Liston Trophy and one of the early spring weight-for-age races is the Liston Stakes, run at Sandown.

LOCHIEL

1882 br horse Prince Charlie – Nelly Moore

Sired in England, but foaled in New Zealand, Lochiel excelled first as a racehorse, then as a sire. His versatility was such that he won the Newmarket in 1887 and the following year took the New Zealand Cup. In 1889 he ran second in the Newmarket to Sedition (with Carbine third), and won the Auckland Cup and the Australian Cup in which he beat Carbine. In that season Lochiel also won the V.R.C. Autumn Handicap. Standing at the Widden Stud, he proved an immediate success and was four times champion sire of Australia.

LONG, WILLIAM (1839-1915)

A convict's son, Long went to school in Australia before reading law in England and returning to New South Wales. He chose to practise as a member of State Parliament rather than as a lawyer. A keen owner of racehorses, and devoted in his desire to improve the quality of Australian thoroughbreds, Long's best horse was the unbeaten Grand Flaneur. He owned many other good quality gallopers in the 1880s and 1890s, who were trained at his private track, Chipping Norton, near the present day Warwick Farm racecourse. Long was chairman of the Australian Jockey Club from 1898-1900 and is properly remembered for his faith in the future of thoroughbred breeding and racing in Australia. The Chipping Norton Stakes is named after his training establishment.

LONGFELLA

1969 b horse Shy Boy – Longhill

A brilliant juvenile in New Zealand, Longfella's wins at two began at Paeroa, but he quickly progressed to take the Breeders' Plate, Eclipse, Sires' Produce at Manawatu, Champagne Stakes and Ellerslie Sires' Produce. Brought to Melbourne to race as a three year old, and put under Des Judd's care, Longfella was unplaced in the 1972 Freeway Stakes, but then beat Abdul in the Memsie; won the Rosehill Guineas, was second in the A.J.C. Derby to Gold Brick and then third in Dayana's Victoria Derby. In the autumn of 1973, Longfella reeled off victories in the Orr and St George Stakes in Melbourne, the Tulloch in Sydney, before running third to All Shot in the All Aged Stakes. In the spring of 1973 Longfella won the Warwick and Chelmsford Stakes and was third in the George Main. But his form gradually fell away, even though he was third in the 1974 Caulfield Stakes to Igloo and Asgard.

LONG PRICED WINNERS

Most of the winners at extravagant odds on the Australian turf have been equine non-entities, Anntelle and Pablo's Pulse for instance – who started at 500/1, the longest odds of all. But some outstanding horses and Group One races have featured in upset results. At the start of his three year old campaign in September 1978, Dulcify won at 300/1 at Morphettville. Next year he took the Australian Cup at 80/1 from Manikato and Family of Man. This was the race, in 1988, where Dandy Andy at 125/1 spoiled the supposed match in two between Bonecrusher and Vo Rogue. The Caulfield Guineas developed its recent reputation as a suspect race because of such winners as Abaridy at 250/1 in 1986, but long before, in 1952, Bayside had been victorious at 200/1. Mighty Manitou won the A.J.C. Sires' Produce at Randwick in April 1982 at 200/1. Three Melbourne Cup winners have saluted at 100/1: The Pearl (1871), Wotan (1936) and Old Rowley (1940), while Saint Warden won the first division of the 1943 Caulfield Cup at the same odds. Social Upstart at

100/1 brightened a mid-week Randwick meeting for this author in 1977; while Oxford Prince returned an even better result, winning at odds of 172/1 at the same track in June 1994.

LORD
1954 br gelding Targui – Broadway

Owned by W.R. Kemball and trained by Ken Hilton, Lord was a fine and durable galloper of the late 50s and early 60s. If his best performances were reserved for Caulfield (where he recorded 21 of his 28 wins) and weight-for-age races (20 victories), Lord competed with distinction in an era of high quality horses. He had three wins as a two year old, but then disappointed Hilton in the spring of 1957. Brought back in the autumn, he won the Victoria Handicap with Geoff Lane up and followed with his first weight-for-age win in the Liston Stakes, then run at Flemington. The first of a remarkable four Memsie Stakes wins followed. Next Lord won the Underwood Stakes before beating Prince Darius in the Caulfield Stakes by a half head in course record time. This was another of his favourite events: he won it twice more, including a dead-heat in 1960 with Dhaulagiri. In the autumn of 1959 Lord won the Orr, St George and Futurity Stakes, before making his lone interstate trip. In Sydney he was second in the Chipping Norton but won the All Aged Stakes.

The following spring the Memsie and Caulfield Stakes fell again to Lord, as did the Orr and St George in the autumn. He was beaten by useful horses in the Futurity and Queen Elizabeth Stakes: Todman and Tulloch respectively. Further weight-for-age successes followed in the spring of 1960, but in the autumn he won only once, although this was a triumph over Dhaulagiri and Tulloch in the Queen's Plate. After a fourth Memsie and then a Craiglee Stakes win in

the spring of 1961, the ever-green Lord went amiss in the Underwood and was spelled. But he was not done with: in the autumn of 1962 he won the Queen's Plate again and the Queen Elizabeth Stakes. The toll of racing was finally evident and his only other win was in the Queen Elizabeth Stakes a year later. A grand career closed with a fourth to Summer Fair in the Fisher Plate in November 1963.

LORD REIMS
1981 ch gelding Zamazaan – Right On

This tough New Zealand-bred stayer was trained to victory in four Group One handicaps by Cliff Fenwick. The biggest win for Lord Reims came on a bog track in the 1987 Caulfield Cup when Brent Thomson sent him to the front at the 1800m and he just lasted to beat the unlucky Beau Zam. There was no fluke about Lord Reims on any occasion that he turned up at the Morphettville track. He won the Eagle Blue Stakes (a Group Three lead-up to the Adelaide Cup) in 1988 and 1989. More remarkably he scored an unprecedented three successive wins in the Cup: from 1987-9. In the last of these victories (which gave Lord Reims five from five starts at Morphettville) he won by four lengths under 57kg with Grant Cooksley in the saddle. Lord Reims had gone amiss while in training for the Melbourne Cup the previous year, and he was retired some time after his third Adelaide Cup win without the chance to extend his record in staying events.

LOTS OF TIME
1964 br gelding Powerhouse – Bulandi

When in the winter of 1969, the jumper Lots of Time won the Toolambool Hurdle, he recorded his eighth victory in a row over hurdles, breaking the Victorian record of Le Mattan (set in the 1918-9 season) and equalling Air Fox's 21 year old Australian record. At his next start, and his first at the Sandown track, Lots of Time won the Port Philip Hurdle to claim the record. He carried 72kg to victory, came from five lengths behind on the turn and gathered in Brother Bart, who was in receipt of 11kg from him. Trained by Norm Creighton, and ridden in his succession of wins by George Costello, Lots of Time was owned by G. Eccles and Sally Wood. His wins were recorded at Kyneton, Geelong, Moonee Valley, Moe, Pakenham, Flemington, twice at Caulfield and then at Sandown. But the 10th in a row eluded him and Lots of Time went under to Brother Bart in the Grand National Hurdle. In the following season he was prepared for a steeplechasing career, but was put down after a fall in the 1970 Hiskens Steeple which was won by Crisp.

LOUGH NEAGH

1928 ch gelding Bachelor's Persse – Terentia

Sired by the 1915 Queensland Cup winner, this durable and most popular gelding raced 127 times in eight seasons, winning 32. The horse was trained by Tim Brosnan, and most often ridden by Frank Shean. At two he won the Q.T.C. Sires' Produce Stakes, while his class was confirmed in the next season with wins in the Queensland Guineas and Derby. At four, Lough Neagh made the first of his 11 trips south of the border. He raced for five years in Sydney with notable success, but his only two forays to Melbourne resulted in disappointing runs in the 1934 Caulfield Cup and the 1932 Melbourne Cup, won by Peter Pan. In the autumn of 1933, Lough Neagh won the first of three Rawson Stakes and was then narrowly beaten by Peter Pan in the A.J.C. Plate. In 1934 he won the B.A.T.C. Newmarket (at one stage in the 1930s Australia's richest sprint race, and forerunner of the Doomben 10,000). At

six he won the Canterbury Stakes and two sprint races in Brisbane.

In the autumn of 1936, at seven, Lough Neagh enjoyed one of his most successful patches, winning his second Chipping Norton and Rawson Stakes. In the former he beat no less than Peter Pan; in the second, Hall Mark. Back home, he showed the doubters that he could stay with a Brisbane Cup win by four lengths, carrying 58.5kg. Lough Neagh was still fresh enough at eight to add a remarkable third Chipping Norton and Rawson Stakes to his record, besides the A.J.C. Cumberland Plate and the Q.T.C. King's Plate. In his last season, at nine, Lough Neagh added a second Tramway to that which he had won in 1937, but this was his only success. Brosnan now retired a horse who was perhaps the most popular Queenslander to race between the wars.

LOWLAND

1965 b mare Agricola – Impeccable

After Light Fingers and Let's Elope, Lowland was probably the best staying mare Bart Cummings trained. Chosen Lady beat her in the V.R.C. Oaks of 1967, but in the autumn of 1968 she found her best form. After a win in the Kewney Stakes, Lowland went to Sydney and fancied that way of going. She decisively won the A.J.C. Oaks. Back in the spring of 1968, her best win was the Underwood Stakes at Caulfield. In the following autumn, she ran thirds in the St George Stakes and then the Queen Elizabeth Stakes behind Rain Lover and Future. Now Lowland was sent once more to Sydney. Her run of minor placings continued with a second to Roman Consul in the Autumn Stakes after she had run third to Rain Lover and Roman Consul in the Chipping Norton Stakes. With Roy Higgins up, the mare had her turn in the Sydney Cup which she won by more than a length to Rain Lover.

Lowland carried 54.5kg, the biggest weight for a mare since Wakeful humped 60.5kg to victory in 1902. Given one more race start, in a short and brilliant career, Lowland recorded her 10th win in the Queen Elizabeth Stakes at Randwick from Roman Consul and the odds-on favourite Rain Lover. It was the seventh time in 13 starts that she finished in front of that grand stayer. After this race, Lowland was sent to stud.

LURLINE

1868 br mare Traducer – Mermaid

Not the first New Zealand horse to be nominated for the Melbourne Cup, Lurline was the first to run in the race. A two-time winner of the Canterbury Cup over 3600m she carried 56kg but finished among the tail-enders in the 1874 Melbourne Cup which Haricot won. After the Cup run, Lurline was sold to Victorian breeder Samuel Gardiner. Her wins for him in the autumn of 1875 included the Australian Cup, two weight-for-age races at Randwick, a third in the Sydney Cup and victory in the Adelaide Cup, when she carried 57.5kg to beat Barmaid and Gloom. A successful broodmare, Lurline's best foal was Darebin, winner of the 1881 Victoria Derby. She was found dead in her paddock near Melbourne in April 1890, having apparently been shot accidentally by boys who were hunting nearby.

LUSKIN STAR

1974 ch horse Kaoru Star – Promising

One of the most brilliant winners of the Golden Slipper Stakes, Luskin Star was trained by Max Lees. Early success came in the Silver Slipper Stakes. In the main event he was taken on by the Blue Diamond winner, Blazing Saddles, but left him far behind. Luskin Star completed the two year old Triple Crown with authoritative victories in the A.J.C. Sires' Produce and Champagne Stakes. In the spring of 1977, Luskin Star ran second in open company to Romantic Dream in the Canterbury Stakes. Taken to Melbourne, he won the Caulfield Guineas from Princess Talaria with Roy Higgins up, but failed to stay in Family of Man's Cox Plate. In 1978 he won the Phar Lap against his own age group and was retired after victory in The Galaxy with the record of 13 wins from 17 starts. Luskin Star went to the Newhaven Stud at Boorowa in New South Wales, where he proved to be a prolific sire of versatile winners (from 1,000 to 3,200m) if of few champions.

M

MACDOUGAL

1954 b gelding Marco Polo II – Lady Fox

Bred at the Trelawney Stud in New Zealand, the tough stayer Macdougal was trained in Australia by Dick Roden. As a three year old, Macdougal showed his staying promise by running third in the 1957 Brisbane Cup. In the same race in 1959, he defeated Grand Garry (who would win the 1960 Sydney Cup) and Baystone (who had won the 1958 Melbourne Cup). Roden took the horse to Sydney, where Macdougal beat Royal Jester and Foxmara in the Metropolitan. A Melbourne Cup campaign was planned, but the horse travelled poorly and was then injured. Ron Hutchinson, regular rider of Macdougal, got off the horse to ride Trellios who won the Mackinnon Stakes. But on the same afternoon, Hutchinson rode Macdougal into second place in the Hotham Handicap behind Grand Garry and reckoned this the better of the two Cup trials. So it proved, starting at 8/1, Macdougal won the Melbourne Cup by three lengths, thus becoming the only horse to win the Brisbane Cup-Metropolitan-Melbourne Cup handicap treble in a single season. Macdougal trained on the next spring when he finished second in the Sandown Cup to Ilumquh.

MCCARTEN, MAURICE (1902-71)

Born in New Zealand, McCarten was twice leading jockey there in the early 1920s. He first came to Australia in 1923 with Ballymena, on whom he won the first of four A.J.C. Derbies. In 1926 he became one of the earliest of the many New Zealand riders to settle in Australia. Besides his victories in the A.J.C. Derby he won six A.J.C. St Legers and six A.J.C. Sires' Produce Stakes. He also won four big Randwick miles (two Epsoms and two Doncasters), two Sydney and four Brisbane Cups, and two Victoria Derbies. The New Zealander Limerick was one of the best horses that McCarten rode. In 1942 he retired from race-riding and made a successful switch to training. His best horse was probably Todman, but he also trained Columnist, Delta, Noholme and Prince Courtauld, and won the Sydney premiership on four occasions.

MCCARTHY, RICHARD LAWRENCE ('DARBY') (1944-)

This gifted jockey was one of the few Aborigines to reach the top of the profession. Son of a stockman at Cunnamulla, in outback Queensland, McCarthy served his apprenticeship in Brisbane. He won his first race there at 13. The Newcastle Gold Cup was his first big win, in 1962, followed by the first of three Stradbroke Handicaps the next year, on Mullala. He also won the Brisbane Cup of 1966 on Apa, the Doomben 10,000 on Gay Gauntlet in 1968. In successive rides in the spring of 1969 at Randwick he won the A.J.C. Derby on Divide and Rule, the Epsom on Broker's Tip. The low point in McCarthy's career came when he was suspended for 10 years (later reduced to two years, and then to 10 months) for allegedly pulling a horse at Hamilton in rural Victoria in 1976. McCarthy made an unsuccessful comeback in 1978, but in 1984 he was able to set up as a trainer at Toowoomba. With the assistance of the Department of Aboriginal Affairs, McCarthy also ran a riding academy for young Aborigines. In 1990 he ventured another, short-lived return to race-riding.

MCGINLEY, TOM (1936-)

Born at Clydebank in Scotland, Tom McGinley rode 45 winners over the jumps in Britain (including one at Aintree) before emigrating to Australia in 1964. In an eight year stint in Victoria, McGinley's fearless and dashing style made him a pin-up rider with punters, and he brought home more than 200 winners. His most notable successes included a Grand National Hurdle on Call Again in 1970 and no fewer than five Grand National Steeplechases in seven years: on Royal Rennie, Black Butt, Valgo and with McEwan in 1966 and 1968. McGinley was also the regular jockey for Australia's greatest jumper of this period, dual Hiskens Steeple winner Crisp. McGinley retired in 1972 after he finished fourth on Yawander in the Australian Steeple. He became a steward with the V.R.C.. After five years he made a brief and unsuccessful return to the saddle and then took up training. Eventually he became a full-time racing official in Macau.

MCGRATH FAMILY

Frank McGrath (1865-1946), a coal-miner's son who became a jockey and won the Epsom in 1886 on Zeno, retired from race-riding because of injuries received after a fall in the Caulfield Cup of the previous year. McGrath trained at Goulburn and Canterbury, before setting up stables at Randwick in 1900. Soon successful, McGrath won the A.J.C. Derby with Abundance in 1902 and the St Leger with the same horse in the next year. Later victories for the trainer included two Caulfield and three Melbourne Cups. In 1932 and 1934 the champion Peter Pan won the Melbourne Cup for McGrath, who believed his horse to be Phar Lap's superior. When Phar Lap won his Melbourne Cup, in 1930, McGrath's splendid galloper Amounis took the Caulfield Cup and set up a disastrous pay-out for doubles bookmakers.

Against his father's wishes, Frank McGrath junior (1915-) became stable foreman in 1935. After being demobilised from the army in 1945, he took over his father's stables at Randwick. While he won a Sydney Cup with On Line in 1959, times became increasingly hard for McGrath, who gave the game away altogether in 1966.

MCGROWDIE, NOEL ('DIGGER') (1920-61)

Born on Christmas Day 1920, McGrowdie was the son of the Brisbane trainer Charlie McGrowdie, and grew up on racetracks. During the Second World War, only the Albion Park sand track was kept open for racing in Brisbane, so jockey McGrowdie headed south to try his luck. His first big race success in Sydney (and the first for trainer Maurice McCarten) was on Kiaree in the 1943 Epsom. The first of three Metropolitan victories came in 1944 with Nightbeam. A natural lightweight, and superb distance rider, McGrowdie won that race again the following year with Murray Stream and in 1957 with Straight Draw. That under-rated stayer gave McGrowdie the rare Sydney-Melbourne Cups double in 1958. One of McGrowdie's biggest setbacks occurred at the end of 1945, when he was sacked as Bernborough's jockey after running fourth on the horse at Canterbury. Athol Mulley replaced McGrowdie and was on the champion in 15 consecutive wins. McGrowdie had plenty of compensatory success, winning an Epsom, two Doncasters, a Newmarket, three Sydney and two Brisbane Cups, three Doomben 10,000s among many big race victories. In 1960 he moved with his family to ride in Malaya, and took the jockeys' premiership with 59 winners in that year. McGrowdie was killed in September 1961 when his car was hit by a truck while he was on his way to ride at Penang.

MACKINNON, L.K.S. (LAUCHLAN) (1861-1935)

Born on the Isle of Skye, Mackinnon emigrated to Melbourne in 1884 and set up practice as a solicitor. Later he would be a company director and a rich Western District property-owner as well. He served on the committee of the V.R.C. for 26 years, the last 19 of them as chairman, from 1916-35. Racing horses under the pseudonym 'K.S. MacLeod', he owned the versatile Realm who won the Grand National Hurdle in 1906, and the Sydney and Australian Cups in the next year. Woorak was one of his best horses, although he won the 1914 Melbourne Cup with Kingsburgh, the first horse that Mackinnon raced under his own name. His term as chairman of the V.R.C. was marked by the consolidation of that club's power over racing in Victoria; by the passing of a by-law disallowing women trainers; by attempts to have geldings barred from

running in the Derby. Mackinnon's horse Carradale had run second to the well-performed gelding Phar Lap in the A.J.C. and Victoria Derbies of 1929. Soon after his death, the Melbourne Stakes was renamed the L.K.S. Mackinnon Stakes in his honour.

MACKINNON STAKES

The traditional weight-for-age lead-up to the Melbourne Cup three days later, the L.K.S. Mackinnon Stakes is a Group One event over 2000m. It was added to the Flemington spring carnival programme in 1869 as the Melbourne Stakes, under which name it continued until 1936 when the V.R.C. renamed it in honour of its former chairman. Glencoe won the first Melbourne Stakes, while the evergreen Tim Whiffler was victorious in the following year. Dagworth was the first of numerous multiple winners in 1873-4. Succeeding him have been Chester in 1878 and 1880, the top Queensland horse Battalion in 1897-8; the great mare Wakeful who won three years in a row from 1901-3, Cetigne (1917 and 1919), Eurythmic (1920-1), Phar Lap (1930-1), Peter Pan in 1932 and 1934 (the years in which he followed on with his two Melbourne Cups), Beau Vite (1940-1) and the top mare Tranquil Star who equalled the performance of Wakeful by winning in 1942 and again in 1944-5. She was second in 1943. Comic Court won twice, in 1949-50, going on to an unexpected Melbourne Cup win on the second occasion. Rising Fast and Belmura Lad are other dual winners. And this roll-call omits some of the greatest names of the Australian turf who have won the Melbourne/Mackinnon Stakes: Robinson Crusoe, Malua, Abercorn, Carbine, Poseidon, Magpie, Gloaming, Manfred, Gothic, High Syce, Rogilla, Ajax, Flight, Delta, Dalray, Hydrogen, Sailor's Guide, Tulloch, Sky High, Tobin Bronze,

Winfreux, Rain Lover, Family of Man, Dulcify, Rubiton, Empire Rose, Horlicks, Better Loosen Up, Let's Elope and Veandercross. No race on the Australian calendar has a more distinguished line-up of winners.

MCLEOD, DONALD ('BIG MICK') (1882-1906)

Born at St Arnaud in country Victoria, 'Big Mick' McLeod was an unsuccessful small-time bookmaker, in an era in which controls over them were lax, even though punishments for defaulting could be violent. McLeod fielded at the Grand National Steeple meeting at Flemington in July 1906 and laid Decoration heavily in the main race. When it won, he 'scaled' – offering punters their stake money back, together with an I.O.U. Accused by his outraged clients of welching, McLeod was chased across the course and bashed. He died of suffocation and a broken neck, in perhaps the ugliest incident in Australian racing history. No prosecutions were made over his death.

MAGIC RULER

1964 ch gelding Orgoglio – Magic Slipper

A tough and brilliant sprinter, who performed season after season at the highest level despite intermittent leg trouble, Magic Ruler recorded his first big win in the 1968 Oakleigh Plate. Thereafter he carried 58.5kg into third place in the Victoria Handicap. In that autumn, Magic Ruler was also third in the Alister Clark Stakes; second in the Futurity. During the spring of 1968, he was third to Winfreux and Fileur in the Freeway Stakes, third in the Invitation Stakes. Still highly competitive, Magic Ruler had to be content with a second to Regal Rhythm in the Linlithgow, and third in the Craven 'A'. His best year was 1969. He carried 61.5kg

into second place in the Standish Handicap behind Ridicule, and then won the William Reid Stakes before running second to Mister Hush in the Lightning Stakes. Back at Caulfield, Magic Ruler went one better than 1968 when he won the Futurity with 62kg from Snub and Bunratty Castle. In the spring he gave weight and finished second to Crewman in the Toorak Handicap. As his form gradually tapered off, Magic Ruler was still able to run second to Alrello in the 1970 Oakleigh Plate; second in the Victoria Handicap of 1971.

MAGISTRATE

1971 b gelding Stipulate – Our Jan

An ill-tempered horse, but a remarkably durable stayer, Magistrate was capable of winning a Group One race – his second successive Perth Cup – as a 10 year old. Owned and trained in New Zealand by I.H. Steffert, he was unplaced in one start at two, won one minor event at Paeroa from 15 outings at three. One more win came when Magistrate was four, but he was nothing if not a slow developer. Next season he won four good races, including the Avondale Gold Cup, and was placed in top company as well. He did not race at six, but returned as a seven year old to win a Cambridge Cup, a second Avondale Gold Cup and run third to Big Gamble in the Wellington Cup. At eight he crossed the Tasman, and was second to Hyperno in the 1979 Queen Elizabeth Stakes and third behind Hauberk in the Sandown Cup. One win at Auckland was Magistrate's best result for the year. But at nine he had a new lease of life, beating Family of Man in the Moe Cup, Favoloso in the Werribee Cup, and then travelling west where he triumphed in the Perth Cup in the New Year of 1981 with the light-weight of 49.5 kg. And he was not done with yet: this moody, tough campaigner was back in Perth the next summer, where he handled the weight rise of three kg to win the Perth Cup once more.

MAGNIFICENT
1942 ch horse Ajax – Complete

One of the best sons of Ajax, Magnificent won four races at two, including the A.J.C. Breeders' Plate, Sires' Produce and Champagne Stakes. At three he won the Hobartville as a lead-up to victory in the A.J.C. Derby of 1945. Sent to Melbourne, he was slow to adjust, running fourth in the Caulfield Guineas and nowhere in the Cox Plate. Accordingly supporters of Magnificent helped themselves to odds of 15/1 in the Victoria Derby and thought the colt well-named when he completed the classic double. Thereafter Magnificent's form fell away and at four he went 12 starts without a win, although he was second to Bernborough in the Warwick Stakes, and was placed in the George Main and Caulfield Stakes, and the Cox Plate of 1946 behind Flight and Star Act.

MAGPIE
1914 blk horse Popinjay – St Frusquin

Magpie raced in top company in England. From six starts he won only the Rous Memorial at Newmarket, but was second in the classic Two Thousand Guineas. Brought to Australia, he won the 1918 Caulfield and Melbourne Stakes. It was at the Kia-Ora Stud that he made his real mark on Australian racing. From his first crop came the New Zealand Derby winner Black Ronald. He was leading sire in 1928-9 and runner up on three other occasions. Among his fine progeny were dual Derby winner Talking, Loquacious, who won an A.J.C. Oaks and Metropolitan, and the Doncaster

winners Karuma and Jacko. Magpie headed the broodmare table three times, and such fine gallopers as Delta and Hydrogen were out of Magpie mares. His three best horses would have been outstanding in any era: Amounis, Chatham and Windbag.

MAHOGANY
1990 br gelding Last Tycoon – Alshandegha

Bred in the purple, Mahogany is also owned and trained in that hue: his connections are Lloyd Williams and Kerry Packer, while Lee Freedman is his trainer. At his second start in the spring of 1992, he was a four and a half length winner at Moonee Valley and was then put away until the autumn. Two Melbourne placings earned him a trip to Brisbane for the winter, where he won three races in four starts, two at Group One: the 1993 Q. T. C. Sires' Produce and the Castlemaine Stakes. In the spring of that year, Mahogany won the Up and Coming Stakes at Randwick. It was a fair omen. Back in Melbourne he beat stablemate Port Watch in the Caulfield Guineas, before running an inexplicable and disappointing third at Moonee Valley. Mahogany was back in form in the Derby, spreadeagling the field to win by five lengths. In the autumn of 1994 he narrowly won the Vanuatu Stakes before showing his class with another Group One win, this time in the Australian Guineas. Durbridge, his older stablemate, then decisively beat Mahogany in the Australian Cup. Sent to Sydney he had three lengths to spare in the Tulloch Stakes. In the A.J.C. Derby Mahogany capped his three year old career. Regular jockey Greg Hall shouldered the horse to the front early in the race and Mahogany became the first three year old since Dulcify in 1978-9 to win the Derby double.

MALT KING

1906 ch horse Maltster – Patrona

Out of a daughter of the champion Grand Flaneur, Malt King was bred at the Widden Stud in New South Wales. As a two year old he defeated Prince Foote in the 1909 Champagne Stakes at Randwick. Later in the year he won the Caulfield Guineas. Malt King grew better with age. He won a V.R.C. All Aged Stakes, while in the Randwick version of that race, ran third in 1910 and won in each of the next two years. Mixing his distances, he was good enough to run second in the 1910 Newmarket Handicap. Next year he carried 57.5kg to victory in the Metropolitan. In addition, Malt King won a Tramway Handicap, the Rawson Stakes in both 1911 and 1912, while in 1911 he took the Caulfield Stakes from a small, but select field which included Comedy King and The Parisian.

MALTSTER

1897 br horse Bill of Portland – Barley

The highlight of the career of this high quality horse came during the Spring Carnival at Flemington of 1900. Maltster had already proved his class by winning an Ascot Vale Stakes and A.J.C. Derby. Now he added a second Derby on the first day of the Spring Carnival; ran second in the Melbourne Cup to Clean Sweep (who received 5kg from him), won the Flying Stakes over six furlongs and on the final day took the C.B. Fisher Plate. This was a per-formance of brilliance and versatility which has never been equalled. Sent to the Widden Stud, Maltster was leading Australian sire on five occasions between 1909-15. His best progeny were Malt King, the Victoria Derby winner Alawa and Couronne, who was the dam of Valicare.

MALUA

1880 b horse St Albans – Edella

The most versatile of all Australian gal-lopers, Malua won in the best company from three and a half furlongs to three and a quar-ter miles. Bred in Tasmania he is – with Sydeston – one of the two greatest horses to come from that State. Racing as Bagot he won the Entally Cup in Tasmania. Thomas Reibey then sold him to John Inglis, who renamed the horse Malua. Taken to Melbourne, Malua won the 1884 Newmarket and the first Oakleigh Plate, with 60kg. He then jumped drastically in distance, but took the Adelaide Cup at his next start, with 57kg. Before the end of the year Malua added the Melbourne Cup, under 61.5kg, to his varied and imposing record. Shortly before he had won the Melbourne Stakes. The Geelong Cup and the 1886 Australian Cup, where he carried 61.5kg, now fell to Malua. A record already incredi-ble in these days was further and improbably enriched when Malua, ridden by Inglis, car-ried 73kg to beat The Yeoman and The Victim in the 1888 Grand National Hurdle at Flemington. Inglis also rode the horse when – with big weights – he finished down the line in the 1887 and 1888 Melbourne Cups. Nor was Malua finished with: he had begun stud duties in 1886 and a son, Malvolio emulated his sire by winning the 1891 Melbourne Cup.

MANIFOLD FAMILY

This wealthy family of Western District pastoralists has had a long association with racing in Victoria. Edward Manifold (1868-1931) was a noted owner of jumpers and a long-time member of the committee of the V.R.C. He won the Great Eastern Steeplechase in successive years (1895-6) with Waterloo and Dungan. The V.R.C.

named in his honour the Edward Manifold Stakes, which was first contested in 1932 and is now a Group Two fillies' semi-classic run over 1600m in the spring at Flemington. Edward's nephew Chester, later Sir Chester Manifold (1897-1979) ran the Talindert Stud at Camperdown. His best horse was the great steeplechaser Crisp. Sometime chairman of the V.R.C., Sir Chester Manifold served as first chairman of the Victorian T.A.B. from 1961 until 1968.

MANIHI

1964 ch horse Matrice – Beauteous

Bred by his owners in South Australia, Manihi was Matrice's best son. A roguish but brilliant galloper, he won 11 of 16 starts. In his home state he won the Breeder's Stakes of 1967. In Melbourne he disgraced himself by running off the track in the Merson Cooper and Sires' Produce Stakes of that year. But in the Newmarket of 1968 Manihi kept his mind on the job, brilliantly defeating Nebo Road and Begonia Belle. Retired to stud in 1970, he produced one of Australia's greatest ever sprinters in Manikato.

MANIKATO

1975 ch gelding Manihi – Markato

One of the most durable of all champion Australian racehorses, the top-heavy, cantankerous Manikato triumphed over bad legs, a bleeding attack, and the demands of campaigning for six seasons. A bargain buy, he was purchased for $3500 by Bob Hoysted for Mal Seccull and was first trained by Bob's brother Bon. Cranbourne was the humble setting for Manikato's first start, in January 1978, which he duly won by six lengths. Karaman then beat him in town, but Manikato scored at Caulfield before taking his place in the Blue Diamond field. Ridden

by Gary Willetts, and starting at 12/1, Manikato won decisively. The reluctant Hoysted was persuaded to take him to Sydney, where he won the Golden Slipper at 7/2 favourite, before failing behind Karaman in the A.J.C. Sires'. Bon Hoysted died suddenly, and Bob Hoysted began his famous association with Manikato.

In the spring of 1978 Manikato won the Ascot Vale Stakes and the Marlboro Cup, and survived a protest from Karaman (one of the many splendid rivals whom Manikato would take on, defeat and outlast) to win the Caulfield Guineas. Willetts received a three months' suspension. On 29 January 1979, Manikato came to Moonee Valley and won the first of an amazing five successive William Reid Stakes, beating King of the Stars and Family of Man. The first of three C.F. Orr and first of four Futurity Stakes followed, as Manikato stamped his authority on Australian sprint racing. Tried at 2,000m in the Australian Cup, Manikato ran a gallant second to Dulcify. In Sydney he was fourth to that horse in the Rosehill Guineas, before coming back to the more suitable distance of 1400m in the George Ryder Stakes, which he won in race record time. Manikato then carried 57.5kg (a record for his age group) when dead-heating for third in the Doncaster, won by Belmura Lad in Australian record time. Hoysted kept Manikato going, and his campaign ended in Queensland, where in July 1979 he carried a record weight for a three year old (58kg) to victory in the Doomben 10,000, starting at 5/4.

In the spring Manikato began with a victory in the Freeway Stakes (the race now named in his honour); was put away and came back in the new year with his now traditional wins in the Reid, Orr and Futurity Stakes. He took a second Ryder Stakes in Sydney but ran down the line in the Galaxy after a severe bleeding attack. He then enjoyed a long spell, not returning to racing until January 1988 when he celebrated Australia Day with his third William Reid Stakes, followed by a third Orr, and third Futurity. Spelled, Manikato was beaten to the million dollar prize-money target by Kingston Town. At six Manikato carried the Bernborough-like weight of 63.5kg to win the Bernborough Handicap at Sandown, then lumped 60.5kg into second place in the 1981 Marlboro Cup. With Roy Higgins up he won the Queen Elizabeth Cup over 1600m in track record time before going lame in the Chirnside, in which he was second. Back in the autumn of 1982, with Willetts again in the saddle, Manikato won his fourth Reid Stakes before running second to Galleon in the Futurity, breaking that sequence, although he was not yet done with the race.

Taken once more to Sydney, Manikato won the Canterbury Stakes but pulled up sore after a third in the All Aged. Again he returned, winning the Freeway and Memsie in the spring of 1982. A couple of beaten efforts led some to think that the champion was past his best, but on 23 October, the day that Kingston Town won his third Cox Plate, Manikato topped the $1,000,000 mark by winning the Moir Stakes from Razor Sharp. In the new year an astounding fifth Reid victory came, and a fourth Futurity. Manikato was beaten a head in the Lightning Stakes in between, while in Sydney he ran second to the brilliant mare Emancipation in the Ryder. Finally his legs gave out. Hoysted retired the champion, whose health worsened so quickly that he died on 13 February 1984. Manikato is buried in a memorial garden at Moonee Valley, the track which was the scene of his greatest deeds.

MANNERISM
1987 b mare Amyntor – Northwood Manor

This top-line mare's career began modestly with a win in a Kyneton maiden in September 1990. Over the summer of 1990-1, Mannerism – trained by Lee Freedman – strung together wins at Sandown, Flemington and Moonee Valley. Freedman sent her to Adelaide where she won the Australasian Oaks, first of her four Group One victories. Back in Melbourne she won the Kewney Stakes. Kept on the move, Mannerism was third in the Storm Queen at Randwick and then third to Triscay in the A.J.C. Oaks. Back in the spring of 1991, the mare was third in the Memsie Stakes, before showing her relish for a wet track when Darren Gauci sent her home by four lengths in the Feehan Stakes at Moonee Valley. After that win she bled, and had to be spelled. Returning in the autumn, Mannerism's big win was the Futurity Stakes. Then she was off the scene again until the spring, when regular jockey Damien Oliver partnered her in successive victories in the Milady Stakes, the Group One Show Day Cup and the Caulfield Cup. In that race, Mannerism scored by a short half head after Veandercross' jockey, Shane Dye, had steered his mount to the centre of the wet track. Back in the autumn of 1993, Mannerism was third in the Blamey, then won the Matron Stakes. She then ran third in the All Aged Stakes at Randwick to Rough Habit and Naturalism, before earning an honourable retirement later in the year.

MARAUDING
1984 ch horse Sir Tristram – Biscalowe

The Golden Slipper was always the target for the beautifully bred Marauding after he was narrowly beaten by Maizcay in the Silver Slipper Stakes. Resuming in the autumn of

1987, Marauding beat Snippets by two lengths in the Penfolds Classic at Newcastle before accounting for Lygon Arms in the Todman Slipper Stakes. In the Golden Slipper, the Brian Mayfield-Smith trained Marauding scraped home by a short head from Lygon Arms. This was jockey Ron Quinton's fourth win in the race. The colt was then third behind Snippets in the A.J.C. Sires' Produce. Stepping up in class in the spring, Marauding was unplaced behind Campaign King in the Premiere and Chelmsford Stakes and was retired after a fifth to Sky Chase in the Gloaming. An early success at stud, he has produced the glamour filly Burst, who won the 1992 two year old Triple Crown in Sydney and King Marauding, winner of the V.R.C. Sires', Manikato and Chirnside Stakes.

MARITANA
1962 ch horse Power House – Carbon Flight

This game, durable and talented horse is better known for his many changes of trainer and for the controversy surrounding one of his starts as a three year old. Trained by Tommy Hughes, Maritana had won three races in succession and run a close third in open company in the Standish Handicap on New Year's Day 1966, so that he went out even money favourite two weeks later in the Argyle Handicap at Moonee Valley. Ridden by Mick Mallyon, Maritana had little luck in running, but stewards opened an inquiry which ended in the disqualification of Mallyon, Hughes and the owner, William Pigram for three years. Hughes and Pigram successfully appealed against the decision, but Pigram sold Maritana; Mallyon's suspension was eventually reduced by six months and Geoff Murphy took over as the horse's trainer.

Maritana won four of his next eight starts and was also second in both the Stradbroke and Doomben 10,000. With Roy Higgins up he won the Invitation Stakes (now the Show Day Cup) at Caulfield. Transferred to Doug Murdoch's stables, Maritana suffered leg problems and was unraced at six. Tony Lopes was his next trainer and under his care Maritana won the Liston Stakes of 1969 by three lengths from Winfreux and Rain Lover. The horse soon found himself in another stable, that of A.F. Honeychurch, for whom he won races at Benalla and Wagga. Back in town, Maritana took a Sandown welter and ran second to Black Onyx in the C.F. Orr Stakes. In 1971 he won six of nine races, including four in town, one of which was the weight-for-age Linlithgow Stakes. Few weight-for-age races have fallen to nine year olds. Maritana raced on in 1972, before finally being deemed to have earned retirement.

MARLBORO CUP
  see INVITATION STAKES

MARSCAY
1979 ch horse Biscay – Heart of Market

Trained by Jack Denham, Marscay burst onto the racing scene with a five lengths win at Rosehill on debut in the spring of 1981. On the strength of that run he was 8/1 on two weeks later and scampered home by eight lengths. Put away with the Golden Slipper in mind, Marscay resumed in January 1982. He beat Hot Opera by a length with the third horse 10 lengths adrift and then cantered in at odds on in his next two runs. The fine New Zealand colt Mr McGinty had his measure in the Todman Slipper, scoring by a short half head, but then broke down. This cleared the way in the Golden Slipper, which Marscay won by two lengths from Vaindarra and Grosvenor. The colt was spelled after running third behind the 200/1 chance Mighty Manitou in the A.J.C. Sires' Produce. He resumed on a winning note at three in the Up and Coming Stakes; won the Hobartville, but was then retired to stud after being unplaced in the Canterbury and Rosehill Guineas. At stud he has already sired the winners of more than $16 million. Two of his best have been fillies Triscay and the 1993 Golden Slipper winner Bint Marscay although the Marscay colt March Hare scored in the 1993 Champagne Stakes.

MARTINI-HENRY
1880 b colt Musket – Sylvia

Bought in New Zealand by the Hon. James White, Martini-Henry was with Trenton among the best sons of the imported English sire Musket. The champion Carbine was of course, the pick of them. Martini-Henry did not race at two, but his track work created a sensational impression at Randwick the following year. Unfortunately illness saw him miss a start in the A.J.C. Derby. Sent to Melbourne, Martini-Henry was set for the Derby-Melbourne Cup double and duly obliged White, who had backed his colt to win 25,000 pounds. Having easily won the Derby, Martini-Henry took the 1883 Melbourne Cup in record time, starting at 3/1 favourite, and then scored in the Mares' Produce Stakes on the last day of the spring carnival. He was never to reach these heights again. While he won the 1884 V.R.C. St Leger, he was unplaced in three starts in Sydney that autumn and broke down later in the year in the Caulfield Cup. Sent to White's Kirkham Stud, Martini-Henry again proved his mettle, siring Litigant, who won the 1890 V.R.C. Oaks, the 1889 Caulfield Guineas winner Rudolph, Singapore who won that year's A.J.C. Derby and Mons Meg (bred to northern hemisphere time) who won the Ascot Gold Vase in England.

MARVEL
1897 blk horse Marvellous – La Belle

An outstanding performer of the late colonial period of Australian racing, Marvel's record boasts a four length win over Carbine in the 1891 All Aged Stakes. In that year his other victories included the Epsom, Craven Plate and in Victoria the Melbourne, Royal Park and Caulfield Stakes. Next year he was third in the All Aged Stakes at Randwick, before turning out later the same afternoon to win the Cumberland Plate over two miles. The 1892 Doncaster saw Marvel hump 65.5kg to a notable victory. Marvel was still a top performer at seven when he was beaten a head in another Cumberland Stakes after recording a second victory in the All Aged Stakes from Loyalty and Carnage.

MARVEL LOCH
1899 ch mare Lochiel – Marvelette

The best daughter of the top sire Lochiel, Marvel Loch was a brilliant staying mare. She won the Tramway in 1903 and the Metropolitan. In 1905 she scored in the Chelmsford Stakes before being set for the Caulfield Cup by her trainer T.F. Scully. Unwell in the month before the race,. Marvel Loch recovered sufficiently to run second in the Caulfield Stakes. Scully kept the work up to the mare, running her in the middle day of the Caulfield carnival. She was second in the Eclipse Stakes to Emir, but was granted the race when he weighed in light. In the Caulfield Cup Marvel Loch was at the generous odds of 10/1 but she won convincingly. Nor was that the end for her, as she took the 1906 Rawson Stakes in her next campaign as a rising seven year old.

MATRICE

1951 ch horse Masthead – La Patrice

Not only a top-line galloper, Matrice became in 1974 the first Australian-bred stallion since Spearfelt to win the Australian sires' premiership. On the track he won 27 times, often carrying huge weights. For instance, in his second successive win in the Cheltenham Christmas Handicap, in 1956, Matrice had 65.5kg. As a three year old he won the Adelaide Guineas. At four he was second in the Goodwood at Morphettville, then went one better the next year, when he carried 60.5kg. Matrice also proved himself against the best weight-for-age company in Melbourne, where he won the Cantala (now Nissan) Stakes in 1956 and consecutive Linlithgow Stakes in 1956-7 at the Flemington Spring Carnival. His best son was Manihi, who in turn sired Manikato.

MAYBE MAHAL

1972 b mare Maybe Lad – Faithfully Yours

An outstanding sprinter-miler of the 1970s, Maybe Mahal won no less than five Group One handicaps. A precocious two year old, she won seven of 12 starts, but at three she lost all form. From nine starts Maybe Mahal failed to win and owner D.H. Reid retired her to stud. When she was unable to get in foal, Bart Cummings persuaded Reid to put the mare back into training. It was a decision richly rewarded. In the spring of 1976 Maybe Mahal won the Craven 'A'-George Adams double, while in the autumn of the next year she won the Lightning Stakes and was beaten a short half head by Desirable in the Newmarket. Wintering in Brisbane, she won the Doomben 10,000 with 56.5kg from Romantic Dream. Her Melbourne career was capped off in the autumn of 1978 when she won a second Lightning Stakes and the Newmarket in 1.9, again under 56.5kg. At

Flemington, Maybe Mahal won five times and was placed on three occasions from 11 starts. Finally in Sydney she beat Always Welcome, who had also finished second to her in the Newmarket, in the A.J.C. Doncaster. In all she won 14 of her 44 starts, before being sent back to stud a second time.

MELBOURNE CUP

'The Australasian Nation Day' was how the American author Mark Twain justly styled the carnival of the Melbourne Cup. For, he added, it 'commands an attention, an interest, and an enthusiasm which are universal and spontaneous, not perfunctory'. The Melbourne Cup, as Twain discerned, is the true Australian folk festival, in which scores of thousands mingle at Flemington on the first Tuesday in November; many millions more watch on television around the nation, around the world. All this for a 3200m quality handicap, which has been won by champions and occasionally by ordinary horses; a race which often spells the end of its winners' careers; that has been won by jockeys as inexperienced as Ray Neville, while eluding the likes of Scobie Breasley and George Moore.

The Melbourne Cup originated in 1861 as a result of one upmanship between the Victoria Jockey Club and the Victoria Turf Club. In 1861 the Turf Club decided to introduce a two mile handicap, to be called the Melbourne Cup. Club members met at the Albion Hotel in Bourke Street on 9 September 1861 to approve the programme for the spring meeting. Four races were framed for the first of the three days: a Maiden Plate, Two Year Old Stakes, a Handicap Hurdle – and the Melbourne Cup. Prize-money for the Cup was 710 sovereigns and 4,000 people came to Flemington to see Archer win the inaugural running. As one spectator observed:

"There was no grandstand, there were no ladies except for the wives of a few bookies, no fashion parades – and the course itself was just a long path in long grass which had been roughly scythed down for the occasion."

Archer won the Cup again in 1862, but when his late nomination was refused in the following year, New South Wales trainers boycotted the race and only seven starters presented themselves. Banker won the Cup. With the V.T.C. and V.J.C. in the doldrums, their members decided to dissolve each club and constitute a new one. From 1864, the fortunes of the Melbourne Cup have been in the hands of the Victoria Racing Club.

The V.R.C. committee determined to make the day one of high fashion. Under the secretaryship of Robert Bagot, the facilities of the course were rapidly improved, so that a feature of Cup Day has long been the vast crowds which come to the course – by car, by rail, on foot, by boat up the Maribyrnong River. Crowds routinely top 90,000 on Cup Day. When Spearfelt won in 1926, almost 120,000 came to Flemington. Cup Day is also the highpoint of the gambling mania that early established itself in Australia. Vast sums are wagered on the race and on the Caulfield-Melbourne Cup double (usually to the enormous profit of bookmakers, although not in 1930 when Amounis and Phar Lap cleaned them out). Cup Day has since the late 1860s been a public holiday in Melbourne (in one of the smartest of the initiatives of the V.R.C.). Elsewhere, it proverbially is 'the race that stops a nation'. The Melbourne Cup is the only Australian race with a truly international reputation, fit to be spoken of in the same breath, if not in the same terms, as the Derby at Epsom, the Prix de l'Arc de Triomphe at Longchamps and the Kentucky Derby.

Great winners dot its roll-call: The Barb in 1866, the filly Briseis 10 years later, the unbeaten Grand Flaneur in 1880, Malua in 1884, the champion Carbine, who in 1890 carried 63.5kg to victory. Poseidon became the first horse to complete the Caulfield-Melbourne Cup double, in 1906. Poitrel, Windbag and Nightmarch were sterling winners in the 1920s, while the incomparable Phar Lap saw in the new decade. One of Australia's greatest stayers – Peter Pan – became the first dual winner since Archer when he won the Cup in 1932 and 1934. It was in that decade that Wotan (in 1936) became the second 100/1 winner of the Cup, following The Pearl in 1871. Old Rowley was at the same odds in 1940; Rimfire at 80/1 in his controversial photo finish victory over Dark Marne in 1948. Comic Court ushered in a vintage group when he won the Cup in record time in 1950. He was followed by Delta and Dalray, by the champion Rising Fast in 1954. That horse came back in 1955 to suffer a desperately unlucky loss that robbed him of the first double Cups double. In 1965 the superb mare Light Fingers narrowly gave trainer Bart Cummings the first of what is so far a record nine Melbourne Cups. Another came with the top stayer Galilee the next year, with Light Fingers second. Quinellas have also been a Cummings' Cup specialty: he has recorded an astonishing five of them. Rain Lover was a dual winner in 1968-9; the Cummings-trained Think Big in 1974-5 (having gone without a win in between). Van Der Hum ploughed through a bog in 1976 in slower time than had been taken for the Cup Hurdle. Gurner's Lane completed the Cups double in 1982, while Kiwi was one of many New Zealand-bred champions to salute, coming from last to win in 1983. Jockeys have set their seal on the race as well: Bobbie Lewis won four times from 33 rides; Harry White has also had four victories in the race.

After a period in the 1970s especially when the Cup was often won by plodding stayers, it has again become in the last decade a race of the highest quality, with winners of the calibre of the imported At Talaq in 1986, the grand mares Empire Rose (1988) and Let's Elope (1992), while the hit and run raid by the Irish-trained Vintage Crop in 1993 showed that he was a stayer of the highest order, and gave an international savour to a race which was won by an imported horse (Comedy King) as long ago as 1910. Sadly the Cup is no longer the province of top three year olds. None has won since Skipton in 1941, although Tulloch would have been very skinny odds if he had started in 1957.

A great horse race, the Melbourne Cup is also the centrepiece of a grand democratic Australian carnival, a truer expression of the national spirit than any imposed celebration could be. It has featured in numerous novels and in film: several of Nat Gould's racing novels use the Cup as background – *The Double Event* (1891) and *A Racing Sinner* (1902) among them, while Arthur Upfield's first assignment for the Melbourne *Herald* was to write a racing serial, 'The Great Melbourne Cup Mystery' (1932).

The Melbourne Cup will continue to claim a decisive and richly expressive place in the national culture.

MELBOURNE RACE CLUB/ RACING CLUB

The Melbourne Race Club was formed early in 1838 after a meeting at John Pascoe Fawkner's Market Street hotel, with Henry Allen as the first chairman. A course was marked out from the site of the present North Melbourne Station to where Spencer Street Station now stands. The first meeting was held on 6-7 March 1838. A longer-lived Melbourne Racing Club was established

after the post-war racing rationalisation which led to the merger of the Williamstown Racing Club and the Victorian Trotting and Racing Association in 1948. The M.R.C. was given the right to stage meetings at the other three metropolitan courses. To the merger the W.R.C. had brought cash, the V.T.R.A. land at Springvale where eventually the new Sandown Park track was built. However the M.R.C. proved not to be viable, and from the start of the 1963 racing season it merged with the V.A.T.C.

MELBOURNE STAKES
see MACKINNON STAKES

MERMAN
1892 ch horse Grand Flaneur – Seaweed

Bred at the Hobartville Stud by W.R. Wilson, who raced the horse himself, Merman had one of the most curious careers of any Australian horse. He showed little promise early, winning minor races in Melbourne and Adelaide. Some staying ability was evident when he ran fourth in Cremorne's Caulfield Cup in 1896. Later in the spring he won the Yan Yean Stakes and the Williamstown Cup. The latter win attracted the attention of the actress Lily Langtry, erstwhile companion of the Prince of Wales, but now Lady de Bathe. She had bought the Newmarket winner Maluma during an Australian tour in 1896 and sent him to race in England. Merman was her next, inspired purchase.

Quickly finding his feet in the northern hemisphere, Merman won three races in the 1897 season, including the famous distance race, The Cesarewitch, at Newmarket. He was third in the same event the next year, to Bay Ronald, with another Australian galloper, Newhaven, in second place. In 1899 he won the Goodwood Cup and Goodwood Plate, besides crossing the Channel to run second in the Grand Prix de Deauville under 66kg. Merman was now set for the Ascot Gold Cup. The odds on favourite was the French Triple Crown winner, Perth II, but Merman – at 25/1 – won handily by two lengths. Another Australian horse, The Grafter, was third, while Perth II struggled into fourth place. After this staying triumph, Merman was sent to stud, where he met with scant success.

METRICATION

Decimal currency had been introduced to Australia on 14 February 1966, and six years later the racing industry was nominated to turn metric before the rest of the country. Race-callers complained bitterly. Traditionalists lamented the slight but significant cropping of distances for the great races on the calendar (the 3200m Melbourne Cup, for example, was twenty and a half yards shorter than the two mile version). All previous time records carried the awkward sobriquet 'metrically adjusted'. Nevertheless the racing industry did the bidding of the Metric Conversion Board and weights and distances for all Australian races turned metric forever on 1 August 1972, first day of the new season.

METROPOLITAN HANDICAP

One of the longest established, and – at the turn of the century – richest of Sydney's races, the Metropolitan is now a Group One event over 2600m at the Randwick spring carnival. Bylong, in 1866, is usually recorded as the first winner, although forerunners of the event had been run since 1862, when Talleyrand won the Randwick Grand Handicap. Tim Whiffler won once (in 1867) and was placed on three other occasions, while The Barb scored in 1868. Since then sound stayers more often than champions have won the race, although the good horse Malt King was first home in 1911; Beau Vite

won in 1940; Delta, Dalray and Carioca won between 1951-3 and Redcraze in 1956; Tails scored in 1969-70; the mare Analie in 1973; Battle Heights in 1976 and Ming Dynasty two years later; Belmura Lad in 1981; Hayai in 1983-4. The Metropolitan has been a reliable form guide to place-getters in the two big spring cups in Melbourne, most recently when the 1993 winner Te Akau Nick went on to second behind Vintage Crop in the Melbourne Cup of that year.

MIDSTREAM
1933 b horse Blandford – Midsummer

In three seasons of racing in England, the beautifully-bred Midstream won only four times. But his bloodlines appealed to Percy Miller of the Kia Ora Stud. On his behalf, Clarrie Hailey bought Midstream for 3,500 guineas at a sale at Newmarket in 1937. Midstream arrived in Australia early in 1938 and stood here for the first time in the 1938-9 season. In a distinguished career, Midstream produced such classic winners as Deep River (1952 A.J.C. Derby) and Waterlady (a dual Oaks winner). From Midstream's third crop came Murray Stream, who won two Metropolitans, and one of the greatest of Australian milers, Shannon, who went on to race with distinction in the United States. Midstream was leading Australian sire in 1947-8, 1950-1 and 1951-2, second on four occasions, third on two. He produced 31 individual stakeswinners.

MIGHTY KINGDOM
1976 ch horse Planet Kingdom – Madam Borough

The Tommy Smith-trained colt Mighty Kingdom, by the Star Kingdom sire Planet Kingdom, gave early indications of quality. At two he won the 1979 V.R.C. Sires' Produce from Bold Diplomat and then finished second to Charity in the A.J.C.

Champagne Stakes. Returning in the spring of 1979, the colt won the Chelmsford Stakes from Gypsy Kingdom in record time, but was then beaten five lengths by his stablemate Kingston Town in the Spring Champion Stakes. Smith sent the pair to Melbourne where they staged some sterling battles. Mighty Kingdom beat no less than Shivaree in the Caulfield Stakes, while Kingston Town was third in the Caulfield Guineas. Smith set Mighty Kingdom for the Caulfield Cup and the colt obliged with a win, at 10/1, from Warri Symbol. In consequence Mighty Kingdom started favourite in the Victoria Derby, but was fourth behind Big Print and the desperately unlucky Kingston Town. While the latter was readied for Sydney and Brisbane campaigns, Mighty Kingdom travelled west. It was a profitable jaunt: he won the Marlboro 50,000, the Western Australian Derby and was then third to Lloyd's Gold and Brava Jeannie in the Australian Derby. Returning in the spring of 1980, Mighty Kingdom's best was a second to Grey Sapphire in the Liston Stakes. He was then sent to stud.

MING DYNASTY
1973 gr gelding Planet Kingdom – Chow Mien

Slow to mature, this popular grey gelding became a first rate handicapper and weight for age performer. As a two year old he won once from six outings, but his six wins from 16 starts at three included the A.J.C. Summer Cup and the S.T.C. Tulloch Stakes. Trained and part-owned by Bart Cummings, Ming Dynasty came into his own at four, when he won the 1977 Caulfield Cup, the Australian Cup, the Craiglee and Queen Elizabeth Stakes. At five he added the Chelmsford Stakes, Craven Plate and Metropolitan to his imposing record in two states, besides running fifth in the 1978 Caulfield Cup under 61kg. Thereafter his

form tapered off and in his third try in the Caulfield Cup of 1979 he could finish only 15th to Mighty Kingdom. But Ming Dynasty had one shot left in his locker. His only victory in 12 starts at seven came when he beat no less than Hyperno and Kingston Town in the 1980 Caulfield Cup. Ming Dynasty started unfancied at 50/1. He went on to enjoy a second racing career as a clerk of the course's horse.

MOLLISON
1925 b gelding Seremond – Molly's Robe

A brilliant young horse, Mollison was out of the fine sprinter Molly's Robe. As a two year old, in Fred Foulsham's care, he was unbeaten in seven starts. His wins included both the A. J. C. and V. R. C. Sires' Produce Stakes, and the A.J.C. Champagne Stakes. Mollison began his three year old campaign with wins in the Hobartville Stakes and the Rosehill Guineas, after which he failed in the A.J.C. Derby. In the autumn, Mollison campaigned successfully in Melbourne, where he won the Futurity and C.M. Lloyd Stakes. Back in Sydney, the All Aged Stakes of 1929 fell to Mollison. When he then beat Phar Lap in the Chelmsford Stakes, his quality was confirmed, but it proved to be the last race that Mollison won.

MOLLY'S ROBE
1915 ch mare Syce – Microbe

One of the best performed and popular sprinting mares to come out of Queensland, Molly's Robe raced in the period just after the Great War. As a two year old she won five of seven in her home state, including a victory in an Open Flying Handicap. Sent to Melbourne, Molly's Robe was beaten a half head in the 1919 Oakleigh Plate by Cielo, but made amends with victory in the Newmarket. The following year she carried

58.5kg to victory in the Oakleigh Plate, and won with up to 63kg on Melbourne tracks. She was never as successful in Sydney, although she finished second in the 1920 All Aged Stakes and fourth in a Doncaster. Primarily a sprinter, Molly's Robe was versatile enough to win two Q.T.C. King's Plates over 11 furlongs. She retired with 16 wins and 15 placings from 45 starts, and then further distinguished herself as the dam of the brilliant juvenile, Mollison.

MOLONEY, JIM (1924-)

Son of a Western Districts trainer, Jim Moloney set up in his own right at Warrnambool in the 1940s. His first success came over the jumps, with Llandrillo, winner of the Grand National Steeple in 1950 and the Australian Steeple in the next year. Swynphilos was Moloney's first big winner on the flat, when he won the 1955 Newmarket. The trainer moved to Epsom in the 1950s, but continued to battle for a living, having his main successes in Warrnambool or across the border at South Australian tracks. His fortunes forever changed when the champion Vain came into his yard. Brilliant winner of the 1969 Golden Slipper, Vain capped his career by winning on three days of the Spring Carnival at Flemington that year. Now good horses came Moloney's way. Vain was retired in 1970, not long before Arctic Symbol won the Sydney Cup for Moloney. Plush was a prolific winner for the stable, his biggest successes being in the Ascot Vale and Moonee Valley Stakes, and the Toorak Handicap of 1975. Sou'wester won the Caulfield Guineas for Moloney in the same year. He had to wait until 1982 for a classic winner, when Rom's Stiletto took the Thousand Guineas and V.R.C. Oaks; four more years for a Derby winner, when Raveneaux scored at Flemington. In between Pat Hyland, appren-

ticed to Moloney in 1958, and associated with him for more than 30 years, combined with the trainer to win the 1984 Caulfield Cup on Affinity. Moloney was able to put Hyland, just recovered from a bad fall, on to Mighty Avenger to win the 1985 Centenary Goodwood Handicap. Moloney continues to train at Epsom, and two of his sons have gone into that taxing business as well.

MOONEE VALLEY CUP

A Moonee Ponds Cup was first run at W.S. Cox's Moonee Valley track in 1883, and was won by the filly Castaway. Traditionally the race was run on the Saturday before the Derby. It has proved a solid trial for the Melbourne Cup, although only four horses: Clean Sweep (1900), Blue Spec (1905), Wodalla (1953) and Kingston Rule (1990) have won the double. Until 1900 a sprint race, the Moonee Valley Cup is now a Group Two event over 2600m, overshadowed by the Cox Plate which is held the same day. This is a development that dates from after World War Two. Earlier the Cup had been the richer race. In 1891 such interest was attracted in the event that it was divided into a Cup and a consolation Purse. Little Bob won the first of successive Moonee Valley Cups in that year. Gladwyn (1914-5), Gilltown (1939-40) and Valcurl (1945-6) are other multiple winners of an event that has attracted strong, rather than brilliant stayers. Shadow King had a deserved change of fortune when he won in 1930. Better winners of the race have included Ngawyni in 1977, Sydeston in 1989, near the start of his mainland career, and the brilliant, lightly-raced Kingston Rule who won the Moonee Valley-Melbourne Cup double in 1990. Clear Day was the controversial winner from Hyperno in 1978 when Roy Higgins dropped his hands and failed to ride his mount out near the post.

MOONEE VALLEY RACING CLUB

Established in 1917 at a meeting in the inner city Hosies Hotel in Melbourne, the M.V.R.C. had as its first chairman Alister Clark, who served for 42 years; as its first secretary A.V. Hiskens, who held his position until 1935. The club leased the Moonee Valley racecourse from the Cox family; built a new grandstand there in 1925 and was able to buy the freehold in 1929, for 160,000 pounds. While the Moonee Valley Cup remained its principal event until after the Second World War, the Cox Plate – established in 1922 – and the William Reid Stakes (1925) are now feature events on the M.V.R.C.'s programme. The club is perhaps the most astutely self-promoting in the Melbourne racing scene, turning to advantage the physical limitations of such a small racing circuit, albeit one so centrally situated.

MOONEE VALLEY RACECOURSE

Smallest of the Melbourne metropolitan tracks, Moonee Valley is situated by the Moonee Ponds creek a few kilometres to the north-west of the city. The site was originally Feehan's Farm (a name remembered in the Group Two Feehan Stakes run at Moonee Valley in the spring). W.S. Cox, owner of the nearby Kensington track, purchased what is now Moonee Valley in 1882 and gradually shifted his main racing operations there. The Cox family was to control Moonee Valley for decades. Its first meeting was held in September 1883. Cox ensured that the prime date between the Caulfield and Melbourne spring carnivals was kept by Moonee Valley: it is now Cox Plate day, and that race has been run there since 1922. The course was extended and its grandstands improved from 1906-9; a new stand was built in 1925 and further extensions occurred five years later, but Moonee Valley is still an intimate amphitheatre with a short straight that

tests jockeys' skills. Control of the course passed from the Cox family to the Moonee Valley Racing Club in 1917. Moonee Valley was the first metropolitan course in Melbourne to have a totalisator and has been in the forefront of racing promotion since the 1970s, when it also became home to Melbourne's harness-racing industry, by means of a track inside the turf circuit.

MOONEE VALLEY STAKES

This Group Two race over 1600m has now established itself as a crucial lead-up event to the Caulfield Guineas and Victoria Derby later in the Melbourne spring. First run in 1934, when Titanium won, it was not until the 1960s that the Moonee Valley Stakes began to attract winners of distinction. Lady Sybil won in 1960, New Statesman the year after that, while from 1966-9 the winners were Storm Queen, Always There, Fileur and Daryl's Joy, the latter in an upset victory over Vain. Eastern Court beat Gay Icarus in 1970. The winners in the succeeding years were Beau Sovereign, Century, Taj Rossi, Plush, Denise's Joy and Surround. Since then, top-line winners have been more scarce, although Red Anchor, Broad Reach, Sky Chase and Zabeel saluted in the 1980s, Canny Lad in 1990. The race is now named in honour of a former M.V.R.C. committeeman, Bill Stutt. It was the first Melbourne feature event to be moved to Sunday, in order to follow the A.F.L. Grand Final.

MOORE, FRANK ('TIGER') (1925-)

Perhaps the most successful of all Western Australian jockeys, 'Tiger' Moore rode more than 2,000 winners in Australia and in Malaysia. He is best remembered for his multiple classic wins in his home state. While only the 1956 Perth Cup fell to him, Moore rode seven W.A. Derby winners, and scored his eighth Oaks winner (on Our Pocket) and ninth St Leger winner in 1974, the year in which he announced his retirement.

MOORE, GARY (1952-)

The son of one of Australia's greatest ever jockeys, Gary Moore proved his ability to compete in top international company for decades. He rode briefly in France for Alec Head in 1967 before completing his apprenticeship with Tommy Hill in Sydney. In 1970 he was back in France to ride for Maurice Zilber. When his father set up as a trainer in Hong Kong, Gary Moore joined him and won four consecutive premierships in the mid-1970s while his father was taking out training honours. Back in France, where his wife had been born, Moore scored his biggest race win on Gold Iver in the 1981 Prix de l'Arc de Triomphe. He returned to Hong Kong, where a long disqualification ended his riding career.

MOORE, GEORGE (1923-)

Born in Mackay, Queensland, the son of a sugar farmer, George Moore became one of the greatest of all Australian jockeys. Apprenticed to Jim Shean in Brisbane, he rode his first winner at Eagle Farm on New Year's Day 1940. Soon afterwards he shifted to Sydney, but army service caused a three year hiatus in his career. After the war, Moore became associated with the battling Sydney trainer Tommy Smith. Moore's first big race win was in the 1946 Metropolitan on Cordale; his first classic on Smith's colt Playboy in the 1949 A.J.C. Derby. A long, often stormy partnership was thereby established. The worst check to Moore's career occurred in 1954 when he was disqualified at the A.J.C.'s pleasure (he served two and a half) for allegedly giving misleading evidence concerning the running of a race at Hawkesbury in which he was said to have

had a proprietary interest in one of the horses. Moore returned to racing a harder man. The measure of his determination – and of his exceptional ability – is that he averaged a winner in just over every three rides which he took.

He rode the champion Tulloch for Smith in the 1957 season and thereafter. His tally of big race wins in Australia included five A.J.C. and two Victoria Derbies; Cox Plates on Redcraze (1957) and Rajah Sahib (1968); three Doncasters and two Epsoms; three Sydney Cups; Golden Slipper Stakes on Baguette and Fairy Walk in 1970-1. In his home state Moore won three Queensland Derbies, three Stradbrokes, five Doomben 10,000s, three Doomben Cups and a Brisbane Cup. In 1957 Moore decided to try his luck in Europe, riding principally for the Freddie Head stable in France. In 1959 he won the Prix de l'Arc de Triomphe on Saint Crespin; the French Derby the following year. After a spell back in Australia, Moore returned to ride for Noel Murless in England. He won the Epsom Derby on Royal Palace in 1967. Other big race wins in England included the 1,000 and 2,000 Guineas and the Ascot Gold Cup.

Back in Australia, Moore emphatically showed his detractors that he was far from done with by riding 15 winners at the 1969 Randwick autumn carnival. In 1970 he retired after winning the Champagne Stakes on Baguette but was lured back for one more campaign. In 1971 he won his second Golden Slipper, the Newmarket on Baguette, Doncaster on Rajah Sahib. His final big race triumph as a jockey came when he won the 1971 Victoria Derby on Classic Mission. This time Moore retired for good. He had been premier jockey in Brisbane as an apprentice; won 10 senior riders' premierships in Sydney; never won a Caulfield or Melbourne Cup. In the mid-1970s, Moore was for a number of seasons leading trainer in Hong Kong (while his son Gary was leading jockey). He retired in the early 1980s and moved to the Gold Coast, thus concluding one of the most skilled and lucrative careers that any Australian jockey has enjoyed.

MOORE, HENRY BYRON (1839-1925)

Born in England, Byron Moore came to Australia with his family in 1852. He worked as a surveyor and land commissioner in Victoria. Varied interests saw him establish the Melbourne Electric Light Company and the Melbourne Telephone Exchange Company. In June 1881 he became secretary of the Victoria Racing Club, a position which he held until the year of his death. Moore succeeded Robert Bagot. During the term of his office, Flemington was extended through a shrewd land purchase by Moore, new grandstands were built and lawns created. The fame of the Melbourne Cup continued to grow through assiduous promotion. He was instrumental not only in private charitable work but in the creation of the V.R.C. Benevolent Fund 'for racing men in necessitous circumstances'. The V.R.C. named a race in Byron Moore's honour.

MORPHETTVILLE RACECOURSE

Named after Sir John Morphett, on whose Adelaide land the course was built, Morphettville was taken over by the S.A.J.C. in September 1875. In 1881 the first Goodwood Handicap was run there and in the next year a new stand was built. Disaster soon followed: the ban on totalisator and off-course betting jeopardised racing in South Australia and Morphettville fell into disuse by 1884. Eventually it was purchased by a syndicate of self-styled sportsmen who intended to make it available to any reconstituted S.A.J.C. They leased the course back to the club in 1889 and confi-

dence had so far returned to South Australian racing that a new stand was built before the end of the century. Morphettville now hosts the classic races in South Australia, as well as the Adelaide Cup.

MOSSTROOPER

1921 ch gelding Kenilworth – Keego

A much-loved and legendary jumper of the Depression era, Mosstrooper was a duffer on the flat, being placed only once in 18 starts. In 1927 he was sold to Gus Powell, who also trained the horse. His jumping career had an inauspicious beginning, for he fell at his first steeple start. But a golden period began in 1929 when Mosstrooper took the Australian Steeple at Caulfield and the first of consecutive Australian Hurdles. The following year he won the Grand National Hurdle and Steeple double, scoring in the latter with 74.5kg. At Moonee Valley he won the Brunswick, Commonwealth and Travancore Steeplechases. As a 10 year old he was third in the Grand National Hurdle, when conceding 19kg to the winner. In 1932 and 1933 (when 12) he was third in the Grand National Steeple, carrying 80kg on the first occasion, and losing to the champion Redditch on the second.

MOUNTAIN GOD

1914 br gelding Mountain King – Demoiselle

Mountain God is one of the few dual winners of the Grand National Steeplechase at Flemington. He achieved that feat in 1921-2 and it would not be done again until Sir Cameron in 1963-4. In the 1920 running of the race Mountain God lost his rider near the abattoirs, but next year he jumped safely and saluted at 5/2. In 1922 he was asked to carry 80kg but was up to the task and won again, from Resembler, to whom he had to give 21kg.

MOWBRAY RACECOURSE

Situated in the northern suburbs of Launceston, Mowbray was the scene of top quality racing in the 1860s. Panic won the Australian Champion race there in 1865; Fishhook the Champion Cup in 1867; while in 1868 Fireworks despatched probably the best ever field assembled in Tasmania, when Tim Whiffler, Strop and The Barb finished behind him. In 1876 the course was sold to a group which leased it back to the Tasmanian Turf Club. Extensive renovations followed, and when the course re-opened horses and jockeys were required to run the Melbourne rather than the Sydney way. A rail service to the course was introduced in 1887. In 1900 control of Tasmanian racing was Solomonically divided across the middle and the T.T.C. took charge of racing in the north of the state. In 1905 the club bought the freehold to Mowbray and a new grandstand was erected in 1914. The course survived a visit by the Prince of Wales in 1920, a bad flood of the Tamar in 1929. In a rationalisation of Tasmanian racing in the late 1980s, Mowbray became a centre of both trotting and galloping.

MOZART

1879 b horse Napoleon – Queen Mary

Mozart's biggest race win was the Brisbane Cup of 1883. He was to prove his worth at stud in Tasmania, where his best effort on the track had been a second in the Hobart Cup of 1885. Mozart sired a succession of fine stayers. Named with their sire in mind, Amadeus, Music and Timbrel were all Hobart Cup winners. Amadeus won the Hobart-Launceston Cup double in 1894; Music won the Hobart Cup the next year, was third in the Launceston Cup shortly afterwards and won the Williamstown Cup later the same year. Timbrel, a Hobart Cup

winner in 1901, was placed in no fewer than four Launceston Cups.

MR MCGINTY

1979 b horse One Pound Sterling – Ernader

A brilliant juvenile in New Zealand, the Colin Jillings-trained McGinty (he became Mr to avoid confusion with another horse when he travelled to Australia) was set the unprecedented task of becoming the first New Zealander to win the Golden Slipper. In the 1982 Todman Slipper Trial, Mr McGinty won brilliantly from Marscay, but fractured a cannon bone and was turned out, his racing future seemingly doubtful. Marscay went on to win the Slipper. Mr McGinty recovered and a year later was back in Sydney, where he won the Canterbury Guineas in record time, before finishing third in the Tancred Stakes. Mr McGinty was then second in the Rosehill Guineas to no less than Strawberry Road. In the spring of 1983, Mr McGinty was second to Emancipation in the George Main Stakes before being taken to Melbourne. There he won the Caulfield Stakes; was third in the Cox Plate behind Strawberry Road and Kiwi Slave and wound up the spring carnival with a second to Fountaincourt in the Queen Elizabeth Stakes. In the autumn of 1984, Mr McGinty won the Air New Zealand Stakes before being taken to Sydney where he was third in the Chipping Norton behind Emancipation. Mr McGinty recorded another big race win when he beat Trissaro in the Rawson Stakes. Subsequently Mr McGinty was retired to stud, where he resumed his former name.

MULLEY, ATHOL (1924-)

Son of a Grafton dairy farmer, Mulley was apprenticed to Bayley Payten at Randwick. Eventually he succeeded Darby Munro as

Payten's stable jockey. Mulley rode his first winner, at Canterbury, in July 1940 at his eighth race ride. In his first season as a senior rider, 1945-6, he won the Sydney jockeys' premiership, a feat he repeated in 1960-1. Mulley rode with success in India and Singapore for 10 years; had stints in France and England but found the climate uncongenial. In Australia Mulley won A.J.C. Derbies on Caranna (1955) and Persian Lyric (1960); Epsoms with High Law (1952) and Rochdale (1962) and Golden Slippers with Skyline (1958) and Eskimo Prince (1964). His most famous association was with Bernborough, the great horse whom he rode to 15 consecutive victories between December 1945 and October 1946, and to a controversial defeat in the Caulfield Cup. Known for his skills as a raconteur and also for a combative nature, which led to some celebrated jockeys' room altercations with George Moore, Mulley retired after losing the sight of one eye after twice being struck by clods during races. He trained for a while at Warwick Farm, Canberra and Coff's Harbour, before his retirement.

MUNRO, DAVID HUGH (DARBY) (1913-66)

Born in Melbourne, Darby Munro moved to Sydney with his parents when he was one and was subsequently apprenticed to his brother John. His first race win, on Release, was achieved at the expense of another brother, Jim Munro. Venetian Lady gave the jockey his first big race win in the Doncaster of 1930, but Hall Mark was the first of many champions with whom he was associated. He took the A.J.C. and Victoria Derbies of 1933 on Hall Mark, but could not make the weight for the Melbourne Cup which the horse won as well, with J. O'Sullivan riding. In that triumphant spring, Munro also won the Cox Plate, on Rogilla. A Melbourne Cup

followed the next year, when he took the champion Peter Pan wide through muddy going to win at 14/1 by three lengths under 62kg. Other victories in the Cup followed on Sirius on 1944 and Russia 1946. During the war, Munro had been able to ride while enlisted in the Army Service Corps. He was discharged because of ulcers in 1944.

Swarthy of complexion, Munro was known as 'The Demon Darb', and by other less flattering epithets by punters who rejoiced in his victories but gave him a harder time than most when he was beaten. Munro unjustly suffered a vicious demonstration after the 1946 Epsom which he unluckily lost on Shannon, who missed the start by many lengths through the negligence of the starter, not the jockey. In 1948 Munro's career received its gravest setback when he was suspended for two years for his ride on Vagabond in the Burwood Handicap on Caulfield Cup day. While the trainer and owner had their appeals upheld, Munro's penalty stood. In hindsight, he seems to have been unjustly treated after a canny ride on a most difficult horse. It was that suspension which cost Munro the chance to ride in England in 1953, although he rode in the United States and France in that year. Munro's many victories included five of each of the A.J.C. and Victoria Derbies, nine winners at the 1940 A.J.C. Easter carnival, including the Doncaster on Mildura and the Sydney Cup on Mosaic, besides many weight-for-age races. Munro retired in 1955 and trained without conspicuous success. He died after a long period of ill-health, from complications related to ulcers and a diabetic condition. Some posthumous recognition of a great jockey came in 1981 when he featured on an Australian 22 cent stamp.

MUNRO, JIM (1905-74)

Older brother of the jockey Darby

Munro, Jim Munro was an outstanding rider in the great era of the 1920s, before pursuing a successful career overseas. He was apprenticed to his father Hugh Munro, who trained Wakeful and the 1901 Melbourne Cup winner Revenue. Jim's first big winner was the 1922 Sydney Cup on John Brown's Prince Charles. A renowned tactician and judge of pace, Munro partnered many great horses, among them Windbag on whom he won 14 races and Amounis on whom he won 10 times. In 1929 he rode Phar Lap in the horse's first classic success – the Rosehill Guineas.

Troubled by rising weight, Jim Munro accepted an offer to ride in Germany the following year. His retainer was a massive 1,500 pounds. Munro claimed that Alba was the best of any of the horses that he rode. Among his six winning rides on the horse was the Grand Prix at Baden Baden, a Group One race which the Australian champion Strawberry Road would win in 1984. Munro became the third Australian jockey – after Frank Bullock and Brownie Carslake – to win the German Derby. Unhappy with the European cold, Munro returned to ride with success in Australia before weight problems again sent him abroad, this time to India. By 1937 he had retired from riding and trained for a time. He retired to England when his daughter Noelene married the top jockey Geoff Lewis.

MURPHY, GEOFF (1926-1993)

Born in Bacchus Marsh, Murphy strapped racehorses before riding with limited success on the flat and over the jumps. Foreman for Basil Conaghan before setting up to train in his own right, Murphy was based at Caulfield for decades. Known contradictorily for a kind heart and a quick temper, Murphy fell out with most of the leading jockeys who rode for him, but as he explained 'I put my own money on and they don't'. Besides being leading Victorian metropolitan trainer in 1976-7, Murphy was instrumental in popularising the stock of the great New Zealand-based stallions Sovereign Edition and Sir Tristram. Perhaps his best horse was Sovereign Edition's daughter Surround, the only filly to win the Cox Plate, besides taking the Oaks in Victoria, New South Wales and Queensland. Murphy won another Cox Plate with Abdul, the Caulfield and Melbourne Cup double in 1982 with Gurner's Lane and Victoria Derbies with Sovereign Red and Grosvenor. An earlier classic win was denied him in 1961 when Blue Era lost the A.J.C. Derby on protest to Summer Fair in the famous 'leg-pull' incident which saw jockey Mel Schumacher outed for life.

MUSGRAVE, FRANK (1860-1944)

Born at Coleraine, Musgrave rode Goshawk in the 1874 Melbourne Cup as a 14 year old. By 1883 he was established as a trainer at Caulfield. In 1890 Musgrave moved his stables to Ruthen Lodge, Ormond, where he trained for decades. Murmur, owned by John Wren, won the Caulfield Cup of 1904 while trained by Musgrave, but by far the best of his charges was the champion Ajax. In the twilight of his career, Musgrave owned and trained Dark Felt. The horse was still a maiden when Musgrave sold him in 1942 because the war had so limited his stable resources that his hands were full with Ajax. Dark Felt won the 1943 Melbourne Cup.

MYOCARD

1983 b horse Ivory Hunter – Double Game

The New Zealand-bred colt Myocard was taken along patiently by Sydney trainer Dr Geoff Chapman. He won first up, before showing his capacity in good company with wins in the 1986 Brambles Classic at Kembla Grange and then in the Autumn Classic at Caulfield in 1987. His staying prowess was swiftly and dramatically underlined when Myocard went to Sydney for the autumn carnival. First he upset the top New Zealanders Bonecrusher and Our Waverley Star in the Ranvet Stakes. That was no fluke: he had two and a quarter lengths to spare from Our Waverley Star in the Tancred Stakes soon afterwards. Myocard's seventh win came up effortlessly when he beat My Precocious Lad by five lengths in the A.J.C. Derby. Chapman kept him going, but the colt was beaten by the more seasoned stayer Major Drive in the Sydney Cup. He was never to recover the brilliance of that autumn.

N

NAMES OF HORSES

The turf superstition that no good horse has ever had a 'bad' name generally holds true: Archer, Carbine, Let's Elope, Phar Lap, Tranquil Star and Vain among many were named with a potency that their deeds on the track confirmed. Some fine names came by accident. Century, first horse to win the three Group One sprints down the Straight Six at Flemington, was so called because the first 99 names suggested for him had been rejected. Prosaically named gallopers are often ordinary performers. The notorious Drongo apart, Beldale Ball was the least distinguished Melbourne Cup winner of the 1980s. On the other hand, a calypso lilt (and his outstanding achievements) forgave the redundantly named Kingston Town, while the resonantly styled Rubiton derived his name banally from his breeding (Century-Ruby). And who knows what a burden was the vacuous name Big Philou for that controversial galloper?

Names of many classic and feature race-winning horses and of leading sires are reserved forever for the horses that first bore them. Names longer than 18 letters are interdicted. No horse's name can be re-used for 15 years after its first registration. But after that time elapsed, another Snub, another Iga Ninja raced. Australia has also seen at least two thoroughbreds named Abstainer, the first by Tippler, the second by Noalcoholic.

Horses' names have much to say of the social history of the eras in which they raced. Warworn won the Goodwood Handicap in 1944. Prophetically, The Crash won the W.A. Derby in 1891, a race admittedly in which it was the only starter, but on the eve of the disastrous depression of the 1890s. England's Dust saluted in the 1958 renewal of this event, as a portent of England's dismal Ashes cricket tour of 1958-9. Some names are incongruous. Hobart won the Launceston Cup of 1885. Others have given offence. The hurdler Tsipura (spell it backwards) escaped notice, but the Geoffrey Chapman horse Merkin, who won several good races in Sydney, had a change of names when it was belatedly realised that merkins were pubic wigs. The Colin Hayes-trained two-year-old Mohammed endured a change of name after Muslim protests.

By contrast, The Wandering Jew had raced on to victory in the Q.T.C. Derby of 1892. Notwithstanding the deeds of The Phantom and The Phantom Chance, recent superstition has it that horses named The... are non-winners. This was not a belief of earlier years, when The Australian Peer took the 1887 Victoria Derby; The Possible and The Chevalier won the Bagot Handicap in 1895 and 1896; The Harvester the Victoria Derby in 1894; while Melbourne Cup winners have included The Barb (1866), The Pearl (1871), The Quack (1872), The Assyrian (1882), The Grafter (1898), The Victory (1902), The Parisian (1911) and The Trump (1937). It is a daring and varied array of names that makes one long for more venturesome choices to return. Whether there is a distinctive savour to Australian racehorse names is doubtful, although those that prolific English author of racing thrillers, Dick Francis, ventured in his novel, In The Frame, set during a Melbourne Spring Carnival, lacked conviction.

Sardonic humour certainly informs some Australian thoroughbreds' names. Gallops and Stays (Fast Boy-Corset Girl), Shotgun Wedding (Double Bore-Bridal Stream), The Stutterer (Talking-K-K-Katy) and Who-Am-I, by an unidentified sire out of an unidentified dam come to mind.

NASSIPOUR

1980 ch horse Blushing Groom – Alama

Bred and raced in Europe by the Aga Khan, Nassipour was retired for stud duties after an unusually strenuous racing career which saw him start 46 times in five seasons. He was Australian champion sire in the 1991-2 season, when his progeny won about $5 million, buoyed significantly by the Melbourne Cup quinella of Let's Elope and Shiva's Revenge. The latter also won the S.A. Derby, while the champion mare Let's Elope won the Caulfield Cup, Mackinnon Stakes and Australian Cup, together with other weight-for-age races, and the Melbourne Cup in that season. Other significant winners for Nassipour were the 1992 Victoria Derby winner Redding, Lord Revenir (1991 Metropolitan), Grooming

(1992 Brisbane Cup). Sadly for Australian racing, Nassipour died at the Ra Ora Stud in New Zealand on 8 May 1994, of toxaemia.

NATURALISM

1988 b horse Palace Music – Zephyr Souba

With only a sole metropolitan win to his name as a two year old, Naturalism still recommended himself to trainer Lee Freedman as a horse with three year old spring potential. Placed behind Tierce and Hula Grey in his first two runs at three, Naturalism was a close second to Chortle in the 1991 Caulfield Guineas before winning the BMW Vase at Moonee Valley. His main target had always been the Victoria Derby, and despite his inexperience, and after an unsuccessful protest against Star of the Realm, Naturalism ran second. His autumn campaign in 1992 saw him beaten a neck in the Australian Guineas by Jolly Old Mac before posting an easy win in the Alister Clark Stakes. This convinced Freedman to send Naturalism to Sydney. In the Canterbury Guineas he was beaten by Veandercross, but exacted revenge in the Rosehill Guineas and A.J.C. Derby, which he retained after a protest.

In the spring of 1992 Naturalism reeled off wins in the Memsie, Feehan and Turnbull Stakes. He was travelling kindly in the Cox Plate when jockey Mick Dittman was unseated in a rough race. Freedman kept the horse going, and he recorded a strong, narrow win over the good stayer Silk Ali, while carrying 63kg in the Grey Smith Stakes. The next assignment for Naturalism was the most ambitious. Sent to Tokyo for the Japan Cup he ran a gallant second to the top local stayer Tokai Teio, despite being hampered by injury. This was, perhaps, Naturalism's best run. In the autumn of 1993 he resumed with wins in the Apollo Stakes and Canterbury Cup, but went under to Veandercross in the

Ranvet Stakes and to Rough Habit in the All Aged. In the spring Naturalism was placed three times before pulling out a final great run to beat The Phantom in the Caulfield Stakes. He was then fourth in the Cox Plate. Invited back for a second try in the Japan Cup, Naturalism was placed in the Mackinnon Stakes but ran down the line in Tokyo. His fine career on the track now concluded, he was sent to stud.

NAVIGATOR

1879 blk horse Robinson Crusoe – Cocoanut

Trained by Etienne de Mestre, Navigator was in the money at all eight starts at two, running second in the A.J.C. Sires' and winning the A.J.C. Champagne Stakes. Blossoming at three, he won the 1882 A.J.C. Derby and Mares' Produce Stakes, before heading to Melbourne where he won the Victoria Derby and the V.R.C. St Leger. In 1883 he capped an outstanding season by winning the Australian Cup and the A.J.C. St Leger.

NAYLOR, RUPERT (RUFUS) (1882-1939)

Born in Sydney, Naylor was a miner at 12 and a bookmaker at 17. He diversified his interests further, establishing a foot-running team with rich potential for race-fixing, taking athletes to South Africa, buying a sports stadium and picture theatres. After sojourns in South Africa, where he fell foul of racing authorities, and in England and the United States, Naylor returned to Australia in 1925 to work again as a bookmaker. After five years the A.J.C. found grounds for objection to his activities and Naylor turned to punting, and to race-calling for radio station 2KY. He was warned off Sydney racetracks in 1933; had his appeal against this decision upheld, but eventually lost his rights to attend after the A.J.C. successfully appealed to the Privy Council in 1937. Naylor died two years later, enshrined as a battler and survived by two wives. He is responsible for the famous racecourse saying 'shut the gate' (meaning that a horse is travelling like a winner). When one of his well-backed foot-runners defeated a hot favourite, the latter called 'shut the gate' so that bona fides could be checked. Naylor had ensured his man had the right credentials.

NEVILLE, RAY (1932-)

Before he rode in the 1948 Melbourne Cup, the apprentice jockey Ray Neville had had only nine rides, without placing. After several senior jockeys turned down the ride on Rimfire, Neville found himself on the 80/1 outsider. In a desperately tight finish, the camera was used for the first time to adjudicate and Neville's mount beat Dark Marne, ridden by Jack Thompson. The latter could not be convinced that he had lost. Leading jockey Harold Badger, whose mount Howe went amiss when looking a good thing, had to be reconciled to never winning a Melbourne Cup after this, his 17th attempt. Neville never rode another winner. He retired to his native Mallee town of Birchip, becoming a carpenter, but still kept his eye in riding regular trackwork for local trainers up to the 1980s.

NEWHAVEN

1893 ch horse Newminster – Oceana

Among the finest Melbourne Cup winners, Newhaven was one of five winners of the race bred at the St Albans Stud near Geelong, and one of four whom Walter Hickenbotham trained. As a two year old he won the Maribyrnong Plate and was second in the Champagne Stakes. At three he won the Ascot Vale Stakes but was beaten by The Officer in the Caulfield Guineas. Back at

Flemington he won the 1896 Derby brilliantly by six lengths. That was his margin in the Melbourne Cup as well. He carried 50.5kg to victory, the highest winning weight ever for a three year old in the race and 3.5kg over weight-for-age. A racing journalist aptly wrote 'Newhaven first, daylight second'. The 1896 Cup was the first to be filmed, and the footage of Newhaven's victory is some of the oldest that survives in Australia. Next autumn Newhaven won the A.J.C. St Leger and was then sent to stud in England. Because he traced back to Dinah, whose origins were unknown, Newhaven was refused admission to the Stud Book and was sent back to Australia in 1899, where he stood for some seasons with little patronage.

NEWMARKET HANDICAP(S)

The greatest sprinting handicap in Australia was the notion initially of V.R.C. committeeman Captain Robert Standish, who thought that 'a short and merry' event over three quarters of a mile would beef up the club's autumn programme. So it proved. The gruelling sprint down the 'Straight Six' was first run in 1874, when Maid of Avenel beat Atalanta and Poodle. Aspen was the first horse to win the event twice (in 1880-1), and has been emulated by Gothic (1927-8), Correct (1960-1) and Razor Sharp (1982-3). Greenline set a weight carrying record of 64.5kg when he won in 1930. Many champions have taken the Newmarket (named fondly after the English racecourse and breeding centre). The astonishingly versatile galloper Malua was the first, in 1884. Wakeful, in 1901, was one of a group of outstanding mares to win the race. Others include Molly's Robe, Begonia Belle, Ripa, Toy Show, Desirable, Maybe Mahal and Special. Heroic and Ajax were high-class winners between the wars, while in 1946 Bernborough came from last to win

with 62kg. In more recent years, Century, Baguette, Black Onyx and Placid Ark have been distinguished winners of the Newmarket.

There are or have been Australian Newmarkets besides that at Flemington, run in three other states. The Tasmanian Turf Club first ran a Newmarket at Mowbray in 1902. The Brisbane Amateur Turf Club called its feature sprint race the Newmarket from 1933-45, but it was the Ahern Memorial Handicap when Bernborough won in 1946. Newcastle also got into the act, and runs its Newmarket in autumn as well. Nevertheless, the Flemington version is the finest test of speed and strength over a sprint course in this country.

NEWMINSTER
1873 br horse The Marquis – Spa

A first rate young horse, sired by the winner of the English 2,000 Guineas and St Leger in 1862, Newminster won the Maribyrnong Plate and the V.R.C. Sires' Produce, beating the brilliant filly Briseis on each occasion. He also scored in the Ascot Vale Stakes at three from Robinson Crusoe and Briseis. Heavily backed for the Victoria Derby and the Melbourne Cup of 1876, Newminster was injured before the Derby, and then apparently poisoned at trainer F.F. Dakin's Point Cooke stables. It was alleged that a stable lad may have acted on behalf of a bookmaker. In the event Newminster took his place in the Derby, but obviously underdone could only run fifth to Briseis. His disappointing form continued until the eccentric redemption of a Geelong Cup win in 1878. His finest hour was to come: Newminster won the inaugural Caulfield Cup of 1879, when the race was run in the autumn, to the delight of his owner, Andrew Chirnside. Standing first at Newminster Stud, Camperdown and then at St Albans

Stud, Geelong, Newminster was a notable success. Twice he headed the Australian sires' list. Two of his progeny won Melbourne Cups: Newhaven in 1893 and Tarcoola (at 40/1 in 1896), while Lamond, The Dauphine, Vengeance and Wild Rose were the best of his other horses. Newminster was remembered in the V.A.T.C. Newminster Handicap, which in July 1981 was the occasion of an infamous no-race.

NEW STATESMAN

1958 b horse Smokey Eyes – Wilma Joy

Winner of three of his five starts at two, New Statesman progressed steadily through the grades at three. He won the Whittier and Belhaven Handicaps, before defeating Royal Belltor and Native Statesman in the Moonee Valley Stakes. A fourth in the Caulfield Guineas, and second to Dhaulagiri in the Cox Plate indicated that the horse was nearing his peak. In the Victoria Derby, New Statesman beat Sometime and Blue Era (who had won the A.J.C. Derby on protest). Geoff Lane rode the colt and Brian Courtney trained him: the pair would combine again the next year in Coppelius' Derby win. Back in the autumn, New Statesman won the William Reid, was third in the Orr and then carried 55kg to defeat Wenona Girl and My Peak in the Oakleigh Plate, showing a brilliance which had not earlier been suspected. But New Statesman ran second last in the Newmarket and at four his form was more patchy. Seventeen starts at that age included wins in the George Main at Randwick and the Sandown Cup, while he was placed third in the Epsom, Cox Plate and Mackinnon Stakes. Unplaced in his assignments at five, New Statesman was retired.

NGAWYNI

1972 b horse Zvornik – Lamperine

Out of an outstanding Western Australian sire, by a horse that was not able to stay, Ngawyni proved to be one of the most accomplished and versatile horses to go east. In Western Australia he won the Guineas and the Derby while trained by John Davidson. Sent to Victoria, he was put in the care of Bart Cummings. His four year old performances included victories in the 1976 Hill Stakes and Carlyon Cup. In 1977, Ngawyni won the Australian Cup at Flemington, the A.J.C. Queen Elizabeth Stakes, and the Moonee Valley Cup. Equal to the task of winning top quality races in four states, he then took the Prime Minister's Cup on the Gold Coast and the P.J. O'Shea Stakes besides running second to Reckless in the Brisbane Cup.

NICHOLSON, DONALD (1861-85)

Born in Scotland, Nicholson came to Australia with his family at the age of three. At 13 he was apprenticed as a jockey. Before he came out of his time, Nicholson had been twice placed in a Melbourne Cup: third on Timothy in 1876, second on Sweetmeat three years later. It was in Sydney that he set a notable and unequalled riding record by winning the Epsom five years in a row, between 1880-4. His winning mounts were Master Avenel, Waxy, Masquerade twice and Espiegle. His career ended tragically in the 1885 Caulfield Cup in which 16 of the 41 horse field fell in a sickening pile-up. Thrown from Lord Exeter against the rail, Nicholson died as he was being carried from the track.

NICOPOLIS

1959 br horse Landau – Ballater Belle

This under-rated galloper from Western Australia won the W.A.T.C. Sires' Produce Stakes at two, and added the W.A.T.C. Guineas and Derby in the next season. Sent east, he won the Victoria Handicap, the

Liston Stakes and the first of successive Toorak Handicaps at four. In the next season his best win was again the Toorak, where he once more beat Radiant Pine. Nicopolis carried 60kg. Nor were his feature performances over. With Roy Higgins up, he won the Invitation Stakes at Caulfield with 59.5kg as a six year old, before being retired to stud.

NIGHTMARCH
1925 br horse Night Raid – Marsa

By the same sire as Phar Lap, Nightmarch was an outstanding juvenile in New Zealand, where he was bred. He won the New Zealand Derby and the Dunedin Cup before embarking on an Australian campaign. Big punter Eric Connolly persuaded Nightmarch's owner, A. Louisson, to set the horse to win the 1929 Epsom, rather than the Metropolitan for which he was initially fancied. The ensuing plunge was lucrative. Nightmarch won the Epsom, before finishing a gallant second in the Metropolitan. Then he won the Randwick Plate over two miles before heading south. Nightmarch won the Cox Plate, and then ran third to High Syce on the afternoon that Phar Lap won the Victoria Derby. Although Phar Lap started even money favourite in the Melbourne Cup, Nightmarch won decisively, carrying 58.5kg. Among Nightmarch's other feature race wins in Australia were two Autumn Stakes, a Cumberland Plate and the 1930 Rawson Stakes. He continued to impress in his home country as well, winning a Canterbury Cup, a Trentham Gold Cup, two Awapuni Gold Cups and carrying 60kg to victory in the New Zealand Cup of 1930.

NOHOLME
1956 ch horse Star Kingdom – Oceana

A full brother to the champion Todman, and like that horse trained by Maurice McCarten and usually ridden by Neville Sellwood, Noholme's career began less auspiciously, but he certainly did not deserve to live in his brother's shadow. After two wins and a second in his first three starts, Noholme ran seventh in the 1959 Golden Slipper won by Fine and Dandy. In the Champagne Stakes he made amends. Put out until the spring, Noholme returned with a first-up win before running a disappointing eighth to Martello Towers in the Canterbury Guineas. McCarten now switched him back in distance. The horse responded by winning the Hill Stakes by five lengths and then easily took the Epsom in 1.34.9, the fastest time run by a three year old for a mile in Australia. Sent south, Noholme was beaten a half head by Prince Lea in the Caulfield Guineas, but then stamped his class on the spring's racing. He won the Cox Plate by four lengths in record time; took the Linlithgow Stakes by four and then added the C.B. Fisher Plate at 12 furlongs, a distance once thought beyond him. Beaten three times in the autumn of 1960, Noholme concluded his Australian career with a win in the All Aged Stakes at Randwick, his 10th in 17 Australian starts. He was now sold to Gene Goff in the United States. There he raced for three seasons, winning only two races and recording seven placings from 24 starts. Noholme was sent to the unfashionable Verna Lea stud in Arkansas. From his second crop, Noholme produced a then world record of 24 individual two year old winners. Among the best of the many top horses that he sired was Nodouble, twice North American Handicap Horse of the year. The fertile Noholme was still at stud in his 25th year.

NO RACES

The most notorious 'no race' was the 1993 Grand National at Aintree in England, where the bungling starter ensured that the horse and jockey first past the post would end up with nothing but chagrin for their troubles. There have been 'no races' in Australia, most recently at Caulfield in July 1981, when a section of false rail had been left on the track near the 800m mark, and at Moonee Valley in the Noel Mason Steeplechase in May 1990, when three horses failed to jump one fence after being directed around a fallen galloper.

NORTON, EZRA (1897-1967)

Illegitimate son of the newspaper proprietor and politician John Norton, who owned the scandal paper *Truth*, Ezra Norton had to fight for his inheritance. His father left his newspaper empire to his daughter and his niece, but Ezra Norton and his mother successfully contested the will. He was in sole charge of the *Truth* and the Sydney *Daily Mirror* after his mother's death in 1940. The year before he had clashed with rival newspaper baron Frank Packer. On A.J.C. Derby Day in 1939 an argument between the two led to punches being thrown before they were separated and rebuked by racecourse officials. When it came to owning horses, Packer had the upper hand early, for Columnist won the 1947 Caulfield Cup for him. Norton hoped to trump his foe with Straight Draw, a 2,000 guineas purchase in New Zealand. The year that Straight Draw was set for the Melbourne Cup was 1957 – the year when Tulloch was expected to run, and win. In the event trainer Tommy Smith and owner E.A. Haley scratched Tulloch and Straight Draw won by a neck. It was no coincidence that in the lead-up to the scratching Norton's papers emphasised that it was too big a burden on a three year old – which Tulloch was – to run in the Cup. Norton knew that this was his horse's only chance to win and he gained the prize, although was not on hand at Flemington to accept it.

NOVEMBER RAIN
1977 br mare Estaminet – Clystalla

One of the best fillies of the many to go through Neville Begg's yard, November Rain had a purple patch in her three year old campaign. In Melbourne she won the Wakeful Stakes before beating Deck the Halls in the Oaks with Ron Quinton up on an appropriately rainy 6 November 1980. In the autumn she completed the rare Oaks treble with wins in the A.J.C. Oaks (over Deck the Halls once more) and Queensland Oaks. This fine stayer also relegated subsequent Melbourne Cup winner Just a Dash to third in her victory in the A.J.C. St Leger.

NUFFIELD
1935 ch horse Heroic – Belle Gallante

A brilliant youngster, the son of Heroic won the V.R.C. and A.J.C. Sires' Produce Stakes as well as the Maribyrnong Plate. He was second in the Champagne Stakes of 1938 to Pandava and won another two starts of his nine as a two year old. Owned by C.B. Kellow, he had been named after the British industrialist Lord Nuffield. At three, the Jack Holt-trained Nuffield won the A.J.C. Derby, Caulfield Guineas and Victoria Derby in a magnificent burst. He became only the third colt to win this treble. His descent was as sudden: Nuffield was unplaced in one other run at three; did not start at four; was unplaced in two outings at five.

O

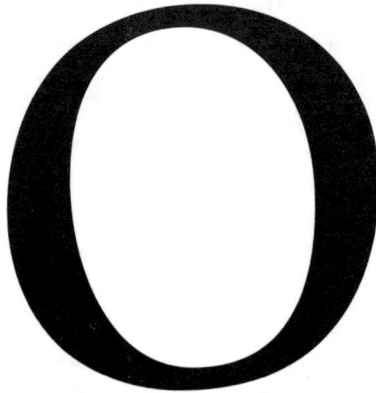

OAKBANK RACECOURSE

Situated in the Mt Lofty Ranges outside Adelaide, Oakbank is the site of the second best attended meeting in the Australian racing calendar, which regularly attracts crowds of 60,000 people. Racing began in the district in the mid-1860s. With the leadership of Alfred von Doussa, the Onkaparinga Racing Club was established in 1876 and held its first meeting in the following year. Since then it has managed, with only brief intermissions, to hold onto Easter racing dates. The Club's most famous race, the Great Eastern Steeplechase, was first run in 1877. By 1880 a grandstand had been built; a railway line linked this Adelaide Hills course to the city by 1883. Traditionally the Great Eastern has been run on Easter Monday as a picnic meeting that attracts huge crowds. A carnival atmosphere in a supposedly 19th century spirit prevails. Jumpers negotiate a road and a fallen log, besides testing fences. Doiran won the race four times early this century, while such tough horses as Vinchiamo and Commission Red are among recent winners. Oakbank has hosted a two day Easter meeting since 1939.

OAKLEIGH PLATE

The once-proverbial expression 'going like an Oakleigh Plater' indicated a horse with a brilliant, even reckless turn of speed. However, what is now a Group One 1100m sprint at Caulfield was first run, in 1882, as the Oakleigh Handicap over 1800m. After a couple of years in which the race was not run, it was reinstated at the autumn meeting of 1886, at the now familiar distance. From 1893-1904, the race was run in two divisions. The first, for horses weighted at 57kg and above was known as the Oakleigh Plate; the other the Oakleigh Purse. From 1905, only the Plate was staged. Champion winners of the Oakleigh Plate include the versatile Malua in 1884, Wakeful (1901), Placid Ark (1987 – as one leg of his sprinting Triple Crown) and Schillaci, who won in course record time in 1992. Two horses have won the race twice – Aurie's Star (1937 and 1939) and Dual Choice (1971 and 1972) – while Pamelus, who split the winning sequence of Aurie's Star in 1938, was second to that horse in 1939 and second again in the next year. For the next four years, 1941-4, the race was run at Flemington. Woorak set a weight-carrying record which is scarcely likely to be approached again when he won with 65.5kg in 1917.

OAKS, A.J.C.

Last of the three year old classics to be introduced to racing in New South Wales, the Adrian Knox Stakes, named for a long time chairman of the Australian Jockey Club was first run in 1922 for fillies over the distance of a mile. Vodka was victorious. In 1946 the race was renamed the A.J.C. Oaks, run over one and a half miles (now 2400m at Group One level) and moved from January to the autumn carnival. Outstanding winners of the event have included Flight (1944), Wenona Girl (1961), Light Fingers (1965), Analie (1973), Leilani (1974), How Now (1976), Surround (1976) and Bounding Away (1987).

OAKS, QUEENSLAND

Maltmaid won the first running of the Queensland Oaks in 1951, but it was not long before a victor in this event set her seal on the wider scene of Australian racing. In 1955 Evening Peal won the Queensland Oaks. She added the V.R.C. Oaks to her record in the same year; the Melbourne Cup a year later. The 1970s saw a procession of brilliant winners of this event, from Analie in 1973 to Denise's Joy, Surround and Show Ego (1976-8). More recently, Triscay added the Queensland Oaks to her 1991 A.J.C. Oaks victory, while the multiple Group One winning filly Slight Chance scored in the Eagle Farm classic in 1993.

OAKS, S.A.J.C.

The South Australian Oaks is a Group One event over 2400m run at Morphettville in May. Gay Comedy took the first Oaks in 1951. Tulloch's best daughter, Valide, was victorious in 1968. Winner in 1975 was Ace Queen, who went on to be first past the post in that year's Australian Derby in Perth, only to lose on protest to Denise's Joy. Since the inauguration of the Australasian Oaks in 1982 as the richest staying race for fillies during the Adelaide late autumn carnival, the South Australian Oaks has been somewhat overshadowed. However the Bart Cummings-trained Our Tristalight became the first horse to win the Adelaide Oaks double in 1993, while Tristalove, also under Cummings' care, won the South Australian Oaks in 1994.

OAKS, V.R.C.

Oldest fillies' classic in Australia, a version of what is now the V.R.C. Oaks (a Group One event for three year old fillies run at Flemington over 2500m on the third day of its Spring Carnival) was first contested in 1861, when Palestine won. As late as 1877, when Pardon beat Device, there were only two starters, but in the previous year the first champion annexed the Oaks when Briseis won. In the same week she took out the Victoria Derby and the Melbourne Cup. Among the best of subsequent winners have been Auraria (1895), Sweet Nell (1903), Carlita (1914), Furious (1921), Frances Tressady (1923), Chicquita (1949), Evening Peal (1955) who won the Melbourne Cup the following year, and Lady Sybil, who cut a swathe through the three year old races in Melbourne in 1960. Other top-line winners have been Light Fingers (1964), a Melbourne Cup winner a year later, Leica Show, who beat Cap D'Antibes in 1974, Denise's Joy and the champion filly Surround in the next two years. Rose of Kingston in 1981, was the last of Roy Higgins' five winners in the race, while Research in 1988 and Tristanagh the following year were other class winners. Bart Cummings and Tommy Smith have the best record of modern trainers in the Oaks, while Bobby Lewis rode seven winners of the event.

OCEANA

1947 b mare Colombo – Orama

By the English 2,000 Guineas winner, Colombo, Oceana was one of the top horses that Stanley Wootton imported to Australia for breeding purposes. Yet, at her first three tries, Oceana failed to get in foal, so a disgruntled Wootton put her up for sale, until she fell sick and had to be withdrawn. Now Oceana's fortunes changed. Mated with another Wootton import, Star Kingdom, she produced the champion Todman. Her next get was Todman's outstanding full brother, Noholme. She also produced the good gallopers Shifnal and Faringdon. While Noholme and Shifnal both stood with success abroad as sires, Todman became a top sire in Australia.

OF THE THUNDER OF HOOVES.

'A Novel of a Wild Horse and the Australian Turf', *Of the Thunder of Hooves* was written in 1943 while Ian H. Sabey was a prisoner-of-war in Germany. The novel was eventually published in 1982. It relates the capture and taming of a wild bush horse, Mountain Rogue, who rewards the patience of its owners by winning the Great Eastern Steeplechase at Oakbank, at 6/1, on protest.

ONCIDIUM

1961 b horse Alcide – Malcomia

A well-performed stayer in England, Oncidium won five times at distances from 10 furlongs to two miles. His best wins were the weight-for-age Coronation Cup over 12 furlongs at Epsom and the Newmarket Jockey Club Cup over two miles. He was also good enough to be placed third in the best English weight-for-age race, the King George VI and Queen Elizabeth Stakes. In 1966 Oncidium was sent to stand at the Te Parae Stud in New Zealand. He proved an outstanding sire of staying horses, as befitted his own record on the track. Best of his offspring were multiple Derby winner Dayana, champion mare Leilani, the unlucky Grand Cidium, V.R.C. Oaks winner Sanderae, Gold Brick, who won the A.J.C. Derby in 1972, and a talented horse who never endeared itself to punters – Taras Bulba. Oncidium died in 1975.

O'NEILL, PAM (1945-)

Born in Brisbane, Pam Rhodes was a trainer's daughter, who married another trainer, Colin O'Neill. Her ambition to be a jockey was eventually realised and she won a women riders' event, the International Stakes in Brisbane on Ropely Lad in 1974. Queensland racing officials were reluctant to give O'Neill a full licence, but successive trebles for her at Southport on the Gold Coast forced their hands. O'Neill responded by winning on Samei Boy in June 1979, thus becoming the first Australian-born woman jockey to beat men on a metropolitan course in a fully-fledged betting race. In 1980 O'Neill won the Qantas-HSV 7 Handicap at Moonee Valley by six lengths on Consular, leaving Roy Higgins' mount well astern. Despite her husband's stable support, her opportunities dwindled. O'Neill's trail-blazing paradoxically showed how hard a road it would be to gain recognition for women jockeys in Australasia.

ORGOGLIO

1949 b horse Nasrullah – Orienne

A 10 time winner up to 1600m in the United Kingdom, Orgoglio stood at stud in Victoria from the late 1960s and proved himself to be a most consistent stallion, especially as a sire of sprinters. His progeny included the brilliant two year old Proud Miss, who won 11 races at that age; Picca, who had 14 wins; the fine sprinter Marmion, whose victories included the Craven 'A' and Lightning Stakes, the Oakleigh Plate and William Reid. Orgoglio also produced the Oakleigh Plate winner Magic Ruler, while Craigola's 13 wins included the Doomben 10,000 in 1973. Other good progeny of Orgoglio were Charltonian, winner of 25 races and Goglio, who in turn sired Goliette, winner of the V.R.C. and S.A.J.C. Oaks in 1969. Orgoglio also produced two outstanding broodmare daughters – Elated (the mother of Vain) and Forego, whose son Tontonan numbered a Golden Slipper, Oakleigh Plate and Doncaster among his wins.

ORR STAKES

The C.F. Orr Stakes is the only Group One event to be staged at Sandown. Named in honour of the chairman, and then the salaried secretary of the Williamstown Racing Club, the Orr Stakes was first run at Williamstown. After the W.R.C. folded, the race withstood translations to Moonee Valley and Caulfield, before its establishment as an integral part of the autumn racing calendar in Melbourne. Great horses have won the Orr: Lord in 1959 and 1960; Wenona Girl and Aquanita; Tobin Bronze and Winfreux; Leilani, Surround, Hyperno and At Talaq. None have set their seal more emphatically on the race (nor done more to guarantee its present status) than three-time winners Manikato (1979-81) and Vo Rogue (1988-90).

OUROENE

1975 ch mare Farnworth – Oenone

The most famous non-winner (apart from Drongo) in Australian racing history, Ouroene raced on 124 occasions. She was second twice, third seven times and won $14,605 in stakes. Owner-trainer George

Chiotis clearly cared for the sport more than for the prize.

OUR POETIC PRINCE

1984 b horse Yeats – Finisterre

Foaled in Australia, at the Woodlands Stud, Poetic Prince (as he was known until his racing days in this country) was sold to New Zealand interests, and trained by J.R. Wheeler. A brilliant young horse, he was brought to Australia as a three year old. In one of the most controversial decisions in Australian turf history, Our Poetic Prince convincingly defeated Marwong in the 1987 Caulfield Guineas and then lost the race on protest. Compensations were ample: in the spring of 1988 he beat Flotilla and Vo Rogue in the Feehan Stakes at Moonee Valley; was second to Sky Chase in the Caulfield Stakes; then beat two champions from New Zealand – Horlicks and Bonecrusher in the Cox Plate. In the autumn of 1989, Our Poetic Prince won the Lion Brown Stakes in New Zealand and was then third in the Air New Zealand Stakes. On this preparation he was sent to Sydney where he decisively won the Tancred Stakes from the European visitor Top Class. Remarkably this was Our Poetic Prince's first win in 10 tries the Sydney way of racing; on left-handed tracks he had won 13 from 19 starts (including the Caulfield Guineas loss). Our Poetic Prince added a Queen Elizabeth Stakes victory at Randwick over Dandy Andy and Beau Zam before being retired to stud.

OXENHAM, HUMPHREY (1854-1923)

Born at Wattle Flat, near Bathurst, this renowned bookmaker early gained a taste for the punt when he won a bet of 200 pounds to sixpence that he could not walk two miles between Bathurst and Kelso, within a specified time, with a pumpkin on his head. He took to bookmaking in his teens and moved to Sydney in 1875. There he established himself as one of the biggest gamblers of his time. He owned horses as well, though often chose to back the wrong one. Cerise and Blue scored for him in the 1886 Sydney Cup; Phaeon (1887) and Alemene (1898) won Epsoms. Waterfall took the 1895 Caulfield Cup, but had nearly ruined him when the colt was beaten by another of Oxenham's horses, Cabin Boy, two years earlier in the V.R.C. St Leger. The mare Acrasia (whose dam was Cerise and Blue) gave him the Melbourne Cup of 1904. Her win cost him 2,000 pounds to buy her back after he had lost her in a poker game two weeks before the Cup. Oxenham lived in sight of Randwick racecourse; loved to gamble on his card-play and billiards, and was ambitious enough to race horses in England as well.

P

PACKER FAMILY

Founder of the Consolidated Press media group, Sir Frank Packer (1906-74) was a keen racing man. He provided a colourful diversion at Randwick on Derby Day 1939 by his fight with rival newspaper proprietor Ezra Norton. Among the good horses which Packer owned were the Tommy Smith-trained dual Derby winner Travel Boy, besides Columnist and Foresight. Evidently Packer never missed the chance to replay his horses' victories on the Channel Nine network that he owned. His son Kerry Packer (1937-) is better known for his interest in polo. When he imported the Ascot Gold Cup winner Longboat, the galloper was given topweight of 59kg in the Melbourne Cup of 1989. He never started: Packer put him to siring polo ponies. Good horses he has owned and sent to the track include the Caulfield Stakes winner of 1987, Drought; Dorset Downs, who won the 1991 Queensland Derby; and Mahogany, a share of which he bought just before that gelding won the 1993 Victoria Derby.

PAGO PAGO

1960 b horse Matrice – Pompilia

A brilliant two year old, Pago Pago won nine of his 10 starts, including six in South Australia. His biggest wins were the V.R.C. Sires' Produce and the 1963 Golden Slipper, where he triumphed on a heavy track. In June that year, he was sold to American interests to stand at stud. In the U.S.A. Pago Pago sired winners of more than $8 million, 35 of whom were stakes-winners. Robert Holmes à Court bought the stallion in 1978 to stand at the Heytesbury Stud in Western Australia, where he did his duty until being retired in 1988 at the venerable age of 28.

PAINT THE STARS

1980 ch horse Luskin Star – Visit

Counterbalancing all the stories of champion racehorses bought for a song is the tale of Paint the Stars. Impeccably bred, he was the most expensive-ever yearling purchased in Australia when Robert Holmes à Court paid $825,000 for him at the Easter sales in Sydney in 1981. When he proved a dud at the track, Paint the Stars was retired to stud with moderate success. This fiasco is put in some proportion by the story of Snaffi Dancer, for whom one of the sheikhs, who sought a racing empire in England, paid $13 million in the early 1980s. That colt was too slow even to see a racetrack.

PARIS

1887 b gelding Grandmaster – Enone

Bred at Havelah Stud near Mudgee, Paris won two of his three starts as a two year old. At three he was unbeaten. The highlight of this campaign was victory in the Doncaster in then record time. Only seventh in the Caulfield Guineas, Paris bounced back to win the 1892 Caulfield Cup. He thus became the first winner of that race to be owned by a woman, in Paris' case, Mrs H.C. White. This hardy galloper won the Metropolitan of 1893 with 58.5kg. The following year, he became the first dual winner of the Caulfield Cup, beating the light-weights Devon and Bruin, under the impost of 59kg. Paris set a weight-carrying record for the race which stood for 30 years. He followed up with an unlucky fifth in the Melbourne Cup. It was decided to send him to England with the long distance Newmarket race, the Cesarewitch in mind. Unfortunately Paris went amiss before the event, but he was successful in other races in England.

PATERSON, A.B. ('BANJO') (1864-1941)

From the time he was taken to the Binalong races at the age of eight, 'Banjo' Paterson was a devotee of the turf. One of the earliest of his poems to appear in the *Bulletin* (on 30 October 1886) was the humorous 'A Dream of the Melbourne Cup'. He wrote of 'Old Pardon, Son of Reprieve' among many turf ballads. Horseracing also moved Paterson to elegy. A wire service account of the death of a 14 year old jockey, Richard Bennison, who was killed when thrown from William Tell, prompted the poem 'Only a Jockey'. Paterson was incensed by the remark in the report that 'the horse is luckily uninjured'. Famously he wrote an elegy for the great jumps jockey, Tommy Corrigan, who was killed in a fall in

August 1894. Paterson saw service as a war correspondent in South Africa and during the Boxer Rebellion in China before the turn of the century; was an officer in charge of remounts in the Middle East during the Great War. In 1921 he was appointed editor of the Sydney *Sportsman*, where he contributed such telling pieces as 'Hints to Urgers'. His racing novel *The Shearer's Colt* was published in 1936, while his poem 'On Kiley's Run' has been adopted as the name of a horse who is a recent Sydney and Melbourne winner.

PATROBAS

1912 br horse Wallace – Sizzle

Bred at Bringenbrong in New South Wales, by Carbine's best Australian son, Wallace, Patrobas was bought by Mrs Edith Widdis, wife of a Gippsland grazier. He had an outstanding spring campaign as a three year old, winning the 1915 Caulfield Guineas before running sixth to Lavendo, who became the first imported horse to win the Caulfield Cup. Patrobas then won the Victoria Derby from the fine horse Cetigne with Westcourt third. His regular jockey W. Smart could not make the Melbourne Cup weight, so the ride went to Bobbie Lewis, his 19th in a Melbourne Cup, and on the horse carrying the 19 saddlecloth. Many of the crowd that year were in khaki. Australian casualties at Gallipoli had risen to 30,000. In a rough race, marred by a bad three-horse fall, Patrobas won narrowly from Westcourt. He thus became the only horse ever to win the Caulfield Guineas – Victoria Derby – Melbourne Cup treble. This was a triumph for his sire, Wallace, for Patrobas was his sixth Derby winner since 1903 and a second successive Melbourne Cup winner. Mrs Widdis became the first woman to own a Cup winner, although was unable to get through the throng to the presentation.

Patrobas, who was trained by C. Wheeler, went on to win the V.R.C. St Leger the following year.

PATRON

1891 ch horse Grand Flaneur – Olga

Best son of the unbeaten champion Grand Flaneur, Patron had 15 starts at two and won four of them, including the V.R.C. Sires' Produce. In the spring of 1893 he won the Canterbury Plate and the Caulfield Guineas. Nonetheless he was friendless in betting for that year's Melbourne Cup and finished near the tail at 100/1. In 1894 he won the V.R.C. St Leger and the A.J.C. Craven Plate in the autumn. Again Patron lined up for the Melbourne Cup and once more was unwanted, at 33/1. His brother, Ruenalf, was favourite at 3/1. But Patron scored, ridden by H. Dawes, whose father – riding under the pseudonym 'H. Chifney' – had steered Banker home in the Cup of 1863. Patron was the first of the four Cup winners which Richard Bradfield trained. He went on to stand at stud in England.

PAYTEN FAMILY

Thomas Payten (1855-1920) began work in 1876 for Michael Fennelly who trained for the leading Sydney owner James White. By 1881 he was foreman of the Newmarket stables and became White's trainer after the death of Fennelly in 1887. Next year he trained nine winners at the V.R.C. autumn meeting, all ridden by Tom Hales. Abercorn, whom he rated a better stayer than Carbine, won the St Leger and later triumphed in the A.J.C. Derby, St Leger and Metropolitan Handicap. Payten won a Victoria Derby for White with Dreadnought in 1889, who went one better than Abercorn who had dead-heated for second with Niagara behind The Australian Peer two years before. When White sold his racing interests, Payten was

able to attract other loyal owners and to take up breeding in his own right. Trident was one of his best horses, while he bred and owned Dewey who won the 1899 Caulfield Cup. Turf journalist Nat Gould found Payten's stables to be a congenial place to gather copy. Payten's horses won five A.J.C. Derbies and four St Legers; four Victoria Derbies and five V.R.C. St Legers.

His son, Bayly Payten (1896-1948) took over his father's Botany Road stables in 1920. He was able to engage Darby Munro as his stable jockey and topped the Sydney trainers' premiership regularly in the 1940s without ever achieving the big race successes that had come his father's way.

PEDRO'S PRIDE

1950 b mare Don Pedro – Gortland

Perhaps the best mare ever to race over the jumps in Australia, the E. Miller-trained Pedro's Pride was also one of the best loved. She won numerous jumps races at Caulfield, Flemington and Moonee Valley, excelling especially over the steeplechase fences. In 1957 Pedro's Pride carried 79kg to victory in the Australian Steeplechase, giving 21.5kg to the second horse, Pagranoma. Next start, she lumped 75.5kg on a heavy track at Flemington in the Grand National Steeplechase, beating Blacksmith (in receipt of 16kg) by 10 lengths. Back again the following winter, Pedro's Pride capped a great career with a win in the Hiskens Steeple. On this occasion she started even money favourite, despite the burden of 79.5kg, and beat Greek Legend (who had 58.5kg) by five lengths.

PERSIAN LYRIC

1957 ch horse Persian Book – Lyrical Lass

By the good sire Persian Book, whose progeny included Book Link and Prince Darius, Persian Lyric showed early promise of being something special. He recorded four wins at two, culminating in the Fernhill Handicap over 1600m at Randwick, so often a good guide to staying potential. At three he took on the best horses in Australia. Second to the brilliant Wenona Girl in the A.J.C. Sires' at two, he had his revenge when he beat the filly and Sky High in the Canterbury Guineas, however Persian Lyric was third to that pair in the Rosehill Guineas of 1960. The one that counted most was the A.J.C. Derby and this time Persian Lyric triumphed, from Le Storm and Sky High. Thereafter Persian Lyric added the Queensland Derby to his imposing record, with Le Storm and Pale Ale filling the placings. Resuming in the autumn of 1961, he beat Tulloch by a head over 2400m at Warwick Farm in record time and then, campaigning in Brisbane once more, added the Stradbroke Handicap to his tally of big race wins, carrying 55kg to victory from Samson and Aquanita. Seconds in the Tatts Cup and to High Society in the Doomben Cup followed, before Persian Lyric was retired to stud.

PERTH CUP

First run at Ascot in 1887, the Perth Cup is the premier staying event in Western Australia. A committeeman of the W.A.T.C., Alexander Forrest, brought First Prince from Melbourne and he easily won the initial staging of the event. The following year Telephone won on protest, thus beginning the controversial episodes which have marked numerous runnings of the race. Wandering Willie was the first dual Perth Cup winner in 1890, and in 1892, when he survived a protest. In that year Wandering Willie was the only horse in the race's history to be ridden, trained and owned by the same man – G.A. Towton.

Sometimes run in December, at others in January, the Perth Cup has consequently had no winners to show in some years, two in others. Top winners have included Eurythmic and Raconteur. The bad tempered, aged black gelding Magistrate was victorious in 1981 at nine years, and the next year, at 10. Most contentious of recent wins in the race was that of Rocket Racer in 1987. After going out to a long lead, Rocket Racer finished in an apparently dehydrated condition, and was judged too distressed to be swabbed.

PETER PAN
1929 ch horse Pantheon – Alwina

One of the greatest of Australian stayers, Peter Pan was bred by R.R. Dangar at the Baroona Stud in New South Wales. As a two year old he did not race until May and was unplaced. Next season he dead-heated in a Warwick Farm Novice. Trainer Frank McGrath sent him straight into the Hill Stakes where he defeated Nightmarch and Veilmond. At his fourth start Peter Pan won the A.J.C. Derby with Jim Pike in the saddle. Travelling to Melbourne, Peter Pan raced ungenerously when fourth in the Caulfield Cup of 1932, being by no means the last high class galloper to find that track a difficult assignment. At his next start Peter Pan – who had not been entered for the Victoria Derby – won the first of two Melbourne Stakes from the Caulfield Cup winner Rogilla. The 1932 Melbourne Cup was only his seventh race start, but with Billy Duncan up, Peter Pan scored by a neck from Yarramba with Shadow King third.

In the autumn of 1933 he won the Randwick Stakes from Rogilla and Lough Neagh before being beaten at 3/1 on in the Rawson Stakes by Lough Neagh after the barrier strand caught in his mouth. He then strung together wins in the A.J.C. St Leger, Cumberland Stakes and the A.J.C. Plate.

Rheumatism kept Peter Pan away from the track in the spring of 1933. In the autumn of the next year he failed to win at his first three starts before reeling off victories in the A.J.C. Autumn and Cumberland Plates. He lost the King's Cup when he savaged Kuvera near the post and in consequence Rogilla won. As a five year old Peter Pan won nine of 13 starts. After a second to Rogilla in the 1934 Chelmsford Stakes, he surprisingly beat Chatham over seven furlongs. Back in Melbourne, he won the Melbourne Stakes from Hall Mark. With 62kg in the 1934 Melbourne Cup and the prospect of a bog track, little seemed to be in Peter Pan's favour. He drifted from 7/2 to 14/1 but in one of the finest performances in Australian turf history, Peter Pan, ridden by Darby Munro won by three lengths. Let down, he returned in the autumn to win the Randwick and Rawson Stakes, the Autumn Plate, All Aged Stakes and the Jubilee Cup. Peter Pan was still a force at six, especially in Sydney, where he won the Rosehill and Spring Stakes as well as the Craven Plate. He could finish only 13th in the Melbourne Cup in 1935 but was burdened with 66.5kg. Only Phar Lap (with 68kg in 1931) had carried more in the race. At his last start, Peter Pan ran third in the Autumn Stakes. His stud career was truncated by an early death after he broke a leg, but this great galloper (who McGrath, among others, believed to be the equal of Phar Lap) sired Precept, the Victoria Derby winner of 1943 and Peter, who ran second in the 1944 Melbourne Cup.

PHAR LAP

1926 ch gelding Night Raid – Entreaty

Lot 41, a rich chestnut bred at A.F. Robert's stud at Timaru, New Zealand, was the last offered at the 1928 Trentham yearling sale. By the English sire Night Raid,

the colt was the second foal of the five year old mare, Entreaty. On the advice of his brother Harry, Hugh Telford paid 160 guineas for the horse. Harry – then a battling trainer renting stables at Randwick – was attracted by the breeding of Lot 41 and had convinced a client, Dave Davis, to buy him sight unseen. Davis reluctantly agreed.

When the colt arrived in Australia, Davis was not attracted by his appearance and leased him to Telford for three years. Phar Lap (it's Singhalese for 'lightning') would become the idol of Australasia. He made seemingly impossible tasks appear easy on the racetrack; beat odds no matter how stacked they appeared; became a symbol of hope in the despairing years of the Great Depression. In his 50 Australian starts, Phar Lap won 36, was second three times and third twice. He sealed his international status by a win in the Agua Caliente Handicap in Mexico on 20 March 1932, which took his stakes earnings beyond 69,000 pounds. Sixteen days later, Phar Lap died at Menlo Park in California, having suffered a severe colic attack (although conspiracy theories of poisoning improbably live on).

Unplaced at his first four race starts, Phar Lap won a maiden Juvenile at Rosehill on 27 April 1929. At his first four runs at three he was out of the money, before showing much improved form to finish second in the Chelmsford Stakes to the good galloper Mollison. Now into his stride, the Red Terror won the Rosehill Guineas, A.J.C. Derby and Craven Plate. Sent to Melbourne he thrashed L.K.S. Mackinnon's Carradale in record time in the Victoria Derby (the horse had been second in the Randwick event as well). In consequence Phar Lap was even money favourite for the Melbourne Cup of 1929. Ridden an impatient race by the veteran Bobbie Lewis, Phar Lap finished third behind Nightmarch and Paquito.

After a spell, Phar Lap ran third first up in the St George Stakes before stringing together nine consecutive wins. These included the V.R.C. St Leger, Governor's and King's Plates, the A.J.C. St Leger and Chipping Norton Stakes. At his first run back at four, in the spring of 1930, Phar Lap was just beaten by the champion Amounis in the Warwick Stakes. He quickly made amends by winning his next eight straight. The Chelmsford and Hill Stakes, Craven and Randwick Plates, the first of two Cox Plates and the Melbourne Stakes at Flemington on Derby Day were among the races that fell to him. Before that win there was high drama when – after morning trackwork – an attempt was made by gunmen to maim Phar Lap as he was leaving Caulfield. Shielded by strapper Tommy Woodcock, the horse escaped injury. The motive of the attack was probably the huge payout which bookmakers faced from the Amounis-Phar Lap Caulfield-Melbourne cup double.

Following his Melbourne Stakes win, Phar Lap was floated in secret to the St Albans Stud near Geelong. At noon on Melbourne Cup day Phar Lap set off for his greatest appointment. Never out of a canter, he won the Cup by three lengths to become its only odds-on winner. Two days later he won the Linlithgow Stakes, while the C.B. Fisher Plate gave him a win on each day of the Flemington Spring Carnival.

Resuming once more in the St George Stakes in the autumn of 1931, Phar Lap won easily and followed with victories in the Essendon and Futurity Stakes. He won the King's Plate and was then beaten by Waterline in the Lloyd Stakes after the weight conditions had been changed to put him at a severe disadvantage. At five Phar Lap was invincible at weight-for-age. He won the Underwood and Memsie Stakes in Melbourne, three races in Sydney, before annexing his second successive Cox Plate and Melbourne Stakes. Connections were disinclined to start Phar Lap in a third Melbourne Cup because of his enormous weight of 68kg, but V.R.C. Chairman L.K.S. Mackinnon insisted that Phar Lap run. In the event he was a gallant eighth, not knocked about by his regular jockey Jim Pike. This was a rare defeat for the combination: Pike had 30 rides for 27 wins on Phar Lap.

Davis now arranged for Phar Lap to run in the Agua Caliente Handicap in Mexico. Woodcock travelled with the horse as trainer; Billy Elliot rode him. Initially advertised as a $100,000 race, the purse was reduced substantially because of the Depression. Phar Lap sustained a cracked hoof in the lead-up to the race, but still romped away in course record time for the 10 furlongs of 2.2.8. And then to the consternation of the sporting world in the United States as well as in Australia, he was dead. Or perhaps not: Phar Lap's stuffed hide is the most popular display in the Museum of Victoria. His mammoth 14 pound heart is in the National Museum in Canberra, while his skeleton is displayed in the Dominion Museum in Wellington. No other figure in Australian folklore is remembered with more unambiguous affection. How would Phar Lap have fared in today's racing? The question is fatuous. He beat the best company in two continents with an ease and authority never seen before or since. His achievements live in the hearts, if no longer the memories, of all who love thoroughbred racing.

PHANTOM CALLS

Long a feature of Melbourne Cup Calcuttas, and a specialty of the late Bert

Bryant, phantom calls are a lively anticipation of the main event. But the most famous phantom call in Australian racing history was altogether more serious, and venal. This was the scam organised by 3XY race-caller Harry Solomons. Before the last race was run at Melbourne's Ascot track on 16 December 1939, Solomons and his confederates had arranged to cut the land-lines which allowed other radio stations to broadcast the race. Because all of them had to do so from outside the course, the job was easier. Solomons had Fred Tupper (3AW), Eric Welch (3DB) and Jim Carroll (3LO) put off air, but could not prevent Tupper's call being relayed to 2GB in Sydney. With the race run and won, Solomons tipped SP punters across Victoria and New South Wales to get on Scobie Breasley's mount Buoyancy in his 'pre-race' comments. Fortunes were won, but Solomons was immediately suspected. Dismissed from 3XY, he was charged with tampering with the land-lines, but did a flit to Suva on the 'Monterey'. Arrested in Fiji he was brought back to Victoria and sentenced to six months in Pentridge in August 1940. Crime hadn't paid for long.

PHOTO FINISH CAMERA

The first use of a photo finish camera to assist judges in placing horses past the line was at the Canterbury racecourse in Sydney on 16 March 1946. The camera was available at Flemington in July of that year, but not at a Western Australian metropolitan track (Ascot) until 1951. The camera has often failed to separate place-getters, as in the famous triple dead-heat in the Hotham Handicap of 1956 at Flemington, while jockey Jack Thompson swore to his grave that he had won the 1948 Melbourne Cup on Dark Marne despite a print which showed Rimfire the winner.

The camera was subsequently realigned.

PIKE, JAMES (1892-1969)

One of the greatest of Australian jockeys, Pike was born at Newcastle; sought an apprenticeship when he was 12; was twice banned for riding under age, but broke through for a winner in 1906. Trainer William Kelso took Pike to England with him in 1908, where he rode only a couple of winners, but gained invaluable experience. In other respects he was a late developer. Although he won an Australian Cup in 1909 with Pendil and the first of six Victoria Derbies in the next year, Pike's golden period began in the 1920s. He won the 1928 Victoria Derby and two St Legers on Strephon for Sol Green. In 1929 his famous association with Phar Lap began when he had the sit on the champion in the 1929 Victoria Derby. Pike rode the horse 30 times for 27 wins, of which the highlight was the 1930 Melbourne Cup. He rode four Victoria Derbies in a row; besides three A.J.C. Derbies; two Epsoms (on Chatham) and two Doncasters, among more than 100 feature races. A heavy-weight jockey, Pike often had to waste severely to take his mounts. What taxed him more was a compulsive gambling habit, notwithstanding that he was at the same time incorruptible. After his retirement in April 1936, Pike trained for a while without success. At the height of his fame he lived in a mansion in Centennial Park, owned a dozen houses and a block of flats. When he died, In October 1969, he was renting a Bondi flat in the block which once he had owned.

PLACID ARK

1983 br gelding Arkenstone – Northern Queen

Perhaps the finest sprinter to come from Western Australia, the imposing brown gelding was bred at the Asprey Stud. He won his first start in the modest setting of Bunbury, but at three won eight of the 11 races which he contested, including the Sir Ernest Lee-Steere Classic at Ascot over 1400m. Then he sought his fortune in the east. In the autumn of 1987, Placid Ark made history by winning the Group One sprint treble of the Lightning Stakes (at 7/1 from Special), the Oakleigh Plate (by three lengths from the same mare) and the Newmarket, where he led all the way down the grandstand side to defeat Princely Heart and Rubiton. Travelling next to Sydney, Placid Ark equalled Manikato's course record in beating the top-liner Campaign King in the Canterbury Stakes. He was then defeated a half neck by Princely Heart in the Galaxy, when giving that horse 6.5kg.

At four, Placid Ark won all five starts, although his record says otherwise. He began with victories in the Rupert Steele, Moir and Linlithgow Stakes in Melbourne. In the latter event he set a new Flemington track record of 1.21.8. Back in Perth he won the Winterbottom Stakes. But his legs caused trouble. Trainer Wally Mitchell treated the horse with an anti-inflammatory drug, depo-medrol. Placid Ark won the Beaufine Handicap, but was disqualified after he returned a positive swab. Mitchell was rubbed out for a year, a suspension later varied to a $20,000 fine. Placid Ark went back to Melbourne and was beaten twice before scoring his 14th and last win from 21 starts in the Bobbie Lewis Handicap. In a track gallop at Flemington in September 1988, Placid Ark broke down in both fetlocks and the horse's brilliant career ended when he was humanely destroyed.

PLANET RULER

1984 ch gelding Kaoru Star – Moon Scent

Originally trained in Brisbane by Bruce McLachlan, Planet Ruler was transferred to

the stables of David Hayes later in his illustrious career. At three he won the Queensland Guineas and was third in the 1988 Stradbroke Handicap. In the spring Planet Ruler scored in the Toorak Handicap, a race in which he would finish third in 1989. In that year his best win was the first of successive Gadsdens during the spring carnival, over 1600m, his pet distance. Second in the Doomben 10,000 in 1990, Planet Ruler showed weight-for-age class by winning the 1991 George Main Stakes at Randwick. Nor was he a spent force the following year, when he ran second to Mannerism in the 1992 Futurity Stakes (a race in which he was third in 1991) and then won the Honda Stakes during the spring carnival, to record yet another Group One victory.

PLANT, HARRY (1894-1978)

Harry Plant grew up in a tough school, as a buckjump rider in outback Queensland. In the more genteel surroundings of the Townsville Show he set a world horseback high jump record of 2.33m. Next he turned to training thoroughbreds. Best remembered for his association with Bernborough, Plant in fact had a number of superior horses through his yard. These included Magic Night and the brilliant sprinter-miler full brothers, Fine and Dandy and Time and Tide. But it was Bernborough, whom he trained to 15 consecutive victories, who made Plant's name, and forever soured his relationship with Athol Mulley, whom he claimed had pulled the great horse in its controversial defeat in the 1946 Caulfield Cup.

PODMORE, GEORGE (1926-)

The Sydney jockey George Podmore retired in 1983 after a career which spanned four decades. His best years were from the mid-1950s until the mid-1960s; the best horses that he rode were Evening Peal and River Seine. On the former he won the V.R.C. Oaks in 1955, the A.J.C. Oaks in the autumn of the following year. He then teamed with the mare to win the 1956 Melbourne Cup. His first big race win had been aboard Suncup in the 1953 Stradbroke Handicap. Podmore won Metropolitans on Beaupa (1955), Duo and General Command (1966-7). On River Seine he won both the Sydney and Doomben Cups in 1965, while an Epsom win came his way courtesy of Even Better in the same year.

POITREL

1914 ch horse St Alwyne – Poinard

Bred at the Arrowfield Stud, Poitrel was a slow developer. Unplaced in three starts at two, he won three of five in his next year. At four Poitrel blossomed at weight-for-age. In the Spring Stakes of 1918 he ended the 19 win sequence of Desert Gold; next year he undid another reputation in that race, handing out the first Australian defeat to Gloaming. Ken Bracken, who rode Poitrel when he defeated Gloaming, then began a long association with the horse. Their big wins included Autumn and Cumberland Stakes and two Randwick Plates. In 1920 Poitrel was beaten by Kennaquhair in the Sydney Cup, where he carried 61.5kg. They met again and dead-heated in Poitrel's favourite race, the Spring Stakes, and both headed south for the spring carnival of 1920. Poitrel was third to Eurythmic in the Melbourne Stakes and then turned out for the Melbourne Cup in which he was burdened with 63.5kg. It was not enough to anchor this top quality galloper who, in winning, became one of only three horses to win with 10 stone or more (the others were Carbine and Archer). Poitrel raced only

twice after the Cup victory, but again proved his class with a second to Eurythmic in the C.B. Fisher Plate and a dead-heat with Richmond Main in the Rawson Stakes. Poitrel was bought by L.K.S. Mackinnon and sent to stud, where his best son was Belgamba, winner of three St Legers.

POON, JIMMY AH

A Chinese market gardener from Canterbury, Jimmy Ah Poon was one of the most renowned and disciplined of Australian punters. Evidently the only horse he backed was the champion Poseidon, and then only on the (numerous) occasions when the horse won. Having amassed a fortune estimated as high as 30,000 pounds, Jimmy Ah Poon vanished from Australian racetracks, and was reputed to have returned to China to enjoy his fortune.

POSEIDON

1904 b horse Positano – Jacinth

One of the greatest of Australian stayers, Poseidon was bred at Neotsfield in New South Wales by R.H. Dangar. After an ordinary two year old term in which he won once from six starts, the Isaac Earnshaw-trained Poseidon had a triumphant three year old campaign. After a second in the Metropolitan, he won 11 times. Those victories included the 1906 A.J.C. and Victoria Derbies, the A.J.C. and V.R.C. St Legers, both the Caulfield and the Melbourne Cups. He won the latter by one and a half lengths from Antonious, ridden by regular jockey T. Clayton. Few better seasons are on record in the history of the Australian turf. And Poseidon went on. As he had been the first horse to win the Caulfield-Melbourne Cups double, so he was the first to land consecutive Caulfield Cups when he carried 58.5kg to victory in 1907 from Apologue who went on to win that year's Melbourne Cup. In between, Poseidon beat Apologue again in the Melbourne Stakes, among his seven victories in the 1907-8 season. In the autumn of 1908 Poseidon's best win was in the Rawson Stakes at Rosehill. An inseparable part of his story is the fortune that the Chinese market gardener Jimmy Ah Poon reputedly made from backing the horse, sufficient – according to legend – to let him retire to his home country. Poseidon went to stud where his best winners were the 1919 Moonee Valley Cup winner Telecles and the Queensland Derby winner of 1915, Rascasse.

PRICE, GEORGE (1878-1950)

This New Zealand-born trainer was apprenticed as a jockey before serving in the Great War. He set up stables in Sydney in 1922, where he was fortunate to have charge of the outstanding horse Windbag, winner of the 1925 Melbourne Cup. He took the Sydney Cup next year with Murray King, and was still prospering in the 1940s when Mildura won a Newmarket and the Doncasters of 1940 and 1941. Price's horses would win two more Doncasters, besides other major races in Sydney and Melbourne. A very short man (150cm), Price was able to secure the services of Maurice McCarten as his principal jockey, while his attentiveness to the needs of his horses placed him in the forefront of trainers. Another specialty was upsetting good things in races. Two of his charges, Warplane and Ballymena beat Gloaming, while it was Price's under-rated galloper Spear Chief who defeated Ajax, shortest priced beaten favourite of the Australian turf, in the Rawson Stakes of 1939. Price retired in 1946.

PRINCE COURTAULD
1950 br horse Sun King – Capricious

Passed in as a yearling in New Zealand, Courtauld (as he was then known) was bought privately and sent to Australia to be trained at Randwick by Maurice McCarten. Prince Courtauld won at Canterbury at his third start and was third in the A.J.C. Sires' Produce behind Cromis. That horse was later disqualified, along with Doncaster winner Tarien for testing positive to the drug Coramine. Prince Courtauld won the Champagne Stakes, but after a fifth in the Rosehill Guineas, Derby plans were abandoned for the colt. In the autumn he had a couple of wins but could only manage seventh in the Doncaster, the race for which he had been set. Thereafter Prince Courtauld won 15 of 21 starts. He won the All Aged Stakes at the autumn carnival. In the spring he was second to Tarien in the Warwick Stakes, before winning the Chelmsford and Hill Stakes, finished second to Connaught in the Epsom and then won the Craven Plate.

Prince Courtauld now headed south where he won the Cantala and Linlithgow Stakes. Kept going, the horse won the Williamstown Cup, proving that 12 furlongs was within his scope. In the autumn Prince Cortauld added the Orr and Blamey Stakes to his record; won the Futurity with 65.5kg; beat Rising Fast in the Queen Elizabeth Stakes. Back in Sydney, Prince Courtauld defeated Rising Fast and Carioca in the Autumn Stakes and won the A.J.C. Queen Elizabeth Stakes. The following spring he beat Rising Fast and Cromis in the Caulfield Stakes of 1955. Then his form tapered off. Prince Courtauld's last Australian win was at Doomben in the winter, his 25th in 52 starts. Invited to represent Australia in the Washington International Stakes, Prince Courtauld returned to something like his old form in finishing third. He raced on for two more years in the United States, before dying suddenly.

PRINCE DARIUS
1954 ch horse Persian Book – Lyrical Lass

Foaled in almost any other year, Prince Darius would have been hailed as a champion. But he had the misfortune to be born in the same year as Tulloch and Todman. Prince Darius soon encountered them both on the track, running second to Tulloch in the Canonbury Stakes and then third – beaten more than 10 lengths – when Todman won his first start in Australian record time for five furlongs. He was third to Tulloch and Todman in the A.J.C. Sires' Produce. Then it was the fate of Prince Darius to encounter Tulloch in the three year old staying classics: he was beaten by four lengths in the Rosehill Guineas, by six in the A.J.C. Derby, by eight in the Victoria Derby, by 20 lengths in the A.J.C. St Leger. In all he ran second to Tulloch on seven occasions, and earned the apt, if unhappy sobriquet, 'Tulloch's Shadow'. When Tulloch was scratched from the Melbourne Cup, on the basis that it was too taxing an assignment for a three year old, Prince Darius contested the race and ran second again, beaten a neck by Straight Draw. Yet he won on 13 occasions, beating Tulloch in the St George Stakes at Caulfield in February 1958 and then finishing in front of him again, but second to Sailor's Guide, in the thrilling Queen Elizabeth Stakes. Prince Darius won two Chelmsford and two Craven Plates, a Colin Stephen Stakes and City Tattersall's Cup. Yet another feature race narrowly to elude him was the 1958 Cox Plate, when he ran into another champion, this time Redcraze.

PRINCE FOOTE
1906 b horse Sir Foote – Petruschka

Bred by John Brown from the imported English stallion Sir Foote, Prince Foote proved to be the best of his sons. Trained by Frank McGrath he had won two minor races in Sydney before easily accounting for Malt King in the A.J.C. Sires' Produce. That horse reversed the placings in the shorter Champagne Stakes. Returned to training in the spring, Prince Foote mocked those who had thought him too small to win a classic race by overcoming difficulties to score in the A.J.C. Derby. Malt King again had his measure over the shorter distance of the Caulfield Stakes, but was not a runner in the Victoria Derby. Starting at 9/4 on, Prince Foote won handsomely. In third place, at 100/1, was his once highly rated but pedestrian stablemate, Lord Foote. In the 1909 Melbourne Cup Prince Foote defeated Alawa, winner of the previous year's Victoria Derby, and was ridden by W.H. McLachlan who won the race again the following year, on Comedy King. Over longer distances Prince Foote was an outstanding performer. In the autumn of 1910 he won both the A.J.C. and V.R.C. St Legers by 12 lengths or more. Other distance wins included the V.R.C. Cumberland Plate and A.J.C. Plate at three miles, and the two mile A.J.C. Cumberland Stakes. At four he won a second Chelmsford Stakes, but thereafter his form fell away and he was retired. His best son was the dual Derby winner Richmond Main, also owned by Brown, who was out of Lord Foote's half sister, Australian Gas.

PRINCE GRANT
1962 b gelding Alcimedes – Chubin

A top campaigner for four seasons, the Tommy Smith-trained Prince Grant was one of the finest stayers of the 1960s. Bought in New Zealand for 2,700 guineas, he had classic form at three, when he won the A.J.C. Derby. In 1966 Prince Grant had an outstanding autumn. He won the V.R.C. St Leger from Tobin Bronze and Midlander, and then beat Craftsman in the Chipping Norton and Queen Elizabeth Stakes at weight-for-age, before triumphing in the Sydney Cup from High Principle. In the spring, Prince Grant won the Colin Stephen Quality Handicap and was second to Trevors in the Chelmsford Stakes. Taken to Melbourne, his best performance was a second to Tobin Bronze in the Mackinnon Stakes. The year of 1967 was less productive, although Prince Grant was second in the Queen Elizabeth Stakes at Randwick to Garcon and second to the champion Galilee while attempting another victory in the Sydney Cup. Two years later, Prince Grant showed that his quality was scarcely dimmed when he recorded a final big race win, in the Tancred Stakes.

PROUD MISS
1959 b mare Orgoglio – Wee Cushla

Proud Miss shares with Surround the Australian record of 10 wins straight for a filly or mare. The New Zealand mare Desert Gold won 19 on end in that country. Proud Miss's winning sequence began at Morphettville on 28 August 1961. This was one of four wins of her 10 in Adelaide. In Melbourne she won six races, including the top two year old events: the Maribyrnong Trial, Debutante, Byron Moore and Merson Cooper Stakes. Sent to Sydney she started 10/9 favourite in the Golden Slipper but wound up second to Birthday Card, who had to equal Todman's race record to beat her. Proud Miss actually won an 11th race as a two year old, the S.A.J.C. Sires' Produce

Stakes. But the long campaign took its toll, and at three and four she managed only three victories in 18 starts.

PROPRIETARY RACING

Fuelled by a mixture of commercial and sporting objectives, proprietary racing began in January 1884 when a syndicate organised a meeting at Canterbury Park. Other Sydney courses established for proprietary racing (that is, run for the owners' profit under the control of private groups, rather than the A.J.C.) were Rosehill (1885), Moorefield (1888) and Warwick Farm (1890). A.J.C. secretary T.S. Clibborn, lamented that racing 'was now a matter of business, while in days gone by it was a sport which we all honoured'. The A.J.C. was concerned that the shorter races favoured at the proprietary tracks would encourage speedy squibs, and affect the quality of horse breeding in Australia. Pony and trotting races were also held at these tracks. The long wrangle between the A.J.C. and the proprietary clubs, plus the declining financial fortunes of the latter, eventually led to their consolidation in 1943 as the Sydney Turf Club.

PURE PAK STAKES
see GADSDEN STAKES

PURSER
1916 b gelding Sea Prince – Paper Money

No high hopes were held for Purser when he was winning picnic races in the Riverina, but gradually the gelding graduated to better things. In 1921 he won the Warrnambool Cup and the Tozer Handicap. Later that year he took the Armidale Cup and was second to Violoncello in the Caulfield Cup. Blossoming in 1922, Purser was third in both the Metropolitan and the Caulfield

Cup, but he beat Whittier in the All Aged Stakes in Sydney; won the Herbert Power (then run at weight-for-age) from the champion Eurythmic and took the Moonee Valley Cup. He finished the season with three handicap wins in Sydney and Melbourne in which he carried between 64 and 68kg. Purser was a brave and well-loved horse, which makes more ironical the sensational events in which he was involved in 1924. The previous season his form had fallen away and he could manage only a few placings from seven starts. At eight he won the A.J.C. Handicap and was taken to Melbourne where he ran a poor 11th in the Coongy. His trainer Cecil Godby had one of the top fancies, The Monk, engaged besides Purser in the Caulfield Cup. To the shock of punters, Godby scratched The Monk on the eve of the race. Despite being burdened with 59.5kg, Purser won easily and broke Paris's 30 year old weight-carrying record in the event. He was also backed from 50/1 to 15/1. The upshot was a stewards' inquiry in which Godby, Purser's owners George Tye and Jack Corteen and his jockey Hughie Cairns (later to die in a hurdle fall at Moonee Valley) were suspended for one year for not allowing Purser to run on his merits in the Coongy. In consequence, the Corteen-owned, Godby-trained crack colt Heroic, had to be scratched from the Derby and Cup, for which it had been a top fancy. Purser went into honourable retirement.

PURTELL, JACK (1921-)

Born at Carlton, Jack Purtell – famous throughout his career both for his prominent nose and his gentlemanly demeanour – was apprenticed to Ted Temby. At Purtell's third race ride, he saw Bonus home at 50/1 at Mentone. Velocity gave him the first of many big race wins when he took the 1941 Caulfield Cup. In the 1948-9 season, Purtell won the first of seven Melbourne jockeys' premierships. He was to win three Melbourne Cups, with Hiraji in 1947, Wodalla in 1953, and the champion Rising Fast in 1954. On Rising Fast he had the perfect record of three wins from as many starts, the others coming in the Cox Plate and Mackinnon Stakes. Purtell won three other Cox Plates in the 1950s: on Alister, Bronton and Ray Ribbon. He rated Comic Court as the best horse he rode (although he preferred Alister in the former's Melbourne Cup win of 1950), and had the seat in 19 of that horse's 21 wins. These included two Craiglee, two Mackinnon, two Memsie and two Turnbull Stakes. Purtell suffered several serious falls during his career, one of which cost him the winning mount on Rivette in her dual Cups-winning year of 1939. Trying his luck overseas during the mid-1960s, Purtell rode with success for the Irish trainer Vincent O'Brien. He won the English Oaks on Long Look in 1965, the Irish Oaks on Ancasta in the previous year. Soon afterwards Purtell retired. His near spotless record (only one suspension as a senior jockey) was – together with his racing acumen – a recommendation to the V.R.C. Committee which appointed him as a stipendiary steward in 1966. Joining the senior panel in 1971, he worked with the V.R.C. until his retirement to the Gold Coast in 1981.

PYERS, BILL (1933-)

Born at Horsham, William Albert Pyers started his riding career in Adelaide and ended it in France. He rode his first winner in 1950 and by the end of the next racing season won the first of seven successive South Australian jockeys' premierships. His initial classic success was in the 1952 South Australian Oaks, a race which he won on six other occasions. Other big home town successes included P.A.R.C. Sires' Produce Stakes, two Port Adelaide Cups and Goodwood Handicaps on Gerante and Scenic Star. Pyers also won the 1953 Adelaide Cup on Royal Pageant. His biggest interstate success was the 1963 Caulfield Cup on Sometime, but other forays saw him win the 1958 Newmarket on Royal Pageant; the V.R.C. Sires' and Golden Slipper of 1963 on Pago Pago; the 1964 Oakleigh Plate on Pardon Me and the 1965 Futurity Stakes on Wenona Girl. Pyers also rode Tulloch when the champion passed the 100,000 pounds mark in prize money in winning the Pullman Select Stakes at Cheltenham. Despite such successes and his big following, Pyers readily accepted a contract in 1964 to ride with Ernie Fellows in France. Quickly Pyers established himself as one of the leading riders in Europe. His big wins included the 1967 Prix de l'Arc de Triomphe on Topyo, the 2,000 Guineas and Ascot Gold Cup in England and the French Derby. He also partnered the great mare Dahlia in such victories as the King George VI and Queen Elizabeth Stakes.

Q

QUEEN ELIZABETH STAKES

The first Queen Elizabeth Stakes (to celebrate the accession to the throne of a new British monarch) was held at Randwick in 1954. It is now a Group One race in the autumn carnival. Tulloch won three times, in 1958, 1960 and 1961. Outstanding subsequent winners have included Gay Icarus (1971), Ngawyni (1977), Ming Dynasty (1978), Shivaree (1979), Tristarc (1986), Our Poetic Prince (1989), Sydeston (1990), Rough Habit (1992), Veandercross (1993) and Durbridge (1994). The Flemington version of the Queen Elizabeth Stakes has not by contrast had a top-line winner since Hyperno's second win in a row in 1980. It is now a Group Two race in the spring carnival programme. The first running in 1956 saw Sailor's Guide home; second the following year, he beat Prince Darius and Tulloch in 1958. Lord was also a dual winner, in 1962-3, besides being placed twice. Craftsman won in 1965-6, and Galilee the next year. Rain Lover was victorious in 1969, but in 1970 was just beaten in the famous match race against Big Philou. Gunsynd also recorded a dual victory: in 1972-3, the latter was his last start in Melbourne, when the race was run in the autumn. By coincidence, Gunsynd's last Sydney start was a second in the Randwick Queen Elizabeth Stakes. The enigmatic Taras Bulba won both Queen Elizabeth Stakes in 1976.

QUEENSLAND DERBY

The first race to be known as the Queensland Derby was held at Gayndah in 1868 by the Queensland Jockey Club. Four horses ran, and The Hermit won. Only two presented in the next year, when Zambesi was first home. The race was then abandoned until 1871, when the Q.T.C. staged a Queensland Derby. In winning, the remarkable filly Florence completed an unprecedented hat-trick for her sex of the eastern states' Derbies. John Tait, her owner, won again with J.L. the following year, but he, too, faced only one opponent. The race was once more discontinued, not resuming until 1878, when Whisker won. Other fine winners were Legerdemain and Fitz-Grafton (who went on to win the Brisbane Cup in 1904 and 1905); High Syce, Lough Neagh and Spear Chief (the best three Queensland-bred gallopers between the wars); the triple Derby winners Tulloch (1957), Royal Sovereign (1964) and Silver

Sharpe (1970); Analie, Kingston Town, Strawberry Road and Rough Habit. It is a race which – at least since the Second World War – loses little by comparison with its Sydney and Melbourne counterparts.

QUEENSLAND RACING

The Moreton Bay Racing Club conducted its first meeting on 17 July 1843 at the Cooper's Plains course on the outskirts of Brisbane. Whig won the Brisbane Town Plate. The M.B.R.C. opened courses at New Farm and at South Brisbane in 1852. In 1859 the North Australian Jockey Club conducted its first meeting at Ipswich in 1859. The Queensland Turf Club was established in 1863; bought land at Eagle Farm and held its first meeting there in 1865. It is the premier racing club in Queensland.

QUEENSLAND TURF CLUB

Formed on 3 August 1863 at McAdam's Hotel in Brisbane, after a meeting of 54 gentlemen, the Queensland Turf Club is the premier racing body in the state. Because of the demography of Queensland: a capital to the south of a vast state, and with less than half the state's population, the Q.T.C. has never exerted the degree of control of its Victorian and New South Wales counterparts. The affairs of the Q.T.C. were set on a more professional footing in 1878 when R.R. Dawbarn became paid secretary, and Joshua Bell Chairman. In that year the Derby was revived; two years later the totalisator operated on the club's autumn meeting. In 1888 the winter meeting (which would prove its most important) was added to the programme of the Q.T.C. The main events that it stages at Eagle Farm, besides the three year old classics, are the Stradbroke Handicap and Brisbane Cup,

together with the Group One two year old races, the Castlemaine Stakes and Q.T.C. Sires' Produce.

QUINTON, RON (1948-)

One of the leading jockeys of the modern era, Ron Quinton came from Mendooran in western New South Wales. His father worked on a property whose owners had a handy horse called Travel On. Quinton senior trained the horse for a time and young Ron occasionally hacked him around the paddocks. His desire to become a jockey was forged and the property's owners arranged for him to be apprenticed to Theo Green in Sydney. Quinton had his first ride at 17. Before coming out of his time, he won the apprentice jockeys' premiership and was second three times. The first of his eight Sydney senior jockeys' premierships came at the end of the 1969-70 season, his first year as a senior rider. A second followed in 1976-7, before Quinton won six on the trot from 1978-9 to 1983-4. In the first year of that run he had his best metropolitan year, recording one hundred and four and a half winners. When he retired, Quinton had ridden about 1,700 winners, many of them for Sydney trainer Neville Begg, but others in Ireland, where he rode with success for three years with the John Oxx stable in the late 1980s.

Quinton's first big race win was the A.J.C. Oaks on Analie in 1973, a race that later he captured with Sufficient and November Rain. The latter filly gave him other big wins in the A.J.C. St Leger of 1981 and the V.R.C. Oaks in the previous year. Quinton won Doncasters on Analie and Emancipation (the latter in 1983), an Epsom on Dalmacia in 1982. North of the border he won the Doomben 10,000 on Burwana in 1976, while in Melbourne he took the 1981 Cox Plate on Kingston Town, the 1986 Victoria Derby on Raveneaux. Quinton shares with R.S. Dye the riding record of four wins in the S.T.C. Golden Slipper Stakes. His victories came on Marscay (1982), Sir Dapper the next year, for Colin Hayes on Rory's Jester following an injury to Darren Gauci in 1985 and in 1987 on Marauding, an especially sweet win as he was returning after injury.

R

RAILWAY STAKES

Run at the W.A.T.C. Christmas meeting at Ascot, the Group One Railway Stakes (1600m) is one of the most important events on the State's racing calendar. First run in 1887 (and until 1921 at 10 furlongs), the Railway Stakes numbers among its winners the versatile Wandering Willie in 1890, Aquanita (1959), dual winner Tudor Mak (1966-7), La Trice (1968) and Marwong (1988).

RAIN LOVER

1964 b horse Latin Lover – Rainspot

Bred by Clifford Reid, who had won the 1945 Melbourne Cup with his horse Rainbird, Rain Lover won only once from five starts at two. Next term he was second to Lowland in the S.A.J.C. St Leger, but won the Adelaide Cup convincingly. When Graeme Heagney went to the United States to superintend the campaign of Tobin Bronze, former Broken Hill miner Mick Robins took over the training of the horse. In the spring of 1968 he was a first-up second at 100/1 to Lowland in the Craiglee. His great staying rival was at the handy odds of 50/1. Rain Lover won the Mackinnon Stakes and with Jim Johnson up, destroyed his opponents by eight lengths (a margin which equalled Archer's more than a century before) in course record time in the Melbourne Cup.

A long sequence of weight-for-age wins followed, in the C.B. Fisher Plate, the St George Stakes, Queen's Plate and the Queen Elizabeth Stakes, before Rain Lover ran second to Lowland in the Sydney Cup. Back in the spring of 1969, Rain Lover won the Craiglee and the Underwood, but seemed to be losing form with fourths in the Caulfield and Mackinnon Stakes. Burdened with 60.5kg in the Melbourne Cup, he nevertheless won gallantly from Alsop, to whom he conceded 13kg. Thus Rain Lover became the third horse, after Archer and Peter Pan, to win the Melbourne Cup twice (Think Big would be the fourth). In the autumn of 1970 he won the St George and the Queen's Plate, beating Big Philou. That horse had his revenge in the famous 'match race' Queen Elizabeth Stakes, when he beat Rain Lover by a half head. Sent again to Sydney, Rain Lover won the Autumn Stakes, failed in the Sydney Cup and was retired after a third in the A.J.C. Queen Elizabeth Stakes. He had won 17 of 46 starts (all at distances of a mile or longer) and been placed on 21 other occasions. He stood, with little success, at Tarwyn Park Stud.

RAJAH SAHIB

1965 br horse Pakistan II – Gay Princess

Champion New Zealand two year old of his year, Rajah Sahib's quality is underscored by the fact that he was placed in the first three in 22 stakes races. In all he won 14 times at distances from six to 12 furlongs. And few horses' wins have been more various. Besides the Caulfield Guineas and Cox Plate in 1968, as a three year old, Rajah Sahib won the Doncaster and the Stradbroke in 1971. To those events can be added wins in the A.R.C. Birthday Cup in Adelaide and the Mornington Cup in rural Victoria. He was also placed in two Doomben Cups, ran second in a Rosehill Guineas and Australian Cup, besides a third in the Newmarket. After this first-rate but perhaps under-appreciated career, Rajah Sahib went to stud duties.

RAMPION

1923 br horse Rossendale – Royal Pet

A top class two year old, Rampion won the A.J.C. Breeders' Plate, the V.R.C. Maribyrnong Plate and Sires' Produce and the A.J.C. Champagne Stakes of 1926. He was left at the barrier in the A.J.C. Sires'. Resuming at three, Rampion won the Hobartville and was then second in the Rosehill Guineas. But he was running into classic form: at his next start he took the A.J.C. Derby, before heading south where he won the Caulfield Guineas and the Victoria Derby. Unplaced in the Melbourne Cup, Rampion never performed again in top company. He won the Bond Cup at Caulfield in the autumn of 1927; at four was unplaced in the Carrington Stakes and was then retired.

RANCHER

1980 ch horse Brave Lad – Awakening

A brilliant juvenile, the Charlie Waymouth trained Rancher won his first three starts by an aggregate of 18 lengths. Not surprisingly the striking chestnut was sent out at 16/1 on in the Maribyrnong Plate and duly won by eight lengths. Back in the autumn, he won three events in the lead up to the Blue Diamond Stakes, before his narrow victory in that event from War Chest and Grosvenor gave him eight wins in succession. Troubled by leg problems as a three year old, Rancher still carried 58.5kg to win the Ascot Vale Stakes and earned prize money in the other three events that he contested. He was now retired and began a successful stud career, siring such top-line gallopers as Rancho Ruler, besides the strong performers Bold Rancher and Strawberry Ranch. The brilliant, but unsound Confederate Lady (now serving as a brood-mare) might have proved to be the best of all his issue. Rancher died at the Arrowfield Stud in March 1994.

RANDWICK RACECOURSE

A training track known as 'the Sandy Course' in its first incarnation, Randwick was in the beginning little more than a tea-tree swamp by the Botany Road, south of the centre of Sydney. Races were held here from 1835-8, but the track surface deteriorated to such an extent that meetings were abandoned. It was not for another two decades that the A.J.C. decided to renovate the course as the base of its operations, establishing Randwick as its racing headquarters from 1863. A revitalised programme saw the Derby run from the spring of 1865 (versions of the event had been conducted since 1861), together with the Epsom (named for the site of the English Derby). The autumn programme, first held in April-May 1866, had the St Leger as its highlight, and also featured the Doncaster (named for the Yorkshire track where the English St Leger is run), the Champagne and All Aged Stakes. Improvements in the grandstand accommodation for racegoers continued throughout the 1870s. In 1873 the A.J.C. was given the right to charge admission fees both to the course and to its stands. In 1876 a continuous running rail replaced the posts set up at five chain (100m) intervals which had marked out the course. Renovations in this century culminated in the opening of the Queen Elizabeth II grandstand in 1969. A total of 40,000 people turned out on a Sunday in July for a preview of the new stand and its facilities. Despite problems in the 1980s with a racing surface susceptible to heavy rain (forcing the postponement of the 1983 Sydney Cup), this grandest and most spacious of Sydney's tracks is now also the most resilient in the face of the vagaries of the harbour city's weather. It became Royal Randwick by grace and favour of Queen Elizabeth II in March 1992.

RANGER, KEN (1908-)

This hairdresser's son, who became one of Sydney's biggest bookmakers, took out his licence to field at the Harold Park trots as well as at provincial greyhound meetings when still in his teens. After a spell on pony tracks, Ranger was granted an A.J.C. licence. By the late 1950s he was the biggest bookmaker on the rails in Sydney. At the end of that decade, he quit while he was ahead.

RANVET STAKES

see RAWSON STAKES

RAWSON STAKES

Known since 1991 as the Ranvet Stakes (and from 1987-90 as the Segenhoe), this Group One weight-for-age race over 2000m is a feature of the autumn carnival at Rosehill. It was the first weight-for-age event to be staged there, in 1903, when Great Scott beat Abundance and Purser. The champion Poseidon was an early winner, while Malt King won twice, in 1911-2. Cetigne scored during the Great War, Artilleryman soon afterwards, while Poitrel and Richmond Main dead-heated in a memorable race in 1921. Other notable winners between the wars included Furious and Whittier, Limerick in 1927-8, Nightmarch, Rogilla and Peter Pan. The Queensland galloper Lough Neagh scored in 1933, 1936 and 1937, and was third in 1934. Bernborough's grand campaign of 1946 contained a victory in the Rawson, while Redcraze and Tulloch saluted in the 1950s. Wenona Girl and Sky High were notable dual winners in the 1960s, Gunsynd and Marceau in the next decade. Balmerino and Hyperno, Mr McGinty and Myocard, Beau Zam in 1988-9, Better Loosen Up (1990), Super Impose (1991) and Veandercross (1993) have recently been added to the honour roll of one of the greatest middle distance races on the Australian calendar.

RAY RIBBON

1951 b horse Pirilous – Lady Yelverton

Ray Ribbon first showed top-line form in the spring of 1955, and he held it for three seasons. Second in the Caulfield Cup to Rising Fast, he was runner-up to that champion again in the Mackinnon Stakes. Some consolation came with victory in the Williamstown Cup. In the spring of 1956 Ray Ribbon enjoyed his most productive campaign. He won the Underwood Stakes at Caulfield before carrying 59.5kg into fifth place in the Caulfield Cup behind Redcraze. He then defeated Rising Fast and Caranna in the Cox Plate, before running third to the upset winner Sir William and Redcraze in the Mackinnon Stakes. Third in the Rawson Stakes in the autumn of 1957 to Redcraze and Kingster, Ray Ribbon notched another big win in the spring when he won the Caulfield Stakes. In the autumn of 1958 he still held his form well enough to run third in the Blamey to Sailor's Guide.

RAZOR SHARP
1977 b gelding Steel Pulse – Sea Holly

Trained by Jim Johnstone, Razor Sharp was brilliant sprinter of the early 1980s. In the autumn of 1981, he was second in the Galaxy at Randwick behind Grey Receiver, who would also beat him home the following year. Razor Sharp won the Challenge Stakes at Randwick in January 1982 and was sent south for a Melbourne campaign. Defeated a short half head by Harpagus in the Oakleigh Plate, he won the Newmarket from Penny Edition. Always best suited in the autumn, he nevertheless ran second to Manikato in the Moir Stakes in the spring of 1982. Next year he won his second Challenge Stakes and headed again for Melbourne. Razor Sharp's form was sound, with a third in the Lightning and a fifth in the Oakleigh Plate before he sought a second Newmarket. Dale Short had the ride again. Since the previous year's triumph he had ridden only one metropolitan winner, but Johnstone kept faith with him. Short saw Razor Sharp home at 25/1 by two lengths from Ideal Planet, so that he became only the fourth horse to win the Newmarket in consecutive years. That was his 12th win, together with 17 placings, from 40 starts. Nor was Razor Sharp done with, he recorded a third win in a row in the Challenge Stakes early in 1984.

READING
1936 b horse Marconigram – Gravure

Noted for his keen duels with the top colt High Caste, Reading's best win at two was in the A.J.C. Sires' of 1938; he was second to High Caste in the Champagne. Trainer J. Cush brought him back at three for a second to High Caste in the Rosehill Guineas. Then he was runner-up to Beau Vite in the Clarendon Stakes. In the A.J.C. Derby, Reading has his turn over High Caste, recording a strong win. He had to be satisfied with placing behind that horse in the Caulfield Guineas and Caulfield Stakes, before running third to Mosaic and Gold Salute in the Cox Plate. Then, with Darby Munro up, Reading won the Victoria Derby from High Caste to complete the classic double. High Caste again had his measure in the autumn of 1940, beating Reading in the Orr and St George Stakes. Reading did, however, complete a successful season with victories in the V.R.C. and A.J.C. St Legers and the Chipping Norton Stakes. But at four he was without a win in 16 starts. At five he recovered a semblance of his best form, with second placings in the Craven Plate and the 1941 Caulfield Cup. Soon after Reading was sold to the film magnate Louis B. Mayer for 2,000 guineas, and ran unplaced in the Moonee Valley Cup for his new owner before being taken to the United States.

REALM(S)

Two horses of this name won the Sydney Cup. The first of them (Archie-Empress) was bred in Queensland and won the 1891 Queensland Cup. In Sydney he won the Autumn Stakes at Randwick besides his victory in the 1893 Sydney Cup. The second Realm (Majestic-Lynette), owned by L.K.S. Mackinnon, was an even more versatile performer. In 1907 he won the Sydney Cup and the Australian Cup. Prior to that he had proved to be a top flight hurdler. In 1906 he won both the Grand National Hurdle at Flemington and the Caulfield Grand National (later Australian) Hurdle.

RECKLESS

1970 br horse Better Boy – Impulsive

The beautifully-bred Reckless was unplaced in five starts at two, placed third at Caulfield in 11 starts at three, and did not win until his 34th start, in the Galilee Handicap, when he was five. Trainer Tommy Woodcock had shown remarkable perseverance with the stallion, and was coming into his reward. In August 1976 Reckless won the Peter Pan Handicap at Flemington. He still went out at 33/1 in the Hotham (now the Dalgety) Handicap but he won well, as had his sire Better Boy two decades before. Bottom weight, but fancied for the Melbourne Cup, Reckless overcame his loathing of a wet track to run fourth to Van Der Hum in the Flemington bog. Woodcock brought him back in the autumn, when he was placed at Flemington and Sandown before being sent to Sydney. Ridden by Pat Trotter, Reckless won the Sydney Cup easily at 20/1 from Gold and Black. Back in Melbourne, Reckless won the Shaggy Ridge Handicap on Anzac Day by five lengths.

In the Adelaide Cup he was at the skinny odds of 10/9, despite the presence of the Perth Cup winner Muros and the dual Melbourne Cup winner Think Big. Reckless duly scored by two lengths. In the Brisbane Cup he faced still stiffer opposition, but defeated Ngawyni and My Good Man to record an unprecedented Cups treble. And Woodcock had a fourth in mind. In the spring of 1977, Reckless was fourth in the Caulfield Cup and then failed by a length – to the intense disappointment of the crowd – to catch Gold and Black in the Melbourne Cup. Thereafter he won the Robinson Handicap and Woodcock took him west for another Cups assignment. In perhaps his greatest run, Reckless broke down but still finished third in the Perth Cup to Golden Circle and Muros in the Perth Cup. He was then retired, ending one of the great sentimental tales of attachment between horse and trainer in Australian turf history.

RED ANCHOR

1981 ch horse Sea Anchor – Decoy Girl

One of the best of trainer Tommy Smith's many Derby winners, Red Anchor's brilliant career was cut short by injury. As a two year old, he won the 1984 Champagne Stakes and was second to Victory Prince in the A.J.C. Sires' Produce. He won the Queensland version of the Sires' towards the end of his two year old season. As a spring three year old, Red Anchor reeled off a series of outstanding efforts. He began with victory in the Roman Consul Stakes before Smith sent him south. Red Anchor convincingly defeated Lord of Camelot in the Moonee Valley Stakes and the Caulfield Guineas, and was installed as favourite at the skinny quote of 11/8 on in the Cox Plate. It was not a vintage field, but Red Anchor won well from another three year old, Street Cafe. In the Victoria Derby he was again odds-on and was too good for his rivals once more, defeating National Gallery and Clovelly Bay. Although he won the Apollo Stakes first up over 1400m at the start of his next campaign, Red Anchor went wrong in preparation for the Chipping Norton and was retired to the Barramul Stud. He had won nine of his 14 starts and was placed in the other five.

REDCRAZE

1950 ch gelding Red Mars – Myarion

One of the greatest and toughest stayers to race in the vintage period of the mid-1950s, the New Zealand-bred Redcraze was by the imported son of Hyperion, Red Mars. At two he did not start and it was not until his four year old days that he showed staying form. By the time he was taken to Australia by trainer Syd Brown, Redcraze had victories in the Wanganui and Awapuni Gold Cups behind him. And he had many miles of racing in front of him (over 100 in the course of his career, or 160+km). Brown raced the horse 14 times in nine weeks and it was no surprise that Redcraze won only once, although it was a significant victory, over Rising Fast at the start of his campaign. He then ran poorly in the 1955 Caulfield Cup to Rising Fast. Even though Brown galloped the horse 10 furlongs on the Melbourne Cup morning, Redcraze was still able to run fourth. He went back to New Zealand after this campaign. In 1956 Redcraze's owner, Mrs J. Bradley, began a famous association when she sent the horse to Tommy Smith.

In the winter of 1956, Redcraze won the O'Shea Stakes and the Brisbane Cup. Spelled he came back with a fourth in the Chelmsford Stakes, won the Hill Stakes in record time, the Colin Stephen Stakes and the Metropolitan with 61kg. Next he defeated Rising Fast narrowly in the Caulfield Stakes (he was in front of that champion on seven of their 12 meetings). Despite having to carry 63kg (which would prove to be a record winning weight), Redcraze was 9/4 favourite for the Caulfield Cup. He won even more authoritatively than that price suggested, by four lengths. Going in to the Melbourne Cup he was beaten a mere half neck by Evening Peal who was in receipt of 14kg from him. In the

autumn of 1957, Redcraze won the St George Stakes, Queen's Plate and Queen Elizabeth Stakes, relegating Sailor's Guide to second on each occasion. Taken to Sydney he ran a race record in winning the Rawson Stakes. Further north, he won a second O'Shea Stakes and was fourth in the Brisbane Cup with 64kg. Redcraze gradually felt the toll of his arduous campaigning and in the spring of 1957 won two of six starts. One was the Hill Stakes, and a final triumph came in the Cox Plate, in which he scored by a half head to Prince Darius. Despite being burdened with 64.5kg, Redcraze still started favourite in the Melbourne Cup, but could only manage an eighth placing. The career of this grand stayer then came to an end.

REDDITCH

1927 b gelding Red Dennis – Kenilworth

Trained by Fred Hoysted, this grand weight-carrier won the Grand National Steeple in 1933 and was second the next year with 80kg. He won the V.A.T.C. Australian Steeple in 1933 and 1934, beating Mosstrooper on the first occasion and carrying 82kg to victory on the second. While he had been second in the 1932 Grand National Hurdle, the bigger post and rail fences suited his extravagant jumping. Redditch fell in the August Steeple at Flemington in 1934 while carrying 86kg and in the Grand National Steeple of 1935 fell again and had to be destroyed. Such was the outcry at his death, that brush fences were brought in to replace the post and rail obstacles over which Redditch had made his name.

REDELVA

1983 ch gelding Romantic Hope – Delvena

The career of the honest and talented galloper Redelva is an abstract of five years of top sprint races in Melbourne and Adelaide. Trained by G.A. Varcoe, and usually ridden by Neville Wilson, Redelva won the 1987 Lightning Stakes in Adelaide, the Irwin Stakes in the following year, the Spring Stakes in the consecutive years 1988-90. In Melbourne Redelva showed his class by winning the 1988 Standish Handicap with 57kg. Later that year he won the Rupert Steele Stakes at weight-for-age (a race in which he was second in the next three years) and was second in the Moir Stakes. Weight-for-age placings in the Manikato and the Linlithgow were his best efforts in 1989, but the following year Redelva's sprint victories included the Lightning, Linlithgow and Stanley Wootton Stakes. He was also second in the Gadsden to Planet Ruler. In 1991 Redelva began with victory in the William Reid, a second to Shaftesbury Avenue in the Newmarket, followed by another Group One victory, in the Futurity Stakes. That autumn he also won the Rubiton Stakes, while in the spring of 1991 he proved both that age had not weakened him and that 1400m was within his scope, by scoring in the Memsie Stakes.

REDLEAP

1884 b gelding Dante – Pandora

One of the greatest of 19th century jumpers, Redleap was usually ridden by the amateur jockey W.S. Cox, and he was owned by Septimus Miller. His weight-carrying feats in victories in the top jumping races are now the cause of astonishment. Redleap won the Grand National Hurdle of 1889 with the light weight of 61kg. Three years on he took the race again with 74.5kg. A week later he won the Grand National Steeple with 84kg, a race in which 11 of the 19 runners fell. Next month, in August 1892, he won the four mile Caulfield Grand

National Steeple by four lengths; started at 6/4 and carried 88kg!

REGO

1949 br horse Nasrullah – Missy Suntan

Winner of three races in England, Rego was to earn renown as a stallion in Australia. He sired Wiggle, a brilliant filly whose 14 wins included the Stradbroke Handicap as a two year old in 1958 before she embarked on her three year old career. She also won six races in the United States. On the strength of Wiggle's performances and following the death in the United States of Nasrullah's sire Noor, a large offer was made to purchase Rego to replace Noor, but studmaster Carl Powell elected to keep the stallion in Australia. Baguette was Rego's best son, numbering among his victories the Golden Slipper, Rosehill Guineas, Newmarket and Doomben 10,000. At stud Baguette got the likes of Romantic Dream, Hit It Benny and Dark Eclipse. Other top progeny of Rego included the Golden Slipper winner Reisling, Thousand Guineas winner Heirloom, V.R.C. Sires' Produce winner Boeing Boy and the 1963 Q.T.C. Sires' winner Kiwanis.

REIBEY, THOMAS (1821-1912)

Born at Entally House, near Launceston, into the Tasmanian gentry, Thomas Reibey went to Trinity College, Oxford, returned home without a degree but with a fondness for the hunt and became the first Tasmanian-born Anglican minister. Accused of attempting to seduce another man's wife, Archdeacon Reibey resigned his position, but soon entered state politics. Although the *Mercury* lampooned him as 'the ecclesiastical debauchee', Reibey was Premier in 1876-7. He is famous also for the Melbourne Cup winners that he never owned. In 1879 he bought Stockwell, who won the 1882 Launceston Cup but could only manage second to The Assyrian in that year's Melbourne Cup. At the 1879 sale he had also been interested in another horse but dropped out when he felt that the auctioneer was running him up in the bidding. That horse, later named Sheet Anchor, won the 1885 Melbourne Cup. In 1880 Reibey went to the sale again and bought Stockwell's full brother, Bagot. After Stockwell's defeat in the 1882 Melbourne Cup, Reibey sold the two horses. Renamed Malua by his new owners, the former Bagot won the Oakleigh Plate, Newmarket and Melbourne Cup in 1884; the Grand National Hurdle four years later. Reibey consoled himself with the presidency of three small racing clubs in northern Tasmania.

REISLING
1962 br mare Rego – Golestan Nymph

In the 1964-5 racing season the filly Reisling gave a taste of fame to two battlers: trainer Jack Norman and jockey Laurie Billett. A winner at her third start, Reisling failed to handle a rain-affected track in the Silver Slipper, although she atoned with an easy win at Rosehill a week later. Back in form she won her next two starts by margins of five and eight lengths, before scoring by 15 lengths at Newcastle. Then her first try over 1200m at Randwick yielded a narrow victory. After a well deserved spell, Reisling returned in the autumn of 1965 and ran a race-record first up to beat the Maribyrnong Plate winner King Star at Rosehill. In the Golden Slipper she was never headed while beating the top-liners Star Affair and Citius in then record time. Three weeks later Reisling was just beaten by Eyeliner in the Champagne Stakes. Norman decided to try

to emulate Wiggle, the filly who won the Doomben 10,000 as a two year old, but Reisling found the older competition too stiff. She never recaptured her two year old form, winning once at three and twice the next season, before being sent to stud. A race is named in her honour at the Sydney autumn carnival .

RESEARCH
1985 b mare Imperial Prince – Outing

The outstanding staying filly of the late 1980s, Research was trained by Clarrie Conners. At two she won her first couple of starts in December 1987. In the autumn she found the best two year olds too slick, although she managed fourth in the A.J.C. Sires' and fifth in the Champagne. At three, Research won seven of 14 starts in the best company; was placed in another five. Her triumphant campaign in the spring of 1988 began with a victory in the Furious Stakes at Randwick; she then lost the Tea Rose Stakes on protest to Glenview, before convincingly winning the Group One Flight Stakes. Sent south, Research was unluckily beaten by Riverina Charm in the Thousand Guineas at Caulfield before decisively reversing those placings, with Mick Dittman up, in the V.R.C. Oaks. In between, Research won the Wakeful Stakes. Back in the autumn, she was placed in top open company in the Hobartville, Chipping Norton and Segenhoe Stakes, behind the likes of Beau Zam. But Research's greatest triumphs were in front of her. She became the first filly to win the A.J.C. Derby-Oaks double. Before then she had won the Storm Queen Stakes by a short half head to Courtalista. So dominant was Research in her age group that she was odds-on in the Derby, where she scored by two lengths from Royal

Pardon. Research was made Australian Horse-of-the-Year for the 1988-9 season.

RICHFIELD LADY

1988 b mare Grosvenor – Sea Princess

Bred in New Zealand, Richfield Lady won four of her five starts there before being sent to Australia to the care of Bart Cummings. In a remarkable spring in 1991 she won every fillies' classic in Melbourne, equalling the feat of Tristanagh three years earlier. Richfield began with victory in the Edward Manifold Stakes. She then won the Thousand Guineas at Caulfield, the Wakeful and the Oaks at Flemington – none of the last three victories was by a margin greater than a neck. Richfield Lady went amiss soon afterwards and was retired to stud.

RICHMOND

1872 br horse Maribyrnong – The Fawn

Trained by Eli Jellett, Richmond was a first-rate horse who campaigned with success in three States. He won the A.R.C. Birthday Cup and Town Plate in Adelaide; the Mares' Produce, Randwick Plate and A.J.C. Derby of 1875 in Sydney; the V.R.C. Champion Stakes, St Leger, Town Plate and Australian Cup in Melbourne. In addition he was second to the top colt Robin Hood in the 1875 Derby and, according to his owner, an unlucky second in the Melbourne Cup of that year. Leading jockey Tom Hales had ridden Richmond to his Randwick Derby victory but declared overweight in the Cup, so that Jellett engaged an inexperienced lad called Williams, whom he blamed for his colt's defeat by Wollomai. Richmond went on to sire The Admiral, who won the 1889 Maribyrnong Plate and the Caulfield Stakes and Victoria Derby in the following year. He also sired Aura, dam of the top-line gallopers Auraria and Aurum.

RIDING THE CARD

The improbable and legendary jockey's feat of riding the card has been achieved or just missed on a number of occasions in Australian turf history. One J. Hayden rode all six at Thangool in Queensland in December 1942 and did the same at the club's next meeting in the following April (although one was a walk-over). Jack Toohey sat out the hurdle race at Canterbury in May 1923, but won the five flat races on the card. Following with the first two at Randwick at the next meeting, he set the Sydney metropolitan record of seven consecutive winners. The Melbourne record is eight in a row, set by Roy Higgins over a remarkable four race days (three wins at Moonee Valley in late December 1977, two at Flemington on New Year's Day, one at Sandown mid-week, two more at Caulfield on 8 January 1978). Usually it has been bush meetings where jockeys have ridden the card: Noel Thompson rode all seven at Cunnamulla in May 1961 and Charles Eaton trained the lot. The estimable *Miller's Guide* gives a lengthy listing of similar achievements. None, however, tops the effort of Tasmanian jockey Geoff Prouse on a metropolitan course. Prouse rode all seven at Elwick on 22 January 1972. He won on Island Prince, Ink Spot and Pyrene King, took the Tasmanian Derby on the odds-on favourite Sabreur, won the next two on Light Rank and Demi God, and scrambled home in the last on Staraire.

RING-INS

see FINE COTTON, ROYAL SCHOOL RING-INS, Bert WOLFE

RIPA

1960 b mare Pride of Kildare – Gold Spi

Trained by Basil Conaghan, Ripa was a

high class sprinting mare in the 1960s. Third to Pago Pago in the Golden Slipper of 1963, she was then second to Time and Tide in the Champagne Stakes. They would meet on seven occasions, with Ripa narrowly securing the advantage. The next was in the Craven 'A' Stakes on Derby Day when Ripa won in race record time. In the autumn of 1964, Ripa was second in both the Oakleigh Plate (to Time and Tide) and the Newmarket (to Rashlore). The latter also had the better of her in the Delaney Quality at Doomben, where Ripa went on a winter campaign. Back in Melbourne in the springtime, she won the Invitation Stakes with Roy Higgins aboard. In the following year she took the Newmarket from Time and Tide in record time, with 55.5kg, more than any other mare has carried to victory in the race. These exertions took a toll, and in seven starts at five, Ripa won only once – but the race was the Toorak Handicap, in which she beat Nicopolis. In 1966 Ripa was bought by American interests as a broodmare.

RISING FAST

1949 b gelding Alonzo – Faster

Leicester Spring paid 325 guineas at the New Zealand yearling sales for a colt called Rising Fast. It was his first thoroughbred purchase and one of the most inspired in our racing history. Trained by Jack Winder, Rising Fast showed little at two, running third once in four starts. As a three year old gelding he gradually improved his performances. Three unplaced runs were followed by a win at Franklin in the Bombay Plate. From this humble start, four more wins came that season. At four, Rising Fast won at Waikato and then ran poorly in the Te Awamutu Cup. Winder and jockey J.T. Anderson were each suspended for a month.

Spring was exonerated. On appeal, Winder's suspension was lifted to one and then to five years! Rising Fast won the Queen Elizabeth Plate at his next start, but Spring vowed never to run him again in New Zealand. Although the horse was frequently paraded in his home country while spelling, racetrack crowds in New Zealand had seen him for the last time. Spring transferred the horse to Ivan Tucker in Brisbane and his first Australian campaign yielded a third in the 1954 Doomben Cup behind Euphrates and Paper Strip.

In his first run at five, Rising Fast trounced the odds-on Euphrates in the Barnes Stakes at Eagle Farm. Sent south, he was fourth in the Memsie, won the Feehan and was then odds-on and beaten a half head by the under-rated Flying Halo in the Underwood Stakes. One of the great winning sequences in Australian racing now began. In succession Rising Fast won the Turnbull and Caulfield Stakes; the Caulfield Cup of 1954 with 55.5kg at 7/4 favourite; the Cox Plate, Mackinnon Stakes and then the Melbourne Cup with 59.5kg at 5/2 favourite. He became the fourth horse to complete the Cups double. Rising Fast rounded off his carnival with victory in the Fisher Plate. His trainers' ill luck continued when Tucker was suspended, so that Spring transferred his horse to Fred Hoysted in Melbourne.

Rising Fast's autumn campaign in 1955 was flat, with a single win from six starts, although he was four times second. As a six year old in the spring of 1955, the horse was beaten at his first four starts as Hoysted struggled to get him fit. But he broke through in the Herbert Power; cast a plate when second in the Caulfield Stakes and then lined up for his second Caulfield Cup. In a sterling performance, Rising Fast carried a record weight of 61.5kg to victory by three lengths. It took some toll, for he was only sixth in the Cox Plate behind Kingster, but Rising Fast was back in form at Flemington and won the Mackinnon Stakes. He had emulated Poseidon's feat of winning the Cups double and then another Caulfield Cup: he almost completed the double double. In a controversial race, Rising Fast carried 63.5kg and was narrowly beaten by Toparoa (who had 48kg). Rising Fast had suffered interference several times in running, most notably from the winner in the home straight. No protest was lodged, but Toparoa's rider Neville Sellwood was outed for three months for interference to Rising Fast. The champion won the Fisher Plate as a consolation prize a few days later.

In the autumn of 1956 he was unplaced in the William Reid Stakes, but then won the Blamey and the Orr before suffering a bleeding attack. Put away till the spring, Rising Fast was never the same horse. In the twilight of his career he won only one of his last 10 starts – the Memsie Stakes – although he ran a top race with 64.5kg when fifth, after again suffering a rough passage, in the 1956 Melbourne Cup. Spring now retired the horse in New Zealand, refusing the calls of Jack Winder (now training again) to ready him for a last campaign.

RIVER ROUGH
1980 br horse Brigand – Romantic Glory

This brilliant sprinter of the mid-1980s has suffered unreasonably from following Manikato into Bob Hoysted's yard. But River Rough, usually ridden by Darren Gauci, won nine of 29 starts and was placed second in another 10. He won successive Pure Pak (now Gadsden) Stakes down the Flemington 'Straight Six' in 1983 and 1984; successive Lightning Stakes in 1984 and 1985. In 1984 he was third in the Newmarket to Heron Bridge. In the spring he was sensationally scratched from the Moir Stakes at Moonee Valley when even money favourite. Hoysted had been refused permission for the horse to urinate in the swabbing stall before the race and took him out. Fined, he took the matter to several courts of appeal before being successful. The next year River Rough was back in action, and he finished second to Vite Cheval in the Futurity Stakes, but had capped his career with a win shortly before in the William Reid. River Rough went to stud after that autumn campaign.

RIVETTE
1933 b mare Ronsard – Riverside

Injury prevented Rivette from racing at two; at three she won a couple of provincial races. Harry Bamber, the former Light Horseman who bred, owned and trained the mare, set her for the Caulfield-Melbourne Cup double in 1938. Injured on the beach at Mordialloc, she had to be spelled instead. Rivette had won only eight minor races for stakes of just over 2,000 pounds before weights were issued for the 1939 Cups and she was assessed at 44kg in each. Down on his luck, Bamber had even tried to sell Rivette as a broodmare. Fortunately that fell through and his patience was rewarded in 1939 when Rivette won the Caulfield Cup handily, overcoming a check. Surprisingly he ran her again in the Moonee Valley Cup where she was a most unlucky third. The form was strong enough for Rivette to be installed at 5/1 favourite for the Melbourne Cup despite a 4.5kg penalty. The riderless Ortelle's Star was first past the post, but Rivette beat the others clearly. Thus she became the first mare to win the Cups double (and the only one besides Let's Elope). Rivette was sufficiently frisky after the event to kick the cup out of Bamber's hands.

ROBERTSON, LOU (1881-1953)

Born in New Zealand, Robertson was a multi-talented horseman who first made a name as a trainer and driver of trotters. In 1900 he moved to Australia to set up a training complex for the Nye brothers. The antipathy of John Wren led Robertson to reconsider his options and he switched to training thoroughbreds, initially for the Nyes. Robertson's career was made with the victory of Lavendo in the 1915 Caulfield Cup. Between the wars, Gothic and Strephon were the best horses through his yard. In 1935 he enjoyed a remarkable run of success in Melbourne, winning the Melbourne Cup with Marabou, the Cox Plate with Garrio, a second Derby (Feldspar), the Oaks (Naida) and Williamstown Cup. Keith Voitre partnered these horses for Robertson. The last big win of Robertson's long career was with the ageing, but popular, Lincoln in the Caulfield Cup of 1949.

ROBINSON CRUSOE
1874 br horse Angler – Chrysolite

The A.J.C. Derby winner of 1876, Robinson Crusoe proved to be one of the most aptly named horses in Australian racing history, when he survived – not marooning – but a foundering ship. In September 1876 the S.S. 'City of Melbourne' sailed south from Sydney with a cargo of 11 horses scheduled to take part in the Melbourne spring carnival. A gale struck the ship off Jervis Bay. Several horses were washed overboard, others were crushed, including Robin Hood, winner of the Victoria Derby of 1875. Only Redwood and the Chrysolite colt (as Robinson Crusoe was then usually known) survived. Taken

ashore in a parlous condition, Robinson Crusoe was revived with gin and beer administered by his race jockey, Joe Morrison. Melbourne bookmakers were delighted that so many well-backed runners would no longer be liabilities, so they presented a purse to the unhappily named Captain Paddle, skipper of the 'City of Melbourne'. Sent to stud, Robinson Crusoe was a notable success. He sired Insomnia, the dam of Wakeful; Navigator, who won both Derbies and St Legers and the Australian Cup and Trident, who won both St Legers and the Victoria Derby.

ROGILLA
1927 ch gelding Roger de Busli – Speargila

Owned and trained by L. Haigh, Rogilla found the best form of his career when a mature horse, winning the 1933 Cox Plate as a six year old. The following year he beat Peter Pan in the Rawson Stakes. In Sydney he also won the A.J.C. Autumn Plate, two Spring Stakes, a Randwick Plate and Warwick Stakes. In the autumn of 1933 he won the Sydney Cup. Going the Melbourne way, he was victorious in the Caulfield Cup of 1932. Next spring he won the Melbourne Stakes and C.B. Fisher Plate besides his Cox Plate triumph. He dead-heated with Chatham in a Tramway Stakes and was placed behind that horse in the 1932 Epsom and 1934 Cox Plate. A gelding of iron constitution, Rogilla took out successive Chipping Norton Stakes in 1933 and 1934, proving his durability at the highest level. No other horse has won the unusual Caulfield Cup, Sydney Cup and Cox Plate treble.

ROISEL
1915 br gelding Blankney II – Cooyeanna

A champion jumper of the 1920s, Roisel had a particular affinity with Caulfield.

With G. Dally up he won the Australian Hurdle there at 12/1 in 1921. The next year he ran second to Fiscom in the Grand National Hurdle at Flemington. Evergreen, Roisel won the Australian Hurdle and Steeplechase double in 1924. Two years later, and five years after his first victory, he won the Australian Hurdle for a third time. Next week he fell while attempting a second win in the Australian Steeple, but remarkably he made up for that when he won the 1927 renewal of the race under the burden of 80kg.

ROSEBERY RACECOURSE

A privately owned pony-racing course in Sydney's inner south, run under the auspices of the Associated Racing Clubs, Rosebery was taken over as a military camp during the Great War. Its fortunes gradually declined in the inter-war period, and the course was closed forever in 1940 when again requisitioned for the use of the army.

ROSEHILL GUINEAS

Now a Group One race over 2000m run during the autumn carnival, the Rosehill Guineas was first contested in 1910 when Electric Wire beat Desert Rose. It was not until the 1920s that the race began to be won on a regular basis by high quality three year olds. Furious, Amounis, Mollison and Phar Lap took the Guineas in that decade; Ajax and High Caste in the 1930s. Hydrogen won in 1951, while Tulloch as usual had plenty to spare over Prince Darius in 1957. Students of unlikely happenings enjoyed the 1961-3 runnings of the Rosehill Guineas in which the second place-getters were successively Summer Fair, Summer Prince and Summer Fiesta. The 1970s saw such fine winners as Royal Show, Imagele, the moody Taras Bulba and – in 1979 –

Dulcify. The Guineas was another procession for Kingston Town in his triumphant 1980 campaign. More recently Strawberry Road won in 1983, while Spirit of Kingston became one of the relatively few fillies to win the Guineas when she was first home in 1985. Surfers Paradise, who would win a Cox Plate at good odds before the year was out, won in 1991, while Naturalism turned the Canterbury Guineas tables on Veandercross when he won in 1992.

ROSEHILL RACECOURSE

Opened as a proprietary racetrack on 18 April 1885, Rosehill is situated in western Sydney, near Parramatta. G.W.S. Rose was the first secretary of the course and held that position until his death. A branch railway line to the course ensured its popularity from the late 1880s. Ambitious early programming led to clashes with the A.J.C., when for a time pony and trotting races were held at Rosehill. In 1903 the Rawson Stakes was first run at the course, while the Rosehill Guineas was inaugurated in 1910. In 1943, under a rationalisation of racing in New South Wales, Rosehill was taken over by the latest club to be called the Sydney Turf Club. Its autumn carnival is highlighted by the B.M.W. and Ranvet (formerly Rawson) Stakes and the Golden Slipper.

ROSE OF KINGSTON
1978 ch mare Claude – Kingston Rose

This brilliant staying filly, trained by Bob Hoysted, won the Bloodhorse Breeders' Plate at Flemington at two, before being sent to campaign in Sydney. After places in the Reisling Slipper Trial and the Golden Slipper (third to Full on Aces), Rose of Kingston won the Champagne Stakes from

Birchwood. In the spring of 1981 she began with a victory in the Ascot Vale Stakes at Flemington. Third placings followed in the Moonee Valley Stakes, Caulfield Guineas and Thousand Guineas. She then attempted to become the first filly since Frances Tressady in 1923 to win the Victoria Derby, but could only finish fifth. However, she showed her best form in winning the V.R.C. Oaks. Spelled, Rose of Kingston was brought back for the Sydney racing in the autumn of 1982. She was second to Rare Form in the Canterbury Guineas and to Isle of Man in the Rosehill Guineas. Hoysted's ambitions for the filly included the A.J.C. Derby, which she won from Our Planet and Gurner's Lane. Rose of Kingston was the first filly since Tea Rose in 1944 to win the Derby. Her next assignment was the inaugural Australasian Oaks at Morphettville in South Australia, in which she also triumphed. Rose of Kingston campaigned on as a four year old, being placed second in the 1982 Underwood Stakes, before being retired to stud.

ROTHMANS 100,000
see DOOMBEN 10,000

ROUGH HABIT
1986 b gelding Roughcast – Certain Habit

A plain-looking gelding by parents who never won a race, the New Zealander Rough Habit was a multiple Group One winner. Unraced at two, he won six starts as a three year old in New Zealand and earned a trip to Brisbane for the late autumn of 1990. Second to Stargazer in the Grand Prix, he won the Queensland Derby from Ray's Hope, and was third in the Doomben Cup, a race upon which he would soon set an indelible seal. Following the same pattern in 1991, Rough Habit had two autumn wins in

his home country and then headed for Brisbane. He won the Sir Byrne Hart Stakes, the first of successive Southport Cups and then started at 6/4 and carried 55kg in winning the Stradbroke Handicap. Next he won the first of an unprecedented three Doomben Cups in succession.

Back in New Zealand, his 1991-2 season yielded four more wins. This time, trainer John Wheeler took Rough Habit to Sydney first, where he was second in the Ranvet and third in the B.M.W. Stakes, but won the Queen Elizabeth and All Aged Stakes. Another Southport Cup, Stradbroke and Doomben Cup followed in a triumphant campaign. In the spring of 1992 Rough Habit – who had proved himself a champion the Brisbane and Sydney way of going – finally won a race in Melbourne over 1400m in the Myer Stakes at Caulfield. He was knocked out of the Cox Plate and then was placed in the Mackinnon and Queen Elizabeth Stakes. In the autumn of 1993 he came up yet again, running second in the B.M.W. to Kaaptive Edition and then defeating Naturalism in the All Aged Stakes. A third Doomben Cup victory capped his career. Later in the year Wheeler took the gamble of sending Rough Habit to California for the Hollywood Gold Cup on dirt, but he finished eighth. This tough and talented galloper has won more than $3 million, two thirds of it in his adopted Queensland home.

ROUS, ADMIRAL HENRY JAMES (1795-1877)

Known as the 'dictator of the English turf' (and by extension of horse-racing round the world), Rous was the younger son of the Earl of Stradbroke. In his 40 year association with the English Jockey Club, his most famous achievement was to draw up the weight-for-age scale, the measuring stick for thoroughbred horses world wide. The scale brings together horses of differing sex and age on 'equal weights', so that in theory the best horse will win the contest in question. Rous drew up the weight-for-age scale in the 1850s and except for minor changes (for instance, as affect horses travelling to race in the other hemisphere) the scale has long been ratified for world use. Rous was elected a steward of the Jockey Club in 1838. Twelve years later he published *On the Laws and Practice of Horse Racing* which traced the development of thoroughbred racing, and included his theory on standard weights according to the age of a horse. Five years later Rous was appointed handicapper of the Jockey Club, a position which he held for the next 22 years. He watched races through a telescope (in memory of his naval background) and was a regular astride his hack on Newmarket Heath most mornings. Rous was also instrumental in securing a 99 year lease on the Newmarket training grounds, while the revenue of the Jockey Club increased six fold under his direction.

ROYAL GEM

1941 br horse Dhoti – French Gem

Winner of 23 of his 51 starts, Royal Gem was out of the top brood-mare French Gem. Her other metropolitan winners included Crown Gem and Regal Gem, the Victoria Derby winner of 1947 Beau Gem, Solar Gem and Austral Gem. Owned in Adelaide by G.W. Badham, Royal Gem won four of his five starts at two. In the other, his first, he dislodged his rider at the start. Trained by G.R. Jesser, Royal Gem won eight times at three. He took the Goodwood Handicap in Adelaide and dead-heated with Attley in the Caulfield Guineas of 1945. He won the A.R.C. City Handicap with 61kg and proved himself a tough sprinting colt. At

four he warmed up again in Adelaide with wins in the Port Adelaide Royal Park and the Benson Quality. Taken to Melbourne in the spring of 1946, Royal Gem won the Toorak Handicap. Nevertheless he was friendless at 33/1 in the betting for the Caulfield Cup a week later. There were two reasons. Royal Gem had been dubbed a non-stayer. Bernborough was in the race. Notoriously, this was the event that ended Bernborough's winning sequence of 15. As a result, the qualities of Royal Gem have been overlooked. Ridden by Reg Heather, he scored well in the Cup, carrying weight-for-age. Nor was he done with yet. The Ascot Vale and Linlithgow Stakes were among other set-weight wins for Royal Gem. He also carried big weights to victory in the Cantala Stakes, and as a five year old in the Futurity of 1948 (where he had 64.5kg; Attley had won with 66kg the year before) and the Newmarket later that autumn with 61.5kg. Thereafter, Badham sold Royal Gem to the United States where he began a career at stud.

ROYAL SCHOOL 'RING-IN'

One of the notorious ring-ins of the Australian turf was perpetrated by a former used car dealer, Vittorio David (Rick) Renzella. Late in 1971 he paid $350 for the moderately performed New South Wales country galloper Royal School. Soon afterwards he bought the former top line sprinter Regal Vista for $6,000. Both were brown horses with a notable resemblance to one another. After racing Royal School around the Western District of Victoria with a predictable and desired lack of success, Renzella rang in Regal Vista for that horse in the Muntham Handicap at Casterton. He took every horse in the Casterton Cup with 'Royal School' in the daily double. 'Royal School' was backed from 50/1 to 7/4 and with Stephen Wood up, beat the favourite Apex Star, hard held, by three lengths. Renzella headed for the border; Regal Vista went missing; inquiries began by police and racing officials. Eventually Renzella was arrested and jailed for two years. His horses' trainer and the jockey received suspended sentences.

ROYAL SOVEREIGN
1961 b horse Chatsworth II – Sabah

Trained by J.B. Page, Royal Sovereign won at Rosehill and Randwick in ordinary company as a two year old, but then finished second to Farnworth in the 1964 Champagne Stakes. At three his steady improvement continued, with thirds in the Canterbury and Rosehill Guineas. Staying was his go, and he beat Strauss narrowly in the A.J.C. Derby. Second to Yangtze in the Caulfield Cup on a heavy track, he struck firm going for the Victoria Derby. With Ray Selkrig up, Royal Sovereign ran a race record to beat Strauss again. The A.J.C. Derby margin of a short neck was stretched to a neck on this occasion. Unplaced in the Melbourne Cup, Page kept the horse going and Royal Sovereign became one of the few horses to complete a Derby treble when he won the Q.T.C. Derby by 10 lengths. After one more unplaced run, at Canterbury, he was retired.

RUBITON
1983 br horse Century – Ruby

Trained by Pat Barns, Rubiton enjoyed one brilliant season as a spring four year old. He beat Military Plume at his first start, in August 1986, on a wet track in Adelaide, having been prevented by shin soreness from racing at two. Taken across the border, Rubiton beat subsequent Derby winner Raveneaux at Sandown. He had not been entered for the Derby. Reserved for sprinting, Rubiton won the Red Anchor Stakes at Sandown by five lengths, and then went amiss. Back in the autumn of 1987, he was unplaced in the William Reid behind Canny Lass, only third in the Autumn Stakes but then – with Harry White in the saddle – a fine third to the champion sprinter Placid Ark in the Oakleigh Plate. Backed up again at Caulfield, Rubiton won the Futurity Stakes the next Saturday, for his first Group One success. Rematched with Placid Ark in the Newmarket, he ran third again, and then was beaten unluckily in his one Sydney start. Now he was spelled before his great, brief and final campaign. In the spring of 1987 Rubiton won the Manikato Stakes at 10/1 first up at Moonee Valley in race record time. Wins in the Memsie and the Feehan Stakes from Vo Rogue followed. Next start, Rubiton won the Underwood Stakes at Caulfield in track record time – two minutes dead. Accordingly he was 3/1 on in the Caulfield Stakes, but could only finish third to Drought and Fair Sir. But he was back at Moonee Valley, winning the Cox Plate in track record time from Our Poetic Prince, Fair Sir and Vo Rogue (who had set the pace). Training off, Rubiton struggled to win the Mackinnon Stakes from King of Brooklyn and Military Plume and was spelled. He never raced again, having broken down in preparation for the autumn carnival. Thereafter he was sent to stand at Mike Willesee's Trans Media Park Stud at Cootamundra.

RUSSELL, KEN (1951-93)

One of the most skilled and popular of modern Australian jockeys, Russell served his apprenticeship as a compositor on the newspaper in his home town, Monto, in Queensland. Evidently his mother did not want him to become a jockey, although her husband combined training with dairy-farming. She relented, and Russell rode his first winner, Frosty Val, at the splendidly named Queensland town of Banana in 1972. He won numerous jockeys' premierships in the Central Queensland and Rockhampton districts. A move to Brisbane in 1977 was unsuccessful, but Russell came down to ride at the Gold Coast in 1979, and quickly established himself. He was leading jockey on five occasions and the Southport course saw later triumphs for him in the Magic Millions of 1988 and 1989 on Sea Cabin and Malibu Magic respectively. In the 1986-7 season, Russell won the Brisbane jockeys' premiership, and was then tempted to Sydney. He was stable rider for Doctor Geoff Chapman, but suffered a severe fall from Killer Khan at Orange in February 1988. Russell returned to the saddle in May with a win at Canterbury, but was sacked as Chapman's stable jockey a few days later. Resilient and good-humoured, he won big races for a number of other stables: the Doncaster of 1989 on Merimbula Bay, two Goodwood Handicaps in Adelaide, the Spring Champion Stakes on Sakana, two Queensland Oaks and a Queensland Derby. Riding Tuig at Rosehill on 9 October 1993, Russell was killed in a fall after his mount broke down and was cannoned into by another.

RUSSIA

1940 ch horse Excitement – Lady March

A top quality, durable stayer, trained by E. Hush, Russia won both handicap and weight-for-age events in a long career. His record shows twenty two and a half wins and 27 placings from 89 starts. Twice placed in the Sydney Cup (second in 1945, third the next year) and third in the 1945 Metropolitan, Russia had support in the 1945 Melbourne Cup but could finish no

closer than fifth. But it was his turn next year. Carrying 57kg and at the odds of 16/1, Russia won by five lengths. He was briefly sent to the stud, but lack of concentration saw him return to the track, where he won the Ercildoune and Carbine Stakes at Flemington. His stud career was resumed in the United States, with some success.

RYDER, GEORGE (1905-89)

Born at Tingha in June 1905, George Ryder started work as a truck driver and soon owned his own bus company. A horse who he bought for 100 pounds and named Jan, after his daughter, ignited Ryder's interest in racing when she won a Trial Handicap at Newcastle in 1937. He began to race horses in earnest during the 1940s and such was his fervour that he bought the Woodlands Stud in 1946. This was the base for one of the most far-reaching and imaginative of all contributions to thoroughbred breeding in Australia. In particular, Ryder began to import top-line stallions and mares from Europe, beginning with the speed sire Newtown Wonder. Ryder was a foundation committee member of the most recent incarnation of the Sydney Turf Club, and conceived the idea of a great race to rival the A.J.C.'s main events. Thus the Golden Slipper was born, although Ryder weathered carping criticisms from those who thought he had set up the event for one of the horses that he would breed himself. In the event, that never happened, but the Slipper is one of the most important, richest and influential events in the Australian racing calendar. Pipe of Peace (sire of Always There and Black Onyx) and Sostenuto were other top sires who Ryder brought to Woodlands; Tarien among the best of his imported mares. Sky High stood there after his retirement.

In 1971 Ryder sold Woodlands to Lord

Derby and the King Ranch, but quickly purchased the Kia Ora Stud at Scone, where Slipper winners Baguette and Imagele stood. Treasurer, Vice-Chairman and from 1977-80 Chairman of the S.T.C., Ryder also pioneered syndication in Australian racing. He died in May 1989, after the Slipper's 33rd running. The George Ryder Stakes (a Group One weight-for-age event), named in his honour, is contested at the S.T.C. autumn carnival.

S

SAILOR'S GUIDE
1952 br horse Lighthouse II – Jeanne

This game, talented galloper took on the best in a vintage period of Australian racing. His two year old campaign yielded little – one win on a heavy track in June, 1955, from six starts. Trained at Bendigo by George Daniel (a former primary school headmaster), Sailor's Guide found form quickly at three, running fourth at 25/1 behind Rising Fast in the 1955 Caulfield Cup, third in the Cox Plate and then winning the Victoria Derby. A successful spring ended with a fourth in the Williamstown Cup. Highlights of the autumn of 1956 were wins in both the V.R.C. and A.J.C. St Legers, a half head victory over Cromis in the Queen Elizabeth Stakes and a narrow victory at 11/4 favourite in the Sydney Cup. The following spring began well, with a second to Rising Fast in the Memsie Stakes and a win in the Craiglee before Sailor's Guide's form fell away. He redeemed himself with wins over Rising Fast in the Pentathlon Stakes and Redcraze in the C.B. Fisher Plate.

In the autumn of 1957, Sailor's Guide won the Blamey from Sir William, but then ran six consecutive seconds in top races in Sydney and Melbourne, four of them to Rising Fast. The spring saw better dividends for Sailor's Guide: victory by five lengths in the Craiglee, third in the Caulfield Cup with 60kg to Tulloch and a victory over Syntax in the Mackinnon Stakes. This campaign ended with a win in the Williamstown Cup. The autumn of 1958 saw Sailor's Guide score a win in the Blamey before a heroic and narrow win over Prince Darius and Tulloch in course record time for the 14 furlongs of the Queen Elizabeth Stakes. Wintering in Brisbane, Sailor's Guide won the O'Shea Stakes and at his last Australian race ran third with 61kg in the Doomben Cup. Sent to the United States, he scored a famous, if controversial, victory (on protest) in the Washington International at Laurel. Other wins followed, and Sailor's Guide earned a further $100,000 in the States before going to stud.

SAMSON
1957 b gelding Nilo – Hora

Best known in racing trivia quizzes as the first horse to win at the new Sandown track in 1965, Samson was a class performer over a long period. Samson carried 62.5kg in his first Sandown victory on 19 June 1965, and subsequently won five more races there, including the 1965 Liston Stakes from Craftsman. A winner of the Healy Stakes in Brisbane in 1962, Samson also won the Doomben Cup that year. His wins in that spring included the Craven 'A' Stakes at Flemington. Then in the spring of 1963, Samson beat Rashlore and Future in the Invitation Stakes and also took the Lloyd Stakes, from Ripa. Samson also beat Captain Blue in the 1965 Victoria Handicap at Caulfield before his Sandown spree began. Retired in 1967, Samson was a long-time holder of the record for most wins at Sandown until surpassed by Luther's Luck, (Acidity-Proserpina II) whose 19 wins from 79 starts included nine at Sandown. Both Samson (who became a police horse after his retirement from the track) and Luther's Luck have races named in their honour at Sandown.

SAN DOMENICO

1946 br gelding Hua – Arpina

Despite being by the 1937 Victoria Derby winner, Hua, San Domenico proved himself to be a high quality sprinter over a number of seasons. Trained by F.P. Formosa, he won the 1949 Oakleigh Plate as a three year old in what was then Australian record time. Next start he was an unlucky second in the Newmarket, a race in which he was third in 1952 with 62.5kg. Big weights were no worry to San Domenico, who won the 1952 Futurity with 65.5kg. He was equally at home in Sydney, where he won the Canterbury Stakes in 1950 and 1951, and was second in the following year; the George Main in 1950, before being placed again in 1951 and 1953, and the 1951 Hill Stakes. The Group Two 1000m San Domenico Stakes run at Warwick Farm in the early spring is named after him.

SANDOWN CUP

In line of descent from the Williamstown Cup, first run in 1888, when Mara beat Pakeha and Chicago, the Sandown Cup has the distinction of being the only event to be run (under whichever name) at five Melbourne metropolitan venues. From 1888-1939 it was staged at Williamstown, except for 1919 when the race was run at Caulfield. In 1940, the Williamstown Cup was shifted to Flemington, where it remained until 1950. From the next year until 1964, Caulfield was again the venue for the race, save for 1956, when it was run at Moonee Valley. From 1965, when the new Sandown track was opened, it has hosted the Sandown Cup, which is now a key race in the course's biggest race day of the year, following the spring carnival at Flemington. The Williamstown Cup was always a top staying event, won by the likes of Merman and Battalion in the 19th century. Between the wars, Richmond Main, King Ingoda and Amounis were victorious. Second Wind won in successive years (1930-1), while Shadow King had some recompense for his frustrating run of Melbourne Cup placings when he took the Williamstown Cup of 1933. The versatile mare Claudette won from the top-liner Skipton in 1943, having taken the Grand National Hurdle earlier that year. Peter Pan's son, Peter, beat her the following year. Columnist won in 1947, Morse Code in 1950 and 1952. In that decade Prince Courtauld and Sailor's Guide were distinguished winners of the race. Ilumquh and New Statesman won early in the 1960s, while Red William won the first Sandown Cup proper in 1965. No less a horse than Light Fingers saluted the next year, carrying 56kg. In the 1970s Gunsynd, Baghdad Note and Salamander won the Sandown Cup; Arwon and Sydeston saw the 1980s in and out. If the Sandown Cup is something of a spring consolation prize, it has come again slightly to overshadow the Moonee Valley Cup, as had its predecessor, the Williamstown Cup.

SANDOWN GUINEAS

Now a Group Two event run over 1600m at the end of the Melbourne spring carnival, the Sandown Guineas was run at Caulfield from 1957-64. Between 1957-67 it was restricted to three year old fillies. Some of them were outstanding. From 1960-4 the winners were Lady Sybil, Indian Summer, Birthday Card, Ripa and Light Fingers. Fire Band won the first running of the event at Sandown in 1965. In the last fillies' only Guineas, the quality of the race was indicated when Begonia Belle beat Quezette and Lowland. In 1968-9, the first two years when the race was open to all three year olds, its distance was extended to ten and a half furlongs and the winners were Always There and Top Flat. Abdul won the following year when the distance went back to 1600m, Taj Rossi in 1973, Better Draw in 1975 (proving that this could still be a good race for fillies), So Called in 1977, Galleon in 1981 and Durbridge in 1990.

SANDOWN PARK RACECOURSE

The only metropolitan course to be opened in Australia in the 20th century, Sandown Park was modelled on American tracks: sweeping turns, cambered corners, plentiful undercover accommodation were features. It has survived much bad early press (as an indifferent wet track course, as one where swoopers inevitably cut down leaders in the straight) to become a serviceable venue. There was a track near this site as long ago as the 1880s, when W.C. Cullen opened Oakleigh Park. Its name was changed to Sandown Park in 1892, after the course outside London. It

was at the Australian Sandown that J.W. Scott's starting machine was first used at a registered Victorian meeting, in January 1894. The fortunes of the course declined, and it was closed on 9 May 1931.

Work began on a new track to ease the pressure on Melbourne racing in the early 1960s and Sandown opened in July 1965. An unexpected 52,000 people strained facilities, and Samson (who became a course specialist) was the only favourite to salute. Sandown hosts the Australian Hurdle and Steeple, and a week after the end of the Flemington spring carnival its Cup and Guineas are run at the course. In 1993 the C.F. Orr Stakes was classified as a Group One race, the only one presently run at Sandown.

SANGSTER, ROBERT (1936-)

One of the world's leading race-horse owners and breeders, Sangster manages the Swettenham Stud. His interest in the turf was enabled initially by the inheritance of the fortune which his father had made as a pools magnate in England, but Sangster soon showed himself to be a shrewd judge of thoroughbreds. His *Who's Who* entry (devoted almost entirely to horses rather than to himself) notes among his big race winners The Minstrel (1977 English Derby), Alleged, who won the Prix de l' Arc de Triomphe in 1977 and 1978, Detroit, an Arc winner in 1980, Golden Fleece, the 1982 winner at Epsom, besides Assert, Lomond and Caerleon. Sangster was the leading owner in Britain in the 1977, 1978 and 1982 seasons. He diversified his operations to Australia in the late 1970s, placing his horses with such trainers as Colin Hayes, Bart Cummings, Tommy Smith, Brian Mayfield-Smith and John Hawkes. Over the next decade, Sangster became arguably the most influential owner in the southern hemisphere, trading as the Swettenham Stud. In the mid 1980s, his Australian thoroughbred stock was valued at c$30 million. He sold much of it in 1986, but still plays a role, despite this diminishment of his interest. Sangster's best Australian wins were with Beldale Ball in the 1980 Melbourne Cup; Our Paddy Boy in the A.J.C. Derby in the following year.

SASANOF

1913 br gelding Martian – Ukraine

A top-line performer in New Zealand, where he won the Great Northern Derby, Sasanof was brought to Australia in 1916. He won the Chelmsford and the Spring Stakes before being taken to Melbourne. There he was third in the Caulfield Cup. Set for the Melbourne Cup, the lightly weighted Sasanof did not get his chance until the Saturday after the first Tuesday in November. The Maribyrnong River flooded following heavy rains and the Cup was postponed. Sasanof won the race easily, becoming the first victor to be bred, owned and trained in New Zealand. He campaigned for years in his home country, winning a Trentham Gold Cup, the 1918 New Zealand Cup and – a week later – beating the champion Gloaming. A stud in N.Z. is named in Sasanof's honour.

SCHILLACI

1988 gr gelding Salieri – Biscarina

Dominant sprinter of the early 1990s, especially in Melbourne, the Lee Freedman-trained Schillaci became the second horse to win the autumn sprint Triple Crown of the Lightning Stakes, Oakleigh Plate and Newmarket, in 1992. Thus he emulated the feat of Placid Ark in 1987. Schillaci, named for a flamboyant star of Italian soccer, went north where he scored in the Galaxy at Randwick. If he beat no champions, he beat the best around. His authority over sprint distances was such that he won 13 of his first 19 starts for stakes of about $1.75 million. Schillaci failed in the 1992 Stradbroke but came back in devastating style to win the Moir Stakes on Cox Plate day from Mookta in the spring of 1992. Spelled because of dislike of wet tracks and a lack of suitable races, he was back in the autumn of 1993. First he scored again in the Lightning Stakes and was then stepped up to the 1,400m of the Futurity. He won again, comfortably, from the good mare Excited Angel. A winning hat-trick followed with the Stanley Wootton Stakes at Moonee Valley, where he beat Umatilla and Soho Square. Schillaci now extended the scope of his performances by winning over 1500m at Randwick in the George Ryder Stakes. Remarkably, this was his last victory. In the Doncaster he faded to run 11th. Then in the spring of 1993 he was beaten a breath by Sports Works in the Moir and spelled again. The autumn of 1994 saw him just fail to make history when he was beaten in his bid for a third successive Lightning Stakes. Thereafter his form – in Melbourne, but more especially in Sydney – tapered off, and it appeared that a grand sprinter's career had finished anticlimactically.

SCHUMACHER, MEL (1937-)

Brought up at Boonah, in rural Queensland, inland from Brisbane, Mel Schumacher was one of the most brilliant and controversial of Australian jockeys. Initially apprenticed to Kevin Young, Schumacher rode his first winner at Laidley, in 1952. After a dispute with Young, Schumacher's indentures were transferred to Dick Roden. By 1957 he had moved to Sydney, where he became leading apprentice. As soon as he became a senior jockey, Schumacher shifted to the Jack Green stable. The first of his top mounts was Skyline, on whom he won the 1958 Hill Stakes and A.J.C. Derby. On the same afternoon that he won the Derby, Schumacher saw Turkestan home in the Epsom. Down in Melbourne, he rode Baystone to victory in the Hotham Handicap and Melbourne Cup. It was the start of a great, if short-lived, time at the top for Schumacher. In the autumn of 1961 he rode the filly Magic Night to victory in the Golden Slipper Stakes. But that spring Schumacher's career was cut down. In the A.J.C. Derby he rode Blue Era to a narrow win over Tommy Hill on Summer Fair. Hill protested, alleging that Schumacher had impeded him by pulling his leg near the post. Unfortunately for Schumacher, a fuzzy head-on film seemed to support the allegation and he was rubbed out for life. Schumacher headed back to Brisbane, where he worked in the fruit markets. After five and a half years, the suspension was lifted, and Schumacher returned with success to race-riding, if never to the extent that he had known, in Sydney and Brisbane. More recently, he has ridden in the Gold Coast area.

SCOBIE, JAMES (1860-1940)

The great racehorse trainer James Scobie began his career in the industry as a jumps jockey. His first metropolitan winner came in 1880. Soon afterwards he began training at Miners' Rest near Ballarat. Combining race riding with training, Scobie won a series of feature jumps races in Victoria and South Australia in the 1880s, notably the Grand National Steeple on Blue Mountain in 1887 when the race was run at Caulfield. In 1900, he trained his first A.J.C. and Victoria Derby winners when Maltster took

the double, and the first of his four Melbourne Cup winners, with Clean Sweep. Scobie's eighth Victoria Derby winner, Hua, came in 1937, towards the end of his long and distinguished career. Keen on the punt until his marriage, Scobie enjoyed the support of such rich patrons as Sir Rupert Clarke. For decades his stable jockey was Bobbie Lewis who rode scores of big race winners for Scobie. It was because of his admiration for the trainer that jockey Arthur 'Scobie' Breasley earned his famous nickname. In 1929 Scobie published his professional reminiscences, My Life on the Australian Turf.

SECOND WIND

1925 ch gelding Psychology or Grandcourt – First Blow

One of the best horses to be owned by Ernest Lee Steere, Second Wind began his racing career in Perth, winning the 1928 W.A.T.C. Derby and St Leger. As was his habit, when he had a horse good enough to race in the east, Lee Steere sent Second Wind to Jack Holt at Caulfield. The gelding won the King's Plate and the Herbert Power Handicap, but achieved a share of the limelight by chasing Phar Lap home at 50/1, to run second in the 1930 Melbourne Cup. Second Wind also ran second to the champion in the C.B. Fisher Plate on the last day of the carnival, a race in which – remarkably – there was no betting at all. Good wins came the way of Second Wind: successive victories in the Williamstown Cup (1930-1) and – in 1932 – success in the King's Cup with Billy Duncan up, when the race was run for the first time in Tasmania, at Elwick.

SEGENHOE STAKES

see RAWSON STAKES

SELKRIG, RAY (1930-)

Son of Frank Selkrig, who was foreman to Sydney trainer Bayly Payten, Selkrig rode for decades with success in Sydney and interstate. His biggest win was the 1961 Melbourne Cup on Lord Fury; his first big winner was with Grey Boots in the 1950 Doncaster. He won the Brisbane Cup on Fair Patton in 1964, the Australasian Champion Stakes on Latin Knight in 1972. Selkrig also won four A.J.C. Derbies on Prince Delville (1954), Swift Peter (1967), Gold Brick (1972) and Royal Sovereign, with whom he teamed in 1964 for the rare Victoria, A.J.C. and Queensland Derby treble.

SELLWOOD, NEVILLE (1922-62).

Son of a battling jockey, Sellwood was born in the Brisbane suburb of Ascot. He served his apprenticeship with Frank Shean, before going into the army. Most of his war service was in the postal unit at Townsville, but he was able to ride work and at the nearby Cluden track, where he won 140 races from 290 mounts during the war. Thereafter he became stable jockey for Maurice McCarten in Sydney, where he was six times premier jockey. On 24 occasions he rode four winners in a day; had five at Randwick on one occasion in 1954. Feature race wins came early: Melbourne Cups on Delta (1951) and Toporoa in 1955, (when he beat the champion Rising Fast and incurred a two month suspension); Sydney Cups on Gold Scheme, Sailor's Guide and Grand Garry; the Caulfield Cup on Tulloch and Basha Felika. A ride for which Sellwood was perhaps most criticised was on Tulloch in the Centenary Melbourne Cup of 1960, when he rode the horse near the rear of the field and could finish no closer than seventh. Other Australian champions with whom he was associated included Todman, on whom he won the inaugural Golden Slipper by eight lengths. Todman started at 6/1 on.

In the late 1950s Sellwood accepted a retainer to ride in England, and took the Two Thousand Guineas at his first ride, besides the 1962 English Derby on Larkspur. Based next in France, he was riding a filly called Lucky Seven at Maison-Lafitte outside Paris on 7 November 1962 when she fell and rolled on him. Sellwood died of his injuries. He tied for the French jockeys' premiership in that season with Yves St Martin, on 102 winners. The latter gave Sellwood's widow the gold whip awarded to the premier jockey.

SHADOW KING

1925 b gelding Comedy King – Beryllion

No horse had such a long, honourable and unlucky association with the Melbourne Cup as the fine stayer Shadow King. He ran in the event six times, and became such a Cup institution that scores of people crowded round his stall before the race. At his first try, in 1929, he was sixth to Nightmarch. Next year he ran third to the first of the champions who would finish in front of him – Phar Lap. In 1931 Shadow King was runner-up to White Nose, to whom he gave 10kg. Peter Pan took his turn to beat Shadow King in 1932, when the seven year old ran third. A fourth consecutive placing followed in 1933, and his narrowest defeat, when second by a head to Hall Mark who had 7.5kg on Shadow King. At some stage in this sequence, a journalist coined a phrase now lost to idiomatic memory: 'as unlucky as Shadow King'. Injury prevented the horse turning out for the 1934 Cup but he was back as a 10 year old in 1935. Shadow King was given the honour of leading out the field. Behind him were two champions who had finished in front of him before – Peter Pan and Hall Mark. Not this time: the grand old galloper ran fourth at 100/1 (Hall Mark and Peter Pan were mid-field) and his days of striving in the Melbourne Cup were at last concluded. In a long career, while trained by Elwood Fisher, Shadow King won the 1930 Moonee Valley Cup (and ran third in 1929 and 1932); took the Herbert Power Handicap in the next year; won the Williamstown Cup with Scobie Breasley up in 1933 at his fifth attempt. After a well-merited retirement, Shadow King became a trooper's horse, in which capacity he served until his death in 1945.

SHAFTESBURY AVENUE

1986 ch gelding Salieri – Lady Upstage

The handsome chestnut Shaftesbury Avenue is the best son of Salieri. Trained by Bart Cummings, he won two minor races at Rosehill in the spring of 1989 and was placed in the Brian Crowley and Stan Fox. In the autumn of 1990 he seemed on the verge of top class with victories in the Royal Sovereign and Hobartville Stakes over Majestic Boy, but was relegated to second in the Canterbury Guineas by Interstellar, the Doncaster by Super Impose, the All Aged Stakes by Eastern Classic. Put away until the spring, Shaftesbury Avenue came back with a win at Warwick Farm. This was the first of seven victories from his 10 starts that season. He won the Tramway, then defeated Super Impose in the George Main Stakes to record the first of six Group One victories. In Melbourne he won the Honda Stakes to round off his spring campaign. Back in the autumn of 1991, Shaftesbury Avenue won the Lightning Stakes before carrying 58kg to victory in the Newmarket with Darren Gauci up. Super Impose finished in front of him again in the 1991 Doncaster, but Shaftesbury Avenue then beat him in the All Aged Stakes.

Regular jockey John Marshall had lost the ride on Shaftesbury Avenue (and his position as Cummings's stable jockey) by the spring of 1991. Gauci was back on the horse when he scored a brilliant win in the Caulfield Stakes from Super Impose and Sydeston. Starting favourite in the Cox Plate despite a greasy track, Shaftesbury Avenue slipped and nearly fell on the first turn and was out of contention. In the Honda Stakes he carried 60.5kg into second place behind Pontormo, and protested without success. While Shaftesbury Avenue had proved his brilliance between 1000-2000m, the Japan Cup at 2400m on a traditionally fast track was thought beyond his scope. In the event he finished hard for third behind Golden Pheasant. Recurrent leg problems now kept him off the scene for almost a year. He resumed with a victory (over Super Impose, his old foe) in the Warwick Stakes in the spring of 1992, but soon went amiss again and was retired with winnings of more than $2 million and a grand record in an era of outstanding gallopers. Trainer Bart Cummings entertained plans for a Shaftesbury Avenue comeback in the spring of 1994.

SHANNON

1942 b horse Midstream – Idle Words

The English horse Midstream was brought to Australia in 1938 and was four times leading sire. His progeny included Delta and True Course, besides Shannon – who was one of Australia's greatest 'milers'. Trained by Peter Riddle, Shannon was an unlucky second at his first start, then recorded two good wins over the high quality filly Tea Rose. After being spelled he came back to narrowly defeat Tea Rose in the A.J.C. Sires' Produce. As a three year old Shannon won the Hobartville Stakes, but then finished out of a place after being kicked by another horse, Vermeil, before the start of the Rosehill Guineas. The Derby distance proved beyond him and Shannon was turned out for a spell of 10 months.

At four, Shannon won first up, then scored a lucky victory over Flight in the Tramway Handicap. He followed this with a win in the Hill Stakes that saw him sent out at 2/1 in the Epsom, which he won after missing the start. A year later, Shannon turned in one of the most sensational runs in Australian racing history. Starting at 4/5 in the Epsom of 1946, he missed the jump by many lengths (stretched into a furlong in legend) only to lose by a mere half head to Blue Legend, following a brilliant and desperate riding display by jockey Darby Munro. Blue Legend was a good enough galloper to win back-to-back Doncasters in 1946-7. Shannon's unofficial time was reckoned, with some warrant, to be the fastest mile ever run in a race in Australia. Munro's reward was to be roundly jeered by a crowd which did not appreciate that the starter, J. Gaxieu, had been at fault. Next start Shannon beat Flight in the 1946 George Main Stakes by six lengths in Australian record time for a mile, then won the King's Cup in race record time. At six he won the Canterbury Stakes and another George Main.

After Riddle's death, the horse was sold to America. A promising first up third in January 1948 was followed by dismal runs, as Shannon was slow to acclimatise. When he did, his brilliant and sustained speed was put to good effect. He won the San Francisco Handicap by 12 lengths and broke the course record of the champion Sea Biscuit. His owners pocketed big cheques for the Argonaut Handicap, the Fortyniner Handicap (won in world record time for nine furlongs) and the Golden Gate

Handicap. Retired to stud, Shannon had a brief but successful career before he broke a leg and was put down in 1955.

SHARP AS
1984 b gelding So Sharp – Royal Lace

Sold for $500 as a yearling in New Zealand, Sharp As did not race in Australia until August 1988, when he won a hurdle at Werribee. In March the following year he lost his rider in a Bendigo Hurdle, but thereafter took with avidity to the jumping caper, winning four of his next five starts, including two in town: at Caulfield and Flemington. A discouraging run of five seconds followed, although one of these was to the fine jumper Sir Agrifo in the 1989 Grand National Hurdle. After a string of country wins on the flat, the versatile Sharp As added the Bond Handicap in town to his victories, besides running third in the Duke of Norfolk Stakes in the autumn of 1990. Veteran trainer Jim Houlahan thought that he had a potential Melbourne Cup as well as a Grand National winner in his stable. In the winter of that year, Sharp As won the Colonel Sanders and Lachal Hurdles before triumphing in the Grand National by five lengths at 7/4 favourite. From 14 hurdle starts, he had recorded eight wins and five seconds. There were to be no more successes: shortly afterwards, Sharp As was killed while schooling at Moonee Valley, ending a career which saw him earn $335,000 from 15 wins and 13 placings in only 32 starts.

SHIVAREE
1974 ch gelding Sharivari – Just a Lark

This tough and talented New Zealander competed with the best Australasian horses at the end of the 1970s, notably with Dulcify. Trained by Dave O'Sullivan, he was without a win at two. At three he won his maiden at Matamata, and then six other races including the Championship Stakes at Avondale. His four year old campaign was outstanding: Shivaree won five races in New Zealand, including the International Stakes at Waikato, and was second to La Mer in the Air New Zealand Stakes. In Sydney in the autumn of 1979 he beat Dulcify in the Tancred Stakes, besides winning the Queen Elizabeth Stakes. He also ran second to Belmura Lad in the National Stakes at Canberra. Back in Melbourne in the spring, he endured a frustrating run of seconds in top class events: to Mighty Kingdom in the Caulfield Stakes, Dulcify in the Cox Plate (when Shivaree was seven lengths adrift) and to that horse again, when he went under by only a neck in the Mackinnon Stakes. Shivaree continued to compete at the highest level and was victorious three times in New Zealand at six, before his career ended.

SHOW DAY CUP
see INVITATION STAKES

SHOWDOWN

1961 ch horse Infatuation – Zanzara

One of the most successful British horses ever imported to the Southern Hemisphere to stand at stud, Showdown won four of five starts at two, including the Middle Park Stakes at Epsom. Without a win at three, he nonetheless was good enough to run fourth in the 2000 Guineas. Later he won the Coventry Stakes at Ascot and the Queen Anne Stakes. In Australia he sired a number of outstanding gallopers, prime among them Toy Show, Leica Show, the unlucky Leica Lover, the brilliant sprinting mare Dual Choice, triple Derby winner Silver Sharpe, Royal Show and – perhaps best of them all – Tontonan.

SHRIMPTON, JEAN (1943-)

The world's highest paid photographic model, English-born Jean Shrimpton was invited in 1965 by the Victoria Racing Club to present its Fashions on the Field Awards on Derby Day. On a scorching afternoon, when the temperature rose to 34°C, Shrimpton, whose trip had been sponsored by the fashion house of Du Pont, shocked those who cared to be by her attire. She wore neither gloves, hat nor stockings, but attracted most attention for sporting what now seems like a demure, white, not-so-mini-dress. Tobin Bronze won the Derby that day, while Shrimpton reappeared for the Cup in more conservative attire, together with her 'companion', the actor Terence Stamp.

SIEVIER, ROBERT (1860-1939)

One of the most flamboyant of Australian bookmakers, gamblers and philanderers, Sievier was reputedly born in the back of a London hansom cab. Son of a well known sculptor, he served with the British military forces in South Africa before taking to the punt. Financial embarrassment saw him decamp to Australia. Under the name Bob Sutton he fielded first at Adelaide in 1882; won a fortune at the end of that year when The Assyrian triumphed in the Melbourne Cup. He married into society, but his disposition to spread his favours led to divorce. Resented by more stolid competitors, Sievier was responsible for a number of crucial innovations in bookmaking: he bet from a stand, rather than wandering through the crowd; framed a market on a price board; wrote bets on serially numbered tickets. In 1887 he returned to England, where again he married into quality. This time he was able to take over his wife's stable of horses. As a gambler he had big wins on the Australian imports The Grafter and Merman (who Lily Langtry owned). Sceptre – a multiple classic winning three year old – was the best horse he owned. A succession of libel suits led him to be warned off English race courses. Richard Wootton, who had such a dramatic impact on Australian thoroughbred breeding, was one of those with whom Sievier particularly feuded. Sievier carried the attack to his enemies by means of his sporting paper *Winning Post*, and had outlived many of them by the time of his death in 1939.

SILVER SHARPE

1967 b gelding Showdown – Snowline

One of the few triple Derby winners in Australian turf history, Silver Sharpe is remarkable in that he won no other race. Trained by Tommy Smith, he was placed in four of five starts at two; had two more placings at three and then ran down the line in the Rosehill Guineas. But his stout breeding eventually won out and Silver Sharpe defeated Planet Kingdom and Gunsynd in the A.J.C. Derby of 1970. Taken to Melbourne, he was unplaced in the Caulfield Cup before beating no less than Gay Icarus in the Victoria Derby. Silver Sharpe completed the treble with victory in the Queensland Derby, in which Gunsynd was again third. In the autumn of 1971 he was placed in the Blamey Stakes and the St Leger; had no runs at four and one unplaced start at five, to conclude a curious career.

SIR AGRIFO

1979 b or br gelding Agrifo – Truejoy

The P.J. Bullock-trained Sir Agrifo was one of the best hurdlers of the modern era, and few horses have equalled his feats in the toughest of these races – the Grand

National Hurdle at Flemington. Sir Agrifo won the race in 1987, beating Nymphus and Prince Lyndal; paid the penalty by carrying 68.5kg next year when he was third behind Barry's Gold and My Court Jewel. But Sir Agrifo was far from done with: although rising 10, he returned in the winter of 1989 with a win and then a third in the Moonee Valley Hurdle. To win the National with 70kg, he had to equal a weight carried to victory as long before as 1947, by Eudunda. Sir Agrifo did so triumphantly, scoring by 12 lengths to the dead-heaters Sharp As and Purposefully. He was the first horse since McEwan (1980 and 1982) to win the race twice and in 1990 he tried again, but weight at last beat him and he was unplaced behind Sharp As.

SIR BLINK

1955 br horse Blue Coral – Inky

Sir Blink was the first horse the fortunate Mrs W. Kellett had raced. Trained by Jack Godby, he was unplaced at his first outing, in the 1957 V.A.T.C. Debutant Stakes, but then won the Kempton Handicap at Flemington. In the autumn of 1958 Sir Blink had victories at the three Melbourne metropolitan tracks, ending with a Flemington win under 58kg. Godby was hopeful that he had a horse well in for both Cups the next spring. Sir Blink's first two starts in that campaign were uninspiring, but then he won the Heatherlie Handicap against open company and was sent to Sydney for the spring classics. In both the Rosehill Guineas (where he was third) and Derby (when second to Skyline in record time), Sir Blink was most unlucky. Back in Melbourne he was fourth in the Caulfield Stakes. On Caulfield Cup day Sir Blink was backed from 12/1 to 6/1 and took the race convincingly, with the favourite Skyline weakening to ninth. Starting at 2/1 on, Sir Blink then won the Victoria Derby, and was a respectable seventh in the Melbourne Cup. He should have won a second Caulfield Cup in 1959, when Regal Wench was most fortunate to beat him, and in 1961 he ran a creditable fifth.

SIR DANE
1960 b gelding Summertime – Casa

Sir Dane, trained by R.J. Shaw, showed plentiful signs of class in the spring of 1963 when he was runner up to Proteus in the Moonee Valley Stakes, to Craftsman in the Victoria Derby. In the autumn he recorded another frustrating second place, this time to Better Lad in the V.R.C. St Leger. Sir Dane's luck turned in the spring of 1964. While he suffered some of his familiar minor placings – third in the Liston Stakes to Craftsman and Nicopolis, second to Future in the Memsie, second in the Caulfield Stakes to Contempler, third in the Underwood to Contempler and Royal Duty – Sir Dane had his share of big wins. He took the Craiglee and the Turnbull Stakes with authority and started favourite at 4/1 in the 1964 Caulfield Cup. The distance was beyond him and Sir Dane was ninth. With Roy Higgins up he had his revenge soon afterwards, defeating Contempler and Nicopolis in the Cox Plate and then rounding off his spring with a win in the Mackinnon Stakes. Sir Dane was back in the autumn of 1965. He won the Blamey, was second to Yangtze in the St George Stakes, won the Futurity with 66kg from Nicopolis, was second to Craftsman in the Queen Elizabeth Stakes. Sir Dane finished this campaign with a win in the Alister Clark Stakes, to stake acclaim among the best weight-for-age horses in a highly competitive era.

SIR DAPPER
1980 b horse Vain – Sikri

Sir Dapper was Vain's best-performed son at the track. As a two year old he won five of six and was second on the other occasion. He won the 1983 Golden Slipper in then record time. In the spring of that year, Sir Dapper won the coveted treble of the Peter Pan, Gloaming and Spring Champion Stakes. He won eight and was second on three occasions from his 12 starts as a three year old. He won the 1984 Canterbury and Expressway Stakes, beating Emancipation in the latter. The mare relegated him to two unlucky second placings in the George Ryder and All Aged Stakes. Injured, Sir Dapper was sent to the Transmedia Park Stud where – unlike his sire – his racecourse prowess has not yet been transferred to his progeny.

SIRES' PRODUCE STAKES (A.J.C.)

First run in 1867, when Glencoe won, the A. J. C. Sires' Produce is now the middle leg of the autumn two year old treble in Sydney. A Group One event over 1400m, its best winners in the 19th century were Robinson Crusoe, Chester, Trident, Abercorn and Autonomy. Furious, in 1921, was one of the many top fillies to win the event. Others include True Course in 1950, Wenona Girl (1960) and Desirable (1976), all of whom had also won the V. R. C. Sires'. Champion colts to take the event include Mollison, Hall Mark, Young Idea, Tulloch, Black Onyx, Baguette, Tontonan and Luskin Star. Mighty Manitou was the longest priced winner of the race when he scored at 200/1 in 1982.

SIRES' PRODUCE (Q.T.C.)

Run in the late autumn/winter carnival in Brisbane, at Eagle Farm, what is now the Group One Q.T.C. Sires' Produce was first contested in May 1881 when Legerdemain won over seven furlongs. The race was abandoned, before being revived under the influence of Greville Pountney. It was also suspended for four years during the Second World War. Top line winners earlier in this century include the Queensland gallopers High Syce (1927), Lough Neagh (1931) and Spear Chief (1937). Tulloch completed the treble of eastern states Sires' Produce Stakes in 1957. Other fine winners include Luskin Star, Red Anchor, Slight Chance and Mahogany.

SIRES' PRODUCE (V.R.C.)

After several early changes of distance and name, the V.R.C. Sires' Produce has established itself as the oldest two year old classic in Victoria. First run over a mile in 1862, when Musidora won, it became a key event in the autumn carnival from 1865, when it was run – together with the St Leger and the Australian Cup – on the first day of a two day programme. Frolic won. In 1866-7 this race was called the Flemington Stakes, next year the Sapling Stakes and – confusingly – it was known as the Ascot Vale Stakes in 1873. From 1864-1919 the Sires' was run over six furlongs, a distance extended to seven furlongs in 1920. Abercorn, Autonomy and Aurum were top line winners last century. Horses such as Sweet Nell, Woorak, Mollison, Young Idea, Hua, High Caste, Tulloch, Wenona Girl, Pago Pago, Citius, Storm Queen, Vain, Dual Choice, Tolerance, Century, Imagele, Lord Dudley, Mighty Kingdom, Grosvenor and Canny Lad have been among the high class winners this century. The Sires' has always been a good race for top fillies, and a better pointer than the Golden Slipper for its winners' potential to race on with success in later years. Bobbie Lewis won the race on five occasions.

SIR TRISTRAM

1971 b horse Sir Ivor – Isolt

By the outstanding racehorse Sir Ivor, Sir Tristram's track performance rose no higher than victory in two minor races in France. He was sold to the Cambridge Stud in New Zealand and soon began one of the most remarkable careers of any southern hemisphere sire. By the end of 1993, he had sired no fewer than 40 Group One winners. His best sons included the Victoria Derby winners Sovereign Red and Grosvenor. Sir Tristram has been even more successful as a sire of fillies. Three were Derby winners: Mapperley Heights (S.A.J.C.), Tristarc (A.J.C.) and Popsy (New Zealand Derby). Among his other outstanding daughters are Riverina Charm, Tristanagh and the 1988 Melbourne Cup winner, Empire Rose.

SKELTON, ROBERT ('THE BARON') (1882-59)

One of Australia's biggest and shrewdest gamblers, Bob Skelton was born at Nhill; moved to Sydney and learned his trade as a plumber. In 1905 he worked his passage to India on the 'Indrado'. There, according to legend, he talked his way into a job training thoroughbreds at Lucknow. Despite his lack of previous experience, Skelton won three trainers' premierships in six years. He went back to Melbourne at first, but after the war set up as the trainer of his own horses for the Sydney pony racing circuit. He soon dominated. When he resigned from the Pony Owners' and Trainers' Association it called a strike which the Associated Racing Club was powerless to prevent. Undeterred, 'The Baron' made sure that the Rosebery meeting went ahead and supplied 38 of the 44 runners. The strike was abandoned. In a long career, Skelton also ran a tipping service and worked as a bookie. But it was his exertions on the punt that finally exhausted him and he died in February 1959.

SKIDMORE, HAROLD (1916-)

Harold Skidmore made his reputation in a riding career that lasted only 12 years. Apprenticed in Melbourne at 12 to Steve Murphy, Skidmore was leading apprentice in the 1931-2 and 1932-3 seasons. On each occasion he was second in the senior jockeys' premiership behind Bill Duncan. The following season Skidmore was premier jockey with fifty two and a half wins, twenty three and a half of which had come while he was still serving his time. Skidmore won three titles on end. His best race wins included a Cox Plate on Young Idea, an Oakleigh Plate, V.R.C. Sires' Produce, Moonee Valley and Williamstown Cups, and a host of country cups. But Skidmore's career ended suddenly in June 1941, when he quit for 'personal reasons'. Although he took out an owner-trainer's licence, that enterprise foundered after a short time. Years later, Skidmore was still in demand as a track rider for such trainers as Tommy Smith. Skidmore, who lives virtually on the doorstep of the Moonee Valley track (where he rode more than 130 winners) is still a regular visitor to the course, but shuns the limelight.

SKIPTON

1938 ch horse Marabou – Cupidity

Sired by a Melbourne Cup winner and owned by Mrs J. Kitson, the wife of a Hamilton publican, Skipton ran three times without success at two, but in his next year won three starts in a row, culminating in the Moonee Valley Stakes of 1941. After a failure in the Caulfield Guineas, Skipton returned to form by decisively beating the A.J.C. Derby winner Laureate in the Victoria Derby. Billy Cook had the Melbourne Cup ride and took Skipton to victory. The colt was the 13th and last horse to complete the Derby-Cup double and he carried the 13 saddlecloth. In 1942 Skipton started at 3/1 favourite for the Caulfield Cup, but could only manage fifth to Tranquil Star. He went winless for more than a year. In the 1943 Herbert Power Handicap he finished midfield, and in consequence was sent out at 14/1 in one of the divisions of that year's Caulfield Cup (run at Flemington for the fourth and last time during the war). Bookies operated enterprisingly on the two Caulfield Cups double. With Scobie Breasley up, Skipton gave them a good result when he carried 58.5kg to victory by one and a half lengths. A stewards' inquiry into his form reversal found no impropriety. Form recaptured, Skipton ran a gallant fifth in the Melbourne Cup of 1943 with 61.5kg.

SKY HIGH

1957 b horse Star Kingdom – Flight's Daughter

The impeccably bred Sky High, full brother to the topline galloper Skyline, was by the imported Star Kingdom out of a mare whose dam (as the prosaic name suggests) was the champion Flight. Trained by Jack Green, he won 29 of 55 starts and was placed in another 19. Sky High's career began with a win in the Randwick Breeders' Plate in race record time in October 1959. Three more juvenile wins in Sydney saw him start odds-on favourite in the 1960 Golden Slipper, where he beat the filly who would become his great and worthy rival, Wenona Girl. She had her revenge in the A.J.C. Sires' Produce, but Sky High won the Champagne at 7/4 on. He was at red figures again when resuming in the Hobartville in the spring, but Wenona Girl beat him and a string of six losses in top class races in Sydney and Melbourne followed. Thus Sky High was at the luxury odds of 12/1 for the Victoria Derby, but he led all the way to beat Persian Lyric. At the end of his campaign, he was narrowly defeated by Aquanita in the George Adams Handicap.

Back in Melbourne in the autumn of 1961, Sky High won the Lightning Stakes, beat Lord in the Futurity, took the C.M. Lloyd Stakes and then the All Aged Stakes at Randwick. In consequence he started at 10/9 on in the Doncaster, but under 55kg could finish only third, in very fast time, to Fine and Dandy. As a four year old, Sky High won 10 of 15 outings. He won the Canterbury and Warwick Stakes with George Moore up, before shouldering 58kg to beat Fine and Dandy in the Epsom. Sky High won the Caulfield Stakes, but was uneasy around the Moonee Valley track and was again beaten at 9/4 on when third to Dhaulagiri and New Statesman in the Cox Plate. Back at Flemington, Sky High set a long-standing Australian record for 10 furlongs when he defeated Dhaulagiri and Aquanita in the Mackinnon Stakes. The Melbourne Cup distance proved beyond him and he ran 19th in his last spring start.

In the autumn of 1962, Sky High was back to show his brilliance by winning another Lightning Stakes at the start of a string of weight-for-age wins (many for the second time) in the C.M. Lloyd, Rawson, and Chipping Norton Stakes. In the spring he won the Canterbury and Warwick Stakes once more and the Hill Stakes before winding up fifth in the Epsom under the burden of 64.5kg. In winning the 1962 Caulfield Stakes he equalled the Australian record, ran second to Aquanita in the Mackinnon and won the Linlithgow. Still asked to take on the best in the autumn of 1963, Sky High won twice more, and set

another Australian record, this time for seven and a half furlongs, in the Rawson Stakes. Retired to the Woodlands Stud, Sky High was shortly afterwards sold to American interests. He went to the prestigious Claiborne Farm at Kentucky, where he enjoyed success from limited opportunities until his death in 1973.

SKYLINE
1955 b horse Star Kingdom – Flight's Daughter

Trained by Jack Green, this outstanding young horse never recovered from a scouring attack of the kind which sidelined Tulloch for nearly two years. However, he had won the 1958 Golden Slipper convincingly and returned as a three year old to beat Prince Darius by six lengths in the Hill Stakes. Triumph of his career was an A.J.C. Derby win in which he broke Tulloch's race record. At his next outing, Skyline won a Rosehill Flying and was second in the 1959 Doomben Cup. Because of illness, Skyline, who Green regarded as a champion, was unplaced in 11 subsequent starts. Fortunately for the trainer, he by then had charge of Skyline's full brother, Sky High.

SLIGHT CHANCE
1989 br mare Centaine – Lady Aloft

The Bob Thomsen-trained Slight Chance was twice first and twice second in her first four starts. A win over 1500m at Randwick in mid-May 1992 earned her a trip to Brisbane, where she scored a hollow win in the Queensland Sires' Produce Stakes and then repeated the dose in the Castlemaine Stakes. Resuming in the spring, the filly won the Roman Consul Stakes and then beat Burst in the Flight Stakes at Randwick. Brought to Melbourne, she was only fifth in the Thousand Guineas of 1992 which Azzuro won, but showed improved form with a fine third in the interference chequered Cox Plate behind Super Impose. The filly's main spring mission had been the V.R.C. Oaks, which she won handily from Mahaya and Burst, in a quality year. After a spell, Slight Chance resumed with a win over Burst at Rosehill; ran second to Mahaya in the A.J.C. Oaks; third in the Queensland Guineas, and then ran up yet another Group One win in the Queensland Oaks. At the conclusion of her three year old career, Slight Chance had won $1.2 million. In the spring of 1993 her only glimpse of form was a third in the George Main behind March Hare. It was not until June 1994 that she won another race, in Brisbane, by the barest of margins from Bright Copper.

SMITH, TOMMY (1918-)

One of the greatest of world trainers, Tommy (T.J.) Smith was born at Jembaicumbene near Braidwood, and grew up on the flat plains near Goolgowi. His father was a boozer, bullocky and butcher, with a keen knowledge of horses. With Desert King the pair travelled to the Hillston picnic races and Smith recorded a profitable win, his first as a jockey. At 13 he left home and was apprenticed to Bill McLaughlin, a down-on-his-luck battling trainer at Mordialloc. Smith took to the punt, and notable successes included backing the card at Rainbow. He gravitated to Sydney, first to the stables of 'Son' Mackinnon at Moorefield, then to Mack Sawyer. He failed as a jumps jockey, but then – to the initial scepticism of those who were wary of his brashness – took to training.

The rogue Bragger, was Smith's first horse, and with Jack Thompson up, Smith finally won a Rosehill maiden with him in March 1942. Within seven years he saddled

his first classic winner, the maiden Playboy in the A.J.C. Derby. George Moore rode the horse, in the first of scores of big race wins during his long and stormy association with Smith. And Playboy's was the first of a world record 35 Derbies for Smith-trained horses. In the 1952-3 season, Smith won the Sydney trainers' premiership, a feat which he repeated for an astonishing 33 years in a row. In 20 of those seasons he trained more than 100 winners, with his record 156 in 1975-6. His strike rate in stakes races is remarkable: besides the Derby wins, 18 Oaks, 13 St Legers, 27 Guineas, 16 Chelmsford Stakes, 14 O'Shea Stakes, 13 George Main and 13 Flight Stakes. Six times his horses won the Golden Slipper, while he won the Cox Plate no less than seven times. Toporoa and Just A Dash were his only Melbourne Cup winners; but he won four Caulfield Cups.

Smith's greatest horse was Tulloch, with the three time Cox Plate winner Kingston Town not far behind. Bounding Away, the 1986 Golden Slipper winner, was a sentimental favourite whom Smith owned and bred. His troubles with racing officials were persistent. He seldom attracted owners from the ranks of the A. J. C. Committee, but was in any case always content to back his own judgment in the purchase of horses. In 1950 he was disqualified for five years over the running of Sunshine Express, but successfully appealed. In 1954 his imported mare Tarien was disqualified after a positive swab following her Epsom win, but Smith escaped further penalty. He was suspended for a month when he did not report Jupiter's bleeding attack, but owners rallied and not a horse left Smith's Randwick Stables. In 1987 he made an ill-judged attempt to turn Tulloch Lodge into a public company, a venture from which he was rescued in part by the intervention of the

American tycoon John Kluge. Smith surrendered his trainers' title in 1985-6 to Brian Mayfield-Smith, but won it for the 34th time three years later. In recent years he has wound down his team, rather enjoying the success of his daughter, Gai Waterhouse. Wife of the former bookmaker Robbie Waterhouse, Smith's daughter had her first Group One victory when Te Akau Nick won the 1993 Metropolitan; followed it with the Doncaster of 1994 with Pharaoh, a horse whose training she had taken over from her father, the larrikin, showman and genius with thoroughbreds, T.J. Smith. A controversial biography of Smith, Kevin Perkins' The Midas Man, was published in 1993.

SOBAR

1969 br horse Sobig – Miss Filou

Lightly raced as a two year old, the Ken Hilton trained colt Sobar won the Orrong Handicap in the autumn of 1971. His first two starts at three saw him unplaced, but then he was stepped up abruptly into weight-for-age class and ran an unlucky third (beaten two short half heads) behind Gossiper and Royal Show in the 1972 Craiglee Stakes. That promising effort was emphatically underlined when Sobar won the Underwood Stakes at his next start. Coming into the Caulfield Guineas, he was second favourite at 6/4 behind Century in what was perceived to be a two horse race. In fact it was a one horse race: Sobar won handsomely by three and a half lengths. Regular jockey Harry White was given permission to ride the horse 2.5kg overweight in the Caulfield Cup. Sobar thus carried 48kg, the same weight as Tulloch in his victory in 1957. And Sobar won with the same conviction as Tulloch had, beating Stormy Seas and Gunsynd in brilliant time. At his next start, Sobar was controversially

beaten at odds-on by Dayana in the Victoria Derby when forced wide. More significant than the loss was the tendon injury which Sobar suffered. In consequence, he was unable to fulfil his potential. Repeated efforts were made to get him back to the track, but these were increasingly unhappy. Although he won the Blamey and St George Stakes in 1974, he was finally retired after running ninth at Ballarat and last in a Toorak Handicap. What might have been a great turf career is now distinguished by a month of brilliance in Sobar's three year old spring campaign.

SO CALLED

1974 b horse Sobig – Calling

This very talented middle distance performer from the Colin Hayes stable won the 1977 Sandown Guineas from Princess Talaria and Show Ego. That was a sign of better things to come. In the autumn of 1978, So Called won the V.R.C. St Leger. Hayes then saved him for the spring. Second in the Spring Champion Stakes to Lefroy, with Belmura Lad third, So Called was taken to Melbourne. There he won the Feehan, the Liston (from Hyperno), the Underwood (from Panamint and Family of Man) and was second to Lefroy in the Turnbull. So Called's biggest day at the races was soon to come: he won the Cox Plate from Family of Man (the previous year's winner) and Karaman, to cap a racing career which had well fitted him for stud duties.

SOMETIME

1958 b horse Summertime – Nereid

Bart Cummings thought Sometime the best looking yearling at the 1960 sales in New Zealand and paid 2,300 guineas for him on behalf of the brothers, Bob and Jack Lee. Cummings brought the horse along patiently, but Sometime showed promise with three successive wins in May and June 1961. At three he won seven races, and although these included the Port Adelaide Guineas and the S.A.J.C. St Leger, Sometime was better known for the top races in which he was narrowly beaten. Second to King Brian in the Caulfield Guineas, he was fourth to Summer Fair in the 1961 Caulfield Cup, third to New Statesman in the Victoria Derby, sixth in Lord Fury's Melbourne Cup. In May 1962, he was second to Cheong Sam in the Adelaide Cup. Sometime was now in the care of Les Patterson, who took over the horse after Cummings was suspended for a year over the running of Cilldara. As a four year old Sometime again proved a solid money-earner, with four wins and a dead-heat, but big races continued to elude him. He was second in the Adelaide Cup, an unlucky fourth in the Brisbane Cup. But he blossomed at five, as many stayers do. Third in the Memsie in the spring of 1963, Sometime won the Feehan and was then third to Havelock and Lord in the Underwood Stakes. He then won the Turnbull Stakes at Flemington before beating Lei (later the dam of Leilani) in the Caulfield Stakes. This saw him start at 5/2 favourite in the Caulfield Cup, and he won almost casually, by four lengths, with Billy Pyers up. Third in the Cox Plate and second in the Mackinnon subsequently, Sometime seemed to have reverted to his old ways. His record of twenty one and a half wins and 18 placings from 70 starts is admirable in one respect; speaks of unfulfilled promise in another.

SOUTH AUSTRALIAN DERBY

The South Australian Derby has had a long, but frequently interrupted history, in keeping with the fortunes of racing in that state, especially in the 19th century. A version of the race was run as long ago as 1860 when Midnight won. Tim Whiffler, who would prove to be one of the most durable stayers of the colonial period, won in 1865. A horse called Rothschild won in 1880. Renamed The Assyrian, he would become the first of several South Australian Derby winners to go on to success in the Melbourne Cup. Gatum Gatum won the Derby in 1961, the Melbourne Cup two years later. Ziema, victor in 1964, had to be satisfied with second places in both the Caulfield and Melbourne Cups in 1965. Mission, who won the Derby in 1965, became perhaps the best jumper with classic credentials in Australian turf history. The South Australian Derby of 1972 gave Dayana the first of an unprecedented four which he would win that year. Stormy Rex (1977) and Brewery Boy (1981) both progressed to victory in the Victoria Derby. Shiva's Revenge, who gave Bart Cummings yet another victory in the South Australian Derby, was second in the 1991 Melbourne Cup, but the 1992 Derby winner Subzero went one better and took the Cup that spring, as well as winning the 1992 Adelaide Cup.

SOUTH AUSTRALIAN RACING

Less than a year after the European settlement of the colony, racing began at Adelaide on New Year's Day 1838. Colonel Light, planner of the city, was one of the stewards for the meeting. In 1856 the South Australian Jockey Club took over the staging of the St Leger. Disappearing briefly in the 1860s and challenged for control of South Australian racing in the 1880s by the Adelaide Racing Club, the S.A.J.C. eventually established its pre-eminence. The club stages its races at Morphettville, while the A.R.C.'s events are run at Victoria Park and Cheltenham.

SOVEREIGN EDITION

1962 gr horse Sovereign Path – Latest Edition

This Irish-bred horse raced with some success in his native country and in England. An ill-tempered stallion, he was sent to stand at the Kia-Ora Stud in New Zealand. There his stock attracted the attention of Australian trainers, and of Geoff Murphy in particular. Among the best horses who Sovereign Edition sired were Abdul and Surround, both Murphy-trained Cox Plate winners; Analie, who won a Doncaster, two Oaks and the Q.T.C. Derby and the Caulfield Guineas winner Beau Sovereign. The latter went on to stand with distinction as a sire in Western Australia.

SOVEREIGN RED

1977 ch horse Sir Tristram – Taiona

This high quality galloper, trained by Geoff Murphy, began his career modestly with a single two year old win at Flemington, and a second to Elounda Bay at his only other start. As a spring three year old in 1980, he proved the best of what was perhaps not a vintage age group. A win at Sandown was followed by a third in the Moonee Valley Stakes, after which Sovereign Red beat Joy in the Caulfield Guineas and Real Force in the Victoria Derby. Murphy kept the horse up, and sent him to Perth for a tough campaign. After a second in the Western Australian Derby, Sovereign Red won the Group One Western Mail Classic; was beaten in the Caris Diamond Quality, but then proved too good for Artist Man in the Australian Derby. He also had Sydney placings that season in the Hobartville Stakes and Canterbury Guineas. In 1981 Sovereign Red was sent north, where he won the Group One Castlemaine Stakes in Brisbane. In the spring he won the Liston and Underwood Stakes, before Kingston Town relegated him to second in the Caulfield Stakes. Sovereign Red's form gradually fell away, although he was second in the St George Stakes in 1982. He went on to a successful career at stud.

SPEARFELT

1921 br horse Spearhead – Lady Champion

By a grandson of Carbine, Spearfelt was bred at the Kurangi Stud in the Goulburn Valley. While being sent to the Widden Stud by steamer, Spearfelt's dam Lady Champion died and the colt had to be bottle-fed. He quickly recovered from these set-backs; winning the Gibson Carmichael and A.J.C Stakes at two. Next season he won the Victoria Derby at 7/4 on before finishing an unlucky third in the 1924 Melbourne Cup. In the following autumn, Spearfelt won the St Leger and the King's Plate, before falling in the Sydney Cup in which Lilypond beat Windbag. Spearfelt's woes intensified when he contracted pneumonia. Brought back to health under the care of trainer V. O'Neill, Spearfelt won the A.J.C. Spring Stakes before being sent for another crack at the Melbourne Cup. In the Melbourne Stakes he ran fourth to Manfred. When that horse and Heroic were both scratched, Spearfelt seized his chance and won by a half length, before a record crowd of nearly 120,000 people. Hughie Cairns obtained the winning ride on Cup eve, after initially being booked for Heroic. George Young, jocked off Spearfelt, obtained a winning percentage in lieu of the glory. Unlike many other Cup winners, Spearfelt was not a spent force. In the autumn of 1927 he won the Australian Cup carrying 63kg. Sent to stud, he sired the 1943 Melbourne Cup winner, Dark Felt.

SPECIAL

1983 b mare Habituate – Sal II

One of the finest sprinters of the 1980s,

Special was trained by Colin Hayes and owned by his wife Betty, until a part-share was sold to Robert Sangster's Swettenham Stud. A minor win at Victoria Park in Adelaide was the only yield of Special's three runs at two. Next season she won first up at Moonee Valley, before succumbing to a virus. This meant that she missed the fillies' classics, but Hayes set her to live up to her taxing name in the 1986 Moir Stakes at Moonee Valley, and she duly beat Campaign King. In the autumn Special ran into Placid Ark, finishing second to him in the Lightning Stakes and the Newmarket. A year later it was the turn of Special, who ran a course record to win the Lightning; took the Newmarket with 56kg and then won the Stanley Wootton at Moonee Valley. In the spring of 1988 Special showed her fondness for the Flemington straight by winning the Gadsden on Derby Day. This made her the first sprinting mare in Australia to win over $1,000,000. Special had her last start when second to Zeditave in the 1989 Lightning Stakes, and went to stud.

SPONSORSHIP

Sponsorship of Australian racing was attempted as long ago as 1873, when the Melbourne firm Buckley and Nunn offered to back a race for fillies and mares at the Flemington spring carnival. The V.R.C. refused. It was not until the 1960 spring carnival at Flemington that races were sponsored. They were the George Adams Handicap, the W.D. & H.O. Wills Hallmark Stakes (renamed the Craven 'A' the following year) and the Black & White Provincial Cup. The consequences of burgeoning racing sponsorship have seen even the Epsom Derby tagged with a brand-name. In Australia, the unhappy outcomes of sponsorship have been regular changes of races' names; the consequent loss of their identity; the grossness of some of the tags which races have worn. None has surpassed the indignity which befell the Toorak Handicap when – in 1993 – it became the Quick-Eze.

SPORTING GLOBE

First published in 1922, Melbourne's *Sporting Globe* for decades has been essential reading for fans of all sports, but principally for punters. Printed on pink paper, it was known as 'Pinky with the Punch' or, less respectfully, as the 'Pink Comic'. Originally published on Mondays and Saturdays, people clamoured for the latter's late edition to get all racing results and prices, together with the football scores, in season. Now published on Mondays and Thursdays, the *Sporting Globe* is principally a racing form paper. Many top writers and colourful characters have worked for it: Geoff Hawksley, Ben Kerville, Hec de Lacy, Jim Bugden, Peter Bye, Tom Moon, Rollo Roylance, Ian McDonald and Merv Williams. Jeff Pemberthy, who started as a copy boy, became editor of the Australian edition of *Time Magazine*. And the literary qualities of the paper were yet more various: John O'Grady ('Nino Culotta') had his best selling novel They're A Weird Mob first see daylight as a serial in the *Sporting Globe* in the mid-1950s.

SPRING CHAMPION STAKES

This Group One event over 2000m is run at Randwick each September. Established in 1971 as the Australasian Champion Stakes (which it remained until 1978), the race has become the main spring three year old staying test in Sydney since the switch of the A.J.C. Derby to the autumn from 1979. It was inaugurated in memorable fashion in 1971 when Gay Icarus beat Baguette and Gunsynd. Top stayers Asgard, Taras Bulba, Cheyne Walk, Lefroy and Kingston Town prevailed later in the 1970s. In the 1980s, Sir Dapper, Beau Zam and Stylish Century were the best to score in a race whose more recent winners have lacked their brilliance.

STAR AFFAIR

1962 b horse Star Kingdom – Royal Lark

Winner of 10 races, Star Affair, owned by Stanley Wootton and trained by Angus Armanasco, had a brief but brilliant career. As a two year old he beat Citius (from the same Star Kingdom crop) in the Merson Cooper Stakes at Caulfield, before finishing second to Reisling in the 1965 Golden Slipper. But in the spring of that year Star Affair was clearly the best of his age group. After winning the Moonee Valley Stakes, he defeated Tobin Bronze (who would go on to win the Derby) in the Caulfield Guineas. Next start Star Affair won the Cox Plate from Winfreux and Yangtze, before rounding off his campaign with victory in the Linlithgow Stakes at Flemington. In the autumn of 1966 he came back as well as ever and recorded high class wins in the William Reid Stakes and in the Futurity where he beat Star Gun. Soon afterwards Star Affair was retired to stud in Japan, although subsequently he returned to Australia.

STAR KINGDOM

1946 ch horse Stardust – Impromptu

Greatest sire to be imported to Australia, Star Kingdom raced in England as Star King. At two he won four of five starts, beaten only by Abernant in the National Breeders' Produce Stakes at Sandown. Only Abernant was ranked above him in that season's Free Handicap. While Star King won first up at Newbury as a three year old, he could only manage 10th in the 2,000 Guineas. He then won at Ascot over a shorter journey, before finishing third to Abernant in the July Cup at Chester. Another Newbury win saw him conclude his three year old days with eight victories from 11 outings. While Star King won first up at four, at Chester, he lost his next four races and was retired. Stanley Wootton chose him to stand in Australia, and he arrived in Melbourne in February 1951. A small colt, Star Kingdom, as he was now known, looked distinctly unpromising as he began duties at the Barramul Stud.

His supporters did not wait long for results. From his first crop Star Kingdom produced the brilliant filly Ultrablue and the multiple Group One winner, (and one of his best sons), Kingster. There were some doubts initially as to whether the Star Kingdom stock trained on, notwithstanding Kingster's deeds. When Skyline, from his fourth crop, won the A.J.C. Derby, and Gold Stakes an Oakleigh Plate and Newmarket, the issue was settled. Most famous of all Star Kingdom's sons – and responsible for carrying his bloodlines into another generation – was Todman, from the third crop. Noholme and Fine and Dandy were brilliant horses from the sixth; Derby winner Sky High from the next crop. Time and Tide and Sunset Hue (sire of Gunsynd) arrived the next season. Nor was Star Kingdom much dimmed by age. Star of Heaven came from his 10th crop; Star Affair and Citius from the 11th; from the 14th came Rajah, and the top sires-to-be, Biscay and Kaoru Star. Star Kingdom died in April 1967, having sired 1,170 winners. He won the Australian Sires' Premiership five times: from 1958-9 to 1961-2, and again in 1964-5. Star Kingdom horses won the first five Golden Slipper Stakes, eight Sires' Produce and seven Champagne Stakes, together with numerous classic and weight-for-age events as older horses. He was also an outstanding sire of sires, so much so, that in 1981 two of his grandsons Bletchingly (by Biscay) and Nodouble (by Noholme) were respectively the leading sires in Australia and the United States. No horse has made a greater impact on Australian thoroughbred racing than Star Kingdom.

ST ALBANS [BOWDEN], PETER (1863-98)

The story of the jockey Peter St Albans is an obscure and tantalising one. For a start his real name was probably Bowden. Apprenticed to James Wilson, he seems to have taken his adopted surname from Wilson's St Albans Stud near Geelong. Rumour has placed him variously as Wilson's illegitimate son, and as an Aborigine. Whatever the truth of his origins, he was the youngest jockey to ride a Melbourne Cup winner when, at 13, he piloted the champion filly Briseis to victory in 1876. And he nearly won again the next year when his heavily backed mount Savanaka was narrowly and unluckily beaten by Chester, upsetting a notorious coup mounted by Wilson and Herbert Power. St Albans rode for a few more years with some success, winning the 1880 St Leger and the 1881 Sires' Produce Stakes, before turning to training. His best horse was Forest King, second in the Caulfield Cup of 1891. Bowden/St Albans died in 1898.

ST ALBANS STUD

Located outside Geelong, St Albans Stud was one of the most famous of Australian racing landmarks. Established at the end of the 1860s by James Wilson, it nurtured such champions as Briseis, Malua, Auraria, First King, Newhaven and Wallace. From 1878 the stud held yearling sales to benefit from the Geelong Cup meeting.

Wilson sold the property to John Crozier of South Australia in 1886. In 1890 William Wilson (no relation to the first owner) bought St Albans. When he decided to sell up in 1895, he dispersed the stud by lottery. The property was the first prize; top sire Trenton the second. Having second thoughts, Wilson paid 24,000 pounds to buy back the stud from the winning ticket holder. He also paid to retrieve the top colt Wallace, then a two year old, who went on to win the Victoria Derby in 1895. Another dispersal of St Albans occurred after William Wilson's death in 1900. A V.R.C. committeeman, Guy Raymond, eventually purchased the stud in 1926, where he bred such big race winners as Sirius and Rimfire. In 1930 the St Albans Stud enjoyed one of its finest hours as the haven for Phar Lap in between the attempt on his life and his win in the Melbourne Cup. After Guy Raymond's death in 1972, his daughter, Ann, continued to manage the St Albans Stud until she moved to New South Wales. The original homestead stands as a reminder of one of the great breeding grounds in Australian turf history.

STAR OF HEAVEN

1961 ch horse Star Kingdom – Magic Symbol

A brilliant sprinter from the 10th crop of Star Kingdom, Star of Heaven won eight of his 14 starts. In the autumn of 1964, the Angus Armanasco-trained colt was third behind Eskimo Prince and Farnworth in the Golden Slipper Stakes. That spring he had an outstanding Flemington carnival, setting a weight-carrying record of 50kg for a three year old when he won the George Adams Handicap (a record that Vain would break a few years later) and then taking the Linlithgow Stakes. Star of Heaven came back again in the autumn of 1965 when his best effort was second to Marmion in the Lightning Stakes. Thereafter he was retired to stud, standing in both the United States and Australia. Star Shower, an unbeaten colt who won the Blue Diamond Stakes in 1979, was perhaps the best of the Star of Heaven progeny.

STEWARDS

Bookmakers and punters alike had similar complaints about racing in the later years of last century: there was a stench concerning some results. It was alleged that jockeys were obeying the orders of unscrupulous bookmakers, while owners were not allowing horses to run on their merits, in order to beat the handicapper in a later event. Club committeemen, who acted as stewards, were generally more interested in the social aspects of the day than events on the track. Newspapers took up the cause, with the result that the V.R.C. appointed Victoria's first full time steward in October 1890. The person charged with cleaning up racing was Harrie Smith, who resigned from the V.R.C. committee to take up the position. The first meeting at which he adjudicated was Caulfield Cup day, 1890. Smith had wide powers, but it was apparent that more stewards were required. In 1912 the V.R.C. established a stewards' panel, and three experienced racing men were employed with salaries of 700 pounds per annum. They had full control of racing on Melbourne tracks, although appeals were heard by the V.R.C. committee. The first A.J.C. stipendiary steward was F.A. Thompson, appointed in 1895. His staff was augmented in 1903. Duties of stewards also increased; a horse name register was begun and the Australian Rules of Racing codified. Public confidence in racing increased and the foundations were laid for practices still followed by stewards today, to keep the public's faith in racing.

ST LEGER, A.J.C.

The notion of running classic horse races at set weights and in one, rather than three heats, apparently originated with Lt Anthony St Leger. The oldest of English classics, the St Leger, first run at Doncaster in 1776, is named after him. Appropriately, the oldest race on the Australian racing calendar is the A.J.C. St Leger, which was initially contested at Homebush in 1841 and won by Eleanor. Despite a number of high class winners, who included Phar Lap (1930), Peter Pan (1933), Sailor's Guide (1956) and Tulloch (1958), the race attracted dwindling fields and was deleted from its calendar by the A.J.C. after Bardshah's win in 1959. The St Leger was reinstated as a weight-for-age race, run at Randwick over 2800m for three and four year olds, in 1980. Since then such top-line gallopers as November Rain, Gurner's Lane, Beau Zam, Tawriffic and Castletown have restored lustre to the event.

ST LEGER, V.R.C.

Now declined to a Group Three event run over 2800m at Flemington in the late autumn, the V.R.C. St Leger was one of the most important three-year-old classic races on the turf calendar in 19th century Australia. Artaxerxes was the first winner, in 1857. Good horses soon stamped their authority on the event: Angler, Fishhook and Fireworks from 1867-9, Hamlet (one of numerous dual V.R.C.-A.J.C. St Leger winners) in 1872, the unbeaten Grand Flaneur in 1881, Navigator in 1883 and Martini-Henry the following year. The 1880s was a sterling decade for the race, as Trident and Abercorn won in 1887-8 respectively. The next decade had the top-line horses Strathmore, Aurum and Bobadil among the winners. Wallace's best daughter, Lady Wallace won in 1906, the champion Poseidon the year after that. Between the wars the race enjoyed another golden period, when its winners included Artilleryman, Furious, Spearfelt, Trivalve, Strephon, Phar Lap. In 1934 Hall Mark deadheated with Limarch. Tranquil Star and Lawrence won during the Second World War, Comic Court and Delta soon after it. During the 1950s Hydrogen, Cromis, Sailor's Guide and Tulloch won the race. Prince Grant won in 1966; Taras Bulba, Lord Dudley and So Called in the mid to late 1970s. The last horse of real quality to win the St Leger was Gurner's Lane in 1982: he went on to the Caulfield-Melbourne Cups double in the spring of that year. Shiva's Revenge, who won the St Leger in 1991 was second in that year's Melbourne Cup; Subzero – second in 1992 – went on to win the Cup. The St Leger is still a sound staying form reference.

ST MAGNUS

1933 b horse Sasovino – Fair Isle

A four time winner in England, St Magnus was imported to Australia and sired a number of brilliant horses. The nearest he came to a sires' premiership was second to Midstream for the 1950-1 season. The crack horse of the 1950s Flying Halo, who won three William Reid and two Underwood Stakes among two dozen victories, was by St Magnus. He also sired St Fairy, the 1945 Caulfield Cup and 1946 Cantala Stakes winner; St Razzle, who won the 1949 and 1950 Futurity Stakes and was second to Lincoln in the 1949 Caulfield Cup; Prince of Fairies, the 1951 Brisbane Cup winner. Morse Code, who won the Williamstown Cup in 1950 and 1952 and two Eclipse

Stakes for good measure, and St Joel, who numbered among his victories the William Reid Stakes of 1954 and the Alister Clark at Moonee Valley the following year were other good progeny. Another good stayer of the St Magnus era, St Warden who won the 1943 Caulfield Cup and the Port Adelaide Cups of 1943-4, was by Lord Warden, despite the similarity of names.

STORM QUEEN

1963 b mare Coronation Boy – Storm Gleam

A brilliant, if temperamental filly, Storm Queen gave jockey Roy Higgins and trainer Bart Cummings their first Golden Slipper winner. Bart's brother Pat, a part-owner, was afforded plenty of fun in the betting ring. After four wins in Adelaide, Storm Queen came to Melbourne where she won the 1966 Merson Cooper Stakes at the handy odds of 8/1. Stepping up to the 1400m of the Sires' Produce Stakes, she was untroubled to score by one and a half lengths. Cummings decided to send the filly further east for the rich pickings of the Golden Slipper and was amply rewarded when – despite having some trouble with the Rosehill turns – Storm Queen scored by a head from Academy Star. An eighth win on end followed in the Champagne Stakes, when once more Storm Queen did not start favourite. Set an ambitious spring campaign, the filly won the Moonee Valley and Edward Manifold Stakes. Then in the Caulfield Guineas she toyed with the opposition to win by five lengths from Pharaon and All High. In the Thousand Guineas a few days later she was surprisingly beaten by Cendrillon, but on the final day of the Flemington carnival Storm Queen was back to her best when she won the George Adams Handicap. In the autumn of 1967, Storm Queen was narrowly beaten by Marmion in the William Reid

Stakes, with Tobin Bronze third, but made amends in the Lightning Stakes. Given the impost of 56kg in the Newmarket she finished a gallant fourth to Nebo Road, while she was ninth in Tobin Bronze's 1967 Doncaster. Storm Queen retired as the first Australian filly to win more than $100,000 in stakes.

STORMY REX
1974 br gelding Storm Ruler – Chelissa

A hardy horse, if not the best of Bart Cummings's Derby winners, Stormy Rex won at his first start at Victoria Park in Adelaide and followed with a Graduation at Cheltenham. Stepping up quickly, he scored in the S.A. Derby. Taken to Melbourne, he was unplaced in the Cox Plate, but a top ride by Roy Higgins saw the gelding narrowly home in the 1977 Victoria Derby from Jury and Lefroy. An unplaced run in the Sandown Guineas followed, but Cummings kept the horse up, sending Stormy Rex to Western Australia. He took the W.A. Derby at 4/5 and added the Marlboro 50,000 to his big race tally. Stormy Rex was then beaten at 4/7 in the Australian Derby by Show Ego. He had already passed his best – to come was a forlorn, if busy, four year old season in which he won once and was placed three times from 17 starts, in one of which he finished last in the 1978 Caulfield Cup.

STRADBROKE HANDICAP

First run at Eagle Farm over six furlongs in 1890 (when Pyrrhus won), the Stradbroke Handicap distance was extended to seven furlongs in 1953. Babel was the first dual winner in 1895 and 1896, while in the following year, Dalnair became the first of no fewer than six two year olds to win the race. The most recent of these was the filly Wiggle in 1958. The race was suspended

because of the war from 1942-5, after which Darby McCarthy and George Moore each won three times. In 1970 Divide and Rule won the race as the first leg of a double with the Doomben Cup which was ruinous for bookmakers. Sir Wisp took the event in 1977 at 100/1, odds well justified by his previous form, while Ducatoon was first past the post in 1980, but was disqualified after returning a positive swab. The race went to Bemboka Yacht. The top line Queensland horse Daybreak Lover won the race in both 1984 and 1986, while other accomplished recent winners include Campaign King, who scored from Rancho Ruler and Planet Ruler in 1988.

STRAIGHT DRAW
1953 b gelding Faux Tirage – Sunbridge

Bred in New Zealand, and trained by Jack Mitchell in Sydney, Straight Draw was the best horse that volatile newspaperman Ezra Norton owned. He is remembered, somewhat unfairly, for winning the 1957 Melbourne Cup upon which Tulloch had a mortgage, before being controversially scratched. Even after Straight Draw won the Metropolitan from Gallant Lee and the Ted Best-trained Queenslander Book Link, Mitchell was reluctant to run him against Tulloch, but Norton prevailed. After a sixth in the Hotham Handicap, Straight Draw was kept safe at 13/2 third favourite in the Cup. Ridden by Noel McGrowdie he scored by a neck from Prince Darius who had been beaten eight lengths by Tulloch in the Derby. And there were good horses behind them: Syntax, Redcraze, Book Link, Baron Boissier and Monte Carlo. Straight Draw became the fourth horse, after Tim Whiffler in 1867, Delta and Dalray (1951-2) to win the Metropolitan-Melbourne Cup double. He underlined his quality by going on to complete a rare treble when he won the

Sydney Cup in the autumn of 1958, carrying 56.5kg, from the luckless Caranna.

STRATHMORE

1888 b horse Nordenfeldt – Ouida

By the 1885 Victoria Derby winner Nordenfeldt, Strathmore emulated his sire when he took the 1891 running of the classic. This was the first of three successes in the race for his owner W.R. Wilson, who also had Carnage and Wallace. Earlier in the spring Strathmore had won the Caulfield Guineas from Stromboli, who was also second in the Derby. Later he was a fast-closing third in the Melbourne Cup which Malvolio won. In the autumn of 1892 Strathmore trained on successfully to win the V.R.C. St Leger, the Champion and All Aged Stakes.

STRAWBERRY ROAD

1979 b horse Whiskey Road – Giftisa

First trained in Queensland by Doug Bougoure, Strawberry Road is remembered for his outstanding performances not only in Australia, but in four other countries and two other continents. As a three year old he won five restricted races in a row in Brisbane and was sent south for the autumn carnival in Sydney. After a close second to Marscay in the Hobartville Stakes, two disappointing runs followed. Then, striking form, Strawberry Road beat Mr McGinty in the Rosehill Guineas. Next start, on a bog track, the horse won the A.J.C. Derby by five and a half lengths from Veloso with Chiamare 20 lengths further adrift. Strawberry Road campaigned on to win three races at the Queensland winter carnival, including the Derby.

His successes in the spring as a four year old all came at Moonee Valley, culminating in the W.S. Cox Plate of 1984. It was then that the horse was bought by John Singleton and Ray Stehr with the ambitious plan of running him in the Prix de l'Arc de Triomphe. The owners persevered, despite Strawberry Road's poor campaign in the autumn of 1984. Trained by Patrick Biancone at Chantilly, Strawberry Road ran sixth in the Arc, but then took the Group One Grosser Preis von Baden in Germany. Next year he won the Group Two Prix d'Harcourt and the Group One Grand Prix de Saint-Cloud in France and was an unlucky second to Pebbles in the Breeders' Cup in America. In 1986 he won at Group Two level in California and was retired to stud the next year. From his first crop Strawberry Road produced Dinard, winner of the Group One Santa Anita Derby and Fowda, winner of the Group One Hollywood Oaks. He remains a horse perhaps more honoured outside Australia than in his own country.

STREAKERS

Racing has had to endure or enjoy fewer streakers than football or cricket, but two made headlines on Doncaster day in 1974. Entering the course in raincoats and sandshoes (and nothing else, as was revealed), a man and woman stationed themselves by the furlong pole. As the Doncaster field entered the Randwick straight, they sprinted across the track, in plain view of disconcerted jockeys. Friends ensured their escape. Roy Higgins made sure that Tontonan got home first, regardless. Melbourne's now defunct Francis Hotel once sported a full frontal of the streaking pair that was never translated to newsprint.

STREPHON

1925 ch horse Saltash – Soldier's Love

Strephon's mother died while foaling, but the horse survived and was bought by Sol Green who sent him to Melbourne to be trained by Lou Robertson. Unplaced at one start at two, Strephon came back at three to win his first two starts, before running fifth to Balmerino in the Caulfield Guineas. He won the Herbert Power Handicap at his next start, before easily winning the Victoria Derby, ridden by Jim Pike, by three and a half lengths from Yodelist and Balmerino. Second to Statesman in the Melbourne Cup, Strephon was turned out before coming back for a sensational autumn. In succession he won the V.R.C. St Leger, Governor's and King's Plates. In Sydney he took the Chipping Norton Stakes, A.J.C. St Leger, Cumberland Stakes and the A.J.C. Plate by 15 lengths. Remarkably, Phar Lap would win the same seven races in the following year. But they never met on the track. After a dispute with stewards, Green sold all his horses. Strephon was sent to England with the Ascot Gold Cup in mind, but suffered severe debilitation when the ship carrying him broke down in the Red Sea. His English programme began in July 1930 with a second at Kempton Park, but thereafter the form of a horse who had been a champion in Australia, declined so sadly that he ended up running over hurdles.

STROP

1861 b gelding Panic – out of a Littlejohn mare

Sired by the imported English stallion Panic, who won the 1865 Launceston Cup (or its effective forerunner), Strop was one of the hardiest horses ever to race in Australia. He had no fewer than four starts in the Melbourne Cup, of which the most successful was when he ran second to the good horse Glencoe, beaten a length, at 20/1 in 1868. Strop's record-breaking deeds were reserved for his home state of Tasmania. Owned by William Field, Strop made the Launceston Cup his pet event to a degree rarely rivalled in any good handicap race in Australian turf history. He won four Launceston Cups: in 1866, 1869, 1874 and 1876, when he was 14! In addition he was fourth to Fishhook in 1867, third in 1868 to Fireworks, with no less than Tim Whiffler second and The Barb in fourth place. Strop also ran second in 1875. At 14 he won the Hobart Cup, while two seasons later he was able to beat an admittedly poor lot in the 1878 Miners' Gift. Soon afterwards Strop was deemed to have earned an honourable retirement.

STYLISH CENTURY

1986 blk horse Double Century – Stylish

The handsome black horse Stylish Century was one of the most accident-prone to race in Australia in recent years. A $6,000 yearling purchase, he won his first start at Doomben at the end of November 1968 by 11 lengths and won at his next three starts as well. Second to Mercury in the Todman Slipper Trial, he won the Brambles Classic at Kembla Grange before running down the line in the Golden Slipper and A.J.C. Sires' Produce Stakes. When Stylish Century began his three year old campaign with five starts without a win, he was transferred briefly to Bart Cummings, who discerned that the key to the colt was allowing him to lead. Ridden that way, Stylish Century took the Spring Champion Stakes from Stargazer and Procul Harum. But Cummings' tenure was brief, for Stylish Century's owner Dick Monaghan had arranged for the horse to be sent to Bill Mitchell.

Taken to Melbourne, Stylish Century was unplaced in the Caulfield Guineas but then ran a brilliant race in the Cox Place at 33/1. He was beaten a head by Almaraad (a seasoned and top quality weight-for-age performer) but chiefly because he had had to work across from the outside 14 barrier. Stylish Century was 11/4 favourite for the Derby and won handsomely, with Kevin Moses up, breaking the race record in his three lengths' victory from Zamenof and Dr Grace. Monaghan paid a late entry fee of $37,650 to ensure a Melbourne Cup start for the colt. Stylish Century was the first of his age group to run in the race since 1974, but disappointed by finishing 21st out of 23 runners. Back in the autumn of 1990, he was third to the sprinters in the William Reid, second in the Alister Clark Stakes to Zabeel and to Dr Grace in the A.J.C. Derby, but he won the Autumn Classic at Caulfield and the Doomben Classic. The horse's misadventures now intensified and he lost form. However, in the autumn of 1991 he was third in the All Aged Stakes at Randwick to Shaftesbury Avenue and Super Impose and then beat Royal Creation and Livistona Lane in the Queen Elizabeth Stakes. His best performance in the spring of 1991 was second to Big Colony in the Sandown Cup, but he ended up winner of the race when the mare was disqualified for returning a positive swab. In 1992, Stylish Century nearly drowned in the training pool at Flemington and his future was soon afterwards directed to duties at the stud.

SUMMER FAIR

1958 b horse Summertime – Reuter

A highly credentialled galloper in his own right, Summer Fair is best known as the beneficiary of the protest in the 'leg-pull' A.J.C. Derby of 1961. He was awarded the race after Blue Era's jockey, Mel Schumacher, was found guilty of retarding Summer Fair's jockey Tommy Hill, by holding on to his leg near the winning post. Before that season, Summer Fair had won

four times at two, and then at three been placed in the Warwick Stakes besides running second to King Brian in the Rosehill Guineas. After his sensational Randwick victory, Summer Fair ran third in the Caulfield Guineas. In the Caulfield Cup he was surprisingly unfancied at 20/1, but took the prize clearly. Nor were his fine performances exhausted. Among 13 career wins were the 1963 Mackinnon Stakes and the 1964 Chelmsford Stakes.

SUPER IMPOSE

1983 ch gelding Imposing – Pheroz Fancy

One of the greatest of recent turf careers had modest beginnings indeed. Unraced at two, Super Impose managed to win his maiden at Seymour in December 1986 and a Benalla Improvers in May of the following year. In the spring of 1987 he gradually moved into better company, running second in the Grey Smith Stakes at Flemington and second in the Ballarat Cup before winning the Eclipse Stakes at Sandown. Taken to Sydney, Super Impose won at Rosehill then scored in the Summer Cup at Randwick – this was the first indication that the Sydney way of going would be much more to his liking. In the autumn of 1988 he was tried at weight-for-age, and finished second in the Orr and St George Stakes to Vo Rogue, who was then at his awesome front-running best. Super Impose broke two minutes to win the Carlyon Cup at Caulfield, before finishing second again to Vo Rogue in the Australian Cup.

In the spring of 1989, Super Impose steadily moved up another notch. He won the Turnbull Stakes before going down to his stablemate Tawriffic in record time in the Melbourne Cup. In the autumn of 1990, Super Impose had four consecutive weight-for-age placings – behind Vo Rogue and Better Loosen Up – in Melbourne and

Sydney, before finally notching a Group One success when he beat Shaftesbury Avenue in the Doncaster. This was the start of an unprecedented sequence in which Super Impose won the big Randwick double of the Doncaster and Epsom in successive years. In the spring of 1990 he won the Warwick Stakes and then beat Our Poverty Bay in the Epsom. Hopes were high for a brilliant Melbourne campaign, but Super Impose bled after finishing second to Sydeston in the Caulfield Stakes and a three months' lay-off resulted. But he was back better than ever in the autumn of 1991, winning the Chipping Norton and Ranvet Stakes in Sydney, before finishing down the track in the B.M.W. Despite this reverse, and burdened by 59.5kg, he won the Doncaster again, from Royal Creation and Shaftesbury Avenue. The latter gained revenge in the All Aged Stakes.

Set for a second Epsom in the autumn of 1991, Super Impose won the Warwick and Hill Stakes. In the Epsom Darren Beadman switched Super Impose to the inside when it appeared he would be forced wide and the horse responded gamely to defeat Livistona Lane. Racing history was thus made. The Melbourne spring resulted in seconds in the Caulfield Stakes, Cox Plate and Mackinnon Stakes, which were exasperating, but earned good money for the gelding. Attempting to win his fifth Randwick mile, Super Impose was unsuccessful in both the Doncaster and Epsom of 1992, but his biggest win was unexpectedly in store. Against a field of champions, and in one of the roughest runnings of the event, Super Impose won the 1992 Cox Plate at 20/1. Tried once more in the Melbourne Cup, Super Impose finished well back and trainer Lee Freedman retired the champion whose magnificent record stood at 20 wins and 32 placings for Australasian record stakeswinnings of more than $5.6 million.

SWEET NELL
1900 br mare Haut Brion – Novelette II

This brilliant filly was owned by Sir Rupert Clarke and trained by James Scobie. Sweet Nell's story is a rare one in turf history: she won the race for which she had long been set, virtually to her owner's order. Clarke called his Haut Brion filly Sweet Nell after the sentimental heroine Nell of Old Drury. The race he had earmarked for her was the V.R.C. Oaks. Plenty of incidental success came along the way. During the 1902 spring carnival at Flemington, Sweet Nell won three races: an Encourage Stakes, the Nursery Handicap and Flemington Stakes. In the autumn, she won the V.R.C. Sires' Produce and the South Australian Stakes. Sent to Sydney, she finished second in the A.J.C. Derby to Belah and ran sixth in the Metropolitan. Back to her own age group, she won the Caulfield Guineas, before becoming the only filly to win the Caulfield Cup. Not content with this wonderful effort, Scobie set Sweet Nell a taxing Flemington programme. Second to F.J.A. in the Victoria Derby, she ran a creditable seventh in the Melbourne Cup. Finally came the race Clarke had waited for. Sweet Nell did not disappoint him, winning the V.R.C. Oaks from Pliable and Brown and Black. She was kept going for another campaign, and carried 54kg into third place in the 1904 Sydney Cup behind Lord Cardigan, winner of the previous year's Melbourne Cup.

SYDESTON
1985 b or br gelding St Briavels – Convatrice

The greatest horse to come from Tasmania since Malua, a century before, Sydeston scored three victories at Elwick as a two year old. His campaign the next season was more ambitious. Five wins came in Tasmania, including the St Leger at

Mowbray, but he was second to Bar Landy in the Tasmanian Derby. A win at Sandown capped the season and indicated a horse of reasonable scope. At four, Sydeston – who was now in the care of Bob Hoysted – recorded wins in a Caulfield Welter and a handicap at Sandown. His staying promise was confirmed with victories in the Moonee Valley and Sandown Cups, but nothing out of the ordinary was expected from the horse until he travelled to Sydney for the autumn carnival of 1990. Second to Better Loosen Up in the Segenhoe Stakes, Sydeston then was an emphatic victor in two Group One races: the B.M.W. and Queen Elizabeth Stakes. His versatility had been underlined by a third in the Futurity before he travelled to Sydney: now Sydeston's weight-for-age class was evident. In the spring of 1990 he won the Liston Stakes and then the Caulfield Stakes from Super Impose and started favourite at 11/2 in the Caulfield Cup. After winning that race with the lack of fuss which was his trademark, Sydeston was a close second in the Cox Plate to Better Loosen Up. He was third in that race in 1991; fell in 1992. By then his form had gone into a steady decline, although he had won the St George in 1991 and – when finally retired – had passed $3,000,000 in stakesmoney. Sydeston's is the story of an unassuming champion.

SYDNEY CUP

Wishing to stage a distance handicap to compete with the Melbourne Cup, the A.J.C. added a Sydney Cup to its autumn programme in 1866 and the race was run on 3 May. The club was blessed with top-line winners in the early years. Yattendon won the first Sydney Cup, Fishhook the next from Rose of Australia. In 1868 and 1869 The Barb beat Stumpy, while Tim Whiffler was third in consecutive years from 1867-9.

The cream of Australian stayers were drawn to this event. Mermaid beat Little Dick in 1871, while in 1879 Savanaka reversed the placings of the 1877 Melbourne Cup when he beat Chester. The fine horse Darebin carried 61kg to victory in 1883, a weight just topped by the champion Carbine when he won the second of successive Sydney Cups in 1890. Wallace beat Toreador in 1896, and early in the new century, in one of the greatest performances in Australian turf history, the mare Wakeful carried 60.5kg to victory from Acetine, who was in receipt of 16kg. Lord Cardigan and Trafalgar were the best of other cup winners before the Great War, while in 1907 a horse called Realm became the second of that name (the other saluted in 1893) to win the Sydney Cup.

After the war Eurythmic won with 61kg in 1921, while the list of beaten horses testifies to the quality of the race: Night Watch, Poitrel, Windbag, Limerick. Mosaic was a dual winner in 1939-40, Veiled Threat in 1942 and 1944. Dark Marne – so narrowly beaten later in the year in the Melbourne Cup – won in 1948. Other fine winners after the Second World War were Carbon Copy, Carioca and Sailor's Guide. In 1961 Sharply beat Tulloch, but was in receipt of 12.5kg. The Cummings-trained pair Galilee (1967) and Lowland (1969) were the best winners of the 1960s, the former completing the unique Caulfield-Melbourne-Sydney Cup treble in one season. Reckless began his cups winning sequence at Randwick in 1977, adding the Adelaide and Brisbane Cups later. Kingston Town, in 1980, was the last champion to win the Sydney Cup, for the race has recently been overshadowed by weight-for-age events earlier in the Sydney autumn carnival.

SYDNEY TURF CLUB

The original Sydney Turf Club was

formed in 1825, when it held meetings at Bellevue and Hyde Park. Its meetings were moved then to Grose Farm. After William Charles Wentworth chose the club's annual dinner in November 1827 to insult the S.T.C.'s patron, Governor James Darling, the latter resigned. Twenty nine members of the club resigned also, forming the Australian Racing and Jockey Club (forerunner of the A.J.C.). The first S.T.C. held its last meeting in 1832 and was wound up in 1834.

From 1880-1905 another S.T.C. leased Randwick racecourse where it staged three or four meetings a year. In 1943, the New South Wales government decided that existing proprietary clubs should be replaced by a single body. Thus the Sydney Turf Club had its third incarnation, and perhaps its last. The S.T.C. was able to purchase Canterbury racecourse in December 1944. The Rosehill course was purchased by the state government in 1945 and given to the S.T.C., which took the Rosehill club's dates for 1946. Other proprietary tracks were taken over: Moorefield (in 1947, sold in 1953) and Rosebery (1949, used as a training track until sold in 1962).

The S.T.C. was intended by Premier McKell to be a more democratic organisation than the A.J.C. and one which would cater for the old proprietary racing club crowds. Its history has been marked by entrepreneurship. Most famously, it announced plans for Australia's premier two year old race in November 1953. The Golden Slipper Stakes was run for the first time in 1957. The S.T.C. resumed mid-week racing in Sydney in 1954 and has continued to conduct most of these meetings, despite disputes with the A.J.C. In other respects, the relationship of the clubs has been marked by co-operation, notably when the S.T.C. shifted the Canterbury and Rosehill Guineas to match the A.J.C.'s shift of the Derby from spring to autumn.

SYNTAX
1952 ch horse Count Rendered – Night Girl

As a three year old in New Zealand, Syntax had an outstanding classic record. He won the New Zealand and Great Northern Derbies and St Legers, besides the Gloaming Stakes. On a second trip to Australia, as a five year old, he came under the care of Fred Hoysted, who had had such success with Rising Fast. In the spring of 1957, Syntax won the Liston Stakes, beat Sailor's Guide in the Memsie, won the Underwood from Lord Gavin and again beat Sailor's Guide, this time in the Turnbull Stakes. This high class weight-for-age form made Syntax the logical danger to Caulfield Cup favourite Tulloch, but Syntax went amiss before the race and was scratched. He was second to Sailor's Guide in the Mackinnon Stakes before finishing a creditable fourth, with 60.5kg, to Straight Draw in the Melbourne Cup.

T

TAILS

1965 ch horse Dalray – Dolled Up

Owned by Ceb Barnes, sometime Federal Minister for Territories, Tails began his career at Toowoomba, under the care of Hiram Philp. After three Brisbane wins and a second to Rajah in the Q.T.C. Sires' Produce, he was sent to Sydney and ran fifth in the A.J.C. Derby, before going back north to win the Q.T.C. Derby. Transferred to the Sydney stables of Pat Murray, Tails, ridden by Neville Voigt, struck a purple patch of form, winning four in a row: the Rosehill and S.T.C. Cups and Metropolitan, then the Coongy at Caulfield. Unplaced in the Cox Plate, Tails won the Hotham Handicap with 57kg and was installed as 2/1 favourite for the Melbourne Cup. Always slightly suspect at two miles, Tails ran seventh to Rain Lover. In two more runs in the Cup, he finished ninth in 1970, but managed third in 1971 behind Silver Knight and Igloo. He was also fourth in a Sydney and second in a Brisbane Cup. Ridden now by Hilton Cope, Tails came back in 1970 to win a second Rosehill Cup and Metropolitan, with 56.5kg, before running a game second to Abdul in the Cox Plate.

In the winter he added a Doomben Cup to his record. Geoff Howard now regularly had the mount, and to Murray's delight, Tails silenced knockers who doubted his weight-for-age ability by winning the Chelmsford Stakes of 1971. A second S.T.C. Cup followed, and then a gallant second in his third try for the Metropolitan. Tails carried 61kg behind Oncidon, conceding that horse 14.5kg. In 1972 he won the Tancred Cup (then a handicap), before beating the champion Gunsynd at weight-for-age in the Queen Elizabeth Stakes. A final campaign in Brisbane in the winter of 1972 saw Tails win the O'Shea Stakes and run fourth in the Doomben Cup. He was retired to the Canning Downs stud where his sire had stood for 20 years, but enjoyed little success. Tails died in April 1991.

TAIT, JOHN (1813-1888)

'Honest John' Tait was born in Edinburgh. After emigrating to Australia in 1837, he set up as a jeweller in Hobart. In 1843 he moved to New South Wales to become a publican, first at Hartley, then Bathurst. Whalebone gave him the first of many feature wins as a trainer when he took the 1847 St Leger (then run at Homebush). This was a race he was to win on five other occasions, with Cossack, Surplice, Alfred, Glencoe and Goldsborough. By 1853 Tait was running the Commercial Hotel at Castlereagh Street in Sydney. He continued to enjoy success with such horses as Cossack, Sportsman and Surplice. Sportsman won a thousand pound match race against John Eales' Cooramin.

Tait sold his racehorses in 1855 and went to England where he bought sires who he imported to Australia. One of them, Magus, sired Clove, winner of the A.J.C. Derby in 1865. By the early 1860s Tait was training from Byron Lodge at Randwick. His best horse was The Barb, who won the 1866 A.J.C. Derby, and the Melbourne and Sydney Cups in 1868-9. Other fine performers in Tait's hands were the triple Derby winner Fireworks and the top filly Florence. Besides The Barb, Tait won Melbourne Cups with Glencoe (1868), The Pearl (1871) and The Quack (1872). In his own words, Tait 'went into racing as a business'. His financial success (30,000 pounds in stakes between 1865-80) was a model of professionalism for trainers who came after him.

TAJ ROSSI

1970 b horse Matrice – Dark Queen

In 1973, a vintage year for colts, Taj Rossi proved himself exceptional. He missed the great A.J.C. Derby clash between Imagele, Leica Lover and Grand Cidium, biding his time in Melbourne. His three year old campaign kicked off with wins in the Ascot Vale and Moonee Valley Stakes. Unplaced behind Grand Cidium and Imagele in the Caulfield Guineas, he then struck a purple patch. With Stan Aitken up, Taj Rossi won the Cox Plate by a head from Swell Time. Then Roy Higgins and Bart Cummings combined for another Victoria Derby win when Taj Rossi scored from Leica Lover. Aitken was back a week later when Taj Rossi won the George Adams Handicap. The horse

finished the season with another triumph – in the Sandown Guineas. After two unplaced runs at four, Taj Rossi was retired to stud. There one of his best sons was the 1989 Doncaster winner, Merimbula Bay.

TANCRED STAKES

see B.M.W. STAKES

TARAS BULBA

1971 b gelding Oncidium – Entrancing Bell

Trained by George Hanlon, then Tommy Smith, Taras Bulba was a brilliant but inconsistent galloper whose shifts in form rarely endeared him to punters. Nevertheless, his performances in top company include some memorable wins, punctuated by inexplicable flops. As a three year old, Taras Bulba campaigned in Perth, running second to Haymaker in the 1974 Australian Derby before finishing a stout second a few weeks later to Runyon in the 1975 Perth Cup. Hanlon kept the horse up and Taras Bulba rewarded him by winning the V.R.C. St Leger. He then struck classic form in Sydney where, after a third in the Tulloch Stakes, he won the Rosehill Guineas, ridden by Garry Willetts and then the A.J.C. Derby when John Stocker had the ride. Sydney always saw the best of Taras Bulba. He won the Australasian Champion Stakes in the spring of 1975, before travelling to Melbourne where he won the Underwood and was third in the Turnbull Stakes. Returning in the spring of 1976, Taras Bulba was second in the Blamey Stakes at Flemington before beating Shiftmar and Leilani in the Queen Elizabeth. Campaigning in Sydney, he beat Leica Lover in the Chipping Norton Stakes and then added the Randwick version of the Queen Elizabeth Stakes, a feat no other horse has matched. Thereafter his form tapered off and Taras Bulba was retired.

TARIEN

1948 ch mare Tehran – Oriena

The beautifully bred English mare Tarien was imported to race in Australia by George Ryder, and was trained here by Tommy Smith. In England she had won once from eight starts, but Australian racing proved more to her liking. Tarien's imposing record stands at 12 wins and 19 placings from 40 starts, but it could have been much better. She won two Warwick Stakes (the first, in 1953, by five lengths in track record time), beat Carioca in the 1953 Rawson Stakes, won a Craven Plate, a George Main Stakes and the A.J.C. Challenge Stakes. Set for the 1953 Newmarket, she won the Hawksburn Handicap at even money, but burdened with 56 kg could only finish second down the Flemington straight to Cultured. Next year, under the impost of 61 kg, she managed third placing. In between came the sensational Doncaster Handicap of 1953. First past the post in record time, Tarien was swabbed and tested positive to the drug Coramine. She became the first winner of a major race in Australia to be disqualified on a drug test, although she was joined by the A.J.C. Sires' Produce winner Cromis. At her other try at the Randwick mile, Tarien ran a gallant second in the 1953 Epsom to Sir Phantom, who had to run an Australian record to beat her.

TASMANIAN RACING

The first race meeting in Van Diemen's Land was held at New Town in 1814, a four mile match race between Cheviot and Diana over three heats for a sizeable stake. Governor George Arthur became patron of the colony's first turf club. The New Town course was cleared for racing in 1831. In the same year the Cornwall Turf Club was established in Launceston. The Tasmanian Turf Club has existed in its present form since 1871. The principal Tasmanian courses are Elwick in Hobart, Mowbray in Launceston.

TASMANIAN RACING CLUB

Hobart businessman and former politician Sir James Wilson was instrumental in the establishment of the Tasmanian Racing Club in Hobart, in 1874. The T.R.C. held its first meeting at Elwick in 1875, and that track has remained the headquarters of the club ever since. The main events which the club stages there are the Hobart Cup and Tasmanian Derby in the summer. Briefly styling itself the Tasmanian Jockey Club (from 1879), the T.R.C. resumed that name from 1882. Intrastate rivalry between the T.R.C. and the northern body the T.T.C. was resolved in 1900, when responsibility for racing in Tasmania was divided between them.

TASMANIAN TURF CLUB

The controlling body of racing in northern Tasmania, the Tasmanian Turf Club was formed in Launceston in October 1871. It staged a Launceston Cup the next year. The club raced at Mowbray, an unsatisfactory venue then in respect to its amenities and rental. The course was sold to a consortium of racing men who leased it back to the club. Renovated extensively by 1877, racing at Mowbray went the Melbourne way from that year. In 1900 the T.T.C. took over racing in the north of the state; the Tasmanian Racing Club was in charge of the south. The T.T.C. bought the freehold to Mowbray in 1905; erected a new stand before the Great War and substantially renovated it in 1987. The T.T.C.'s main event, the Launceston Cup, is run in the summer, together with the Tasmanian Oaks.

TAUTO

1965 br gelding Good Brandy – San Patricia

From a modest bush start to his career, Tauto's progression to the highest levels of Australian racing was both swift and sustained. He first showed the signs of indomitable courage and quality which would mark his long career when second in the 1970 Newmarket to Black Onyx. The R.M. Agnew-trained gelding gained his first big race victory that spring, when he won the Toorak Handicap. At Flemington he was second to his perennial adversary, the brilliant mare Dual Choice, in the Craven 'A' Stakes. In the autumn of 1971 he was second in the Lightning Stakes and then third in the Newmarket to Baguette and Dual Choice. Tauto travelled to Sydney and was second to Rajah Sahib in the Doncaster: an unfortunate pattern was being established – Tauto's placings at top grade would well outnumber his wins. But the spring of 1971 was kinder. He won the Liston Stakes and the Invitation Stakes (both wins which he would repeat the following year), before carrying 61kg into third place in the Toorak Handicap behind Gunsynd and Sky Call. Unfancied at 12/1, and over what was supposed to be the unsuitably long distance of 2000m in the Cox Plate, Tauto recorded one of his biggest wins, defeating the unlucky Igloo. He rounded off the spring with a second in the George Adams to Gunsynd.

In 1972 Tauto was second in the Lightning, Futurity and Linlithgow Stakes, besides his Liston and Invitation Stakes victories. Next year he was second in the William Reid and again in the Linlithgow, carried 60kg into second place in the Victoria Handicap behind Nicopal (who had 48kg) and was taken to Adelaide for a third in the Goodwood with 59.5kg. There was the consolation of the first of consecutive Freeway Stakes victories. And in 1974 that race provided the last of

Tauto's big wins, although the gallant galloper was second in the William Reid again, third in the Futurity and then second – giving Coolalinga 6.5kg – in yet another crack at the Newmarket. The rising nine year old had earned retirement.

TAYLOR, 'SQUIZZY' (JOSEPH LESLIE THEODORE) (1888-1927)

This Melbourne racketeer worked first as a jockey on the pony-racing circuit, where some of his earliest criminal connections were formed. Race-fixing was one of his main sources of income, together with robbery and prostitution. In 1922 he was suspected of involvement in the fire on Caulfield Cup morning that burned down the members' stand as revenge for being ejected from the track the previous Wednesday. The meeting went ahead with emergency assistance from the V.R.C. and Whittier won the Cup.

With his second wife, Ida Pender, Taylor co-starred in an autobiographical film called 'Riding to Win' which took a generous view of his exploits. Banned in Victoria, it was released in Brisbane in 1925 with the more confident title 'Born to Win'. Taylor died in 1927 from wounds received in a gun fight in Fitzroy with the Sydney gangster, 'Snowy' Cutmore.

THE ASSYRIAN

1877 br horse Countryman – Tinfinder

One of the most versatile horses of his era, The Assyrian, trained by J.E. Savill, won high class races in four southern states. They included the Randwick Autumn Stakes, the S.A.J.C. Derby of 1880, the 1882 Melbourne Cup when he beat 34 opponents at 33/1 under the riding of C. Hutchens and the Hobart Cup in the following year. The Assyrian originally raced in South Australia as Rothschild, where besides his classic win, he was second in the Adelaide Cup. Favourite for the Caulfield Cup of 1882, he was checked and ran down the field. On a heavy track he made amends decisively at Flemington, beating the Tasmanian horse Stockwell. Thereafter he was sold to Tasmanian interests, and carried 67kg to victory in the Hobart Cup of 1883.

THE AUSTRALIAN PEER
1884 br horse Darebin – Stockdove

Named perhaps in the hope of the 'Bunyip Aristocracy' which never came to be in Australia, The Australian Peer was a son of the top class galloper Darebin. As a three year old he won the Victoria Derby from the good horse Abercorn, ran third in the Melbourne Cup and also won the V.R.C. Canterbury Stakes. The next year he won the Sydney Cup and the A.J.C. Spring Stakes; took the Melbourne Stakes during the spring carnival and ran ninth in the Melbourne Cup under 58kg.

THE BARB
1864 blk horse Sir Hercules – Young Gulnare

Owned and trained during his racing career by John Tait, this brilliant, ill-tempered horse, nick-named the Black Demon, nearly failed to make it to the track. As a foal he was stolen from Bathurst by bushrangers, and eventually was recovered at Caloola. A classic winner (of the 1866 A.J.C. Derby), The Barb also won an A.J.C. Metropolitan, the 1866 Melbourne Cup (first of four for Tait) as well as two Sydney Cups in succession. The second of these, in 1869, he won with 67kg, which is still a record winner's weight. From 23 starts The Barb won 16 times. His career at stud was indifferent, but a daughter, Melodious, was the dam of Carbine's best son, Wallace. The Barb was the greatest horse to race in Australia before Carbine.

THE FELINE
1943 br gelding Solar Bear – Chauchat

By the imported English stallion Solar Bear, The Feline proved to be one of the finest jumpers in the period immediately after the Second World War. Trained by Alex Fullarton and owned by W. Graham, The Feline was a 140 guineas purchase who well and truly paid his way. This small, game horse successfully combined hurdling with steeplechasing. The Feline won the Grand National Hurdle in 1948, the year in which he was also victorious in the first of two Great Eastern Steeplechases at Oakbank. The second came in 1951, when he also ran fourth in the Grand National Hurdle. In between he had won an Australian Hurdle and the 1950 Warrnambool Grand Annual Steeplechase; he was also placed second in two Hiskens Steeples at Moonee Valley. A Melbourne jumping race was named in his memory.

THE GRAFTER (AND GAULUS)
1893 br gelding Gozo – Industry

The Grafter, who won the Melbourne Cup in 1898, was so plain a horse that he was nick-named 'His Ugliness', but he was sound and tough. In 1897 he had run second to his full brother Gaulus (1891 ch horse Gozo – Industry), the only occasion on which horses so related have quinellaed the race; and in 1898 The Grafter ensured another niche in history, for this is the only time that full brothers have won successive cups. Both horses were owned and bred by William Forrester and The Grafter was much the better. He started 8/1 in the 1898 Cup and survived a protest to win, and this was the highlight of a remarkable spring carnival. He contested races on each of the four days, winning three (the Cup, a Flying Handicap and the C.B. Fisher Plate) and running second in the Melbourne Stakes. Previously he had won the A.J.C. Craven Plate. After the Cup, trainer J.E. Brewer took The Grafter to England, and Bobbie Lewis went along for the experience. This was an era of successful raids on the old country, by such horses as Merman, Newhaven and Tornado besides The Grafter. The latter won two big races in England: the City and Suburban and the 2,000 pound Prince Edward Handicap at Manchester. Former Australian bookie Robert Siever had a grand killing on the first event: the win by The Grafter netted him 33,000 pounds.

THE TRUMP

1932 b gelding Manfred – Koanie

Winner of the V.A.T.C. Stakes at two, The Trump ran third in the Caulfield Guineas at three and was impressive enough to be promoted to favouritism for the Caulfield Cup. But his weak knees led to him being scratched, and then it was decided to geld him. Lightly raced at four, he came back in 1937 and won at Moonee Valley and Caulfield. This was a purple patch for The Trump, who won the Toorak at his next start. After that victory, the horse was off-colour, but heavy rain led to the postponement of the Caulfield Cup. Held the following Wednesday it was delayed long enough for The Trump to recover and he won convincingly. Next assignment was the Mackinnon Stakes in which The Trump triumphed again. Winning the Melbourne Cup three days later, he became the first horse since Poseidon in 1906 to take the Cups double. He lost form thereafter and was retired after breaking down in the 1937 Melbourne Cup. Sent to a country property, his duties there

were no more onerous than being ridden to school by the owner's children.

THOMPSON, JACK (1922-1992)

This tall, poker-faced jockey rode with success for almost half a century, and retired at the age of 62 with more than 3,000 winners behind him. The first came at Tamworth in May 1938, the last at Wyong in January 1985. Son of a stock inspector, Thompson was born at Macksville on the New South Wales coast and apprenticed to Frank Dalton at Randwick. Initially Dalton was concerned that Thompson was too tall to make a career in the saddle, but those doubts were soon allayed. In 1939 Thompson won the Summer Cup on Bunga. In the 1940-1 season he became the first apprentice to win a senior jockeys' premiership in Sydney, and rode 106 winners to do so. Four times leading apprentice Thompson also won five senior premierships. Thompson's many big race wins included four Doncasters and two Epsoms, a Golden Slipper and a Sydney Cup. He won both the A.J.C. and Victoria Derby. It was in Melbourne that he lost a race that he swore ever afterwards he had won: the 1948 Melbourne Cup. The newly installed photo finish camera gave Rimfire at 80/1 the nod over Thompson's mount Dark Marne. Whether or not cameras lie, its angle was changed soon after, but too late to help Thompson's cause. In 19 Cup rides he would manage three second placings. Comic Court, Flight and Russia were among the champions that he rode. After his retirement, Thompson trained for a while at Randwick.

THOMPSON, JOSEPH (1838-1909)

Thompson (originally Solomon) jumped ship in Victoria in 1854 by hiding in a water-cask, and – like many thousands of others – headed to the diggings. After returning briefly to England, he came back to Australia and set up as a country bookmaker in Victoria. By 1862 he was fielding at Flemington. He also bought racehorses, calling one of them King of the Ring, a name by which he was happy to be known. In the mid-1880s he left Australia for England and settled there at the end of the decade. After fielding in England through the week, he crossed the Channel for the Sunday races in France. His fearless punting was complemented by wit. He called another of his horses Argus Scandal, because that Melbourne paper had criticised him. Don Juan won the 1873 Melbourne Cup for him and he named his Albert Park house after the horse in gratitude.

THOMSON, BRENT (1958-)

Born at Wanganui in New Zealand, Thomson was the son of a good jockey, Kevin Thomson. As a 17 year old apprentice Thomson came to Australia to ride Fury's Order who won the 1975 Cox Plate on a bog track. This was the first of four wins from his first four rides in the big race. In 1977 he won on Family of Man. Next year he replaced John Stocker as Colin Hayes' stable jockey and obliged by winning the Cox Plate on So Called and scoring again the next year on Dulcify. The latter was perhaps the best horse who Thomson rode in Australia, giving him the Victoria-A.J.C. Derby as well, in 1978-9. Unhappily he was aboard Dulcify when he broke down and had to be destroyed in the Melbourne Cup, a few days after his fighting win in the Mackinnon Stakes. Thomson's other big victories included Caulfield Cups with Gurner's Lane in 1982 and Lord Reims in 1987. In 1984 he split with Hayes and began a globe-trotting career which saw him ride with success in many countries, notably

the United Kingdom and Hong Kong. He was back in Australia for the spring of 1993 when he partnered the Freedman-trained Rubicon to several weight-for-age successes.

TIME AND TIDE
1960 ch gelding Star Kingdom – Shading

A brother of the Golden Slipper winner Fine and Dandy, Time and Tide was trained by Harry Plant. Winner of 20 of his 45 starts (and placed in 10 others), Time and Tide in the end decisively proved that he was more than a pure speed horse. A precocious juvenile, Time and Tide won the Canonbury Stakes at Randwick and the Debutant at Caulfield before being beaten a half head by Heirloom in the Maribyrnong Stakes. Back in Sydney, Time and Tide won an open Flying Handicap and the next autumn was fourth to Pago Pago in the 1963 Golden Slipper. On that occasion a wet track undid Time and Tide: he hit back with victories in the Sires' Produce and Champagne Stakes. As a three year old, Time and Tide won six times from 13 starts, and in three states: the Theo Marks in Sydney, the Caulfield Guineas in Melbourne and a Lightning Handicap in Brisbane. He was also third in the Epsom.

Lightly raced at four, Time and Tide won four of six starts and was placed at the other two. He took the Challenge Stakes in Sydney and then, in the autumn, won the 1965 Oakleigh Plate (with 56kg) from Ripa. Des Lake rode him that day; was injured subsequently, so that the Newmarket ride went to Roy Higgins. Recovered, Lake had a late pick-up ride on Ripa who won by a short half head after Time and Tide missed the start by three lengths. Campaigning again in Sydney, Time and Tide won the Rawson Stakes with Lake back aboard and then the Doncaster of 1965 from Our Fun and Ripa. Thus he proved that he could run a strong mile in the highest company. The horse's form gradually tapered. Only one win came at five from eight starts – another Theo Marks – because of leg problems, while a third Theo Marks was the highlight of Time and Tide's three wins at six. He lived on serenely into retirement until his death in November 1975.

TIM WHIFFLER(S)

In the late 1860s and early 1870s in Australia, before restrictions were imposed on the names under which horses could run, there were six Hectors (named for an early colonial champion racehorse) and four Tim Whifflers racing. The confusion was highlighted in the Melbourne Cup of 1867. Etienne de Mestre brought his Tim Whiffler (1862 b horse New Warrior – Cinderella) down from Sydney, to find it opposed by a horse of the same name, owned by the Ballarat publican Walter Craig. The bookmakers laid 'Sydney Tim' and 'Melbourne Tim'. Both were well performed. De Mestre's horse had won the Metropolitan in record time, while Craig's horse was an Australian Cup winner. In the event 'Sydney Tim' won easily, although fights broke out when some backers of the other horse (who ran fifth) tried to claim that they had intended to support 'Sydney Tim'. The situation was complicated further when the English horse Tim Whiffler was imported to stand as a sire in Australia in 1871. His produce included two Melbourne Cup winners: Briseis (1876) and Darriwell (1879).

TITAN

1888 ch gelding Chester – Tempe

One of the best sons of Chester, Titan was a brilliant two year old, winning seven of nine at that age. His victories included both the V.R.C. and A.J.C. Sires' Produce Stakes, the Ascot Vale Stakes and the Oakleigh Plate (or Handicap as it was then known) against open company. Titan continued to win top-line races for four more seasons. His best subsequent wins were in the 1893 Toorak Handicap, and the 1894 All Aged Stakes at Flemington.

TOBIN BRONZE

1962 ch horse Arctic Explorer – Amarco

By the imported English sire Arctic Explorer out of V.R.C. Oaks winner Amarco, Tobin Bronze was bred in the purple and raced accordingly. The handsome chestnut was one of the finest and most popular horses to race in Australia in the 1960s. His promise was evident from juvenile days, when, in the care of Graeme Heagney, he won four of seven including the Breeders' Stakes at Morphettville (his early racing was done in Adelaide) and the Gibson Carmichael at Flemington. In the spring of 1965 he was placed behind Star Affair in the Moonee Valley Stakes and Caulfield Guineas, before winning the Geelong Derby Trial and the Victoria Derby. A useful eighth placing in the Melbourne Cup wound up this campaign.

In the autumn Tobin Bronze won the first of many weight-for-age races, the Blamey Stakes, then ran second to Light Fingers in the St George. Next spring he won four weight-for-age races in succession – the Liston, Craiglee, Underwood and Turnbull Stakes – and was accordingly a very short-priced favourite for the Caulfield Cup. Only Tulloch had previously started at odds-on: Tobin Bronze's price was 11/8 on and it was 12/1 bar one in the race. But he galloped ungenerously and was spent soon after the turn, winding up sixth to the great stayer Galilee. Some amends came with victory in the Mackinnon Stakes, before Tobin Bronze ran well down the line in the Melbourne Cup.

Another splendid autumn followed, with wins over Galilee in the Orr and Blamey Stakes and victory in the St George. Taken to Sydney, Tobin Bronze switched back to handicap racing and scored brilliantly with 59.5kg from Cabochon in the Doncaster before winning the All-Aged Stakes. His spring campaign was delayed by injury and then began unusually, with a first-up run in the Nulla Nulla Handicap at Moonee Valley. Tobin Bronze humped 63kg to victory. At even money he carried 62.5kg to victory in the Toorak Handicap. Once again he would start favourite for the Caulfield Cup, but this time at the decent odds of 5/1 and not before he had been sold to Messrs Breliant and Litz to race in the United States. With 61.5kg (only Redcraze had carried more to victory) Tobin Bronze won brilliantly, but narrowly from Red Handed and returned to one of the great ovations that the turf had heard in Australia. It was to be bettered a week later, when with Jimmy Johnson up, he beat Terrific in the W.S. Cox Plate at 6/1 on. Taken hurriedly to the States, Tobin Bronze ran a fine third in the Washington International. Although he won other races in America, he never recaptured his Australian form before being sent to stud where he performed with moderate success. He was put down in April 1994.

TODMAN

1954 ch horse Star Kingdom – Oceana

Most brilliant sprinting son of the imported sire Star Kingdom (with whom he shared an inveterate dislike), Todman ran an Australian record for five furlongs on his debut. Trainer Maurice McCarten set him for the inaugural Golden Slipper Stakes of 1957, which Todman duly won by eight lengths at 6/1 on. His only defeat as a two year old came next start when Tulloch was too strong for him over the 1400m of the Sires' Produce. Todman had immediate revenge. Ridden for speed by regular jockey Neville Sellwood, he easily accounted for Tulloch in the Champagne Stakes. Resuming in August 1957, Todman won the Hobartville Stakes and then beat Turkestan by eight lengths in the Canterbury Guineas. In his lead-up for the A.J.C. Derby in the Hill Stakes, Todman ran for the first time against older horses but broke down badly at the top of the straight. Off the scene for two years, he resumed with a two lengths win in December 1959 in a Flying Handicap at Canterbury. Taken to Melbourne, he won the 1960 Lightning Stakes, and then carried 64.5kg to victory over Gay Port and Lord in the Futurity. Todman went to stud in 1960, where he sired the Golden Slipper winners Eskimo Prince and Sweet Embrace. Other top-line gallopers he produced were Blazing Saddles, Crewman, Imposing and Ricochet. Todman died at the Widden Stud in 1976.

TOLERANCE

1968 ch horse Better Boy – Salma

Another of Better Boy's talented sprinting sons, who later went himself to stud, Tolerance won 10 times. His best victories included such feature race wins as the V.R.C. Sires' Produce Stakes by four lengths from Fairy Walk; the inaugural Blue Diamond Stakes in 1971; the Ascot Vale and Chirnside Stakes as a three year old. At that age he also ran second to Beau Sovereign in the Caulfield Guineas. In lesser events, he showed himself capable of carrying very high weights to victory. Taken to Sydney at two, Tolerance was never comfortable with that way of racing, but was third in both the Champagne and the Sires' Produce Stakes.

TONTONAN
1971 b gelding Showdown – Forego

A brilliant galloper, Tontonan won 12 of 16 starts in a career restricted by injury. Controversy attended some of his biggest wins. In the 1973 Golden Slipper, Tontonan won a race in which the odds-on favourite, Imagele fell. He added the A.J.C. Sires' to his spoils from the Sydney campaign. As a three year old he won the 1974 Oakleigh Plate first-up at the start of an outstanding autumn. Back in Sydney, Tontonan carried 56kg to win the Doncaster. Beating the rest of the field was easier for jockey Roy Higgins than avoiding the two streakers who careered across the straight at the 200m mark. Tontonan added an All Aged Stakes at Randwick to his record, before winning the Delaney Quality at Doomben. Leg problems prevented him from racing at all at four. Trainer Bart Cummings brought him back at five, when he showed that his class was undimmed by winning the Craiglee, Feehan and Chirnside Stakes before breaking down once more, and being retired.

TOTALIZATOR AGENCY BOARD

Legal off-track betting was introduced in Australia on 11 March 1961, when the Victorian T.A.B. began operations with 12 offices and a limited telephone betting service. On course totes had been operating since 1931. The establishment of the T.A.B. followed a Royal Commission convened by the state government, which was concerned with attendant social evils, as well as the financial rewards of this medium of gambling. After hearing evidence from police, social workers and representatives of all facets of the racing industry, the Commission wound up at the end of 1958. It had heard evidence of the proliferation of illegal S.P. bookmakers, and of the bribery and corruption associated with them. In its final report, Commission chairman Mr Justice F.R.B. Martin said that the total illegal off-course turnover was more than $300 million per year. None of this money served to maintain courses, improve facilities or increase stake money for racing. Thus the Victorian T.A.B. was born. In its first year 296 meetings were covered, for a turnover of more than $3 million. Bets were initially recorded by hand and had to be placed well before the start of the race. Dividends could not be collected until the next day. Computers, and a more lenient view of gambling have transformed these early arrangements. Because of deductions from each bet, the racing industry, hospitals and other charities are now beneficiaries of T.A.B. operations. The Victorian T.A.B. was transformed into a Public Company known as TABCORP Holdings Pty Ltd in August 1994, becoming the first such organisation in Australia to be privatised. In Western Australia, the T.A.B. opened a week after its Victorian counterpart. Queensland followed in August 1962, the A.C.T. in September 1964, New South Wales in December of that year, South Australia in March 1967, Tasmania not until January 1975 and the Northern Territory in July 1985.

A new era began when the Victorian T.A.B. was transformed into a public company known as TABCORP Holdings Pty Ltd in August, 1994, thus becoming the first T.A.B. in Australia to be privatised, and making TABCORP the largest wagering and gaming company in Australia.

TABCORP has the sole licence to conduct off-course totalizators in Victoria on racing in Australia and New Zealand, and one of two licences to operate gaming machines in licensed clubs and hotels in Victoria. The wagering and gaming licences are for terms of 18 years.

TABCORP entered into a Joint Venture Agreement with VicRacing, a company established by the Racing Industry, which entitles VicRacing to a 25 per cent interest in TABCORP's conduct of gambling activities.

The future outlook for TABCORP includes opportunities for expansion both interstate and overseas.

TOWTON, GEORGE (1853-1906)

The most successful Western Australian trainer of the latter part of the 19th century, Towton was born at his father's No Place Inn (now the Bedford Hotel) in Perth. From the age of 13 he was a jockey. In 1883 he won the Queen's Plate on Lowlander. But his employment was much more various. Towton was a racehorse trainer, ran a livery stables, was a hotelier and an undertaker as well. His training record included four W.A. Derbies and six Perth Cups. In 1892 he owned, trained and rode the Perth Cup winner Wandering Willie. The G.A. Towton Cup (1800m), a traditional lead-up race to the Perth Cup, is named in his honour.

TOY SHOW

1972 b mare Showdown – Toyland

Toy Show's record is that of a brilliant but unpredictable filly whose race-day performances were often hampered by a back complaint. After winning first-up by five lengths at Canterbury, she injured herself. In order to make the 1975 Golden Slipper field, she had to win the Magic Night Quality. Toy Show obliged – by four lengths. Trainer Tommy Smith's stable jockey Kevin Langby had the choice of Denise's Joy or Toy Show for the Golden Slipper and stuck with Toy Show. She beat her stablemate by two lengths and then went on to defeat the Blue Diamond and

V.R.C. Sires' winner Lord Dudley in the A.J.C. Sires' Produce. Injured again, Toy Show was turned out. She resumed in the spring of 1975 with a disappointing run on a wet track in the Freeway Stakes before winning the Ascot Vale from Lord Dudley. Next Denise's Joy had her measure in the Moonee Valley Stakes. Unplaced at odds-on in the Manifold Stakes, Toy Show disconcerted punters by winning the Thousand Guineas. She then ran second to How Now in the Wakeful Stakes and was spelled after a third placing in the Sandown Guineas. Resuming in the autumn of 1976, Toy Show was well supported but well back in the Oakleigh Plate before winning at good odds from Leica Show in the Newmarket with 54kg. The spring of 1976 yielded only a couple of minor placings, but in the autumn of 1977 Toy Show won the William Reid first-up before being second to Merger in the Oakleigh Plate. After a few more runs she was sent to stud, but none of her offspring had the brilliance that she displayed so abundantly, if erratically, on the racetrack.

TRAFALGAR

1905 ch horse Wallace – Grand Canary

The best son of the champion sire Wallace, Trafalgar was a great stayer of the first decade of this century, most of whose 24 wins were in top company over testing distances. For instance, he won nine races at two miles. He was a specialist at multiple wins as well, annexing two A.J.C. Autumn Stakes, three A.J.C. Plates, two V.R.C. Loch Stakes and two Champion Stakes as well as the Randwick Plate in four successive years from 1909-12. Other weight-for-age victories included the A.J.C. Spring and Cumberland Stakes, the V.R.C. Melbourne and Essendon Stakes, the C.B. Fisher Plate and the V.A.T.C. St George Stakes.

Trafalgar won the Sydney Cup of 1909. A handsome chestnut, with a silver mane and tail, he ran in two Melbourne Cups, starting at 9/2 each time. In 1909 he was fourth to Prince Foote, while the following year he came from well back to go under by a half head to Comedy King, giving that top horse 8.5kg. Retired to stud, Trafalgar failed to produce any outstanding runners.

TRANQUIL STAR

1937 ch mare Gay Lothario – Lone Star

No mare has raced more often, in the highest company, for more seasons than the Ron Cameron-trained Tranquil Star. From 111 starts she was unplaced in just over half, and could turn in a shocker, yet she won 23 times and was placed on 32 other occasions. All her racing was done in Melbourne, during the Second World War. After winning the Edward Manifold Stakes as a three year old, Tranquil Star was second in both the Victoria Derby and the V.R.C. Oaks. In the spring of 1941 she raced in the first of five consecutive Caulfield Cups, finishing midfield, but earlier that year she won the V.R.C. St Leger and the first of three St George Stakes. The others came in 1944 and 1945, while she was third in the St George of 1942. In that year Tranquil Star, ridden by regular jockey Scobie Breasley, won the Caulfield Cup, beating Heart's Desire who had a 10kg pull in the weights. She had taken the Caulfield Stakes at her previous start, and in this top weight-for-age contest she was also placed second twice and third twice. At her next start following the Caulfield Cup victory, Tranquil Star won the first of a pair of Cox Plates. The second would come in 1944. Her great run in the spring of 1942 continued when Tranquil Star scored in the Mackinnon Stakes. She was second in this race in 1943; won again in 1944 and 1945.

In the third win she survived a protest from her great rival Flight, who would finish in front of her on the other five occasions that they met. In that spring she had also won the Memsie Stakes, while in the autumn of 1946 this great mare – now rising nine – won the William Reid Stakes. Tranquil Star was retired at the end of still another splendid campaign.

TREEN, FRANK (1930-93)

Born at Albany, Frank Treen overcame his mother's objections to his choice of career and became one of the finest jockeys in the turf history of Western Australia. Racing was in the family. At 12 Treen was pencilling for his bookmaker uncle. At 14 he rode his first winner, at an Albany picnic meeting. Leading apprentice in Western Australia three times, he also took the senior jockeys' premiership on eight occasions. Treen's 2,000 wins included more than 80 cup races, which has been claimed as an Australasian record. Five of them came in the Perth Cup. In his dominance of riding in his home state, Treen also won six W.A. Derbies and five Oaks, six Karrakatta Plates and the same number of Kalgoorlie Cups. His six winners at Ascot on 25 November 1967 (he came second on his seventh mount for the day), empathically ended a poor beginning to the season for Treen, and still stands as a record for a jockey on a metropolitan course in the state. In the east, he was successful in the Australian, Brisbane and Moonee Valley Cups.

TRIDENT

1883 ch horse Robinson Crusoe – Cocoanut

Bred by Etienne de Mestre, Trident was a full brother to the top quality galloper Navigator. In the autumn of 1886 he won the A.J.C. Sires' Produce Stakes to give token of his quality. First-up in the spring of that year he won the A.J.C. Derby at 2/1 on, following this with wins in the Craven Plate and the three mile Randwick Plate. He took the Victoria Derby at 5/2 on before running fourth in the Melbourne Cup. Trident completed his triumphant progress in that spring with victory in the Canterbury Plate. His deeds in the autumn of 1887 were yet more remarkable. At the Flemington carnival he won the V.R.C. St Leger, the Australian Cup and the Champion Stakes within a week. A month later, at Randwick, he won the A.J.C. St Leger, the Cumberland Stakes and the A.J.C. Plate, also within a week, to stamp himself as one of the great stayers of the 19th century in Australia.

TRIPLE DEAD-HEATS

The first and most famous triple dead-heat in Australian racing occurred in the 1956 Hotham Handicap at Flemington. The photo finish camera could not split Ark Royal (ridden by Reg Heather), Fighting Force (Jack Purtell) and Pandie Sun (Bill Williamson). Subsequently there have been two further triple dead-heats for first in Australian races – at Townsville in June 1985 (Angular, Apollo's Flame and Plenty of Spirit) and at Stony Creek in January 1987 (Chester Field, Fast Seal and Mr Spectre). The only triple dead-heat in New Zealand since the introduction of the camera occurred at Wanganui in February 1967. There have also been several triple dead-heats among minor placegetters. Before the photo-finish camera was widely installed run-offs were the usual way to settle close or disputed race finishes.

TRISTARC

1981 b mare Sir Tristram – Arenarc

Owned by Nick Columb, and trained by

Ross McDonald, Tristarc won only six races from 32 starts but five of them were at Group One level. In the autumn of 1985 she achieved the rare feat of victory in the A.J.C. Derby (although she would be one of the three fillies to triumph in that decade, along with Rose of Kingston in 1982 and Research in 1989). Caulfield proved by far her favourite track, and in the spring of 1985, Tristarc won the Underwood Stakes, the Caulfield Stakes (each time from Lacka Reason) before a narrow win in the Caulfield Cup from another mare, the 5/1 equal favourite with her, Our Sophia. Lacka Reason this time was third. Tristarc had one more big win in store: the Group One Queen Elizabeth Stakes at Randwick in the autumn of 1986.

TRIVALVE

1924 ch horse Cyklon – Trey

Trained by James Scobie, Trivalve won the V.R.C. Flemington and the Gibson Carmichael Stakes as a two year old. Blossoming at three, Trivalve won the A.J.C. Derby first up in 1927, which he followed with victories in the Victoria Derby and the Melbourne Cup. Other wins included the V.R.C. St Leger and several weight-for-age staying races. Bobbie Lewis won his eighth Victoria Derby on the horse (a record that still stands) and his fourth Melbourne Cup. There have been few more distinguished three-year-olds to race in Australia.

TRUE COURSE

1947 br mare Midstream – Urunalong

One of the best of the fillies Fred Hoysted trained, True Course was a brilliant two year old. In the autumn of 1950 she won both the V.R.C. and the A.J.C. Sires' Produce, and the A.J.C. Champagne Stakes. Sent on a classic campaign in the spring of that year, she won the Thousand Guineas at Caulfield; the Wakeful Stakes and then the V.R.C. Oaks by four lengths at 9/4 on with Bill Williamson up. True Course made a strong return in the autumn of 1951, when she added the A.J.C. Oaks to her successes in Melbourne, to prove herself a top filly of the immediate post-war era.

TUDOR HILL

1954 ch gelding Ottoman – Charmeuse

One of the top sprinter-milers of the late 1950s, Tudor Hill first showed his class with a second to Mac's Amber in the 1957 Toorak Handicap. He went one better the following year, when he carried 56kg to defeat Malarno, who was in receipt of 10kg from him. In the autumn of 1959, Tudor Hill was third in the Newmarket. Sent to Sydney, he beat On Guard and Book Link in the Doncaster. In the autumn he was back in Melbourne, running third to Lord in the Memsie Stakes. When the Doncaster came round a year later, Tudor Hill – who had top weight of 57kg – was unfancied at 20/1, but he came from near last on the turn to beat the well fancied In Love by a short neck in race record time. There was still enough sprint in this fine galloper for him to run second to Sky High in the 1961 Lightning Stakes.

TULLOCH

1954 b horse Khorassan – Florida

Bought on spec for 750 guineas by Tommy Smith at the Trentham yearling sales, the smallish, sway-backed Tulloch proved to be a galloper fit to keep company with Carbine and Phar Lap. He was invincible at three, but was then sidelined for what might have been his two most profitable years because of a near fatal stomach illness. In 53 starts, he missed a

place only once, and won 36 of them. Smith sold the colt to long-time client Ern Haley. It was an investment that returned satisfaction known to very few in our racing history.

Second in his first Sydney start, Tulloch was taken to Melbourne where he won two races and was second in the Maribyrnong Stakes. As an autumn two year old in 1957, Tulloch showed his appreciation of a bit more distance by winning the V.R.C. Sires' Produce. Back in Sydney he beat Prince Darius (the horse who would be dubbed 'Tulloch's Shadow', so often did he fill second place behind the champion) in the Fairfield Handicap. Next week Tulloch clashed with Todman in the A.J.C. Sires'. The outstanding colt Todman had won the inaugural Golden Slipper by eight lengths, but Tulloch beat him handily in the Sires'. Over the shorter 1200m of the Champagne Stakes, Todman reversed the placings. Smith sent Tulloch on to Brisbane, where he won a third Sires' Produce.

It was as a three year old that Tulloch claimed his legendary status, winning 14 races. He resumed in late August in the Warwick Stakes, where he began a winning streak of eight races. He moved to the 2,000m of the Rosehill Guineas, cantering home from Prince Darius by four lengths. The 2,400m of the A.J.C. Derby was even more to his liking, and this time he beat Prince Darius by six lengths. His time cut more than two seconds off the record which Phar Lap had held. Brought to Melbourne, Tulloch took the Caulfield Guineas by eight lengths and then – overcoming interference and eased down – won the Caulfield Cup in the Australian record time of 2.26.9. The Melbourne Cup looked a formality, but Smith bowed to owner Haley's wishes and decided to scratch Tulloch. He ran him instead in the Victoria Derby which the colt won by eight lengths from Prince Darius, who was then a narrow second to Straight Draw in the Melbourne Cup. Had Tulloch run...? there is no more intriguing might-have-been in the annals of the Australian turf.

What he did manage was a victory by five lengths over Sailor's Guide on the final day of the Flemington carnival. A third Derby victory, in Queensland, followed. Returning in the autumn of 1958, Tulloch was beaten at his first two starts, but then reeled off six wins on end: in the V.R.C. and A.J.C. St Legers (by 12 and 20 lengths), the Chipping Norton and Queen Elizabeth Stakes at Randwick. Tulloch looked likely to be unbeatable at four, but succumbed to a stomach illness which nearly killed him. He was unable to take food or water without scouring, and it was 23 months before he could return to the track. But he did so with one of the greatest victories that Australian racing has to celebrate, battling the weight-for-age star Lord down the length of the Flemington straight in the Queen's Plate before triumphing by a short half head. In that campaign, in the autumn of 1960, he won a further four races.

In the spring he won first-up and then beat Dhaulagiri and Persian Lyric in the Cox Plate in record time. The Mackinnon Stakes followed, before Tulloch finally had his chance in the Melbourne Cup. With 64kg, he was beaten four lengths into seventh place, after an indifferent ride by Neville Sellwood. Four days later he bolted in with the Fisher Plate. A winner in Adelaide and then second in the 1961 Sydney Cup, Tulloch's racing days culminated in Brisbane. At his farewell he won the Brisbane Cup with 62.5kg. Thus concluded the greatest career of any Australian thoroughbred of the modern era. A relative failure at stud, Tulloch died on his owner's property on 30 June 1969.

U

UNDERWOOD STAKES

Named for E.A. Underwood, long time chairman of the Williamstown Racing Club, this race was originally called the Williamstown Stakes. Now a Group One event run over just less than 2,000m, the Underwood is a feature of the Caulfield spring carnival. It boasts a top quality roll of winners: Beau Gem (1949-50), Flying Halo (1953-4), Lord (1958 and 1960), Aquanita (1961-2), Future (1965 and 1967) all won twice. In addition Syntax (1957) and Tobin Bronze (1966) added lustre to the race, which from 1968-72 was won by near champions: Lowland, Rain Lover, Big Philou, Gay Icarus and Sobar. Then from 1975-8 the winners were Taras Bulba, How Now, Denise's Joy and So Called. These names indicate what a strong pointer the Underwood has also been to the Caulfield Cup. More recent winners include Bonecrusher in 1986, Rubiton the following year, Almaarad, The Phantom and Dr Grace from 1989-91.

V

VAIN

1966 ch horse Wilkes – Elated

Perhaps the greatest of Australian sprinters, Vain was bred by the Johnson brothers and sent to be trained by Jim Moloney in Melbourne. At his first start, in the Debutant Stakes in October 1968, he missed the jump for the only time in his career but soon gathered in the odds-on favourite Shako and won by two lengths. Sent to Flemington he won the Maribyrnong Plate by eight lengths, before returning in the autumn to post authoritative wins in the Merson Cooper Stakes and the V.R.C. Sires' Produce. The Golden Slipper beckoned. Vain started at 9/2 against, because the Sydney money came for the unbeaten Special Girl, but with regular jockey Pat Hyland up, the champion colt burned her off in the first furlong and won eased down by four lengths in front of a then record Slipper Day crowd at Rosehill of more than 40,000. Vain was underdone for his next outing, the A.J.C. Sires', in which he was surprisingly beaten by the 33/1 shot Beau Babylon. Roy Higgins, who would be involved in Vain's only two defeats, had the mount on Beau Babylon. Vain silenced his detractors decisively in the Champagne Stakes, which he won unextended by 10 lengths in the fastest ever six furlongs that had been recorded to that time by an Australian two year old.

Vain resumed in the spring of 1969 in the Freeway Stakes at Moonee Valley where he trounced the Newmarket winner Bowl King by five lengths. At Flemington he easily beat two exceptional three year olds from New Zealand who would share the honours of that spring with him: the filly Woodcourt Inn ran second, the colt Daryl's Joy was third. Higgins rode Vain at his next start, in the Moonee Valley Stakes, but this time Daryl's Joy had his measure. Vain would not be beaten again, while in front of Daryl's Joy were victories in the Victoria Derby and the Cox Plate. The Oaks would wait for Woodcourt Inn. Vain set the record straight in the Caulfield Guineas, defeating Daryl's Joy by three lengths with Woodcourt Inn six lengths away. His greatest exploit was to come. Moloney set him for the spring treble over the Flemington carnival. On Derby Day he won the Craven 'A' Stakes over six furlongs with a record weight of 54kg by 12 lengths! That remains a record margin in a major Australian handicap. On Oaks Day, Vain added the Linlithgow Stakes. He won by six lengths and ran a track record. On final day he was burdened with 55.5kg in the George Adams Handicap, but set a weight-carrying record to beat Our Faith and Cyron. Resuming trackwork in January 1970, Vain knocked a fetlock joint which he had injured as a foal and was retired to stand at the Widden Stud. He had been handicapped to carry 60.5kg in the Newmarket, 3.5kg more than Ajax's burden in 1938. At stud Vain was a notable success, siring 370 winners of almost 1,800 races. Among them were two Golden Slipper winners, Sir Dapper and Inspired, together with other top-liners such as Mistress Anne and Kenmark. Renowned especially as a sire of dams, Vain was champion sire in 1983-4 and runner-up on two other occasions. He was humanely put down on Christmas Day 1991.

VALAIS

1913 ch horse Cicero – Lily of the Valley

Imported sire Valais left an indelible mark on Australian racing. In England he had only four starts, winning the Windsor Stakes at Newmarket and finishing fourth at the same track in one of the Derbies run there during the Great War. Valais had been at stud for one season without much success when he was bought by the Moses brothers for 2,000 guineas to stand at their Arrowfield Stud. In 1924, when he had only two crops racing, Valais became Australian champion sire for the first of five consecutive occasions. His high class progeny included Lady Valais, Fujisan and Valicare, but the best of his sons went on to be champion racehorses and top sires in their own right: Heroic and Manfred. At the dispersal of the Arrowfield Stud in 1924, Valais was bought for 14,400 guineas by Herbert Thompson to stand at the Widden Stud, where he died in October 1928, his outstanding promise only partly fulfilled. While his progeny were inclined to severe

fits of temperament – especially the best of them, Heroic and Manfred – Valais sired 28 stakes winning horses and the winners of 476 races in his brief career.

VALICARE

1922 b mare Valais – Couronne

Trained by Bayly Payten, Valicare did not race until three, when she was backed into favouritism at Warwick Farm and won easily. This began a sequence of four wins which culminated in victory in the 1926 Adrian Knox Stakes (forerunner of the A.J.C. Oaks). Back in work, Valicare was set a stiff task first-up when sent out over nine furlongs in the Rawson Stakes at Rosehill against the odds-on favourite Windbag. Valicare won brilliantly, by eight lengths, in course record time. She then became the shortest priced ever Doncaster winner when she took the race at 5/4 on in near record time. Valicare rounded off the autumn with victory in the All Aged Stakes. Resuming in the early spring of 1926 in the Warwick Stakes, Valicare found Windbag too strong this time, after a duel down the straight. While she won the Hill Stakes and, when taken to Melbourne, the C.M. Lloyd Stakes, Valicare was never the same horse again, and her form tapered away.

VEANDERCROSS

1988 b gelding Crossways – Lavender

The story of this fine racehorse begins as a fairytale. Schoolteacher Chris Turner went to a sale at Levin in New Zealand to buy a mare. When Lavender ambled over to him, he bought her, together with her foal at foot by Crossways and the foal she was carrying, by Wham – all for $1,000. The Crossways foal, named Veandercross, soon showed such ability that Turner sent him to John Wheeler for fine tuning. As a two year old, Veandercross won three from three. In his next season, Veandercross won or was placed in a succession of classic or semi-classic races in his home country. At his last start in 1991, Cavallieri beat him in the New Zealand Derby at Ellerslie. Sent to Australia in the autumn of 1992, Veandercross won the Canterbury Guineas, before being narrowly beaten by Naturalism in both the Rosehill Guineas and the A.J.C. Derby. Jockey Jim Walker had chequered runs, and in the Derby he protested without success.

Wins at Wanganui and Hastings in the spring of 1992 primed Veandercross for another trip across the Tasman. Starting favourite at 5/2 in the Caulfield Cup, he was surprisingly taken to the outside on the turn by new jockey Shane Dye and beaten on the line by Mannerism, who stuck near the rails. Punters jeered the unrepentant Dye who, while missing the start in the Mackinnon Stakes, saw Veandercross home from Rough Habit. In the Melbourne Cup Veandercross was a 9/4 favourite but once more a Lee Freedman-trained horse – Subzero – nudged him out of first place. After a short let-up, Veandercross won the Lion Brown in New Zealand and was back in Melbourne for the autumn, where with Mick Dittman up he won the Carlyon and Australian Cups. Walker had the mount again in the Ranvet Stakes when Veandercross beat Naturalism (and Dittman/Freedman). At long odds-on he disappointed in the BMW, but came back a week later to win the Queen Elizabeth Stakes. His spring campaign in Melbourne in 1993 was poor, possibly because of a back injury sustained in the Caulfield Stakes.

VICTORIA AMATEUR TURF CLUB

The V.A.T.C. was formed after an eight hour dinner at Craig's Hotel, Ballarat, which stretched from the evening of 13 October 1875 into the early hours of the next morning. Prominent in the formation of the club were the brothers Norman and Hector Wilson, Herbert Power and E.C. Moore, who became the first secretary. Further meetings in Melbourne the next month completed the establishment of the club, which was initially intended to give amateur riders the chance to compete against one another, principally in steeplechases. The first V.A.T.C. meeting was held at Dowling Forest, Ballarat, with five of the six races over the jumps. The main event, the Victoria Gold Cup (a three miles steeplechase) was won by Sailor, owned by V.A.T.C. committee member Andrew Chirnside and ridden by his son. Seeking a course in Melbourne, the V.A.T.C. decided on the apparently unpromising bush track in Caulfield, where races had been run occasionally since 1859. Swampy, snake-infested and almost turned over for the purposes of a cemetery in 1861, Caulfield nevertheless hosted its first V.A.T.C. meeting on 5 August 1876. Again the main event was the Victoria Gold Cup and the result was the same: Sailor and the Chirnsides collecting.

The first Caulfield Cup was staged in the autumn of 1879, when Newminster won on an unpleasantly windy day. What would become the V.A.T.C.'s great race was moved to the spring from 1881. New events were programmed that decade, the Toorak Handicap from 1881, the Caulfield Grand National Steeple from 1882 (later the Australian Steeple) and the Oakleigh Handicap (later Plate) from 1884. Fire destroyed the members' stand on Cup morning, 1922, but the race went ahead. In 1963 the V.A.T.C. took over the Melbourne Racing Club and its second metropolitan track – Sandown Park – was opened two years later.

VICTORIA DERBY

Oldest classic race on the Victorian racing calendar, the Victoria Derby is now a Group One event over 2500m run on the first day of the Flemington Spring Carnival. It was first contested in 1855 when Rose of May beat Quiz-the-Wind and Pilot. After Fireworks won the race in 1867, it was decided to change the Derby date to New Year's Day. This opportunity Fireworks gratefully accepted, becoming the only dual winner of the Derby. There were two winners the following year as well: My Dream on New Year's Day 1869 and Charon, when the race was switched to the springtime, where it has remained ever since. Outstanding winners last century included Robin Hood in 1875, the filly Briseis the next year (at the start of her astonishing Derby-Melbourne Cup-Oaks week), Chester in 1877. The unbeaten Grand Flaneur won in 1880. Like Fireworks he was also an A.J.C. Derby winner. Darebin, Trident and The Australian Peer followed him in the 1880s, Wallace in 1895, while the top horse Maltster won in 1900. The champion Poseidon won the Derby in 1906, Patrobas in 1915, while Richmond Main was victorious in 1919 after his dead-heat with Artilleryman in the A.J.C. Derby.

The period 1921-5 saw a run of top winners: Furious, Whittier, Frances Tressady (the last filly to win the Victoria Derby), Spearfelt and Manfred. In 1929 it was Phar Lap's turn, but in reaction against geldings being eligible to win classics, they were prevented from running between 1932-57. In that period the best horses to win included Hall Mark (1933), Hydrogen (1951) and Sailor's Guide (1955). Skipton (1941) was the last Derby winner to go on to victory in the Melbourne Cup. One who might have done, given the chance, was Tulloch who triumphed by eight lengths in 1957. Sky High won in 1960 and Tobin Bronze in 1965, but the Derby has never again seen a consistent line of notable winners. The 1970s did, however, throw up the multiple Derby winners Silver Sharpe and Dayana (1970 and 1972), besides Taj Rossi in 1973 and Dulcify in 1979. The fine colt and top sire-to-be Grosvenor won in 1982; the enigmatic Stylish Century and Star of the Realm had been the best of recent winners until Mahogany, who added the 1994 A.J.C. Derby to his five length spacing of the field at Flemington in 1993, to be the first horse since Dulcify to complete the double. The story of the Derby has been told in Marc Fiddian's *The Victoria Derby* (1991).

VICTORIAN RACING

After a meeting at John Pascoe's Fawkner's Inn in Melbourne at which the Melbourne Racing Club was formed, the first races in the colony were held at Batman's Hill on 6 and 7 March 1838. Postboy won the Town Plate. A hideously ugly carpenter named Curwen won the grinning match. The Flemington racetrack opened in March 1840. It would become the headquarters of the Victoria Racing Club, which in 1864 took over from the Port Phillip Turf Club and the Jockey Club. The Victorian Amateur Turf Club was formed at Ballarat in 1875 and held its first meeting at the town's Dowling Forest course in 1876. In that year the V.A.T.C. bought land at Caulfield, where its principal track was established. Racing in Melbourne is conducted, as in Sydney, at four metropolitan tracks: Flemington (V.R.C.), Caulfield and Sandown (V.A.T.C.) and Moonee Valley (M.V.R.C.).

VICTORIA PARK RACECOURSE

The Old Course, as it was long and affectionately known, is situated in parklands in Adelaide's south-east. At 637m, Victoria Park – as the course has been known since 1897, year of Queen Victoria's Diamond Jubilee – has the longest straight of any Australian track (compare Flemington at 453m). Paddy Coglin, an early South Australian entrepreneur, leased the course in 1864, and the Adelaide Cup was run there on several occasions in the early 1870s. Biggest race at the Old Course, which was the headquarters of the Adelaide Racing Club, was for long the Birthday Cup. Its main races are now the Adelaide Guineas, Auraria Plate for three year old fillies and the Rain Lover Plate. Good winners of the latter event have included Dayana, Mapperley Heights, Kaapstad and King's High. Another Victoria Park racecourse flourished in Sydney as a venue for pony racing until its closure in 1941.

VICTORIA RACING CLUB

The Victoria Racing Club was formed after a meeting at the Scott's Hotel in Melbourne on 9 March 1864. That hotel had been the venue where the Melbourne Cricket Club (in 1838) and the Melbourne Club (a year later) had been established. Prominent in the foundation of the V.R.C. were Henry Creswick, Herbert Power and Captain Frederick Standish. The gentlemen gathered at Scott's agreed to dissolve the financially troubled and competing Victoria Turf and Jockey Clubs, thus to create the V.R.C. Robert Bagot 'was appointed first secretary, and operated from part of his William Street office which he leased to the club. The V.R.C. first had responsibility for the Melbourne Cup in 1864. Thereafter it embarked on an ambitious programme of promotion and of building at Flemington

which saw the course established as one of the greatest of world racing venues; the Melbourne Cup as indisputably the world's greatest handicap event. The V.R.C. has enjoyed a much less hotly contested control of racing in Victoria than its counterpart – the principal club in New South Wales – the A.J.C. A history of the V.R.C., John Pacini's *A Century Galloped By*, was published in 1988.

VINTAGE CROP

1986 ch gelding Rousillon – Overplay

In one of the most remarkable stories in Melbourne Cup history, the Irish stayer Vintage Crop was brought from Europe to contest the race in 1993, together with Ascot Gold Cup winner Drum Taps. The two horses were stabled and trained at Sandown, and neither contested an Australian event before the Melbourne Cup. Dermott Weld had charge of Vintage Crop, who had graduated from victory in a Novice Hurdle at Leopardstown, to taking the great distance handicap race in England, the 3,600m Cesarewitch at Newmarket in October 1992. In the start before he came to Australia, Vintage Crop won the Irish St Leger; earlier in 1993 he had won the Curragh Cup. Accordingly he seemed well weighted with 55.5kg in the Melbourne Cup, if he had acclimatised. In the Flemington straight Vintage Crop set out after the rank outsider, Te Akau Nick at 160/1 and ran to him easily. The victory meant that Irish jockey Michael Kinnane joined Australian Pat Glennon as the only man to win an English Derby, a Prix de l'Arc de Triomphe and a Melbourne Cup. Despite some parochial mutterings, Vintage Crop was a top-line winner who enhanced the international status of the Melbourne Cup. He joined a line of overseas-bred winners of the race that stretches back to

Comedy King in 1910. Early in 1994 Vintage Crop was rated the best horse in the world at 2,800m and beyond in the International Classification of racehorse performance. He won first-up in his next preparation before being beaten in the Ascot Gold Cup.

VIOLONCELLO

1916 ch horse Valens – Catgut

Violoncello was owned in England by Mr A. de Rothschild. There he won three of six starts, finishing with a strong win in a welter at Newmarket. He was bought to race in Australia by Sir Samuel Horden. In three weight-for-age starts in the Sydney spring carnival of 1921, Violoncello recorded a second in the Hill and a fourth in the Spring Stakes. Taken to Melbourne, he ran an ordinary fifth in the Herbert Power Handicap. That effort saw him start at 16/1 in the Caulfield Cup, but he won handily from Purser. Kept going by trainer C.H. Bryans, he was down the line in the Melbourne Cup after finishing second to the champion Eurythmic in the Melbourne Stakes. The following spring, Violoncello enjoyed more success. He was fourth in a roughly run Caulfield Cup, and then won the inaugural Cox Plate in 1922 from the fine gallopers Easingwold and Furious. His excellent form was sustained at Flemington, where during the carnival he won both the Cantala and the Linlithgow Stakes.

VOIGT, NEVILLE (1944-)

After a long and distinguished riding career, Neville Voigt retired in 1984 to take up training in Sydney. His big races wins began in 1969, when he won the Rosehill Guineas on Portable, the Doncaster for Tommy Smith on Bye Bye and the Metropolitan on Tails. Voigt was often to pick up top rides from leading stables, while operating freelance. The following year he won the Sydney Cup on Arctic Symbol and the first of two A.J.C. Derbies, on Silver Sharpe (for Smith). A second would come in 1977 on the Bart Cummings-trained Belmura Lad. Another productive year for Voigt was 1975, with wins on Analie in the Queensland Derby, Lord Nelson in the Doomben Cup and then – in the spring – the Epsom on the same horse, again for Smith. In 1982 Voigt won the A.J.C. St Leger on Gurner's Lane, but did not ride the horse in Melbourne, where he won the Cups double. However, he won the 1982 Stradbroke on Grey Receiver and finally achieved a big race success in Melbourne in 1983, the year before his retirement, when he partnered Hayai to victory in the Caulfield Cup.

VOITRE, KEITH (1913-1938)

The New Zealand-born Keith Voitre was a leading jockey in his home country before the Melbourne trainer Lou Robertson, himself a New Zealander, lured him across the Tasman to ride. Voitre quickly established himself as a top jockey in a remarkably talented era. His best year was 1935, when he won the Newmarket Handicap and C.M. Lloyd Stakes on Count Ito, the unusual double of the Cox Plate and the Williamstown Cup on Garrio. Robertson trained the latter, but that was not the extent of the trainer-jockey combination. Voitre won the Derby-Oaks double on Robertson's horses Feldspar and Nalda. He capped this off by riding another Robertson galloper, the 9/2 favourite Marabou, to a two and a half length victory in the 1935 Melbourne Cup. Few jockeys have had a more remarkable Melbourne spring. Three years later Voitre was dead, killed in a race fall at Moonee Valley in September 1938.

VON DOUSSA, (HEINRICH ALBERT) ALFRED (1848-1926)

By turns gold prospector, clerk to the Echunga Council for 50 years, a liberal Member of the South Australian Legislative Council and a rifle shooter, Von Doussa is best remembered as secretary of the Onkaparinga Racing Club from its formation in 1875 until his retirement in 1924. He instituted the famous Easter meeting at Oakbank outside Adelaide, and his horse Pioneer won the Hack Steeplechase at the first meeting. Von Doussa's name is perpetuated in a steeplechase run at the Easter carnival at Oakbank.

VO ROGUE

1984 b gelding Ivor Prince – Vow

One of the best-loved horses of the 1980s, Vo Rogue was a very fast front-runner who – despite his dislike of wet tracks – established an outstanding weight-for-age record. Trained by Vic(tory) Rail, an advocate of unorthodoxly simple methods, and usually ridden by the unfashionable jockey Cyril Small, the horse's beginnings were inauspicious. Vo Rogue's breeding promised little, and he was so unprepossessing as a youngster as to be nicknamed 'Erky'. He won his fifth start at two and, with gradual improvement, took five of 17 at three. First sign of his true promise was when he was just beaten at 50/1 by Military Plume in the 1987 Australian Guineas. Defeated by a heavy track in the Autumn Stakes, he struck back to win the Creswick Stakes by eight lengths and then the Alister Clark Stakes in record time. After a four year old campaign which began in Brisbane, Vo Rogue won the Turnbull Stakes and was just beaten in the Toorak by Caledonian Boy. In a breathtaking effort he next led a high class field in the Cox Plate by 12 lengths down the Dean Street side, and held on to run a close fourth.

Autumn suited Vo Rogue even better than springtime. He returned to racing to win the William Reid in race record time, the Orr Stakes by six lengths, the Blamey and Futurity Stakes in track record time. His supposed match race against Bonecrusher in the Australian Cup was undone by the 125/1 shot Dandy Andy. He was back for the next two renewals of the race and won them both, beating Super Impose and Our Poetic Prince in 1989, Better Loosen Up the following year. In between he went west and won the W.A.T.C. Winfield Stakes at Group One. His form gradually tapered off, but he was a grand second to Better Loosen Up in the 1991 Australian Cup. At seven he raced 15 times without success and earned well-merited retirement with winnings of more than $3 million.

W

WAKEFUL

1897 b mare Trenton – Insomnia

Arguably Australia's greatest mare, the H. Munro-trained Wakeful did not race until four. At her third start, Wakeful won the 1901 Oakleigh Plate. She followed up with the Newmarket; took the Doncaster at Randwick in record time and then ran a stout third in the Sydney Cup. The next spring she won the Caulfield Stakes, before being unluckily and narrowly beaten by Hymettus in the Caulfield Cup of 1901. After winning the Melbourne Stakes, Wakeful ran fifth to her stablemate Revenue in the 1901 Melbourne Cup. Her deeds in her next preparation earned her huge weights. She won her four starts in Sydney in the autumn of 1902, including the Sydney Cup with 60kg. In the spring of that year she took a second Caulfield Stakes, the Eclipse and Melbourne Stakes, the C.B. Fisher Plate and Champion Stakes. Given 65kg in the Melbourne Cup of 1902, Wakeful was scratched by an owner who put his mare's welfare before the chance of victory in a sub-standard field. After winning a third successive Melbourne Stakes, Wakeful ran in the 1903 Melbourne Cup, finishing a gallant second to Lord Cardigan with 63.5kg. Besides her 19 victories at weight-for-age, the mare also won the Herbert Power Handicap in 1902 and 1903. In all, Wakeful won 25 of her 44 starts and was placed in 16 others.

WALLACE

1892 ch horse Carbine – Melodious

The best of the sons Carbine sired in Australia, Wallace is notable not only for his deeds on the track, but as an outstanding sire. Bred at the St Albans Stud, Wallace won a Flying Handicap at Flemington in open company as a two year old. At three he won the classic double of the Caulfield Guineas and Victoria Derby. Next autumn he won the A.J.C. St Leger and carried 56kg to victory in the 1896 Sydney Cup, a notable impost for a three year old. Racing in the best of company, Wallace dead-heated with Quiver in the Champion Stakes and with Auraria in the C.B. Fisher Plate. At stud, where he stood for 22 years, he sired the winners of 949 races before his death in 1917. Among the big race successes for his progeny were two Melbourne and one Sydney Cups, six Victoria Derbies and six V.R.C. Oaks, and an A.J.C. Derby. The fine stayer Trafalgar was one of his best sons, Patrobas, winner of the 1915 Melbourne Cup (and sixth of Wallace's Victoria Derby winners) was another.

WALTZING LILY

1929 br mare Beau Fils – Robecq

This brilliant sprinting mare first showed signs of her class when second to Dutchie in the Edward Manifold Stakes in the spring of 1932. In the summer of 1933 she won the Standish Handicap at Flemington, then scored her first important weight-for-age win in the William Reid Stakes. Waltzing Lily then carried the testing weight for a mare of 55kg to victory in the 1933 Newmarket over Jacko. In the spring she won the Memsie Stakes, before being tried over more ground in the Cox Plate, where she ran a creditable third to Rogilla and Dermid. In the autumn of 1934, Waltzing Lily ran third in the William Reid before carrying 61.5kg to win the Futurity Stakes. She was back again in the autumn, winning a second Memsie. Retired to the stud, Waltzing Lily was the dam of the 1953 V.R.C. Oaks winner, Waltzing Lady.

WARD, ARTHUR (1920-)

Apprenticed to Frank Adams at Rosehill, Ward was one of the most consistent of Sydney jockeys. He won two premierships in a period when Neville Sellwood was dominant, in 1950-1 and 1954-5. Ward rode with success in Singapore in 1953, but returned for some of his biggest race wins in Australia. He won the Caulfield Cup on Rising Fast in 1954, on Redcraze two years later. Partnering the latter horse he was narrowly beaten in the 1956 Melbourne Cup. Earlier in the year they had combined to win the Brisbane Cup. At the 1957 V.R.C. autumn carnival, Ward won the Sires' on Tulloch, Newmarket on King's Fair, St Leger on Summalu and – with Redcraze again – the Queen's Cup. After retiring as a jockey he became a leading Sydney trainer.

WARRNAMBOOL GRAND ANNUAL STEEPLECHASE

Racing began in the Warrnambool and Port Fairy area in 1848. In 1873 the Warrnambool Racing Club was formed, replacing the defunct Warrnambool Amateur Turf Club. The Club's biggest attraction, Australia's longest and most gruelling race, the Warrnambool Grand Annual Steeplechase, had already been run for the first time, when Prior took the event in 1872. Held each May before very large crowds, in a holiday atmosphere, the Grand Annual now requires horses to jump 33 fences and to cover 5500m. They race on the course proper and through the Brierly and Granters Paddocks. The Tozer Road double commemorates one of the pioneers of racing in the district. Recent distinguished winners include Thackeray, twice victorious in an event which has attracted some of the bravest of Australian jumpers, and deterred some of the most brilliant.

WARWICK FARM RACECOURSE

What is now Warwick Farm racecourse, in Sydney's western suburbs, was originally William Forrester's stud and training track. With a groups of friends Forrester formed the Warwick Farm Race Club which held its first meeting in March 1889. This proprietary club was sold to the A.J.C. in 1922. Pressure on facilities, especially for training at Randwick, was one reason for this acquisition, another was the intention to strike against the power of the proprietary clubs. Renovated from 1923-5, the Warwick Farm track suffered from declining attendances during the Depression and then was taken over as a military camp during World War Two. Racing did not resume at Warwick Farm until 1952, when a record crowd of 37,000 turned up to celebrate.

Closed again for extensive renovations from August 1979 to February 1982, Warwick Farm was able to host crucial meetings for the A.J.C. in the 1980s when Randwick was a poor wet weather track.

WATERHOUSE FAMILY

Waterhouse has been a big name in Australian racing, and particularly bookmaking, for more than a century. Charles Waterhouse began fielding in Sydney in 1890. Three of his sons followed him into the game. By the 1970s, seven Waterhouses were fielding in New South Wales. Most famous of them was Bill Waterhouse, who trained first as a lawyer. His duels with massive punters Felipe Ysmael and Frank Duval in the 1960s were legendary. And Waterhouse finished in front. In 1971 the A.J.C. without explanation refused to renew Waterhouse's licence. That decision was revoked two years later. Waterhouse's son Robbie (who married trainer Tommy Smith's daughter Gai in 1980) also became one of Sydney's biggest bookmakers. Both father and son lost their licences because of alleged knowledge of the Fine Cotton ring-in in 1984. Gai Waterhouse eventually won her long battle to be granted a trainer's licence.

WATSON, GEORGE (1829-1906)

Born in Ireland, Watson emigrated to Australia, arriving in 1850. His diverse business interests included a horse saleyard, mail contracting, for which he purchased two Cobb & Co coachlines, and horse-breeding in the Riverina. Watson became a committeeman of the Victoria Racing Club from its inception in 1864, which he served for many years. A steeplechase rider himself, he established the Melbourne Hunt Club in 1853 and had success with his own horses in some of the earliest classic races run in

Victoria. With Flying Colours he won the 1860 Victoria Derby, and the Oaks with Palestine in the following year. Watson also served as starter at V.R.C. meetings for about 30 years, before being succeeded by his son Godfrey in 1896. Long after his race riding career had ended, he enjoyed riding to hounds besides kangaroo hunting on horseback.

WELCH, ERIC WILFRED (1900-83)

The renowned journalist and race-caller Eric Welch gave up medical studies at the University of Melbourne because 'race meeting and poker schools clashed with the lecture times'. In 1925 he called the first of more than 18,000 races which included 27 Melbourne Cups. After being dismissed from the A.B.C. because of the scandal occasioned by his allegedly 'enticing' a woman away from her husband, Welch began 20 years work with radio station 3DB. While on-course race-calling was banned from the early 1930s until 1945, he found vantage points outside the courses to ply his trade. Races at Flemington were broadcast from the loft of the now demolished Pioneer Hotel. From that spot Welch picked the dead-heat in the 1934 St Leger. In 1948 he paid off his house when Rimfire won the Melbourne Cup at 80/1. A colourful character (who survived a plunge in his car into the waters off Victoria Dock – a passenger drowned), Welch loved to drink, but never on race-days. Retired from race-calling, he became a publican. His advice to punters was 'Never bet on anything that can talk'.

WENONA GIRL

1957 ch mare Wilkes – Golden Chariot

Trained by Maurice McCarten, this marvellous sprinting mare won 27 of her 68 starts and was placed in 26 others. She was able to win up to one and a half miles and is remembered not only for her deeds over a number of seasons, but for her duels with Sky High, which eventually saw the ledger a bare 11 to nine in his favour. In 1960 Wenona Girl won both the V.R.C. and the A.J.C. Sires', beating Perisan Lyric and Sky High in the latter. She had finished one and a half lengths adrift of Sky High in the Golden Slipper. In the spring she won the Hobartville, ran second to Persian Lyric in the Canterbury Guineas and then beat Sky High in the Rosehill Guineas. Taken to Melbourne, Wenona Girl won the 1960 Thousand Guineas and the Wakeful Stakes before finishing third in the V.R.C. Oaks. But the following autumn she won the A.J.C. Oaks. In 1962 her best win was the C.F. Orr Stakes at Caulfield, but 1963 was another vintage year for Wenona Girl. She won the George Main and Gloaming Stakes in Sydney; the first of two successive Lightning Stakes, the Futurity under the burden of 63kg (with Sky High third). In the Melbourne spring carnival she won the Linlithgow Stakes and the George Adams Handicap, carrying 58.5kg. And she was still able to win at the highest level at six, where her victories included another Lightning and the Randwick All Aged Stakes. Sent to stud, Wenona Girl threw a Golden Slipper favourite, Special Girl (by Todman – hence one of the best bred fillies ever to race in Australia). Special Girl's brilliant early two year old form showed that she had inherited her mother's speed but Vain gave her windburn in the 1969 Golden Slipper.

WEST AUSTRALIAN
1848

One of the finest horses to race in England in the 19th century, West Australian was the first to win the three year old Triple Crown of 2,000 Guineas, Derby

and St Leger. His jockey had been bribed to pull the horse in the final leg, but received a better offer from the owners. West Australian is connected to Australian racing not only by the chance of his name, but because one of his daughters was the dam of Musket, sire of the champion Carbine who would in turn sire an English Derby winner.

WEST AUSTRALIAN TURF CLUB

The West Australian Turf Club was formed in October 1852. Gradually it extended its control over racing in the state. Ascot racecourse was leased as the headquarters of the club from 1877. The club conducted meetings at Helena Vale from 1948 until the sale of the track in 1969. Earlier Belmont had been purchased to relieve pressure on the facilities at Ascot. The W.A.T.C. encouraged a notable boom in racing in the state during the 1970s (when the Australian Derby was introduced to its calendar), but recently has been unable to sustain the interest of as many eastern states' trainers in bringing their horses across for the summer carnival.

WESTERN AUSTRALIAN RACING

The first race meeting in Western Australia took place at 'The Downs', South Fremantle, on 2 October 1833, only a few years after the foundation of the colony. Timor ponies contested the events. Thoroughbred racing began three years later at Guilford, in October 1836, but their events were given equal billing with a ploughing match. Racing began at Ascot in 1848, while the West Australian Turf Club was formed in 1852. The controlling body of racing in the state, it holds events at two metropolitan courses: Ascot and Belmont. A strong country racing circuit developed in the goldfields region of Western Australia, particularly around the turn of the century.

Jenny Tomlinson wrote 'a history of thoroughbred breeding and racing in Western Australia since 1833', Born Winners Born Losers

WHITE, HARRY (1944-)

Son of the former jockey Harry White senior (who won a division of the 1943 Caulfield Cup on the outsider, Saint Warden), White was apprenticed to Tony Lopes in 1958. Taking time to adapt to the regimen of the jockey's life, White waited until 4 July 1959 for his first race ride. But it was memorable: he scored on Lopes' horse Alpino at 66/1 in the Braybrook Handicap at Flemington. White's first big win was on Sir Dane in the 1964 Duke of Norfolk Stakes, a race which he was to win on four more occasions. He made a habit of success over the two mile journey at Flemington. Besides the five Duke of Norfolk wins, he notched four Melbourne Cups (equalling the record for a jockey in the race of Bobbie Lewis). White won the great race four times in six years: on Think Big in 1974 and 1975, Arwon in 1978 and Hyperno in 1979. George Hanlon trained Arwon; Bart Cummings the other horses: these were two of the top trainers for whom he rode with most success. Both of the Cummings' mounts now enjoy their retirement on White's property at Gisborne.

White was premier Victorian jockey four times: in 1967-8, 1973-4, 1978-9 and 1980-1. Besides the Melbourne Cup, he won two Caulfield Cups – on Sobar in 1972 and Ming Dynasty in 1977. His most controversial defeat was on Sobar in the Victoria Derby, a race that he won later on Bounty Hawk. He also excelled in sprint races, with three Newmarket, Oakleigh Plate and Futurity successes. Five Australian Cups also came his way. In the later stages of his career, White partnered Rubiton to a series of victories which included the Cox Plate. He regarded Rubiton as the best of the horses that he had ridden. While he won big races in South and Western Australia, White enjoyed no success in Sydney. But he was still riding at 50, as one of the most skilled and tenacious of Australian jockeys. His son Brent has also become a jockey.

WHITE, JAMES (1828-1890)

Pastoralist on a grand scale in the Hunter River district, and sometime New South Wales politician, White was a keen, disciplined and lucky racehorse owner and breeder. In 1880 and from 1883-90 he was chairman of the Australian Jockey Club. He established Segenhoe as the centre of his breeding operations. The first of White's top horses was Chester, who won the Victoria Derby and Melbourne Cup in 1877. Chester gave White the first of six Victoria Derbies. His horses also won, in an astonishingly compressed time frame between 1884-90, five A.J.C. Derbies, five A.J.C. Sires' Produce Stakes and five V.R.C. St Legers. Martini-Henry gave him a second Derby-Melbourne Cup double in 1883. A heavy punter, White was said to have collected 25,000 pounds as a result. His attempts to breed horses by Chester to English time in order to win the Epsom Derby were unsuccessful. White retired as chairman of the A.J.C. and sold most of his horses in 1890, the year of his death. His most famous descendant was the novelist Patrick White, whose father was a keen racehorse owner. Australian racing has a minor but significant role in several of White's novels, notably *The Tree of Man* (1956).

WHITTIER

1919 br horse Woorak – Polacca

Owned by Ben Chaffey, son of the pioneer of Mildura, and sometime

Chairman of the V.A.T.C., Whittier was trained at Bendigo by H. McCalman. He won 17 of 52 starts, many at the highest level, and was placed on another 19 occasions. In the spring of 1922, Whittier won the Caulfield Cup on the day that the V.A.T.C. staged its meeting despite the grandstand having burned down. He went on to win the Victoria Derby and raced with success for four more seasons. Second in the Cox Plates of 1923 and 1924, Whittier won several weight-for-age races, among them the Orr and Rawson Stakes and the St George Stakes at seven. In 1925 he went on better than his sire, Woorak, by winning the Doncaster, and did so in style, under 59.5kg in Australian record time. In the spring of that year Whittier won a second Caulfield Cup, the gap of three years between wins being exceptional for a major Australian race (although Ming Dynasty emulated the feat in 1977 and 1980).

WIDDEN STUD

Established by the Thompson family in the middle of the 19th century, the Hunter Valley Widden Stud is one of the oldest and most prestigious in Australian turf history. Little John was a foundation sire, but the English-bred, New Zealand-born Lochiel was its first outstanding performer. He was four times champion sire in Australia, and was followed by a line of champions. Grafton equalled his feat by finishing on top of the sires' list on four occasions; Maltster went one better. More recently, the champion racehorse Vain stood at Widden. Champion sire on one occasion, his forte was as a sire of broodmares.

WIDDIS, EDITH

Wife of a Gippsland grazier, Mrs E.A. Widdis earned her place in Australian turf history as the first woman to own a Melbourne Cup winner. She bought the colt Patrobas for 300 guineas and watched with pleasure when – at three – he won the Caulfield Guineas and Victoria Derby of 1915. Three days later, he won the Melbourne Cup at 8/1 narrowly from the bolter Westcourt. Edith Widdis watched the race with her daughter from the back of the Ladies' Stand but was unable to get through the crowd to the mounting yard for the Cup presentation. In the event her husband John accepted the Cup. According to tradition, the Cup winning owner attended the Victoria Club the next day to shout the bar. Mrs Widdis turned up, but preferred to donate 200 pounds to the Patriotic Fund, a gesture for which she was roundly applauded.

WIGGLE

1965 br mare Rego – Sweet Nymph

Wiggle combined remarkable success as a two and three year old racing in Australia, with a successful series of campaigns in the United States. Bought cheaply, for 360 guineas, Wiggle was named by her owner Bill Godby on the strength of a backside which he imagined wiggled like Marilyn Monroe's. As a yearling, Wiggle almost died when her legs became entangled in a barbed wire fence, but was saved with a future as a broodmare in mind. Trained by Ron Shirtliff, Wiggle won five races in a row as a two year old, four at Randwick, and one at Doomben. After running sixth in the Lightning Stakes at Eagle Farm, the two year old achieved an astonishing victory in the Stradbroke Handicap of 1958, a Group One race against open company. She remains the only winner of that age in the history of a race, that goes back to 1890.

Back in training at three, Wiggle's

feature wins included the Hobartville Stakes, then in Melbourne the Caulfield Guineas, as well as the Edward Manifold and Linlithgow Stakes. She also ran second in both the Thousand Guineas and the Sandown Guineas. In the autumn of 1959 Wiggle won in succession the Queen's Plate, C.M. Lloyd and Kewney Stakes at Flemington, as well as the Alister Clark Stakes at Moonee Valley. Leased to American interests, the mare won six races and was placed 10 times. Her American performances included two track records.

WILARI

1908 b mare Wallace – Murna

One of the best daughters of Wallace, the W. Risby-trained Wilari showed enough precocity to run second in the Champagne Stakes at Randwick in 1911 to Posadas. But staying was her game. In the spring of that year she became one of the few fillies to win the Victoria Derby-V.R.C. Oaks double. A 50/1 outsider in the Derby, where she beat Cisco and Jacamar, Wilari was at 5/2 on when she defeated Orvieto and Queen of the May in the Oaks. Next autumn she confirmed her quality over a distance by winning the V.R.C. St Leger.

WILKES

1952 ch horse Court Martial – Sans Tares

Imported from France in 1959 by John Kelly, Wilkes stood at the Newhaven Park Stud. Three times Australian champion sire, he produced the top-line filly Wenona Girl from his first crop to race, in 1960-1. In all he sired 48 individual stakes winners, but none to rival the incomparable Vain, out of Elated. Wilkes was put down in 1976.

WLLLETTS, GARY (1943-)

A splendid riding career ended when Gary Willetts was injured in a mounting yard accident at Yarra Glen in August 1991. Already a leading jockey in New Zealand, where he had won a Wellington Cup and two Oaks, Willetts had come to Australia in 1974 to ride the top stayer, Battle Heights. In the autumn he won the Sydney Cup on Battle Heights on his first ride in Sydney and then took the Queen Elizabeth Stakes on the horse. At his first Melbourne ride in the spring of 1974, he won the Cox Plate on Battle Heights. A few weeks before he had won the Rosehill Guineas in a pick-up ride for George Hanlon with Taras Bulba. Hanlon and other trainers took notice of Willetts when he risked his career by moving to Melbourne: in the 1975-6 season he won Group races for Hanlon, Bart Cummings, Colin Hayes, Bob Hoysted and Tommy Smith. Thereafter he moved his family to Australia. In the next 15 years Willetts won almost 1000 races in Australia. 29 of them were cups, including an Australian, two Moonee Valley and two Sandown and a Sydney Cup. Twenty five of his wins came in a fabled association with Manikato. Willetts won 127 of what are now Group or listed races before his retirement in a career total of 1493. Subsequently he has worked as a media commentator.

WILLIAM REID STAKES

This Group One summer sprint over 1200m at Moonee Valley is one of the toughest tests on the Melbourne calendar. It was inaugurated in 1925, a year in which the Moonee Valley Racing Club also added the Alister Clark Stakes to its programme, and the building of a new grandstand was completed. The Night Patrol won the first two runnings of the event, while Heroic and Gothic were other top class winners in the 1920s. From 1930-3 the fine sprinter Greenline was luckless in the William Reid, three times running second and then dead-heating for third. By contrast, Heros found the winning post in 1934 and 1935. Waltzing Lily, Hua and Amiable were other good winners in the 1930s. Tranquil Star won in 1946, while the remarkable galloper Comic Court returned to racing after his victory in the 1950 Melbourne Cup in record time, to score first-up in the William Reid where he again ran a track record.

Flying Halo was second to Comic Court but atoned by winning the next two William Reids and then scoring for a third time in 1955. Golden Doubles joined him as a multiple winner of the race when he scored in 1958-9. The 1960s and 1970s saw the race maintain its lustre. Winners included New Statesman (1962), Star Affair (1966), Winfreux (1968), Crewman (1970), Dual Choice (1972), All Shot in the next two years, Leica Show, Lord Dudley, Toy Show and Family of Man from 1975-8. Numbers of those winners were equally capable up to much longer distances, thus indicating what a test of strength is the William Reid. But the greatest feat in the race was yet to come. The champion Manikato won from 1979-83, to record an unparalleled five successive wins in a major sprint in Australia. He overshadowed subsequent winners, who included horses of the calibre of River Rough, Campaign King, Canny Lass, Vo Rogue and Zeditave.

WILLIAMS, LLOYD JOHN (1940-)

A highly successful businessman, as the major shareholder and chief executive of Hudson Conway and Chairman of the Crown Casino, Lloyd Williams has created a name for himself in racing over a long period. He broke into the game with the filly Cautious Sue, who went on to win the 1969 Kewney Stakes. After early successes with horses trained at Ballarat, Williams increased his involvement in racing and had his first major win with Lord Nelson in the 1973 Doomben Cup. Numbers of other good horses followed, including the Melbourne Cup winners Just A Dash (who had also won the 1981 Adelaide Cup) and What a Nuisance in 1985; Major Drive (Sydney Cup of 1987), Nearest, who equalled the record for the highest number of wins at Sandown and Plush, who won the Moonee Valley and Ascot Vale Stakes, a Toorak Handicap and the Memsie and Orr Stakes. Williams's current star, now part-owned with Kerry Packer, is Mahogany, whose wins include the Victoria and A.J.C. Derbies, the Caulfield and Australian Guineas.

WILLIAMSON, BILL (1922-79)

One of the finest of all Australian jockeys, Bill Williamson was apprenticed to Frank Law. His first winner came at Flemington on Lilirene in his fourth race ride. By coincidence, this was the last horse on which his mentor, and great uncle, the champion jockey Bobbie Lewis had scored. Lewis had persuaded Williamson's reluctant parents to let their son try out as a jockey. Seven times premier jockey in Victoria, Williamson won the 1952 Melbourne Cup on Dalray, the 1958 Caulfield Cup on Sir Blink. In the 1960s he joined the exodus of top Australian hoops to Europe, riding with distinction in England, France and Ireland until his retirement in 1973. Nicknamed 'Wearie Willie' because of his customary deadpan expression, Williamson's top wins in Europe were successive victories in the Prix de l'Arc de Triomphe: on Vaguely Noble (one of the great horses of the century) in 1968 and Levmoss. He returned to Australia in 1977 and died after a long illness two years later.

WILLIAMSTOWN CUP,
see SANDOWN CUP

WILLIAMSTOWN RACECOURSE

Originally a picnic racetrack in a Melbourne bayside suburb, Williamstown gradually established itself as a popular metropolitan course. By 1884 it had three annual meetings and a new grandstand was constructed three years later. The main event on the calendar of the Williamstown Racing Club was the Williamstown Cup, traditionally run after the conclusion of the Flemington Spring Carnival. Many fine horses won the race (which certainly overshadowed the Moonee Valley Cup) including Merman, Richmond Main, Amounis, Shadow King and Second Wind (in 1931 and 1932). In one of the great accidental comic moments in Australian racing, The Tyrant beat The Slave in the Williamstown Cup of 1925. The heyday of Williamstown was in the interwar period, for a decade of which its chairman was J.J. Liston. But when the Second World War broke out, the course was requisitioned by the military. Williamstown's last meeting was held on 10 February 1940 (the day that the fine young jockey Billy Lappin was killed in a race fall in Sydney). In 1948 the Williamstown Racing Club amalgamated with the Victorian Trotting and Racing Association to become the Melbourne Racing Club, whose meetings were held at the other three metropolitan tracks until the M.R.C. was taken over by the V.A.T.C.

WINDBAG

1921 b horse Magpie – Charleville

Bred at the Kia Ora Stud in New South Wales, Windbag was a top-line performer, especially in Sydney. He was raced by Robert Miller, brother of the breeder, who bought the colt after the original purchaser refused to take such a bad walker (as he thought) back to New Zealand. In Sydney, Windbag's big wins included the A.J.C. St Leger, two Craven Plates, a Cumberland Stakes, the Randwick, Autumn and Warwick Stakes (where he downed Valicare after a thrilling duel). He was second in the Sydney Cup in the autumn of 1925, but went one better at Flemington. Windbag's Melbourne Cup preparation had been unusual. After winning a six furlong sprint at Randwick in July with 62.5kg, he was kept in work through to the end of the spring, taking four weight-for-age races in Sydney: the Chelmsford and Spring Stakes, Craven and Randwick Plates. Windbag's first visit to a Melbourne track yielded an unimpressive third in the Melbourne Stakes, but he still started at 5/1 in the Cup behind the champion Manfred, who was favourite at 7/4. This was the first Melbourne Cup to be broadcast on radio, on A.B.C. station 3LO. After a great battle down the straight, Windbag – ridden by Jim Munro – beat Manfred by half a length, running race record time and equalling the Australasian two mile record. Both he and Manfred finished their careers with 18 wins. Sent to stud at Northwood Park near Seymour in Victoria, Windbag's best son was Chatham.

WINFREUX

1961 b gelding Affreux – Winlam

The only decent offspring of the imported French stallion Affreux, Winfreux was bred by George Lloyd and trained at Mentone by C.A. Wilson. What would prove to be an outstanding career both as a handicapper, but more particularly at weight-for-age, was slow to blossom. It was not until March 1965 that he won his maiden, at Bendigo. He soon added wins in town, at Caulfield and Moonee Valley before Wilson took the punt on sending the horse to Queensland for the winter carnival. Specked at 14/1 in the Stradbroke Handicap after a welter win, Winfreux won by three lengths, with the 2/1 favourite Eskimo Prince well adrift. Despite a penalty, he went on to annex the Stradbroke-Doomben 10,000 double at his next start and – having copped another stiff penalty – ran second to River Seine in the Doomben Cup. The pattern of his winter campaigning was now set, and Winfreux won races in Brisbane in each of the next three seasons, including two J.H.S. Barnes Stakes, two Tatt's Cups and – in 1966 – the Doomben Cup, which he won by two and a half lengths in Australian record time for 11 furlongs.

In the spring of 1965 Winfreux won the first of three successive Caulfield Stakes, at 20/1, with Jim Johnson, who would become his regular jockey, riding him for the first time. Back in the spring of 1966, his form was patchy, although a second to Tobin Bronze, besides another Caulfield Stakes victory (over Light Fingers) were highlights. Refreshed by yet another Brisbane campaign, Winfreux posted strong wins in the Hill Stakes and Craven Plate in Sydney in the spring of 1966, setting another Australian record – this time for eight and a half furlongs – in the former. The Melbourne campaign was also highly productive. With Tobin Bronze now racing in America, Winfreux won his third Caulfield Stakes and the Mackinnon Stakes. His versatility was emphasised by an autumn programme which saw him win from the six furlong sprint distance of the William Reid to the 10 furlongs of the Queen's Plate, with Orr and St George Stakes wins in between. Back once more, in the spring of 1968, Winfreux took the season's first two weight-for-age sprints – the Liston and Freeway

Stakes – but pulled up distressed in the Caulfield Stakes; was spelled and then went lame. His twilight years truly entered, Winfreux was sent on a final inglorious campaign which saw him tailed off at Kyneton and last at Ararat. He was eventually retired to a property in rural Victoria and ended his days rounding up stock, a more benign fate than that which has befallen some of the champion geldings of the Australian turf.

WINOOKA
1928 b horse Windbag – Kanooka

A brilliant sprinter of the early 1930s, Winooka was trained by Mick Polson. Characteristically he showed his best form in the autumn. In 1933 he was second in the Oakleigh Plate before running a course record when defeating Kuvera and Gaine Carrington in the Futurity. He also ran record time in the Leonard Stakes at Flemington. Sent to Sydney, he won the All Aged Stakes, a race in which he had been second as a three year old in 1932. He then set an Australian mile record while carrying 63kg to victory in a great performance in the Doncaster. Winooka beat Jacko, winner of the race the previous year. Now the punter and racing entrepreneur Rufus Naylor talked the connections of Winooka into letting him take the horse to race in the United States. The trip went ahead, and Winooka paid his way with three wins, but the big collect came from his far less well performed Trevallion, on whom a successful plunge was launched. Back in Australia, Winooka was burdened by even heavier weights than he had customarily carried. Nonetheless he ran second in the Oakleigh Plate, third to the dead-heaters Heros and Synagogue in the Futurity before finishing fourth in the Newmarket. Injured in another try at the Doncaster, Winooka was retired.

WINTERSET

1936 b gelding Son O'Mine – Winter's Dream

Even in an era where big weights were common in jumping races, Winterset's capacity to carry poundage was remarkable. The D.S. McCormick-trained gelding won 11 steeplechases, and never carried less than 79.5kg to victory. That was the weight which he had when third in the 1942 and 1944 Grand National Steeplechases. The horse's big wins included the Great Eastern Steeplechase of 1945 in South Australia, when L. Meehan saw him home with 81kg and the Hopetoun Steeple at Flemington, which Winterset won two months later, under the burden of 82.5kg, by four lengths.

WITHOUT FEAR

1967 b horse Baldric II – Never Too Late

Sparingly raced in Europe, Without Fear won twice from four starts. His victories came in the Prix de Saint Fermin at Longchamps and the Prix Herod at Chantilly, while he was second in the Prix Djebel at Saint Cloud. Colin Hayes sorely wanted him for stud duties at Lindsay Park and secured the horse in the early 1970s. But Without Fear had travelled badly and was so ill on arrival at Hayes' property that an insurance claim was considered. Meticulous care saw the stallion gradually bloom to such an extent that he achieved a world record for a first season sire in 1975-6 when his progeny numbered 30 winners of 49 races. The best offspring of Without Fear have been Victoria Derby winner Unaware and the brilliant filly Desirable, who won a Lightning Stakes and a Newmarket. Without Fear died in July 1994.

WOLAROI

1913 blk horse Kenilworth – Widden Lass

A brilliant juvenile, Wolaroi won four of seven starts at two, including the A.J.C. Breeders' Plate, Champagne Stakes and the V.R.C. Sires' Produce. At three his form was more patchy. Unplaced in the Chelmsford Stakes, he bounced back to win the 1916 Rosehill Guineas before running out of the money in the A.J.C. Derby. Taken to Melbourne, he was second to Ettefred in the Caulfield Guineas and fourth in the Caulfield Cup. Wolaroi was back in form in the Victoria Derby which he won convincingly. Next he took the then traditional path of Derby winners into the Melbourne Cup, where he came a respectable fifth. Later in the carnival he showed versatility by winning the Linlithgow Stakes. In the autumn Wolaroi won the C.M. Lloyd Stakes before running into Patrobas, who beat him in the St George and the King's Plate. At four Wolaroi failed to run a place, but at five he enjoyed another vintage spell, with wins in the A.J.C. Shorts, a second Linlithgow and a Rawson Stakes. A late highlight of his career was victory in the 1919 Epsom when, as a six year old, he carried 61kg to victory.

WOLFE (HERBERT AUSTIN) BERT ('CARDIGAN') (1897-1968)

This famous turf journalist took his by-line, 'Cardigan', from the 1903 Melbourne Cup winner Lord Cardigan who his grandfather John Mayo bred. Wolfe was also present at the foaling of Lord Nolan, another of Mayo's horses who won the cup of 1908. Racing editor of the Sydney *Referee*, then sports editor of the Melbourne *Argus*, Wolfe spent three years as chairman of stipendiary stewards for the Queensland Turf Club before returning to journalism. He was hired as turf editor of the Melbourne Herald after its proprietor, Keith Murdoch, said that he was seeking the best racing journalist in Australia for the job. 'You're looking at him',

Wolfe replied. He held the job at the *Herald* from 1933-55, covering 21 Melbourne Cups. Wolfe's varied racing activities saw him accompany Phar Lap to Mexico in 1932. Later he was present at the horse's death at Menlo Park in California. Wolfe exposed the notorious Erbie/Redlock ring-in and went to England in the 1930s to buy broodmares for Sol Green. Few racing journalists have been more respected or more influential.

WOMAN IN BLACK, THE

This was the press sobriquet for Johanna Pauline Taks, an emigrant from Estonia who was the most mysterious, yet most observed supporter of the champion horse Bernborough. Following the horse to watch his exploits in person, and to profit from most of his 15 straight wins, Taks bet on him in cash which she carried in a black bag. A total of 6,000 pounds came out of it – and onto the nose of Bernborough in the Caulfield Cup of 1946. When the horse was unluckily beaten into fifth place, the Woman in Black left the course, pleading a headache.

WOMEN JOCKEYS

Despite its politically incorrect name, the Powder Puff Derby for women riders, first run in 1969 at Tauranga in New Zealand, began their advance into professional riding. The winner of the second running of the Powder Puff was Linda Wilkinson, who years later under her married name Linda Jones was a trail-blazer for women jockeys in Australasia. First licensed to ride professionally in the 1978-9 season, Jones was second in the Wellington Cup of 1979 on Northfleet (trained by her husband Alan) and won the Wellington Derby on Holy Toledo. Jones went on to become the first woman to ride against men in an official betting race in Australia, and

to beat them when she won the Labor Day Cup at Doomben on Pay the Purple. In Brisbane in 1974 a series of challenge races for women had been conducted and the best performed jockey was Pam O'Neill, wife of trainer Colin O'Neill. Queensland racing officials at first licensed her to ride only at provincial tracks, but after two trebles at Southport she was cleared to ride in town and scored at Doomben on Samei Boy.

Other women quickly followed the example of Jones and O'Neill. Like that pair, Beverley Buckingham had the benefit of a trainer in the family (in this case her father) to provide opportunities. Nevertheless her feat in winning the Tasmanian senior jockeys' premiership in 1981-2 was remarkable. New Zealander Diane Moseley became the first woman to ride a Group One winner in Australia, when she took the 1982 Doomben Cup on Double You Em. Maree Lyndon was appointed stable jockey for Brian Smith at Rosehill in 1987; and in that year rode a treble at Warwick Farm, won the Adelaide Cup on Lord Reims and became the first woman to ride in a Melbourne Cup. Other women riders to gain notice include Cheryl Neal (unfortunately disabled after a fall), Carol Tucker, Sally Wynne and the sisters Maree and Therese Payne. The Payne sisters and another jockey Christine Puls, between them won the first seven races at Warracknabeal on Friday July 29 1994. (Male riders won the remaining two events). The seven winners by lady riders is believed to be a world first at a registered race meeting. Therese Payne won four, her sister two and Christine, one race.

WOODCOCK, AARON TREVE ('TOMMY') (1905-85)

Born at Uralgurra, Tommy Woodcock was apprenticed to Barney Quinn in Sydney and rode until 1927, when increasing weight meant that he was restricted to riding track work. One of those for whom he rode was Harry Telford, trainer of Phar Lap. His association with that great horse was vividly revived in the 1970s when Woodcock, as trainer of the fine stayer Reckless, gained the surprising place – for him – as one of the best loved characters in the history of the Australian turf. Woodcock's affection for Phar Lap was demonstrated when he shielded the horse from a shooting attempt after work at Caulfield on the Saturday before the 1930 Melbourne Cup. When Phar Lap went to Mexico for the Agua Caliente Stakes, Woodcock accompanied him as the horse's official trainer, and was with Phar Lap when he died at Menlo Park in California in April 1932. Woodcock trained in America for a few months, before returning to Australia where he trained for nearly half a century, from 1934-83. From 1947 he had stables at Mentone.

Knockarlow gave Woodcock an Australian Cup win in 1946, while he won the V.R.C. Oaks with Amarco (1957) and Chosen Lady (1967). With Webster he won the Invitation Stakes, Queen Elizabeth Stakes and Easter Cup in 1959. He was also a noted master. Geoff Lane, who came to Woodcock's stables at Christmas 1952, was the best of his many apprentices. The final triumphs of Woodcock's training career were provided from the unlikeliest source. Reckless went 34 starts before he won, as a five year old. But then his staying prowess was revealed. He won the Hotham Handicap and ran fourth on a bog track in the 1976 Melbourne Cup. In an unparalleled run of staying performances, Reckless now reeled off wins in the Sydney, Adelaide and Brisbane Cups in the autumn and winter of 1977, before running second

to Gold and Black in the Melbourne Cup. Woodcock kept him going for a win at Sandown, but Reckless was retired after being injured while running third in the Perth Cup in January 1978. In 1979, Woodcock was awarded an M.B.E. for his services to racing. Following his retirement, he moved to Yarrawonga, where he died in 1985. In the movie of 'Phar Lap', Woodcock – played by Tim Burlinston – was the co-star. Jan Wositzky wrote his beautifully illustrated biography, *Tommy Woodcock 1905-1985* (1990).

WOORAK
1911 ch horse Traquair – Madam

Owned by L.K.S. Mackinnon, Woorak was a top line juvenile, beating Carlita in the Champagne Stakes and winning the V.R.C. Sires' and Ascot Vale Stakes. At three he was second in the A.J.C. Derby to Mountain Knight, but was at his best over sprint distances and at a mile. In Sydney he won such feature races as the Craven Plate and the Spring Stakes (from subsequent Melbourne Cup winner Westcourt), the 1915 Epsom and the All Aged Stakes in the following year. In Melbourne his wins included the 1917 Oakleigh Plate in which he carried a record winning weight of 65.5kg. He was also second in the Newmarket and Doncaster of 1916. Sent to stud, Whittier was the best horse whom Woorak sired.

WOOTTON FAMILY

No family has had a more significant influence on Australian thoroughbred breeding than the Woottons. Richard ('Dick') Wootton (1866-1946) was born at Moree. He trained in Australia before trying his luck in South Africa. There he set himself up with a plunge on the Goldfields

Cup at Johannesburg, where he put his son Frank (1893-1940) on a long-shot and saw it get home. Frank was not quite 10 years old at the time. Moving his family to England in 1906, Wootton began training at Treadwell House near Epsom. He was leading English trainer in 1913, but his eldest son's successes were more spectacular. Frank Wootton's first big race win was the 1907 Cesarewitch. In 1909 he won the English jockeys' premiership and did so again in the next three years. Classic wins came too: the Oaks on Perola in 1909, the 1910 St Leger on Swynford. Increasing weight and the advent of the Great War led him to give flat riding away, but the war opened a new career. Frank Wootton won the Baghdad Grand National while on active service and after the war turned to jumps riding. He led the English table in 1921; retired in 1924.

Dick Wootton had returned to Australia at the start of the war and set up training in Sydney in a smaller way than had been his custom. After his retirement Frank also came home. But his brother Stanley (1895-1986) remained in England. He had had a brief riding career until weight beat him, and like his brother had served in the British Army. By 1922 he had taken over his father's old stables at Epsom and quickly became one of the leading trainers in England. His interests were also in breeding, fortunately for his native country. Wootton began to send horses to stud in Australia, most famously the well-performed Star King who – as Star Kingdom – became perhaps the greatest single influence on Australian breeding. Standing at the Baramul Stud in the Widden Valley, Star Kingdom sired not only such top-line racehorses as Todman, but was an incomparable sire of sires. He was leading Australian sire on five occasions, and his progeny won the first five

Golden Slippers. Sons of Star Kingdom – Kaoru Star and Biscay – in their turn sired Slipper winners. One of Biscay's best daughters, Bounding Away, won the 1986 Golden Slipper shortly after Wootton's death. He had kept an eye on his Australian breeding interests during annual visits to this country. The Stanley Wootton Stakes at Moonee Valley is named in his honour.

WREN, JOHN (1871-1953)

The most notorious of Australian gambling men, Wren was born in Collingwood. His fortune was made from an illegal tote, and most sports presented him with opportunities for speculation. He won heavily on the 1901 Austral Wheel-race, while the horse who he had imported from Tasmania – Murmur – gave Wren victory in the 1904 Caulfield Cup. Next year the V.R.C. refused all entries from horses which Wren owned. In revenge, he bought up pony tracks at Ascot, Fitzroy and Richmond, soon gaining a reputation for cleaning up a dirty business. In 1906 Wren cheekily attempted to lease Flemington for 30,000 pounds. His racing operations expanded to Brisbane, where he secured the private courses at Albion Park and Bundamba, putting on a 2,000 pound race at the former. He also had interests in Perth racing, in boxing stadiums in Sydney and Melbourne, and in professional wrestling. Frank Hardy's novel *Power Without Glory* (1950) is a sensational treatment, thinly disguised as fiction, of the nefarious activities of 'John West', who stands accused of race-fixing, and – worse still – of securing Collingwood ('Carringbush') football premierships by underhand means. 'The Real John Wren' (as apologist Hugh Buggy entitled his book) died the day after the Collingwood Grand Final victory of 1953.

Y

YANGTZE

1961 b or br horse Ping Ching – Lady Shaw

Bred in South Australia, Yangtze was the only good horse by Ping Ching. He won 15 of 50 starts and competed for years at the highest level. Trained by Ron Dini, Yangtze won the Caulfield Guineas of 1964, before being backed up in the Caulfield Cup, where he defeated his fellow three year old, and triple Derby winner Royal Sovereign. In doing so, Yangtze, ridden by the apprentice John Stocker (whose father had finished second on Segati in the Caulfield Cup of 1932 to Rogilla) became the first horse to lead all the way to victory in the Caulfield Cup. (Stocker emulated that feat on How Now in 1976). A year later Yangtze was fourth in the Melbourne Cup (over a distance thought unsuitable) to Light Fingers. His career record also boasts two Memsie Stakes, in 1965 and 1966, besides the Mackinnon and St George Stakes of 1965.

YATTENDON

1861 br horse Sir Hercules – Cassandra

Part-owned by Etienne de Mestre, Yattendon was trained and often ridden by Sam Holmes. He had 17 starts in his career, all at Randwick, and won 11 of them, including the inaugural Sydney Cup of 1866. Earlier he had beaten one other horse in the 1864 Derby and won the St Leger. Yattendon proved to be an outstanding colonial sire, after going to E.K. Cox's Fernhill Stud. His best sons were Chester and the unbeaten Grand Flaneur.

YOUNG IDEA

1932 br horse Constant Son – Persuasion

Young Idea should be more widely recognised as one of the top horses of the late 1930s. Even though Ajax overshadows him, consider the record of the Jack Holt-trained Young Idea. As a two year old he won the Champagne and Sires' Produce Stakes in Sydney, besides the V.R.C. Sires'. At three he won the Caulfield Guineas, and then continued to perform at the highest level until his fifth season. He won the Caulfield Stakes in 1936 and soon afterwards the first of two Cox Plates, with Harold Skidmore up. He won again the next year when Darby Munro had the ride and was third to Ajax and Royal Chief in 1938. Besides numerous other placings at weight-for-age (third in the Mackinnon in 1936 and the Futurity the next year), Young Idea won the 1937 St George Stakes when Hostage, first past the post, weighed in light.

YSMAEL, FELIPE (1928-84)

Known more or less affectionately as 'The Babe' and 'The Filipino Fireball', Felipe Ysmael was a wealthy Filipino who developed his love of the punt while a university student in California. A supporter of Ferdinand Marcos when he won the presidential election of 1965 in the Philippines, Ysmael brought plenty of political clout as well as cash to Australia in that year. Officially he entered the country as president of Ysmael Steel. His hobby soon became more engrossing. He established a thoroughbred property at Bahilda Lodge (Hilda was his German-born wife) in the Dandenongs outside Melbourne; began to buy racehorses and to bet in a fashion unprecedented in Australia. A clever plunge on the Charlie Waymouth trained Red Diver in January 1968 netted $250,000. On another occasion Ysmael claimed big Sydney bookmaker Bill Waterhouse for an even $100,000 on Silver Strike, who won at Newcastle. He owned the 1968 Victoria Derby winner Always There and the fine two year old filly, Romantic Miss. However it was one of his undistinguished performers who brought Ysmael undone, or rather provided authorities with the opportunity to curtail what they may have considered his egregious presence on the Australian turf. Follow Me ran 11th when favourite in the second Hollymount Handicap at Moonee Valley in December 1968. When it was discovered that Ysmael had backed Dalthing in the race as well, an inquiry began. As a result Ysmael, jockey George Hope, and Waymouth were outed. Ysmael, feeling socially disgraced, left Australia, but was soon angling for official support to return. He was accepted in 1971 as economic attache to the Filipino embassy, but his punting heyday was well behind him. He died of a heart attack in the Philippines in July 1984.

Z

ZEDITAVE
1986 ch horse The Judge – Summoned

This brilliant sprinter was trained by the veteran Angus Armanasco, who had also had charge of his sire, The Judge. After victory in a Blue Diamond Prelude at Sandown in 1988, Zeditave convincingly won the main event from Vitalic and Startling Lass. Towards the end of his two year old season he added another Group One event to his record, with victory in the Castlemaine Stakes in Brisbane. Resuming as a three-year-old in the spring of 1988, Zeditave scored in the Ascot Vale Stakes, but was then spelled after two unplaced runs. However, his autumn campaign in 1989 was outstanding. Zeditave beat the good sprinter Clay Hero in the Rubiton, before adding the William Reid, Lightning and Futurity Stakes to his imposing record at the highest level. As an indication of the colt's quality, Vo Rogue was runner-up in the William Reid; Special in the Lighting; Jet Fighter and Redelva in the Futurity. Zeditave was retired to stud while still a young horse and has enjoyed success.

ZULU
1877 blk horse Barbarian – Maiden's Blush

By coincidence, Zulu was foaled on the eve of the war between Britain and the Zulus. (The names of his sire and dam might have led one to expect a more suggestive one for this black colt). Trained by T. Lamond, Zulu came into the 1881 Melbourne Cup with the unprepossessing record of two wins at New South Wales country meetings and a victory in the Squatters' Handicap at Randwick. Starting at 33/1 in the Melbourne Cup, he carried a mere 36.5kg to victory. Legend has it that Zulu ended his days pulling a milk cart.

TABCORP ▼

Share
the
excitement.

TAB ▼   **TABARET** ▐ ▟   ◢**SPORTSBOOK** THE NATIONAL   **Club KENO**

SIX WINNERS PAY $541,000 FOR 50 CENTS!

A record Australian dividend of $541,920.65 was paid by the Victorian TAB on Melbourne Cup Day, 1991.

The amount was won on a Straight Six bet, which requires selecting the winners of six nominated races.

The Straight Six bet, which is exclusive to the Victorian TAB, jackpots if it is not won and the record dividend was won by a single ticketholder after a series of jackpots.

The Victorian TAB offers the widest choice of bets of any TAB in Australia.

Apart from Win, Place, Quinella and Trifecta bets, there are other alternatives. These include:

Quadrella: Selecting the winners of four nominated races. In quadrellas there are a maximum of nine combinations in each leg, which means that in the event of more than nine starters, runners are bracketed, i.e runner No 10 becomes 9b; 11 becomes 8b, 12 becomes 7b.

This can result in having two runners for the one selection, which is part of the appeal of the Quadrella. The record dividend for a Quadrella is in excess of $92,000.

QuadXtra: This also involves selecting the winners of four nominated races. Unlike the Quadrella, there are no bracketed runners. This means that in a field of 18 starters, the number of combinations for that race is 18 (whereas under the Quadrella conditions it would be nine). The record dividend for a QuadXtra is almost $130,000.

Quinella and **Trifecta** betting are also very popular, and people can improve their chances of winning with these bets, by "boxing" their selections.

What this means is that, in the case of a Trifecta, (which requires the selection of first, second and third in correct order) you fancy the chances of four starters. All combinations of these four starters can be covered by taking a **"Box" Trifecta,** so-called because it "boxes" all the possible winning combinations for your selections. In the case of four runners to fill three placings in order, the number of possible combinations is 24, so such a bet would cost $12 for a 50 cent bet.

It is also possible to take a **Box Quinella** (first and second in any order) if you fancy more than two runners to fill first and second places.

The Victorian TAB also provides a betting service on general sports and AFL football, Customers can place fixed price bets on selected sports or football matches via National Sportsbook or by using their TAB Telephone betting account.

If you require further details, phone (03) 868-2100 to find out how you can be a winner with the Victorian TAB.

A DESPERATES' DICTIONARY

All-up .... wagering the projected winnings from one race on to another

Angora .... rhyming slang for tote

Asparagus .... an abundance of tips, as in more tips than a can of asparagus

Autumn horse .... notion that some horses perform much better in certain seasons, e.g. that Durbridge is an 'autumn horse'

Bag, in the .... a horse known to be running dead

Bank-teller's job .... a certainty – such a good bet that a bank-teller could withdraw substantial funds on Friday, bet and win with them on Saturday, then return the money on Monday. Not a fool-proof system.

Battler .... any punter of modest means and high expectations

Bird .... a certainty

Bit, on the .... a horse which seems to be travelling easily

Black tracker .... a horse tailed off is sometimes said to be so far back that it would take a black tracker to find it (now, perhaps an incorrect form of words)

Blanket finish .... one so close that a blanket could be thrown over the horses contesting it

Blow out the gate .... an alarming drift in a horse's price – its odds have 'blown out the gate'

Boat race .... a rigged race. Afterwards, suspicious punters refer to the 'swishing of oars'. Also known as a 'oney', or 'one-goer'.

Boracic .... rhyming slang for skint, from boracic lint

Brick .... formerly a 10 pound note (because of the red colour), now $20.

Bucking the brand off .... denotes a horse so fit that it performs this improbable feat

Cat	a very weak horse
Cert, dead	a supposed sure thing
Charles Chase	rhyming slang for running a place, from the American comedian of that name
Cockatoo	an S.P. bookmaker's look-out
Compound	a horse which gives up quickly is said to have compounded
Daylight	the proverbial margin which separates a horse that has won by a big space from the runner-up
Dead	a horse known to be not trying, or 'on the go'
Desperate	generic term for punter
Dogs are barking	a hot tip, not necessarily reliable, but so widely broadcast that the very dogs are said to be barking it
Double wraps	a horse well held by its jockey and travelling easily
Drift	when a horse's price lengthens ominously
Drum	rhyming slang for running a place, from drum and mace; a tip is also the drum
Egg flip	rhyming slang for tip
El Golea	rhyming slang for beer, after the good racehorse El Golea, who survived a shotgun nobbling when mistaken for another horse
Emu	from the appearance of an inveterate bender for discarded betting tickets which she or he hopes may be 'live'
Firm	to shorten in the market
Flattened	knocked out of a race, a horse is said to have been flattened
Flip of the coin	odds of even money
Flyblown	condition of a broke punter
Get-out race	nowadays the last in Perth, whereby punters hope to retrieve their fortune

Gizzard	$250 or $300 being the 'guts of a monkey' (i.e. $500)
Goose's neck	rhyming slang for cheque
Gorilla	$1000 (or twice the size of a monkey)
Greet the judge	a winning horse is first to 'greet the judge'
Hands and heels	a horse ridden along without recourse to the whip
Hook	to pull a horse
Hoop	a jockey, from the round arm action of riders when using a whip
Hurricane lamp	implement needed to locate horses which have finished disgracefully far back in a race
Jarred up	new excuse (c1993) for horses which are uncomfortable on very firm going
Jocked off	the unfortunate fate of a jockey who is replaced with little warning on a well-fancied runner
Kembla Grange	rhyming slang for change
Killing	the results of a successful plunge
Lay-off	bookmakers' hedge against a likely bad result by laying off with bets on other runners
Leviathan	genteel slang for punters and book-makers who operate on a grand scale
Mail	a tip
Monkey	$500
Monty	a certain winner, from the British General Montgomery
Morning glory	a brilliant track worker whose deeds are not translated to the racecourse
Mug punter	a punter
Nap	a tipster's best bet for the programme
Nobbled	to dope a horse, as Big Philou was nobbled shortly before the 1969 Melbourne Cup

Odds on, look on	a caution against backing horses which are at odds on, or 'in the red'
Outs, run of	a circumstance which can happen to anyone, but which particularly afflicts horses, jockeys and tipsters
Out the gate	a horse which has blow disconcertingly in the market is said to be 'out the gate'
Oxford Scholar	rhyming slang for dollar
Persuader	jockeys' term for the whip, sometimes extravagantly called the 'shillelagh'
Pony	originally 25 pounds, now $25 – derived from what was long ago the average price of a pony
Pot	to declare that a horse can't win
Prat, cop a	a horse which suffers interference in a race has copped a prat
Pull	when a jockey prevents a horse from running on its merits
Pull the wrong rein	a habit of jockeys, whereby they turn down a subsequent winning mount to ride another horse instead
Puncture	when a horse stops quickly, it is said to have punctured
Rent bet	a supposed certainty
Ridden too well	apparently contradictory, the term indicates that a jockey could not extricate his mount from the excellent position which he had secured
Roughie	a victorious outsider, or – much more often – a horse who starts at well-merited long odds
Run dead	a horse who is not trying runs dead
Salute	a genteel expression to describe a winner – e.g. Crisp has saluted again
Save	an agreement between jockeys involved in a tight and uncertain finish to ensure that the loser gains some reward

Scaler	a welshing bookmaker who offers to return punters' stake money and an I.O.U. It was this practice which led to the violent death of 'Big Mick' McLeod on Grand National Steeplechase Day in 1906.
Snookered	describes the fate of a horse which cannot secure a clear run
Spec	to wager on a horse; for instance 'I "specked" Oxford Prince at big odds'.
Spot	$100, more commonly nowadays, a Mawson
Stipes	the stipendiary students who control the conduct of racing
Stumer	the designated winner in a rigged, or 'boat race'
Till, foot on the	a horse which is ready to win next start proverbially has its foot on the till
Urger	one who cons unsuspecting punters into backing a variety of horses that are bound to win in the same race and then seeks out the victor for a cut
Via the Cape	a horse which has run wide has gone 'via the Cape' (in the manner of sea voyagers last century)
Welsher	one who does not honour a bet, whether as punter or bookmaker
Whip them in	a horse in last place is said to be whipping them in
Write your own ticket	punters are invited, metaphorically, to write their own tickets about very long priced horses as an indication of their likely chances.

Readers wanting to extend their knowledge of racing slang are directed to the splendid compilation by Jack Hibberd and Garrie Hutchinson, *The Barrackers' Bible. A Dictionary of Sporting Slang* (1983), and to Ned Wallish's *Truth Dictionary of Racing Slang* (1989).